「Love Hina」

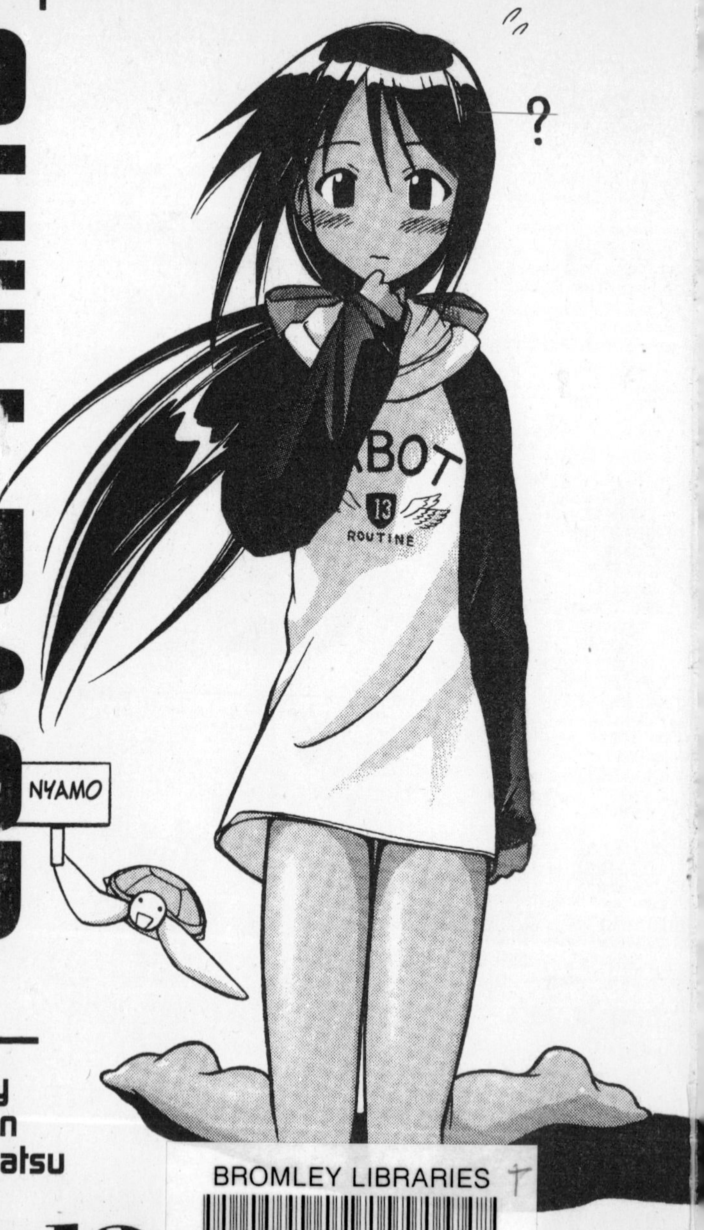
?
13
ROUTINE
NYAMO

By
Ken
Akamatsu

Vol. 12

ALSO AVAILABLE FROM TOKYOPOP®

MANGA

.HACK//LEGEND OF THE TWILIGHT BRACELET (September 2003)
@LARGE (COMING SOON)
ANGELIC LAYER*
BABY BIRTH* (September 2003)
BATTLE ROYALE*
BRAIN POWERED*
BRIGADOON* (August 2003)
CARDCAPTOR SAKURA
CARDCAPTOR SAKURA: MASTER OF THE CLOW*
CHOBITS*
CHRONICLES OF THE CURSED SWORD
CLAMP SCHOOL DETECTIVES*
CLOVER
CONFIDENTIAL CONFESSIONS*
CORRECTOR YUI
COWBOY BEBOP*
COWBOY BEBOP: SHOOTING STAR*
DEMON DIARY
DIGIMON*
DRAGON HUNTER
DRAGON KNIGHTS*
DUKLYON: CLAMP SCHOOL DEFENDERS*
ERICA SAKURAZAWA*
FAKE*
FLCL* (September 2003)
FORBIDDEN DANCE* (August 2003)
GATE KEEPERS*
G GUNDAM*
GRAVITATION*
GTO*
GUNDAM WING
GUNDAM WING: BATTLEFIELD OF PACIFISTS
GUNDAM WING: ENDLESS WALTZ*
GUNDAM WING: THE LAST OUTPOST*
HAPPY MANIA*
HARLEM BEAT
I.N.V.U.
INITIAL D*
ISLAND
JING: KING OF BANDITS*
JULINE
KARE KANO*
KINDAICHI CASE FILES, THE*
KING OF HELL
KODOCHA: SANA'S STAGE*
LOVE HINA*
LUPIN III*
MAGIC KNIGHT RAYEARTH* (August 2003)
MAGIC KNIGHT RAYEARTH II* (COMING SOON)

MAN OF MANY FACES*
MARMALADE BOY*
MARS*
MIRACLE GIRLS
MIYUKI-CHAN IN WONDERLAND* (October 2003)
MONSTERS, INC.
PARADISE KISS*
PARASYTE
PEACH GIRL
PEACH GIRL: CHANGE OF HEART*
PET SHOP OF HORRORS*
PLANET LADDER*
PLANETES* (October 2003)
PRIEST
RAGNAROK
RAVE MASTER*
REALITY CHECK
REBIRTH
REBOUND*
RISING STARS OF MANGA
SABER MARIONETTE J*
SAILOR MOON
SAINT TAIL
SAMURAI DEEPER KYO*
SAMURAI GIRL: REAL BOUT HIGH SCHOOL*
SCRYED*
SHAOLIN SISTERS*
SHIRAHIME-SYO: SNOW GODDESS TALES* (De
SHUTTERBOX (November 2003)
SORCERER HUNTERS
THE SKULL MAN*
THE VISION OF ESCAFLOWNE
TOKYO MEW MEW*
UNDER THE GLASS MOON
VAMPIRE GAME
WILD ACT*
WISH*
WORLD OF HARTZ (COMING SOON)
X-DAY* (August 2003)
ZODIAC P.I. *

*INDICATES 100% AUTHENTIC MANGA (RIGHT-TO-LEFT FORMAT)

CINE-MANGA™

CARDCAPTORS
JACKIE CHAN ADVENTURES (COMING SOON)
JIMMY NEUTRON (September 2003)
KIM POSSIBLE
LIZZIE MCGUIRE
POWER RANGERS: NINJA STORM (August 2003)
SPONGEBOB SQUAREPANTS (September 2003)
SPY KIDS 2

NOVELS

KARMA CLUB (COMING SOON)
SAILOR MOON

TOKYOPOP KIDS

STRAY SHEEP (September 2003)

ART BOOKS

CARDCAPTOR SAKURA*
MAGIC KNIGHT RAYEARTH*

ANIME GUIDES

COWBOY BEBOP ANIME GUIDES
GUNDAM TECHNICAL MANUALS
SAILOR MOON SCOUT GUIDES

5-8-03

Love Hina

By

Ken Akamatsu

Volume 12

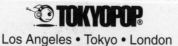

Los Angeles • Tokyo • London

Translator - Nan Rymer
English Adaptation - Adam Arnold
Associate Editors - Paul Morrissey & Tim Beedle
Retouch and Lettering - James Lee
Cover Layout - Anna Kernbaum

Senior Editor - Mark Paniccia
Managing Editor - Jill Freshney
Production Coordinator - Antonio DePietro
Production Manager - Jennifer Miller
Art Director - Matthew Alford
Director of Editorial - Jeremy Ross
VP of Production & Manufacturing - Ron Klamert
President & C.O.O. - John Parker
Publisher & C.E.O. - Stuart Levy

Email: editor@TOKYOPOP.com
Come visit us online at www.TOKYOPOP.com

A **TOKYOPOP** Manga

TOKYOPOP® is an imprint of Mixx Entertainment, Inc.
5900 Wilshire Blvd. Suite 2000, Los Angeles, CA 90036

©1999 Ken Akamatsu. First published in 1999 by Kodansha Ltd., Tokyo.
English publication rights arranged through Kodansha Ltd., Tokyo.

English text © 2003 by Mixx Entertainment, Inc.
TOKYOPOP is a registered trademark of Mixx Entertainment, Inc.

ISBN: 1-59182-118-5

First TOKYOPOP® printing: July 2003

10 9 8 7 6 5
Printed in Canada

Love Hina

The Story Thus Far...

Fifteen years ago, Keitaro Urashima made a promise to a girl that the two of them would go to Tokyo University together. For fifteen long years, Keitaro has slaved away at his books, stumbling through academia until the day he could take the university's entrance exam. Having failed three times, Keitaro unfortunately failed a fourth attempt. But he discovered that the girl to whom he made that fateful promise is the same girl that recently studied with him and helped overcome his fear of tests. At last the saga has ended–the impossible has become reality. Keitaro Urashima has finally managed to pass the entrance exam and accomplish his dream. But fate has a way of intervening. A freak accident during the university's opening ceremonies leaves Keitaro hospitalized with a broken leg. His stay results in a bedside confession of his love for Naru. As the two struggle to find an outlet to express their feelings, Keitaro makes a shocking revelation... he wants to study abroad. With Keitaro gone for six months, the Hinata girls are forced into a colossal tussle for supremacy against Keitaro's own sister, Kanako. But perhaps we are getting ahead of ourselves.

This chapter in Keitaro Urashima's life began well over a year ago, when he inherited a special property from his globe-trotting grandmother. The Hinata House is an all-girls dormitory whose clientele is none too pleased that their new, live-in landlord is a man...or as close to a man as poor Keitaro can be. The lanky loser incessantly (and accidentally) crashes their sessions in the hot springs, walks in on them changing clothes, and pokes his nose pretty much everywhere that it can get broken, if not by the hot-headed Naru–the mystery girl from fifteen years ago–then by one of the other Hinata inmates: Kitsune, a late-teen alcoholic with a diesel libido; Motoko, a swordsman who struggles with her feminine identity; Shinobu, a pre-teen princess with a huge crush on Keitaro; Su, a foreign girl with a big appetite; Sarah, an orphaned ward resentful of being left behind by her archeologist guardian; Mutsumi, an accident-prone lily also studying for her exams; Haruka, Keitaro's aunt and the de facto matriarch of Hinata House; and now Kanako, Keitaro's little sister, who has a knack for impersonations and a bizarre love for her brother.

Just as the Hinata crew begins to get on with life without Keitaro, Kanako Urashima arrives on the scene and institutes a number of changes–the first being the closing of Hinata House as a dorm and its re-opening as Hinata Inn, a full-service bed and breakfast. As tensions mount, the girls are forced to take sides against their tyrannical new landlord and her unlikely cohort, Naru. Just as things are about to get ugly, Keitaro makes his grand entrance. But how will the girls react to his sudden return?

CONTENTS

HINATA. 97   **Please Give Me This Memory!** 08

HINATA. 98   **Blonde Misgivings!!** 28

HINATA. 99   **A Double-Booked Promise!** 48

HINATA.100   **Sister Syndrome** 68

HINATA.101   **A Future Overflowing With Magic** 87

HINATA.102   **Heart Break Crossing** 108

HINATA.103   **Escape En Route With My Stalker** 127

HINATA.104   **Never Give Up!** 148

HINATA.105   **Crazy for You to the Ends of the Earth** .167

LOVE♡HINA

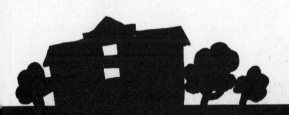

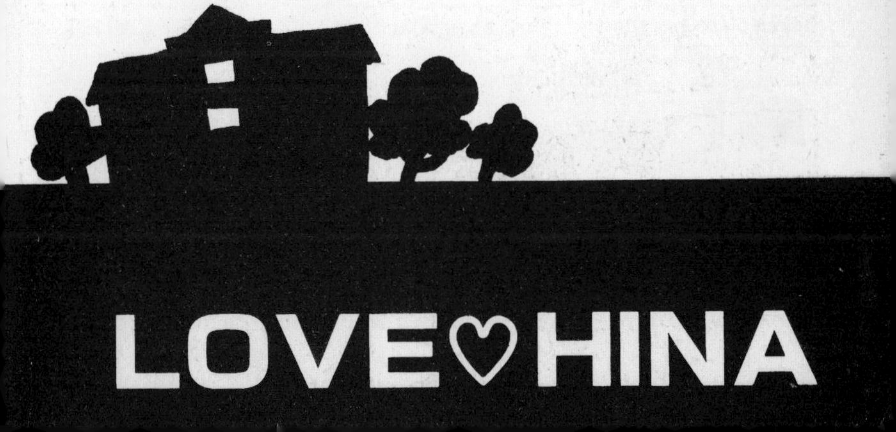

LOVE♡HINA

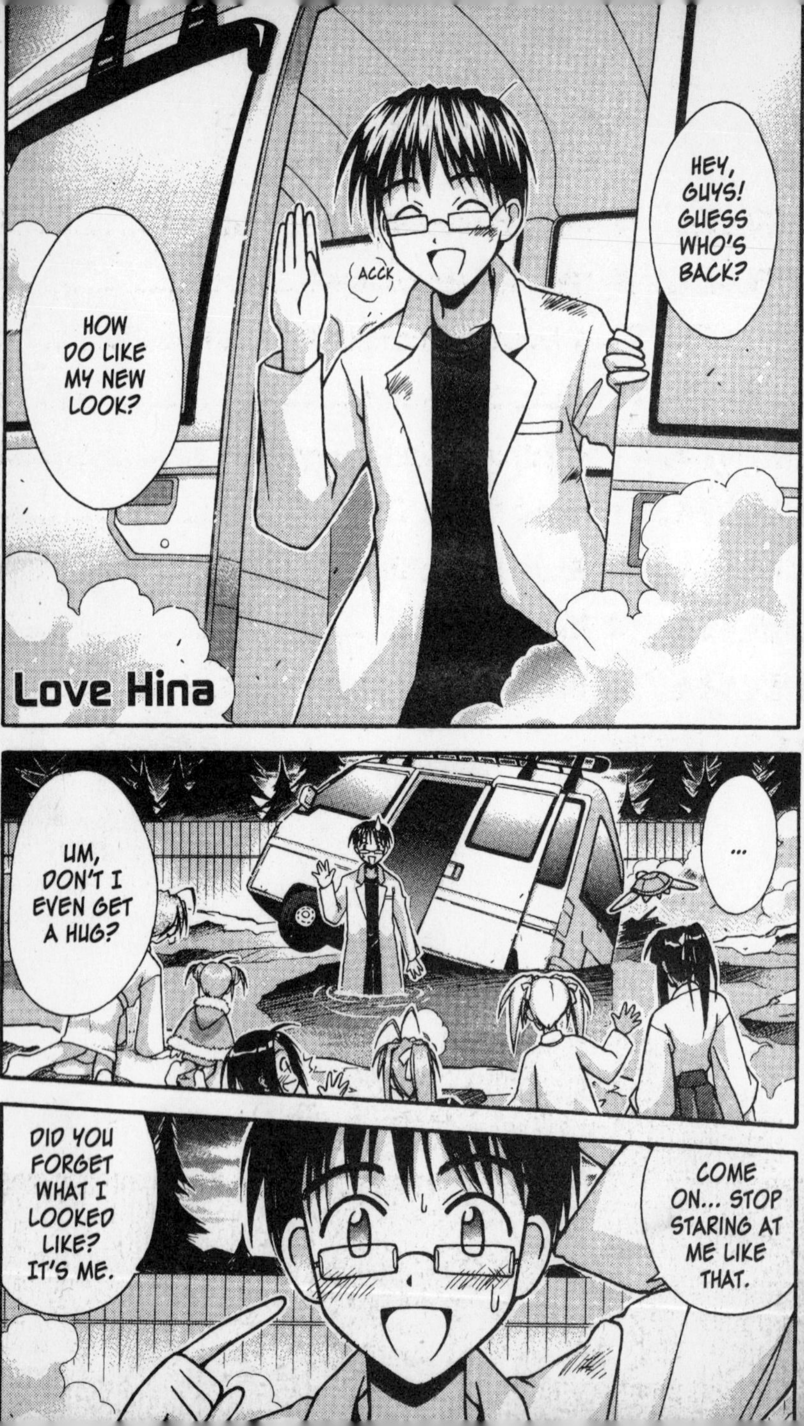
HEY, GUYS! GUESS WHO'S BACK?
ACCK
HOW DO LIKE MY NEW LOOK?
Love Hina
...
UM, DON'T I EVEN GET A HUG?
COME ON... STOP STARING AT ME LIKE THAT.
DID YOU FORGET WHAT I LOOKED LIKE? IT'S ME.

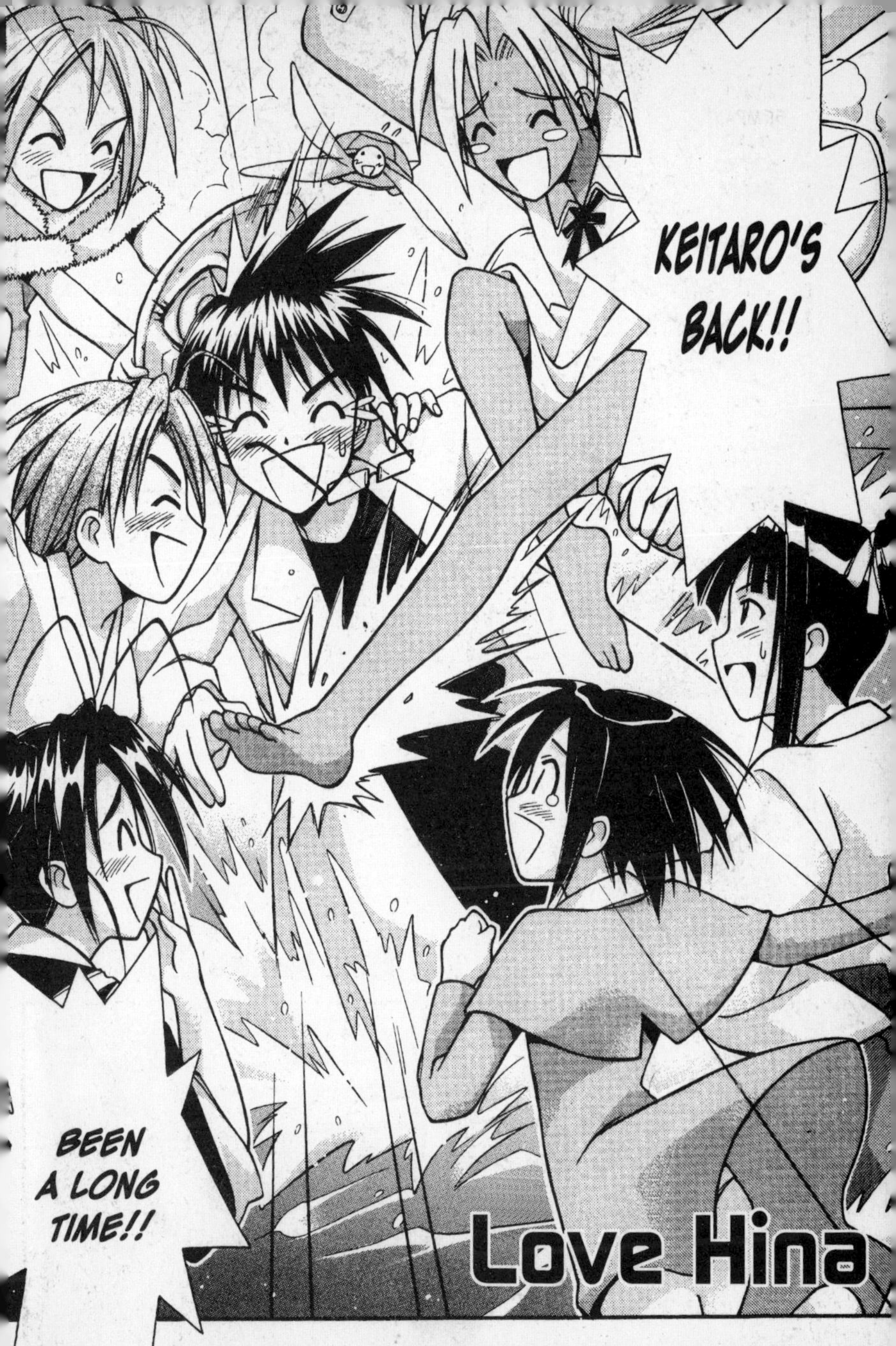
KEITARO'S BACK!!
BEEN A LONG TIME!!
Love Hina

HINATA. 97 Please Give Me This Memory!

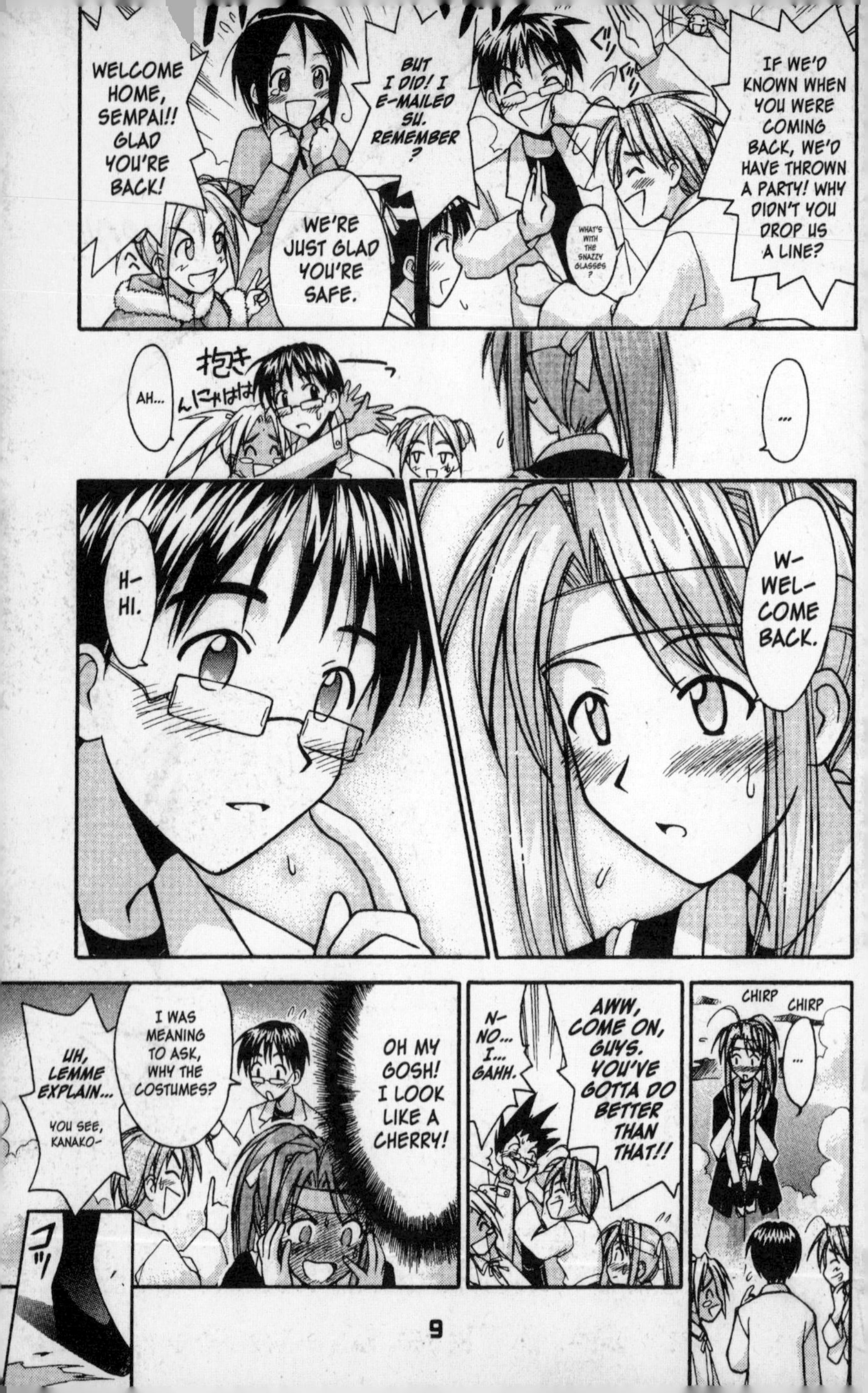
IF WE'D KNOWN WHEN YOU WERE COMING BACK, WE'D HAVE THROWN A PARTY! WHY DIDN'T YOU DROP US A LINE?
BUT I DID! I E-MAILED SU. REMEMBER?
WELCOME HOME, SEMPAI!! GLAD YOU'RE BACK!
WHAT'S WITH THE SNAZZY GLASSES?
WE'RE JUST GLAD YOU'RE SAFE.
...
抱き
んにゃはは
AH...
W-WEL-COME BACK.
H-HI.
CHIRP
CHIRP
...
AWW, COME ON, GUYS. YOU'VE GOTTA DO BETTER THAN THAT!!
N-NO... I... GAHH.
OH MY GOSH! I LOOK LIKE A CHERRY!
I WAS MEANING TO ASK, WHY THE COSTUMES?
UH, LEMME EXPLAIN...
YOU SEE, KANAKO-
ゴッ

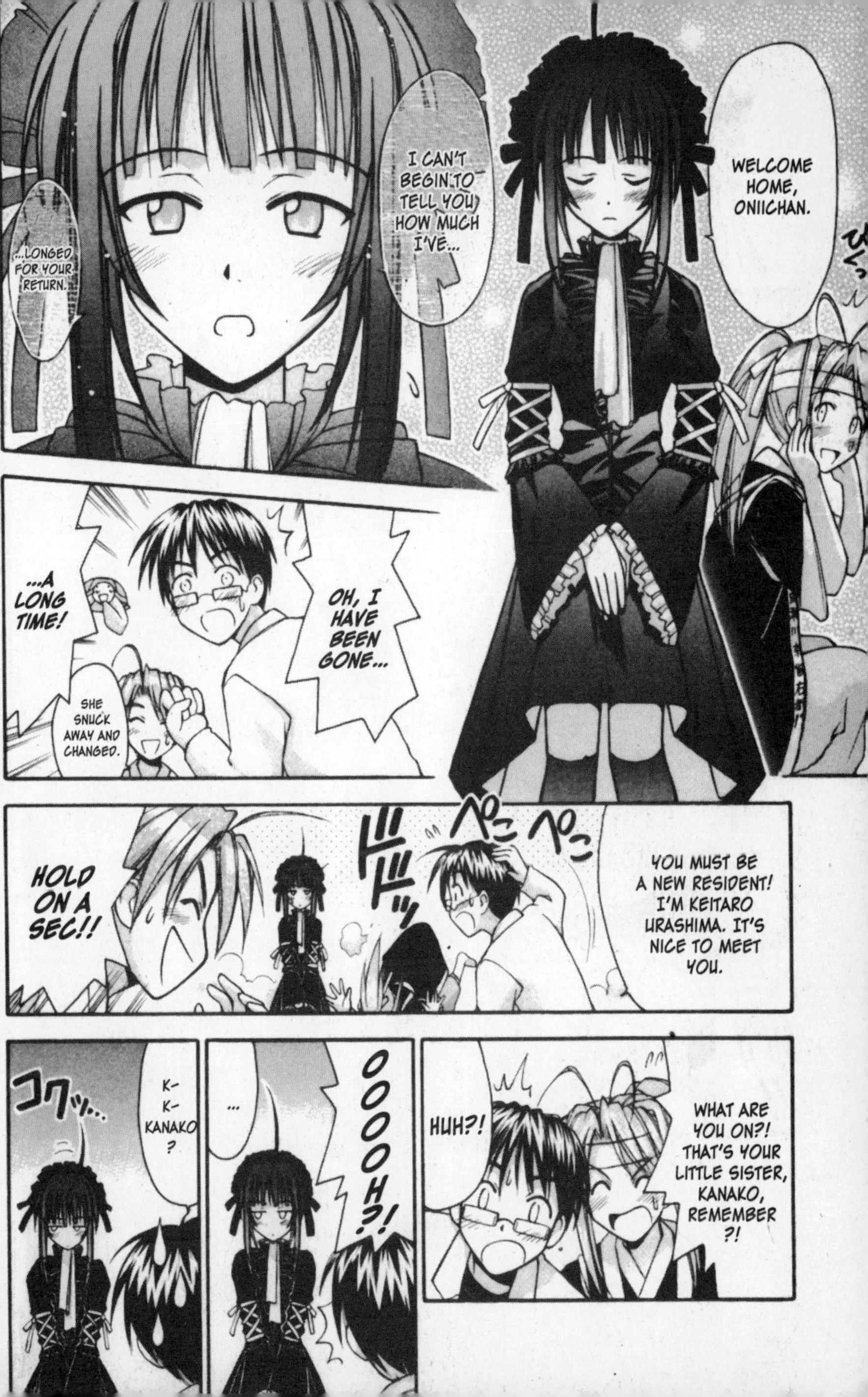
WELCOME HOME, ONIICHAN.
I CAN'T BEGIN TO TELL YOU HOW MUCH I'VE...
...LONGED FOR YOUR RETURN.
OH, I HAVE BEEN GONE...
...A LONG TIME!
SHE SNUCK AWAY AND CHANGED.
YOU MUST BE A NEW RESIDENT! I'M KEITARO URASHIMA. IT'S NICE TO MEET YOU.
HOLD ON A SEC!!
WHAT ARE YOU ON?! THAT'S YOUR LITTLE SISTER, KANAKO, REMEMBER?!
HUH?!
OOOOOH?!
...
K-K-KANAKO?

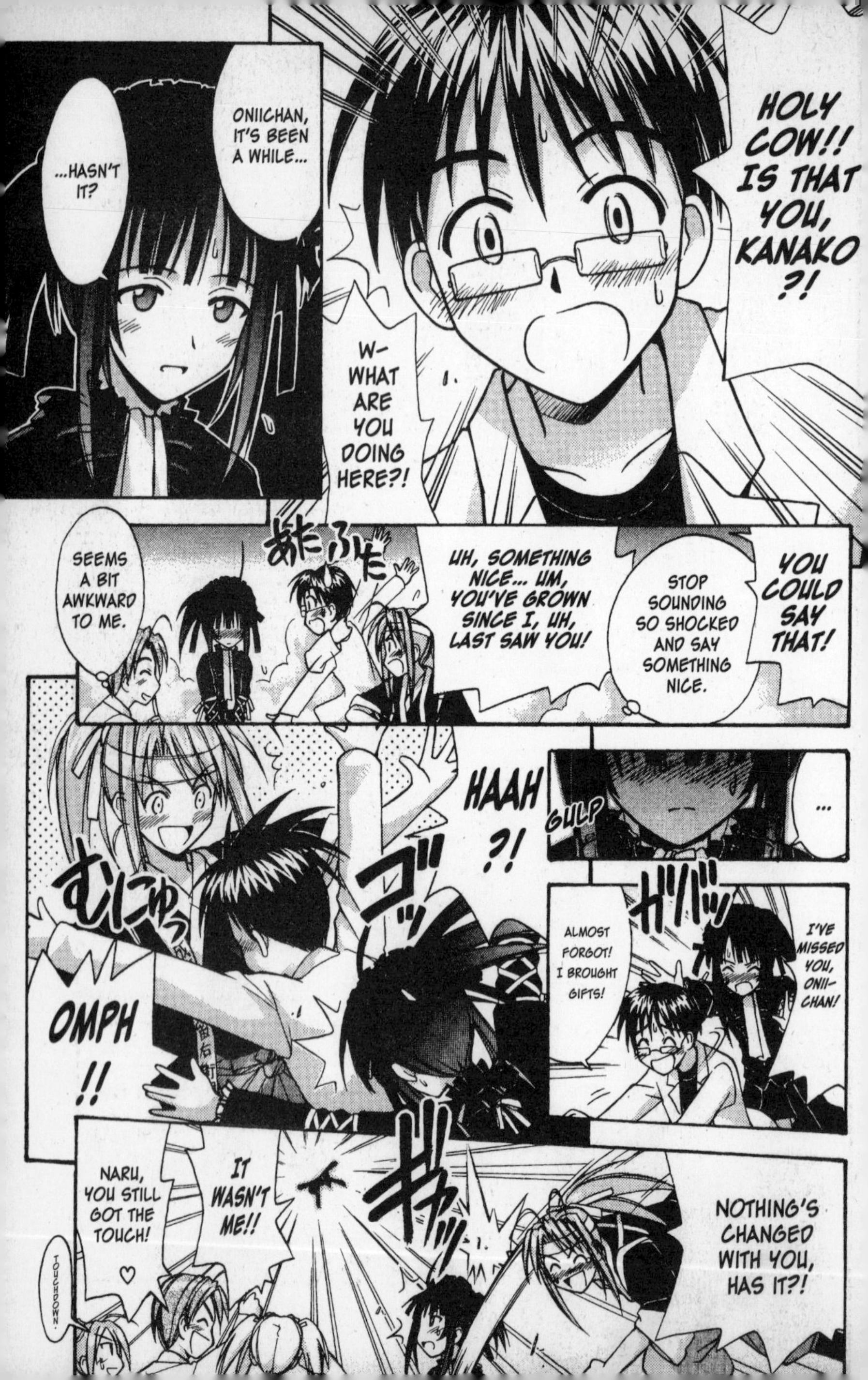
HOLY COW!! IS THAT YOU, KANAKO?!
W-WHAT ARE YOU DOING HERE?!
ONIICHAN, IT'S BEEN A WHILE...
...HASN'T IT?
YOU COULD SAY THAT!
STOP SOUNDING SO SHOCKED AND SAY SOMETHING NICE.
UH, SOMETHING NICE... UM, YOU'VE GROWN SINCE I, UH, LAST SAW YOU!
あたふた
SEEMS A BIT AWKWARD TO ME.
...
GULP
I'VE MISSED YOU, ONII-CHAN!
ガバッ
ALMOST FORGOT! I BROUGHT GIFTS!
HAAH?!
ゴッ
むにゅっ
OMPH!!
NOTHING'S CHANGED WITH YOU, HAS IT?!
ギャッ
IT WASN'T ME!!
NARU, YOU STILL GOT THE TOUCH!
TOUCHDOWN.
♡

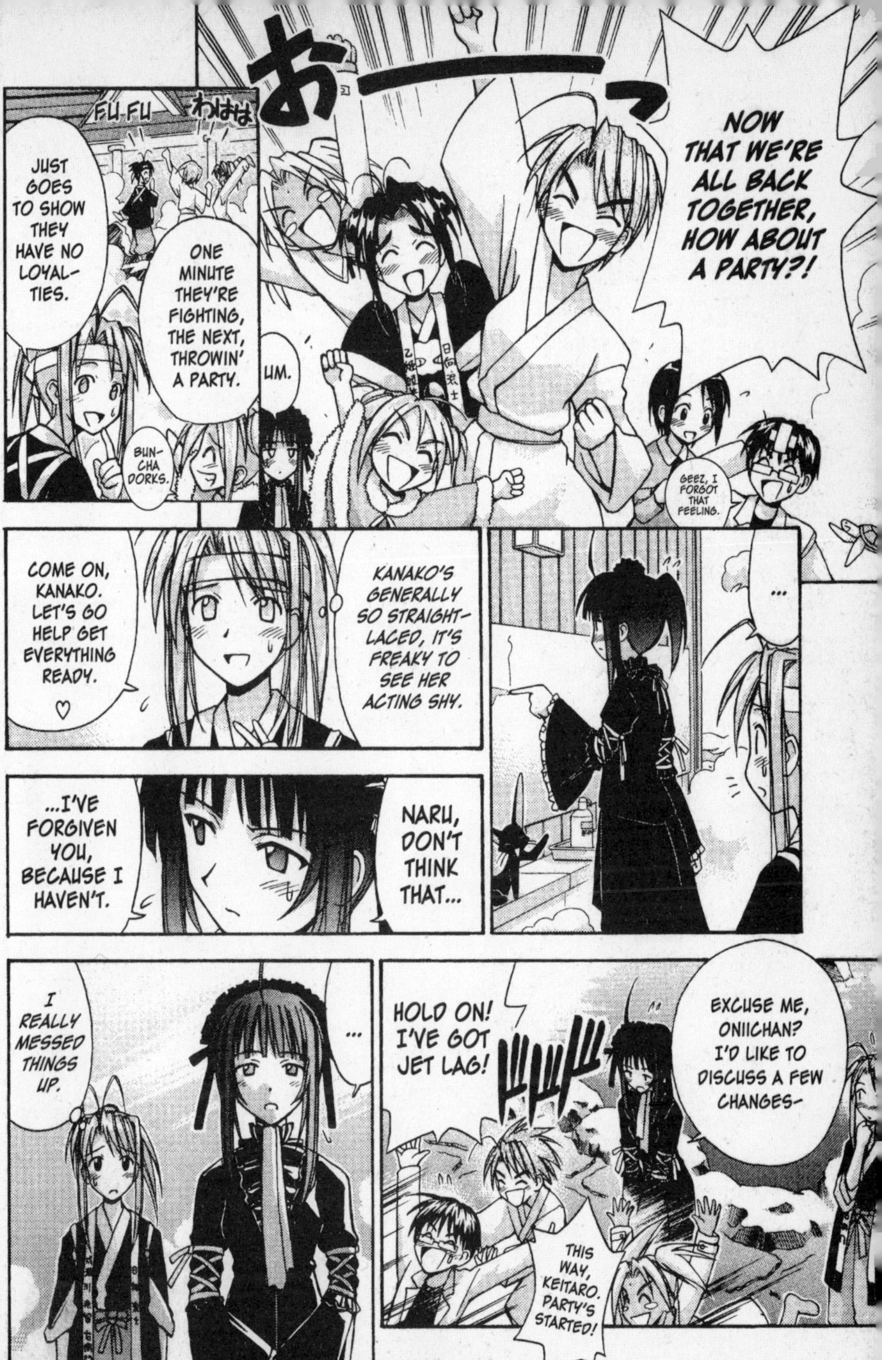
あーっ
NOW THAT WE'RE ALL BACK TOGETHER, HOW ABOUT A PARTY?!
GEEZ, I FORGOT THAT FEELING.
UM.
わはは
FU-FU
JUST GOES TO SHOW THEY HAVE NO LOYAL-TIES.
ONE MINUTE THEY'RE FIGHTING, THE NEXT, THROWIN' A PARTY.
BUN-CHA DORKS.
...
KANAKO'S GENERALLY SO STRAIGHT-LACED, IT'S FREAKY TO SEE HER ACTING SHY.
COME ON, KANAKO. LET'S GO HELP GET EVERYTHING READY. ♡
NARU, DON'T THINK THAT...
...I'VE FORGIVEN YOU, BECAUSE I HAVEN'T.
EXCUSE ME, ONIICHAN? I'D LIKE TO DISCUSS A FEW CHANGES-
HOLD ON! I'VE GOT JET LAG!
THIS WAY, KEITARO. PARTY'S STARTED!
...
I REALLY MESSED THINGS UP.

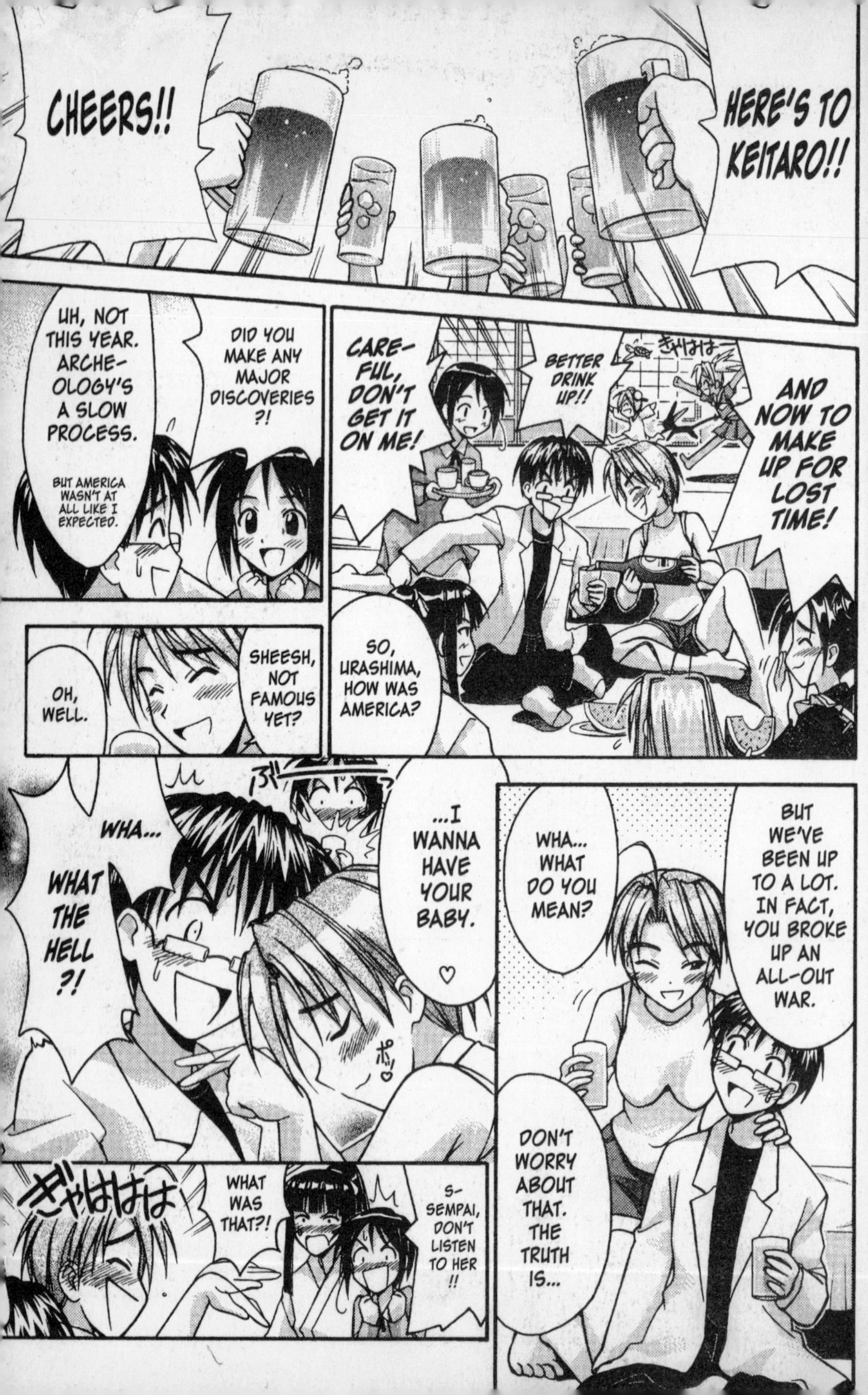

HERE'S TO KEITARO!!
CHEERS!!
AND NOW TO MAKE UP FOR LOST TIME!
きゃはは
BETTER DRINK UP!!
CARE-FUL, DON'T GET IT ON ME!
SO, URASHIMA, HOW WAS AMERICA?
DID YOU MAKE ANY MAJOR DISCOVERIES?!
UH, NOT THIS YEAR. ARCHE-OLOGY'S A SLOW PROCESS.
BUT AMERICA WASN'T AT ALL LIKE I EXPECTED.
SHEESH, NOT FAMOUS YET?
OH, WELL.
BUT WE'VE BEEN UP TO A LOT. IN FACT, YOU BROKE UP AN ALL-OUT WAR.
WHA... WHAT DO YOU MEAN?
DON'T WORRY ABOUT THAT. THE TRUTH IS...
...I WANNA HAVE YOUR BABY. ♡
ぶ
WHA...
WHAT THE HELL?!
ポッ♡
S-SEMPAI, DON'T LISTEN TO HER!!
WHAT WAS THAT?!
ぎゃははは

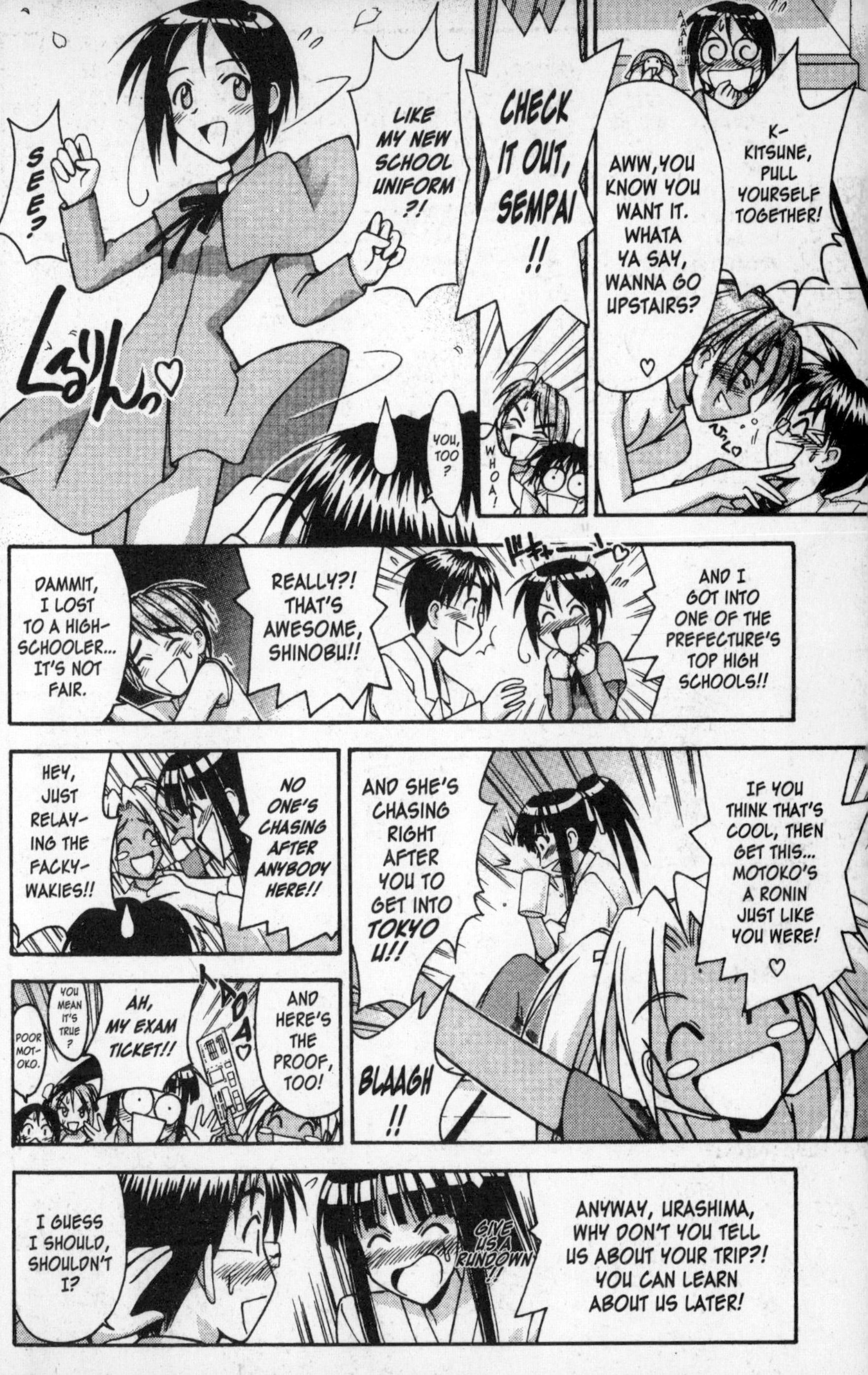
AAAHHH
K-KITSUNE, PULL YOURSELF TOGETHER!
AWW, YOU KNOW YOU WANT IT. WHATA YA SAY, WANNA GO UPSTAIRS? ♡
CHECK IT OUT, SEMPAI!!
WHOA!
LIKE MY NEW SCHOOL UNIFORM?!
SEE?
YOU, TOO?
AND I GOT INTO ONE OF THE PREFECTURE'S TOP HIGH SCHOOLS!!
REALLY?! THAT'S AWESOME, SHINOBU!!
DAMMIT, I LOST TO A HIGH-SCHOOLER... IT'S NOT FAIR.
IF YOU THINK THAT'S COOL, THEN GET THIS... MOTOKO'S A RONIN JUST LIKE YOU WERE! ♡
AND SHE'S CHASING RIGHT AFTER YOU TO GET INTO TOKYO U!!
BLAAGH!!
NO ONE'S CHASING AFTER ANYBODY HERE!!
HEY, JUST RELAYING THE FACKY-WAKIES!!
AND HERE'S THE PROOF, TOO!
AH, MY EXAM TICKET!!
YOU MEAN IT'S TRUE?
POOR MOTOKO.
ANYWAY, URASHIMA, WHY DON'T YOU TELL US ABOUT YOUR TRIP?! YOU CAN LEARN ABOUT US LATER!
GIVE US A RUNDOWN!!
I GUESS I SHOULD, SHOULDN'T I?

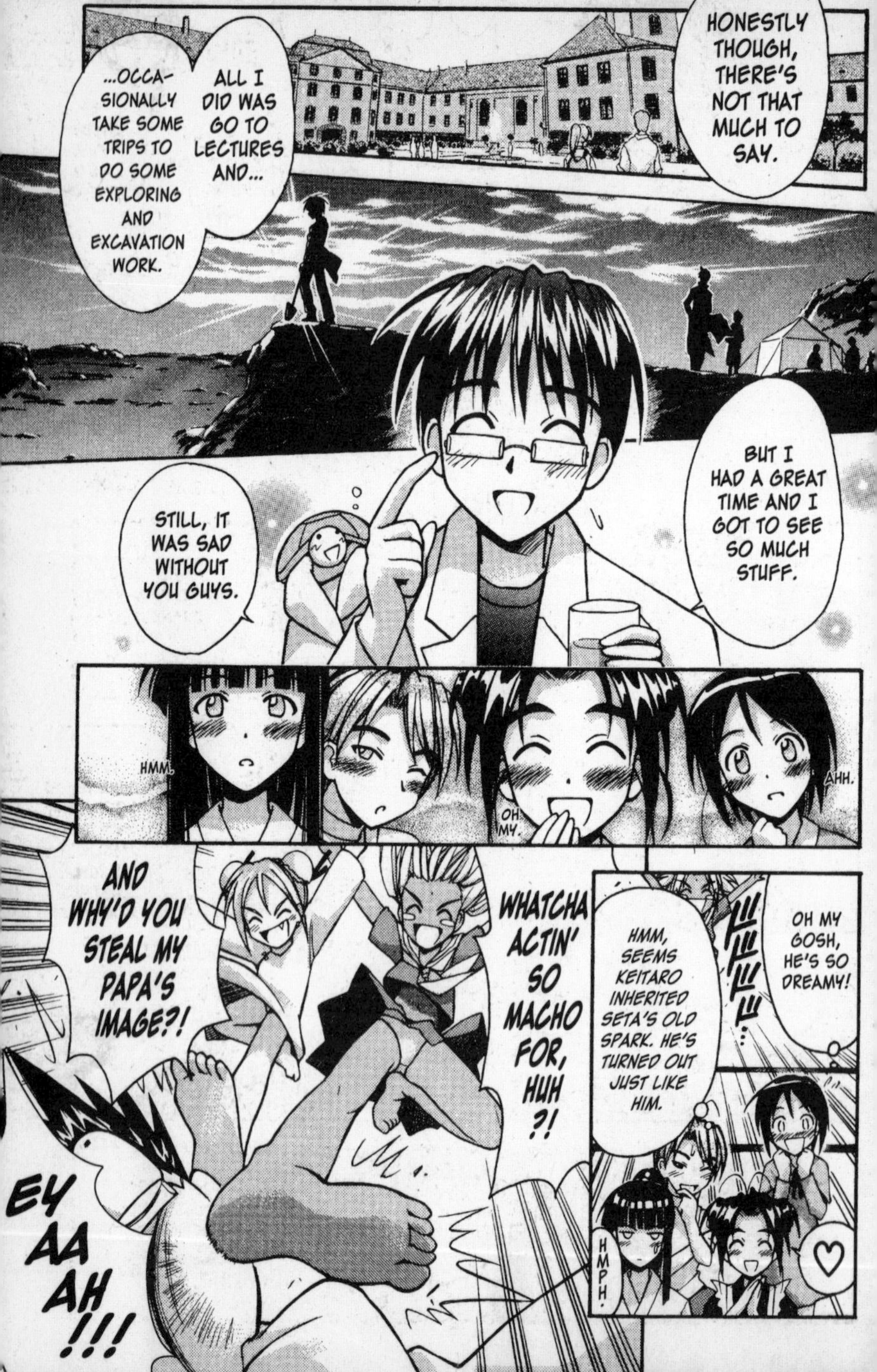
HONESTLY THOUGH, THERE'S NOT THAT MUCH TO SAY.
ALL I DID WAS GO TO LECTURES AND...
...OCCASIONALLY TAKE SOME TRIPS TO DO SOME EXPLORING AND EXCAVATION WORK.
BUT I HAD A GREAT TIME AND I GOT TO SEE SO MUCH STUFF.
STILL, IT WAS SAD WITHOUT YOU GUYS.
AHH.
OH MY.
HMM.
OH MY GOSH, HE'S SO DREAMY!
HMM, SEEMS KEITARO INHERITED SETA'S OLD SPARK. HE'S TURNED OUT JUST LIKE HIM.
HMPH.
WHATCHA ACTIN' SO MACHO FOR, HUH?!
AND WHY'D YOU STEAL MY PAPA'S IMAGE?!
EYAAAH!!!

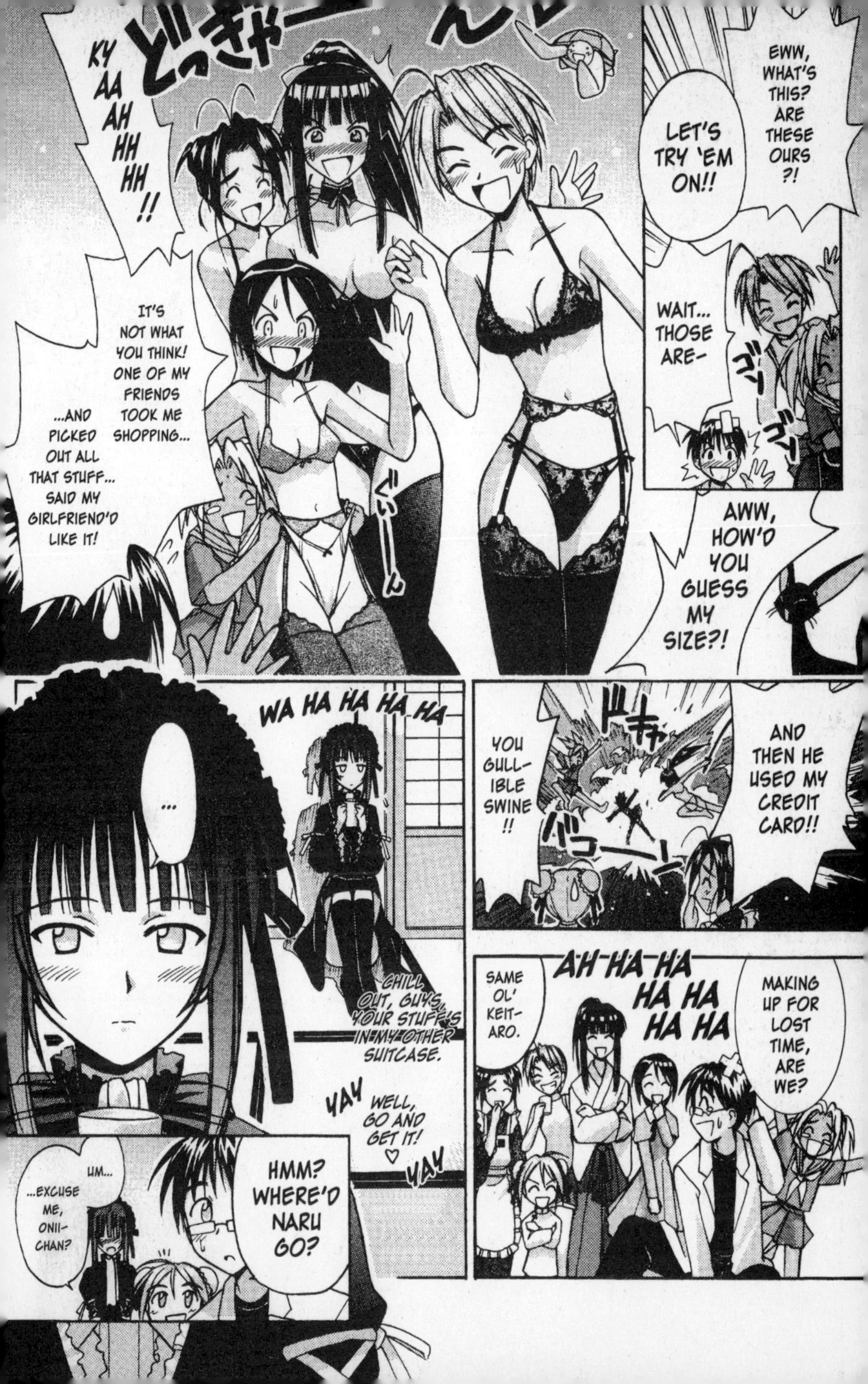

EWW, WHAT'S THIS? ARE THESE OURS?!
LET'S TRY 'EM ON!!
WAIT... THOSE ARE-
ゴン
ゴン
どっきゃーーん
KYAAAHHHHHH!!
AWW, HOW'D YOU GUESS MY SIZE?!
IT'S NOT WHAT YOU THINK! ONE OF MY FRIENDS TOOK ME SHOPPING...
...AND PICKED OUT ALL THAT STUFF... SAID MY GIRLFRIEND'D LIKE IT!
AND THEN HE USED MY CREDIT CARD!!
ドキャ
YOU GULLIBLE SWINE!!
バゴーン
AH HA HA HA HA HA HA HA
MAKING UP FOR LOST TIME, ARE WE?
SAME OL' KEIT-ARO.
WA HA HA HA HA
...
CHILL OUT, GUYS, YOUR STUFF'S IN MY OTHER SUITCASE.
YAY
WELL, GO AND GET IT! ♡
YAY
HMM? WHERE'D NARU GO?
UM... ...EXCUSE ME, ONII-CHAN?

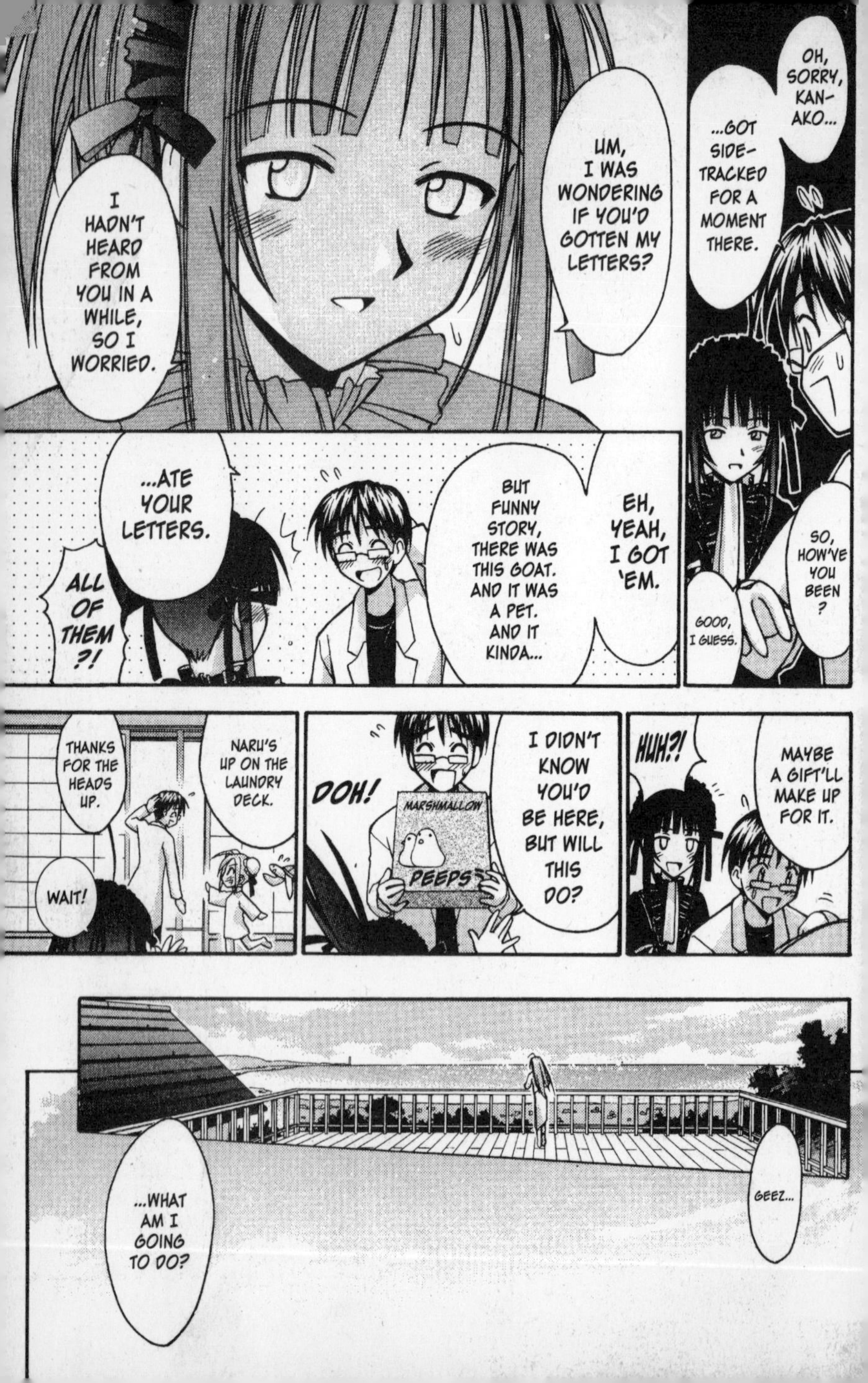
OH, SORRY, KANAKO...
...GOT SIDE-TRACKED FOR A MOMENT THERE.
UM, I WAS WONDERING IF YOU'D GOTTEN MY LETTERS?
I HADN'T HEARD FROM YOU IN A WHILE, SO I WORRIED.
SO, HOW'VE YOU BEEN?
GOOD, I GUESS.
EH, YEAH, I GOT 'EM.
BUT FUNNY STORY, THERE WAS THIS GOAT. AND IT WAS A PET. AND IT KINDA...
...ATE YOUR LETTERS.
ALL OF THEM?!
MAYBE A GIFT'LL MAKE UP FOR IT.
HUH?!
I DIDN'T KNOW YOU'D BE HERE, BUT WILL THIS DO?
DOH!
MARSHMALLOW
PEEPS
NARU'S UP ON THE LAUNDRY DECK.
THANKS FOR THE HEADS UP.
WAIT!
GEEZ...
...WHAT AM I GOING TO DO?

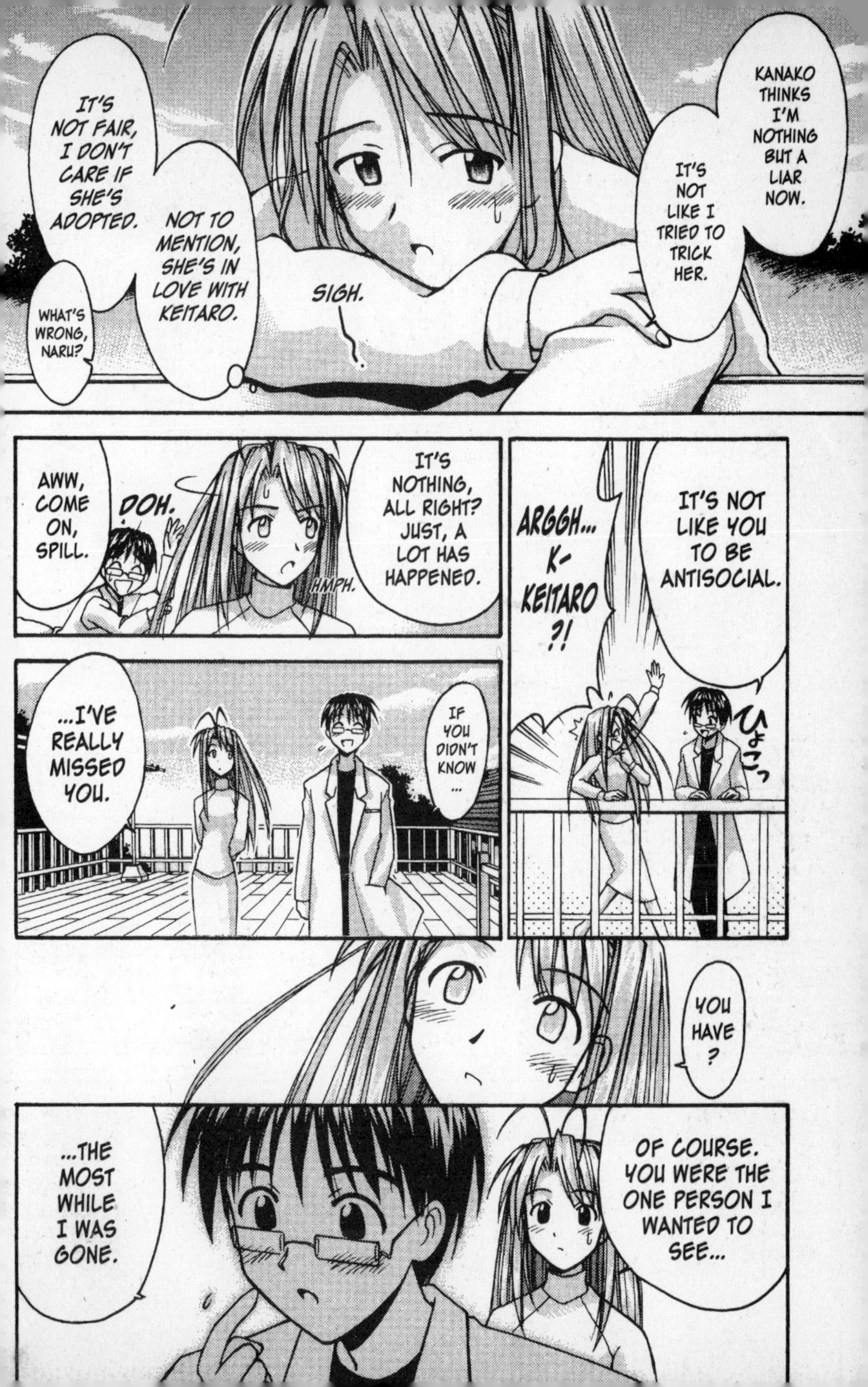
KANAKO THINKS I'M NOTHING BUT A LIAR NOW.
IT'S NOT LIKE I TRIED TO TRICK HER.
SIGH.
NOT TO MENTION, SHE'S IN LOVE WITH KEITARO.
IT'S NOT FAIR, I DON'T CARE IF SHE'S ADOPTED.
WHAT'S WRONG, NARU?
IT'S NOT LIKE YOU TO BE ANTISOCIAL.
ARGGH... K-KEITARO?!
ひょこっ
IT'S NOTHING, ALL RIGHT? JUST, A LOT HAS HAPPENED.
HMPH.
DOH.
AWW, COME ON, SPILL.
IF YOU DIDN'T KNOW...
...I'VE REALLY MISSED YOU.
YOU HAVE?
OF COURSE. YOU WERE THE ONE PERSON I WANTED TO SEE...
...THE MOST WHILE I WAS GONE.

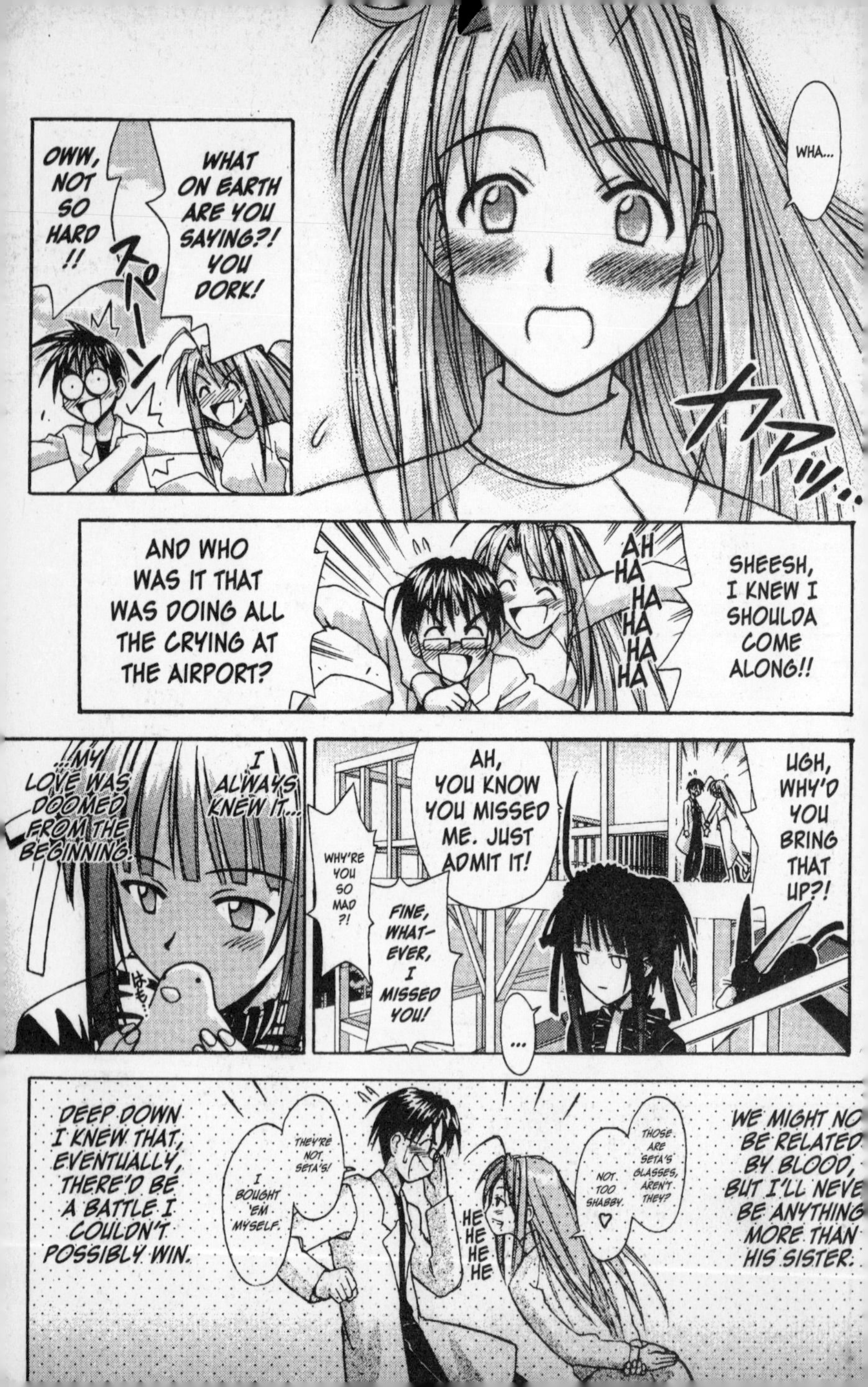
WHA...
カァッ..
WHAT ON EARTH ARE YOU SAYING?! YOU DORK!
スパーン
OWW, NOT SO HARD!!
SHEESH, I KNEW I SHOULDA COME ALONG!!
AH HA HA HA HA HA HA
AND WHO WAS IT THAT WAS DOING ALL THE CRYING AT THE AIRPORT?
UGH, WHY'D YOU BRING THAT UP?!
AH, YOU KNOW YOU MISSED ME. JUST ADMIT IT!
FINE, WHATEVER, I MISSED YOU!
WHY'RE YOU SO MAD?!
...
I ALWAYS KNEW IT...
...MY LOVE WAS DOOMED FROM THE BEGINNING.
WE MIGHT NO BE RELATED BY BLOOD, BUT I'LL NEVE BE ANYTHING MORE THAN HIS SISTER.
THOSE ARE SETA'S GLASSES, AREN'T THEY?
NOT TOO SHABBY. ♡
HE HE HE HE
THEY'RE NOT SETA'S!
I BOUGHT 'EM MYSELF.
DEEP DOWN I KNEW THAT, EVENTUALLY, THERE'D BE A BATTLE I COULDN'T POSSIBLY WIN.

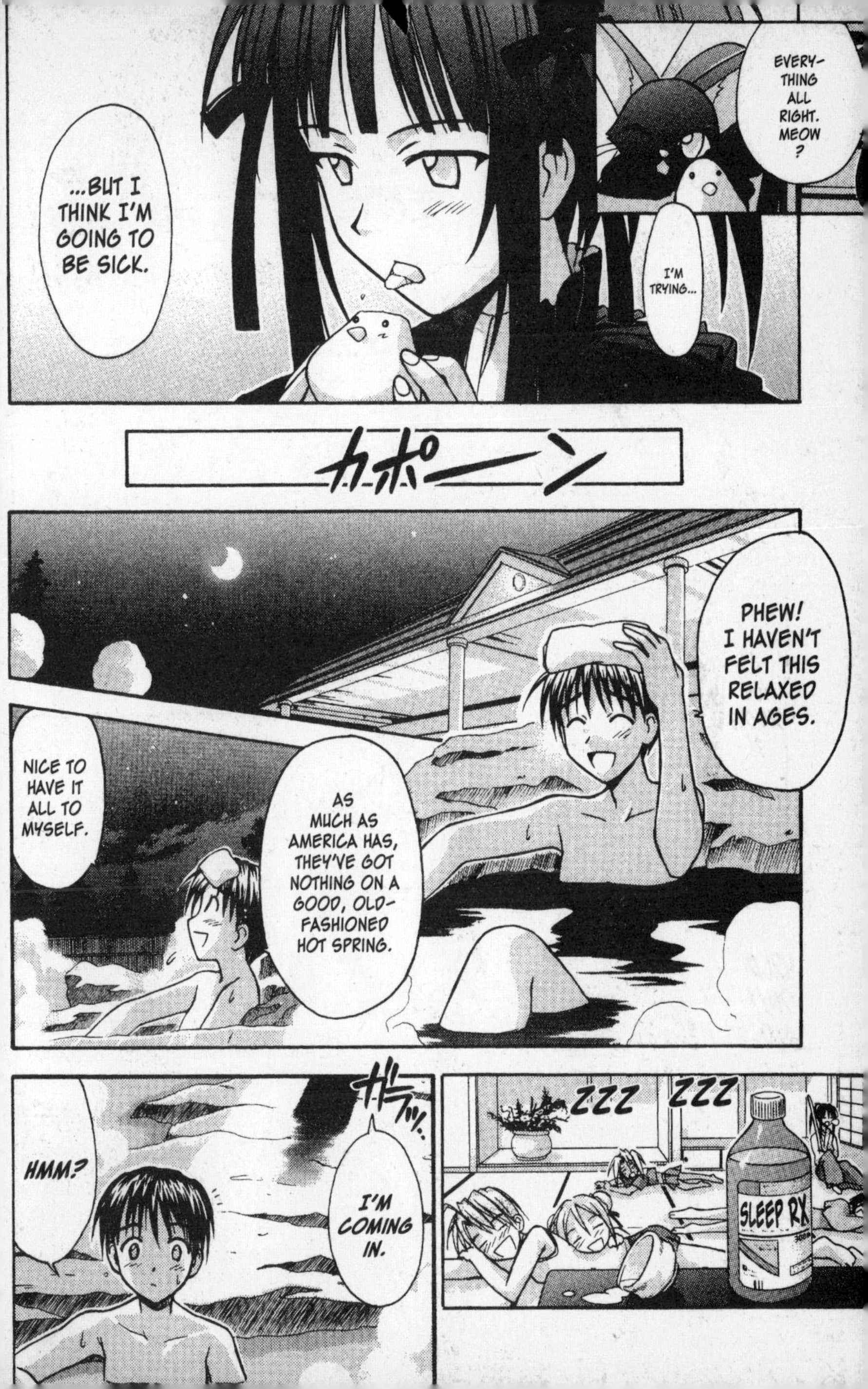
EVERYTHING ALL RIGHT. MEOW?
I'M TRYING...
...BUT I THINK I'M GOING TO BE SICK.
カポーン
PHEW! I HAVEN'T FELT THIS RELAXED IN AGES.
AS MUCH AS AMERICA HAS, THEY'VE GOT NOTHING ON A GOOD, OLD-FASHIONED HOT SPRING.
NICE TO HAVE IT ALL TO MYSELF.
ZZZ
ZZZ
SLEEP RX
ガラッ
I'M COMING IN.
HMM?

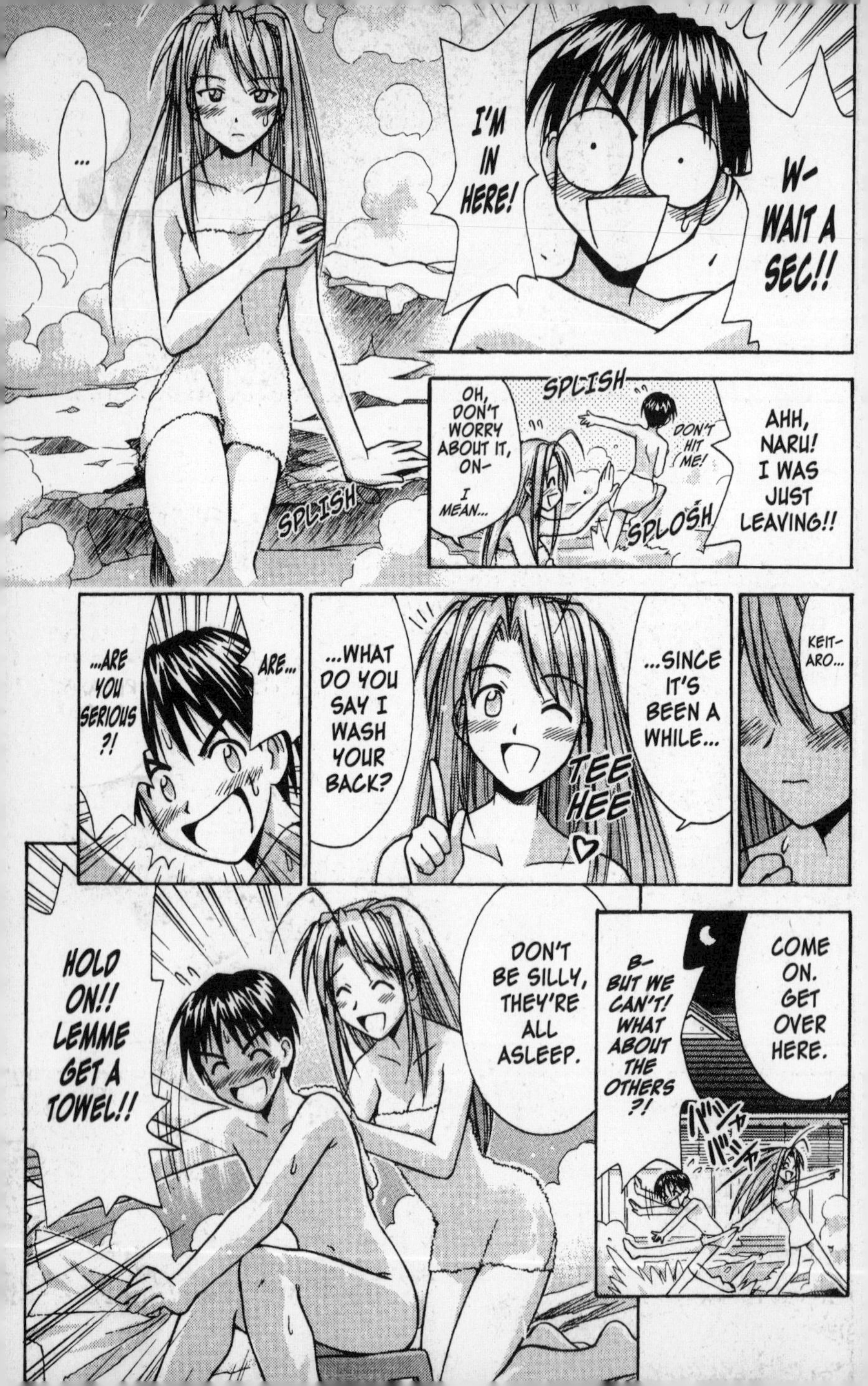
W-WAIT A SEC!!
I'M IN HERE!
AHH, NARU! I WAS JUST LEAVING!!
DON'T HIT ME!
SPLOSH
SPLISH
OH, DON'T WORRY ABOUT IT, ON- I MEAN...
SPLISH
...
KEIT-ARO...
...SINCE IT'S BEEN A WHILE...
TEE HEE ♡
...WHAT DO YOU SAY I WASH YOUR BACK?
ARE...
...ARE YOU SERIOUS?!
COME ON. GET OVER HERE.
B-BUT WE CAN'T! WHAT ABOUT THE OTHERS?!
DON'T BE SILLY, THEY'RE ALL ASLEEP.
HOLD ON!! LEMME GET A TOWEL!!

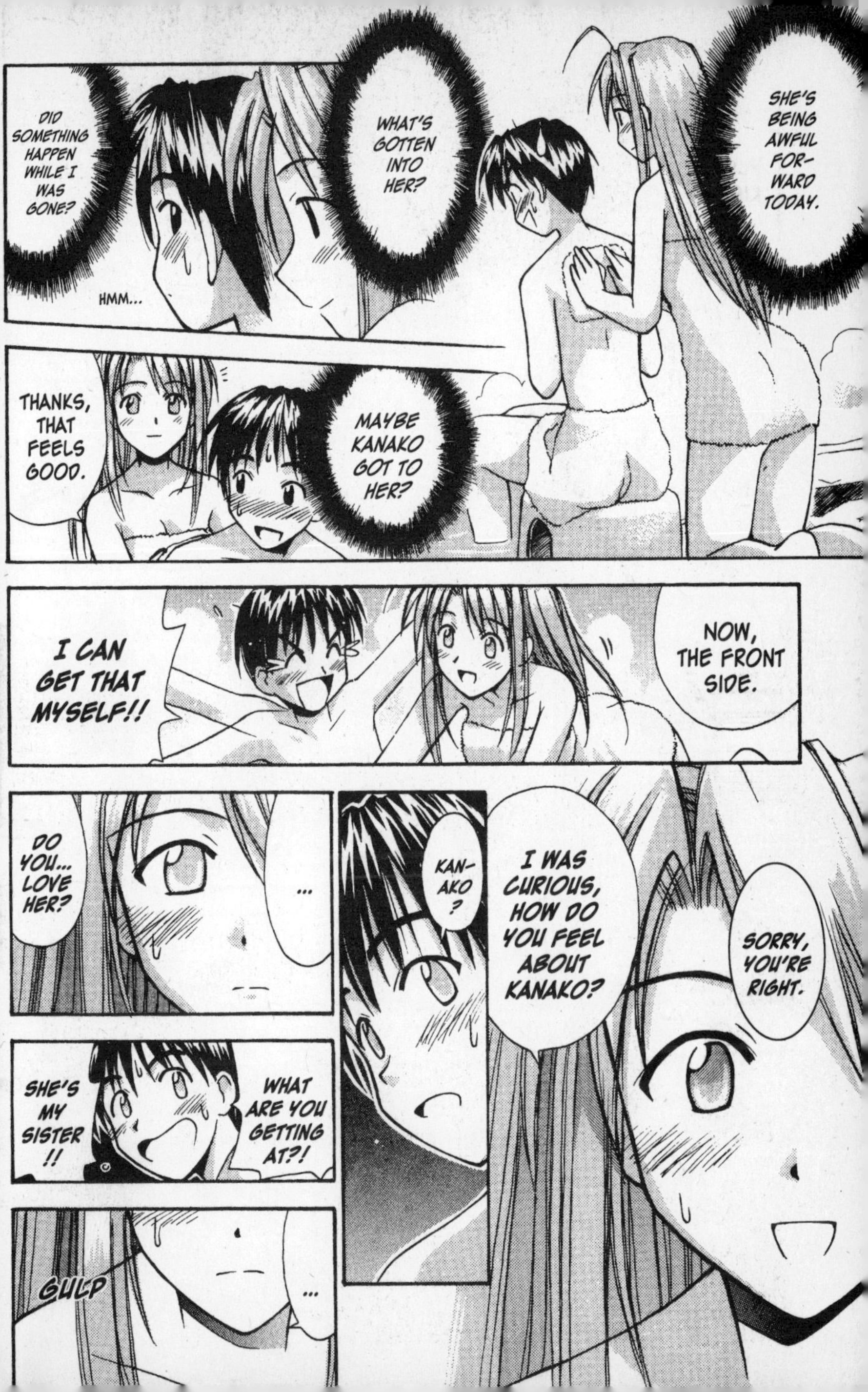
SHE'S BEING AWFUL FOR-WARD TODAY.
WHAT'S GOTTEN INTO HER?
DID SOMETHING HAPPEN WHILE I WAS GONE?
HMM...
MAYBE KANAKO GOT TO HER?
THANKS, THAT FEELS GOOD.
NOW, THE FRONT SIDE.
I CAN GET THAT MYSELF!!
SORRY, YOU'RE RIGHT.
I WAS CURIOUS, HOW DO YOU FEEL ABOUT KANAKO?
KAN-AKO?
...
DO YOU... LOVE HER?
WHAT ARE YOU GETTING AT?!
SHE'S MY SISTER!!
...
GULP

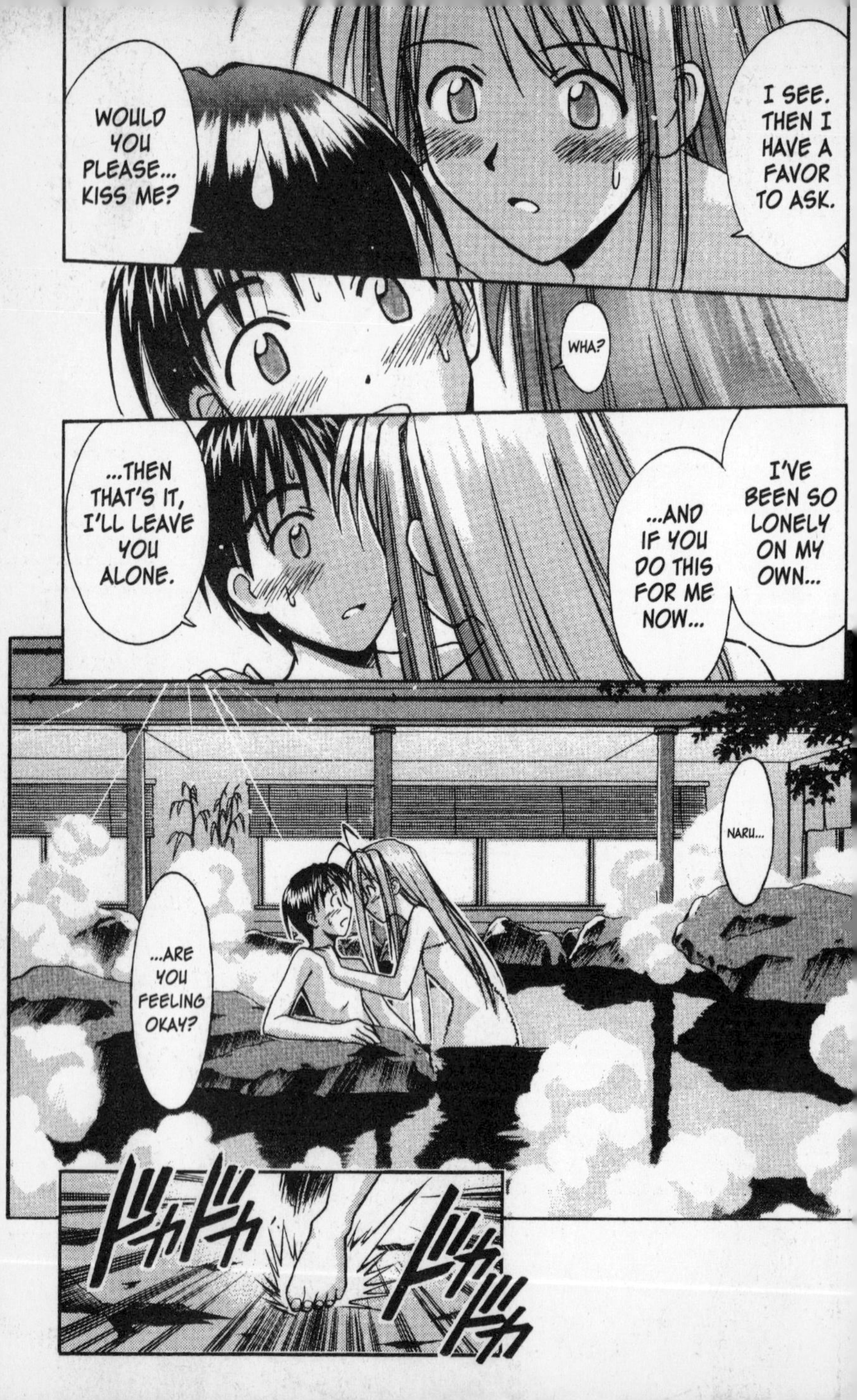
I SEE. THEN I HAVE A FAVOR TO ASK.
WOULD YOU PLEASE... KISS ME?
WHA?
I'VE BEEN SO LONELY ON MY OWN...
...AND IF YOU DO THIS FOR ME NOW...
...THEN THAT'S IT, I'LL LEAVE YOU ALONE.
NARU...
...ARE YOU FEELING OKAY?
ドカドカ
ドカドカ

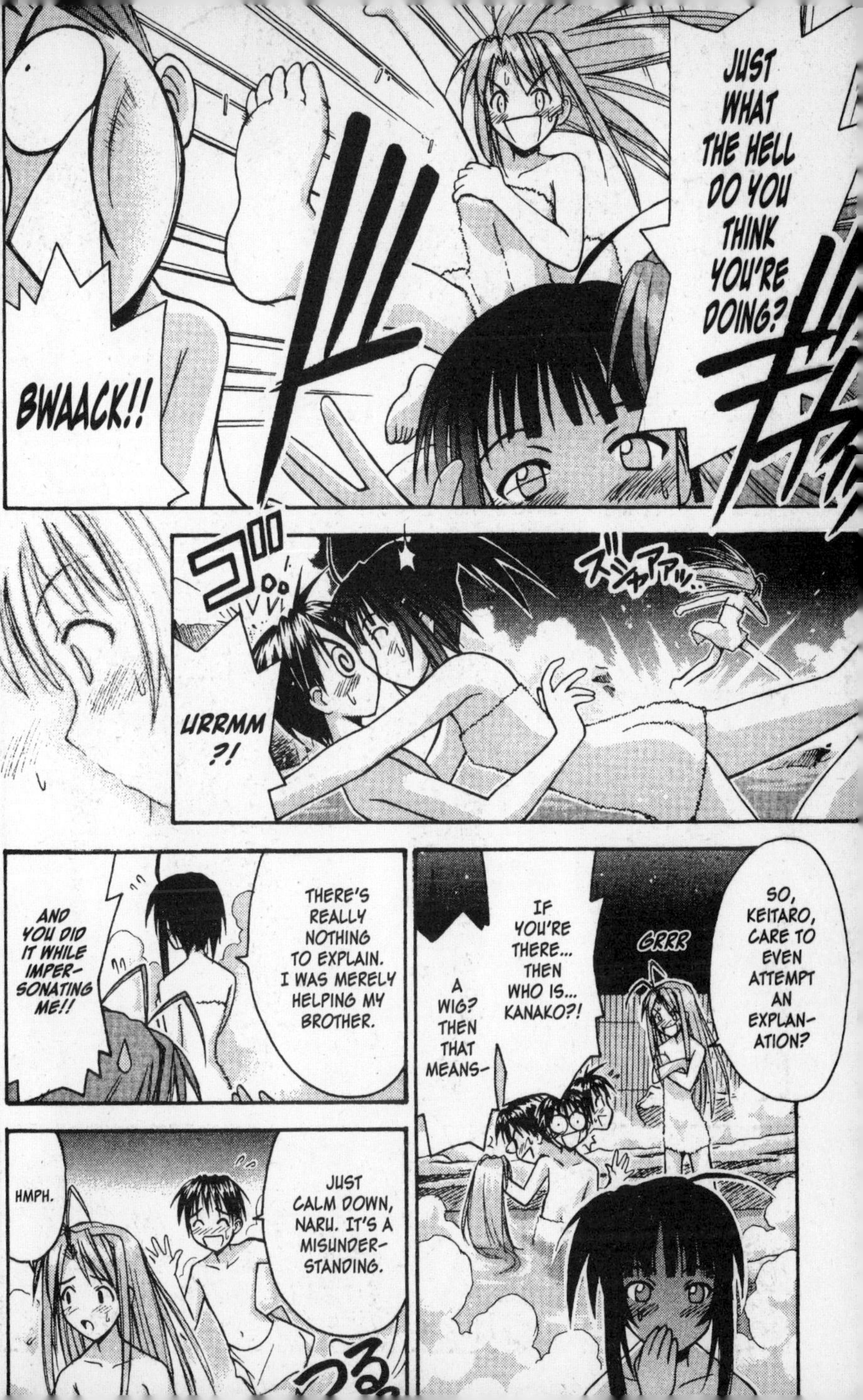
JUST WHAT THE HELL DO YOU THINK YOU'RE DOING?
BWAACK!!
ゴッ
ズシャアッ
URRMM ?!
SO, KEITARO, CARE TO EVEN ATTEMPT AN EXPLANATION?
GRRR
IF YOU'RE THERE... THEN WHO IS... KANAKO?!
A WIG? THEN THAT MEANS-
THERE'S REALLY NOTHING TO EXPLAIN. I WAS MERELY HELPING MY BROTHER.
AND YOU DID IT WHILE IMPER-SONATING ME!!
JUST CALM DOWN, NARU. IT'S A MISUNDER-STANDING.
HMPH.

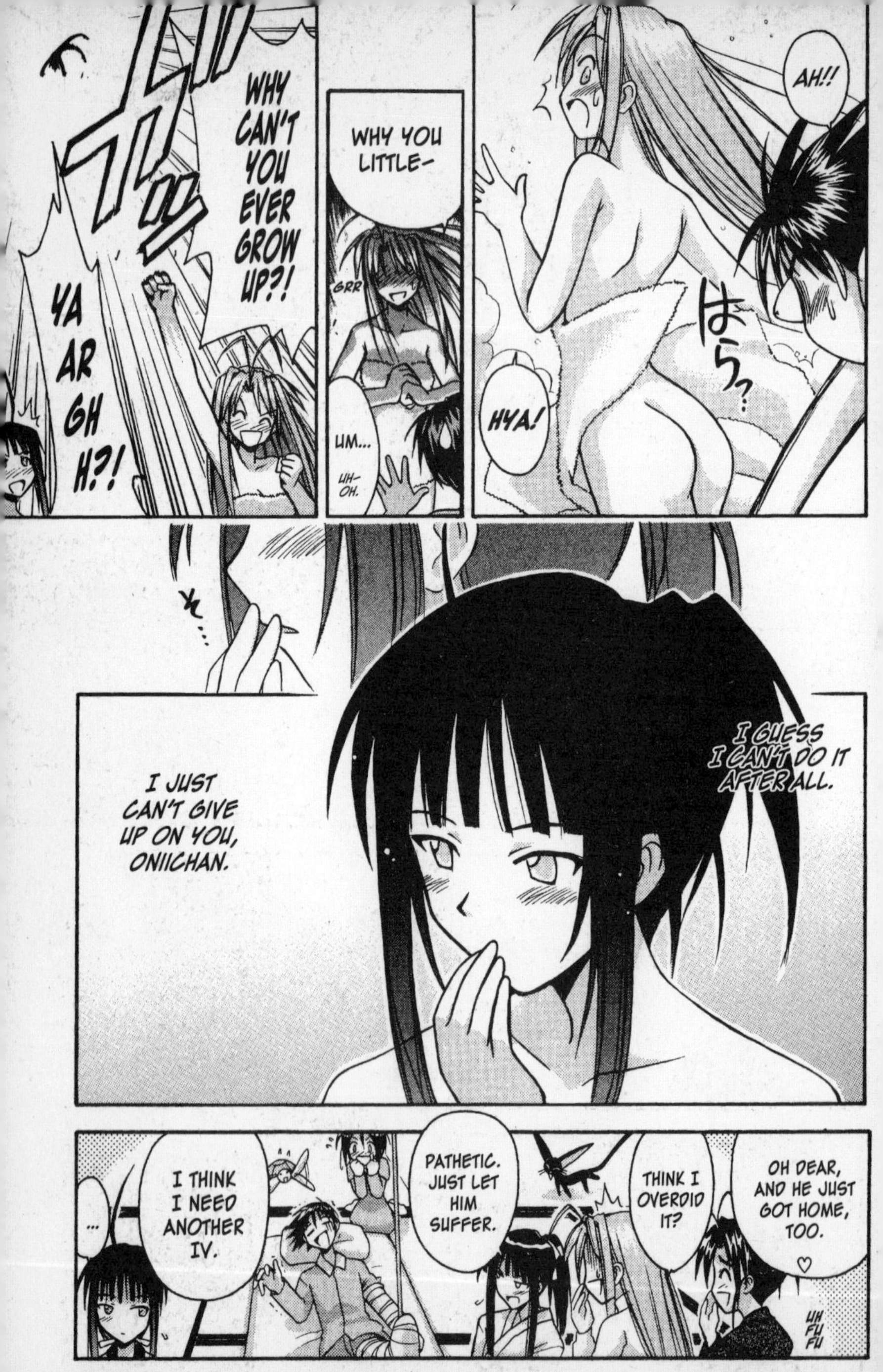
AH!!
はらっ
HYA!
WHY YOU LITTLE-
GRR
UM...
UH-OH.
WHY CAN'T YOU EVER GROW UP?!
YAARGHH?!
I GUESS I CAN'T DO IT AFTER ALL.
I JUST CAN'T GIVE UP ON YOU, ONIICHAN.
OH DEAR, AND HE JUST GOT HOME, TOO. ♡
UH FU FU
THINK I OVERDID IT?
PATHETIC. JUST LET HIM SUFFER.
I THINK I NEED ANOTHER IV.
...

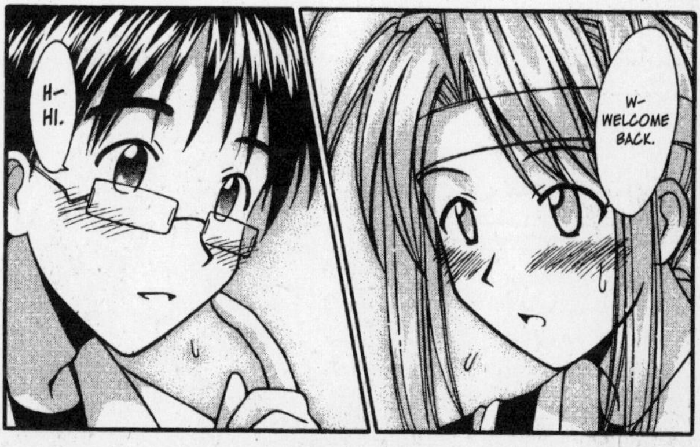
W- WELCOME BACK.
H- HI.

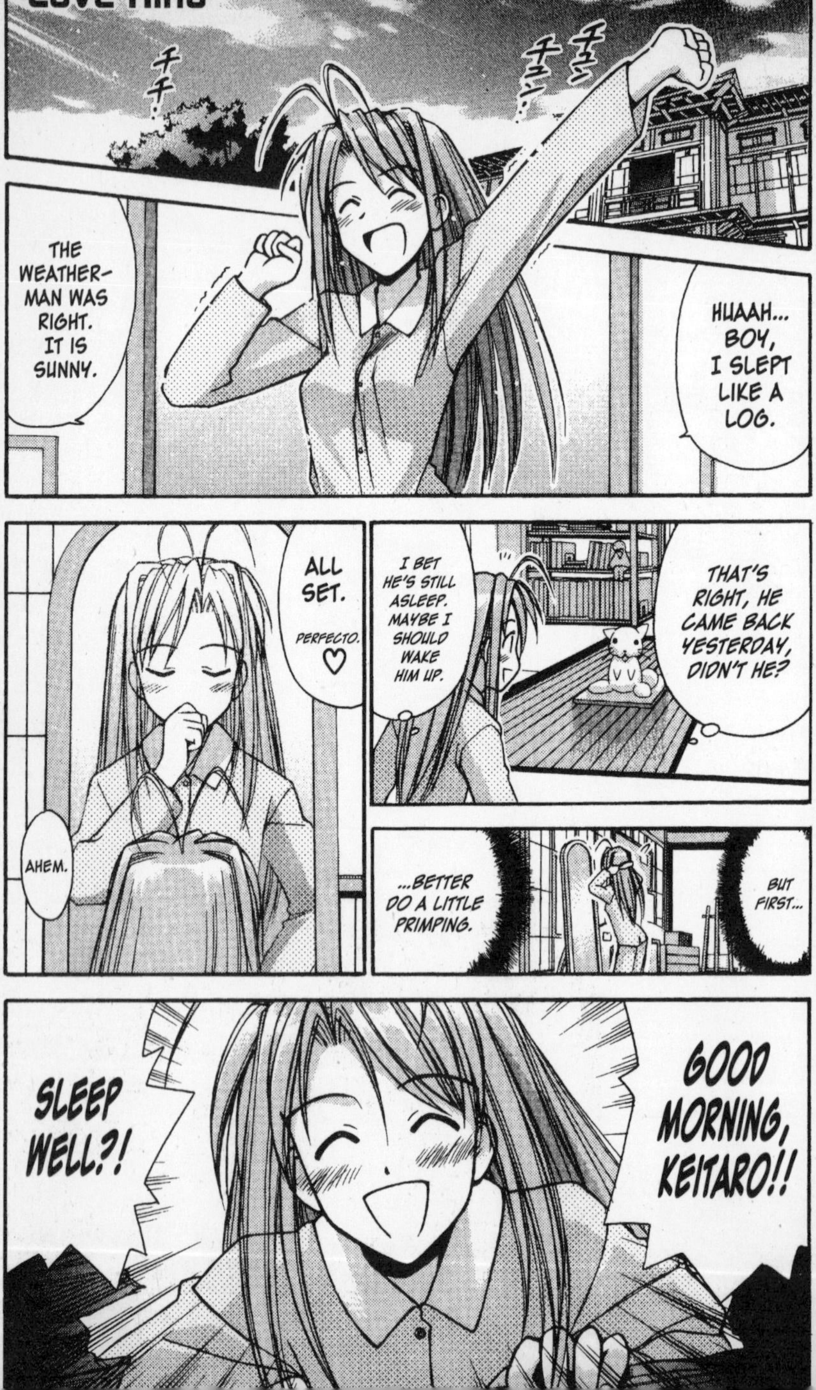
チュン チュンー
チチ…
HUAAH... BOY, I SLEPT LIKE A LOG.
THE WEATHER-MAN WAS RIGHT. IT IS SUNNY.
THAT'S RIGHT, HE CAME BACK YESTERDAY, DIDN'T HE?
I BET HE'S STILL ASLEEP. MAYBE I SHOULD WAKE HIM UP.
BUT FIRST...
...BETTER DO A LITTLE PRIMPING.
ALL SET.
PERFECTO. ♡
AHEM.
GOOD MORNING, KEITARO!!
SLEEP WELL?!

Love Hina

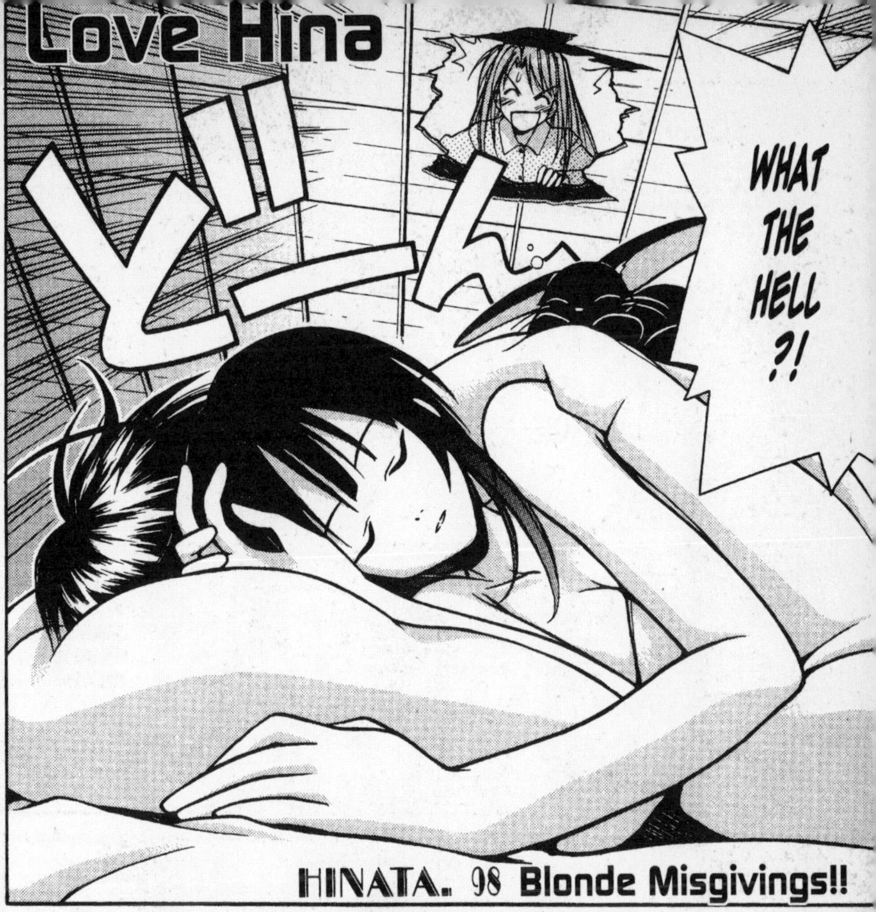
WHAT THE HELL?!
どーん

HINATA. 98 Blonde Misgivings!!

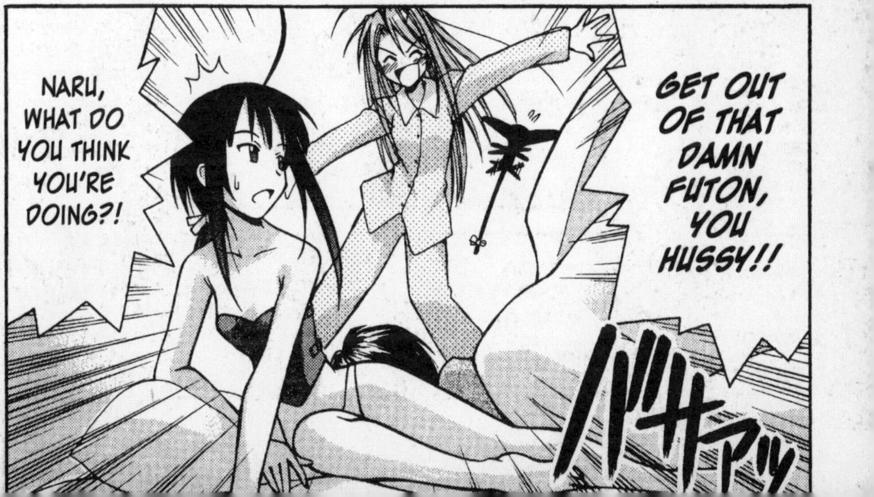
GET OUT OF THAT DAMN FUTON, YOU HUSSY!!
NARU, WHAT DO YOU THINK YOU'RE DOING?!
バサァッ

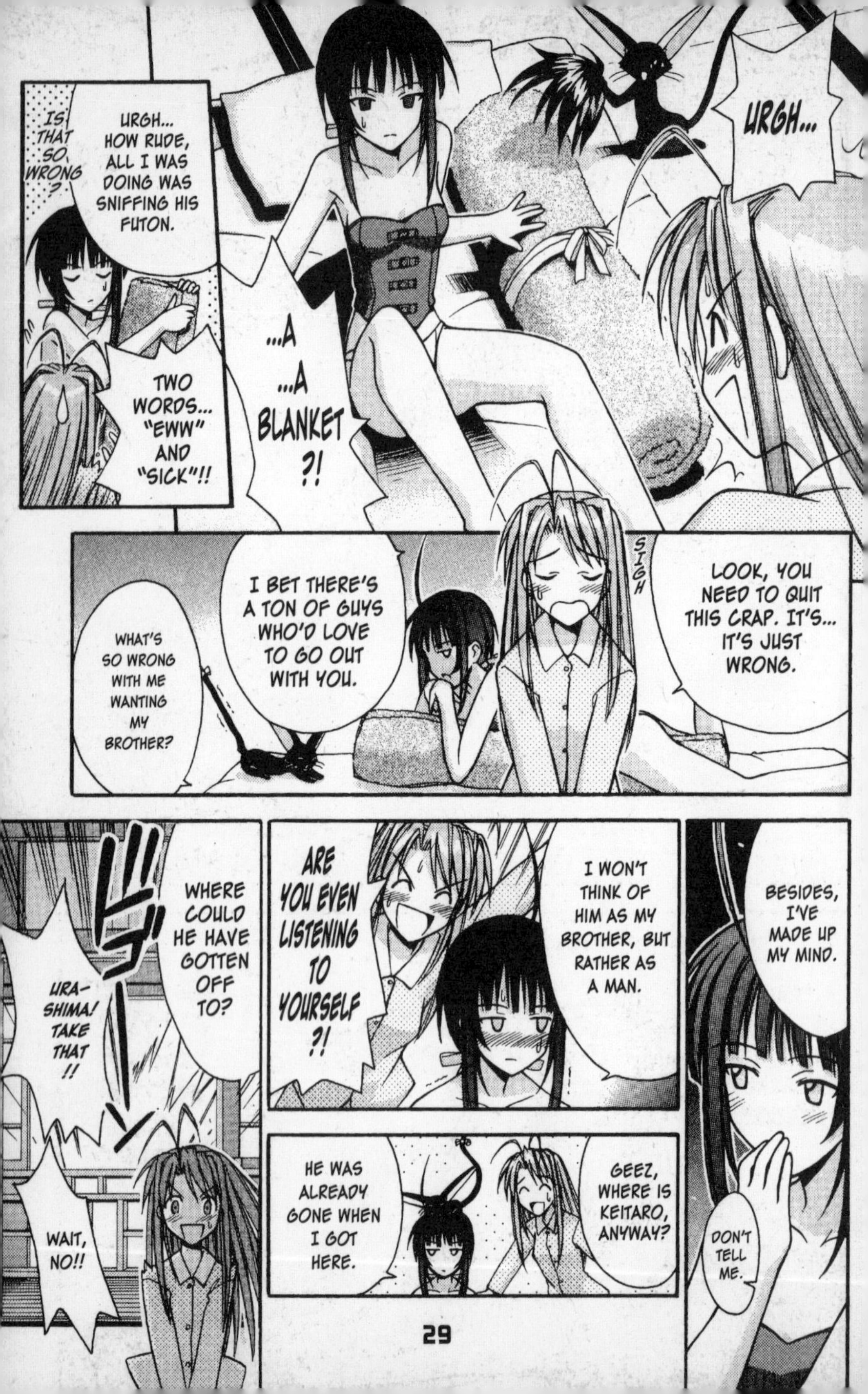
URGH...
...A ...A BLANKET ?!
URGH... HOW RUDE, ALL I WAS DOING WAS SNIFFING HIS FUTON.
IS THAT SO WRONG ?
TWO WORDS... "EWW" AND "SICK"!!
SIGH
LOOK, YOU NEED TO QUIT THIS CRAP. IT'S... IT'S JUST WRONG.
I BET THERE'S A TON OF GUYS WHO'D LOVE TO GO OUT WITH YOU.
WHAT'S SO WRONG WITH ME WANTING MY BROTHER?
BESIDES, I'VE MADE UP MY MIND.
DON'T TELL ME.
I WON'T THINK OF HIM AS MY BROTHER, BUT RATHER AS A MAN.
ARE YOU EVEN LISTENING TO YOURSELF ?!
GEEZ, WHERE IS KEITARO, ANYWAY?
HE WAS ALREADY GONE WHEN I GOT HERE.
WHERE COULD HE HAVE GOTTEN OFF TO?
URA-SHIMA! TAKE THAT !!
WAIT, NO!!

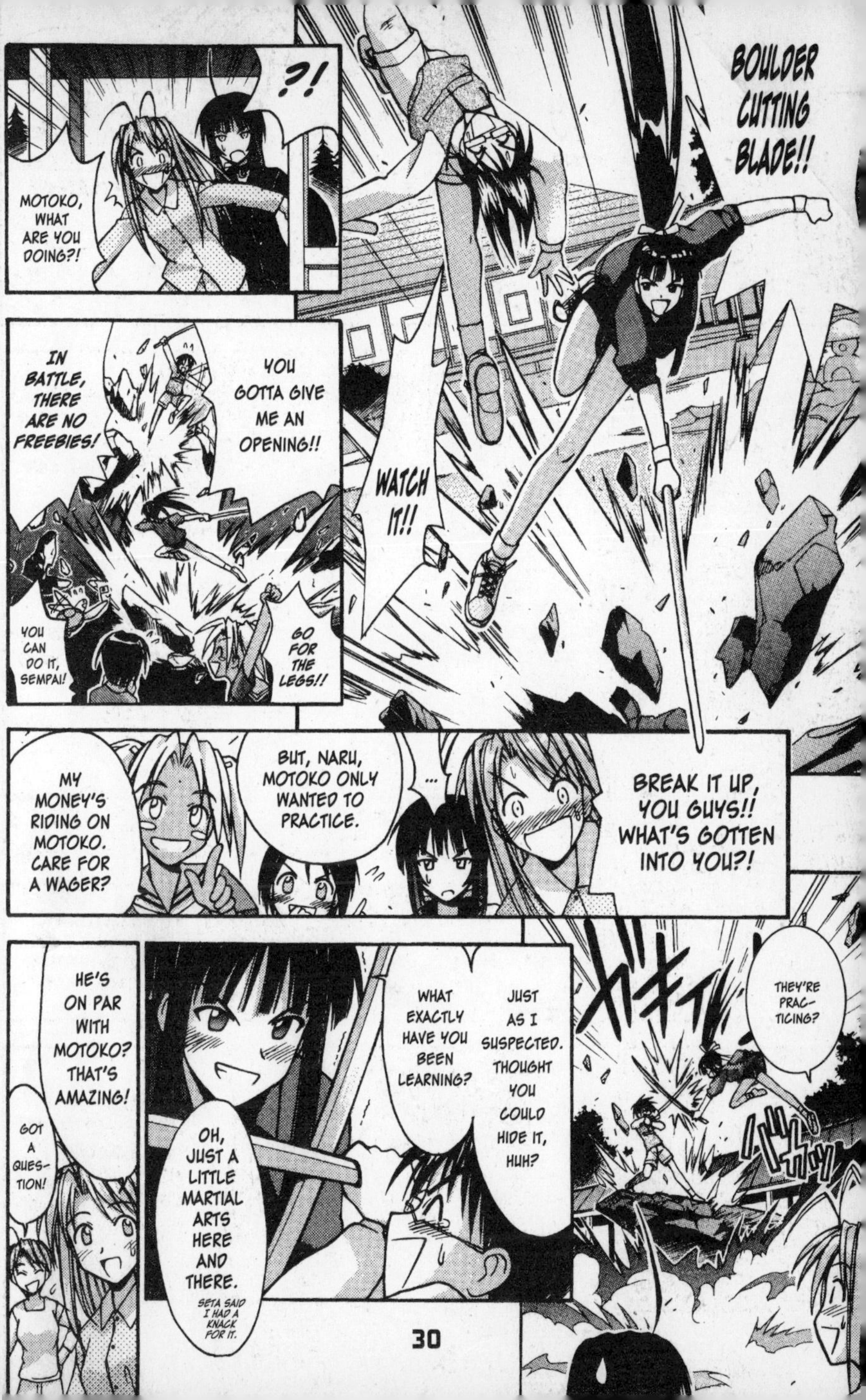
BOULDER CUTTING BLADE!!
WATCH IT!!
?!
MOTOKO, WHAT ARE YOU DOING?!
YOU GOTTA GIVE ME AN OPENING!!
IN BATTLE, THERE ARE NO FREEBIES!
GO FOR THE LEGS!!
YOU CAN DO IT, SEMPAI!
BREAK IT UP, YOU GUYS!! WHAT'S GOTTEN INTO YOU?!
...
BUT, NARU, MOTOKO ONLY WANTED TO PRACTICE.
MY MONEY'S RIDING ON MOTOKO. CARE FOR A WAGER?
THEY'RE PRACTICING?
JUST AS I SUSPECTED. THOUGHT YOU COULD HIDE IT, HUH?
WHAT EXACTLY HAVE YOU BEEN LEARNING?
OH, JUST A LITTLE MARTIAL ARTS HERE AND THERE.
SETA SAID I HAD A KNACK FOR IT.
HE'S ON PAR WITH MOTOKO? THAT'S AMAZING!
GOT A QUESTION!

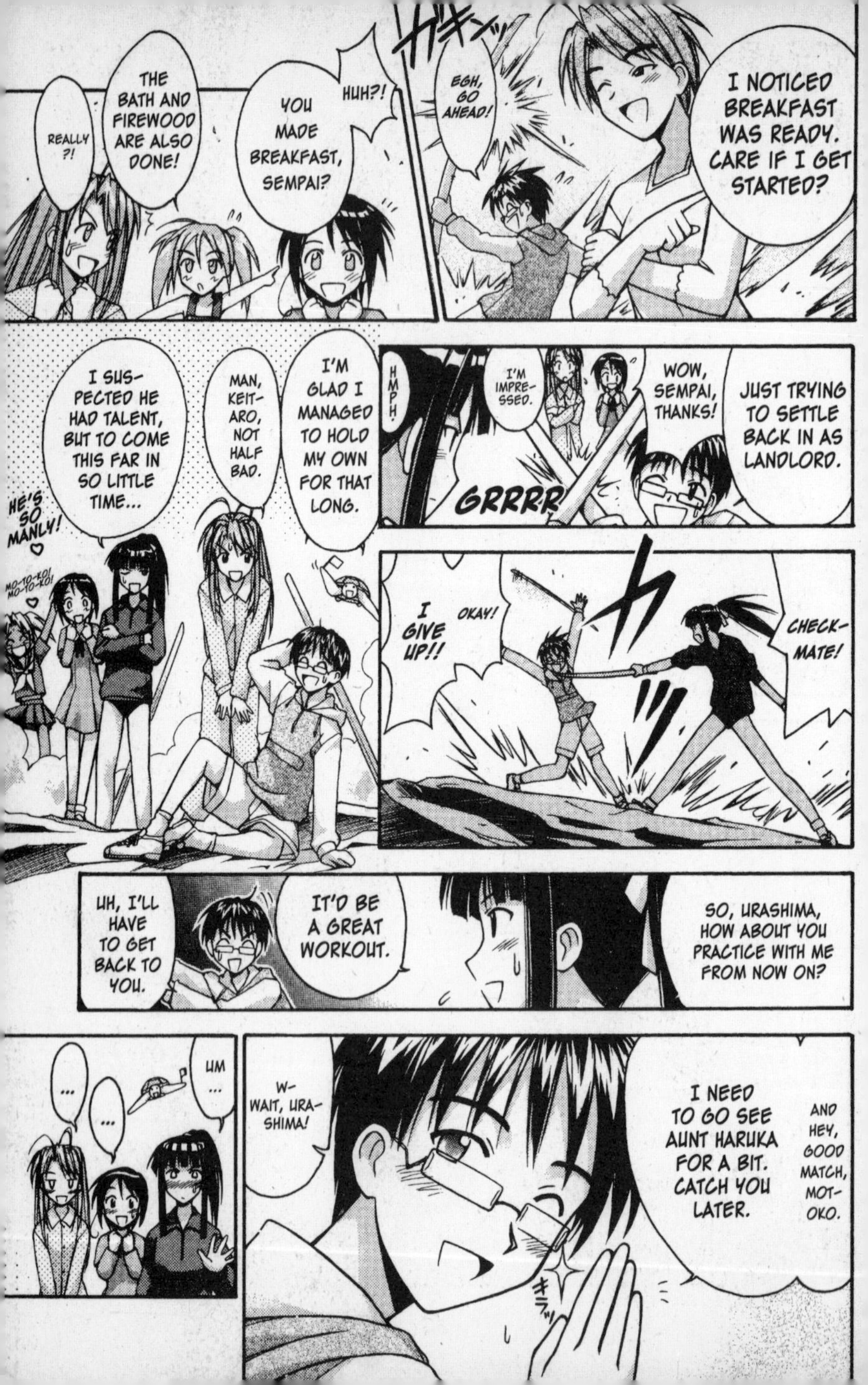
I NOTICED BREAKFAST WAS READY. CARE IF I GET STARTED?
EGH, GO AHEAD!
HUH?!
YOU MADE BREAKFAST, SEMPAI?
THE BATH AND FIREWOOD ARE ALSO DONE!
REALLY?!
JUST TRYING TO SETTLE BACK IN AS LANDLORD.
WOW, SEMPAI, THANKS!
I'M IMPRESSED.
HMPH!
GRRRR
CHECK-MATE!
OKAY!
I GIVE UP!!
I'M GLAD I MANAGED TO HOLD MY OWN FOR THAT LONG.
MAN, KEIT-ARO, NOT HALF BAD.
I SUS-PECTED HE HAD TALENT, BUT TO COME THIS FAR IN SO LITTLE TIME...
HE'S SO MANLY!
MO-TO-KO! MO-TO-KO!
SO, URASHIMA, HOW ABOUT YOU PRACTICE WITH ME FROM NOW ON?
IT'D BE A GREAT WORKOUT.
UH, I'LL HAVE TO GET BACK TO YOU.
AND HEY, GOOD MATCH, MOT-OKO.
I NEED TO GO SEE AUNT HARUKA FOR A BIT. CATCH YOU LATER.
W-WAIT, URA-SHIMA!
UM ...
...
...

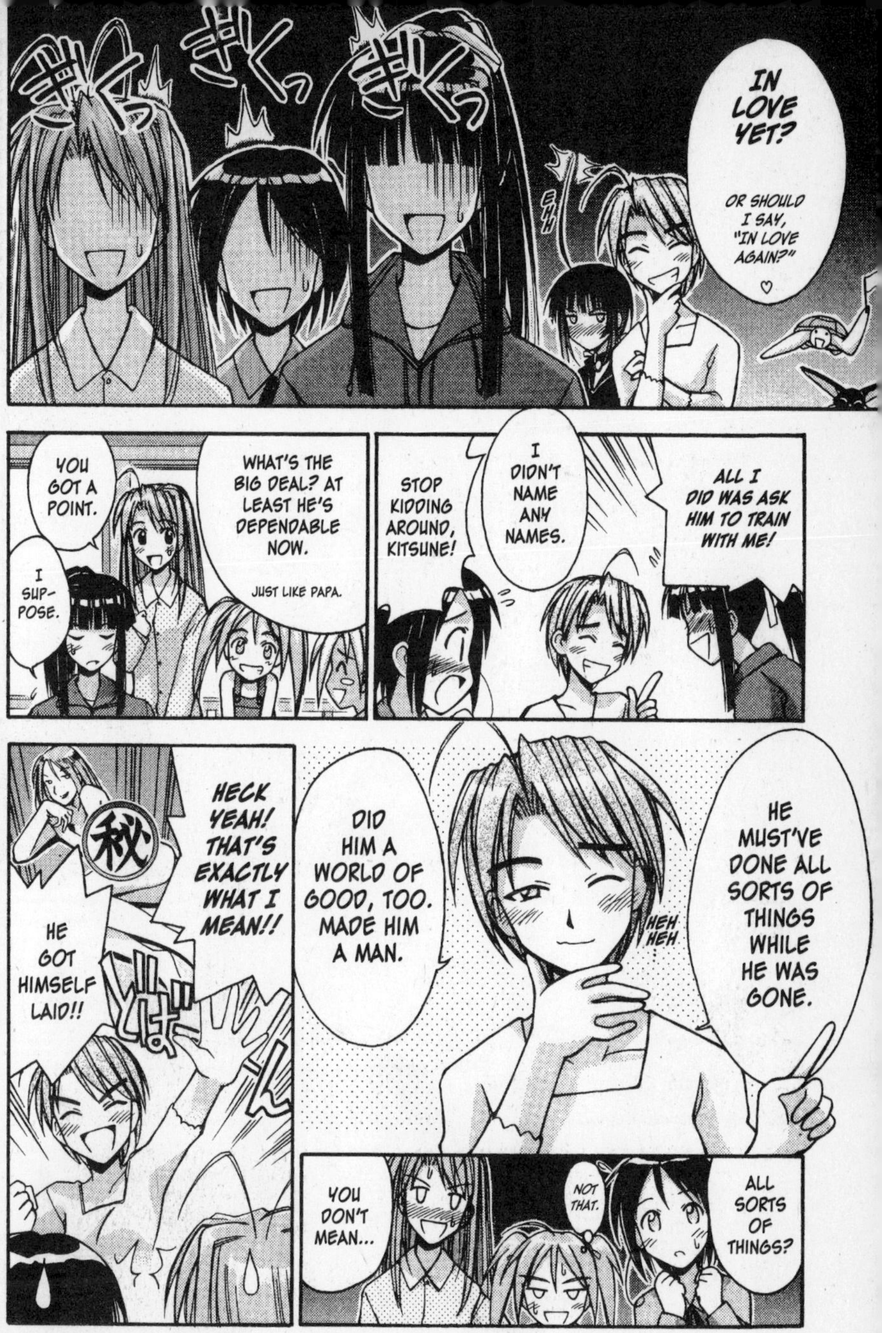
ぎくっ
ぎくっ
ぎくっ
IN LOVE YET?
OR SHOULD I SAY, "IN LOVE AGAIN?" ♡
EHH
ALL I DID WAS ASK HIM TO TRAIN WITH ME!
I DIDN'T NAME ANY NAMES.
STOP KIDDING AROUND, KITSUNE!
WHAT'S THE BIG DEAL? AT LEAST HE'S DEPENDABLE NOW.
JUST LIKE PAPA.
YOU GOT A POINT.
I SUP-POSE.
HE MUST'VE DONE ALL SORTS OF THINGS WHILE HE WAS GONE.
HEH HEH
DID HIM A WORLD OF GOOD, TOO. MADE HIM A MAN.
ALL SORTS OF THINGS?
NOT THAT.
YOU DON'T MEAN...
秘
HECK YEAH! THAT'S EXACTLY WHAT I MEAN!!
HE GOT HIMSELF LAID!!
ばーん

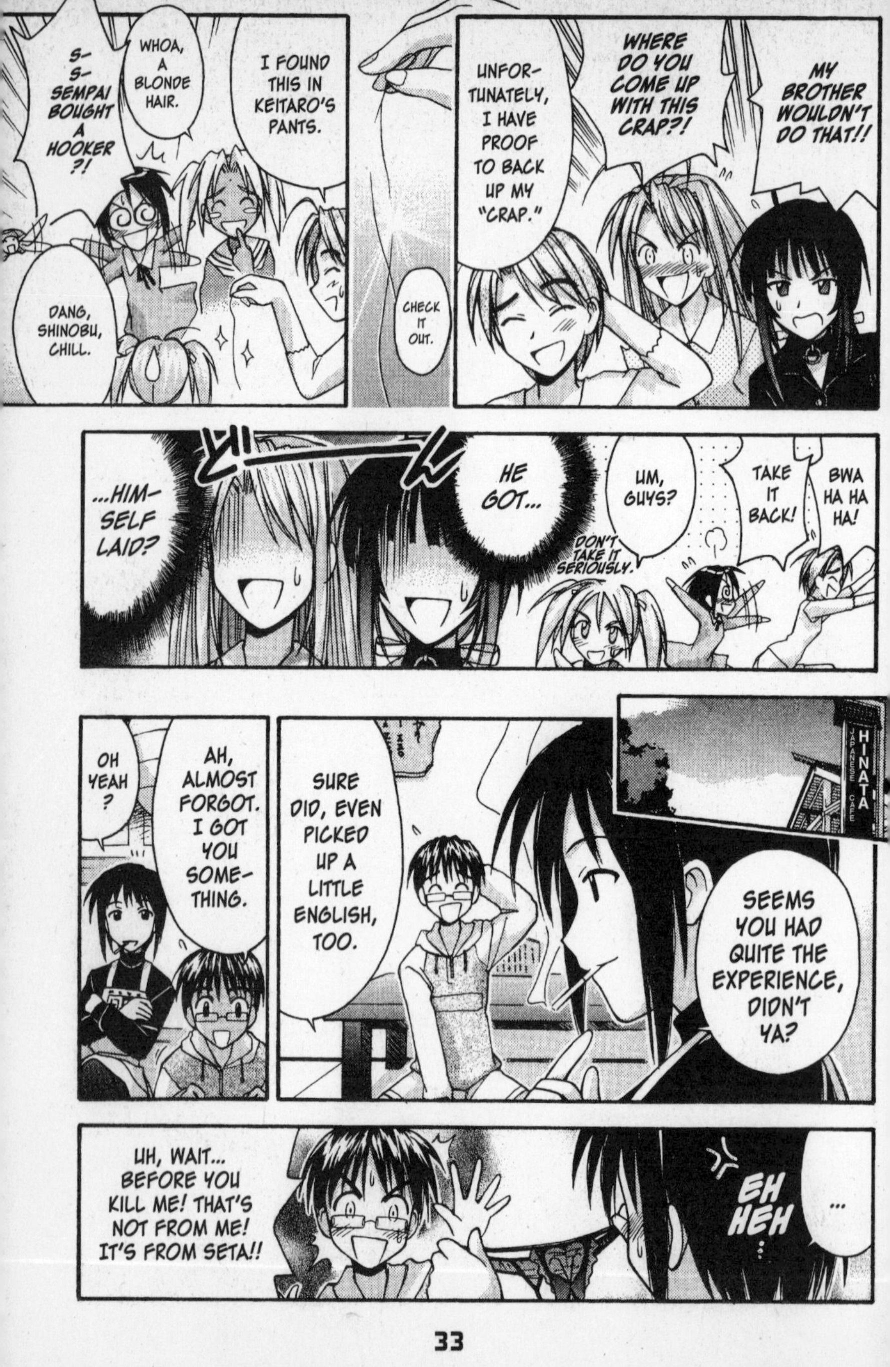
MY BROTHER WOULDN'T DO THAT!!
WHERE DO YOU COME UP WITH THIS CRAP?!
UNFORTUNATELY, I HAVE PROOF TO BACK UP MY "CRAP."
CHECK IT OUT.
I FOUND THIS IN KEITARO'S PANTS.
WHOA, A BLONDE HAIR.
S-S-SEMPAI BOUGHT A HOOKER?!
DANG, SHINOBU, CHILL.
BWA HA HA HA!
TAKE IT BACK!
UM, GUYS?
DON'T TAKE IT SERIOUSLY.
HE GOT...
...HIMSELF LAID?
HINATA JAPANESE CAFE
SEEMS YOU HAD QUITE THE EXPERIENCE, DIDN'T YA?
SURE DID, EVEN PICKED UP A LITTLE ENGLISH, TOO.
AH, ALMOST FORGOT. I GOT YOU SOMETHING.
OH YEAH?
EH HEH...
...
UH, WAIT... BEFORE YOU KILL ME! THAT'S NOT FROM ME! IT'S FROM SETA!!

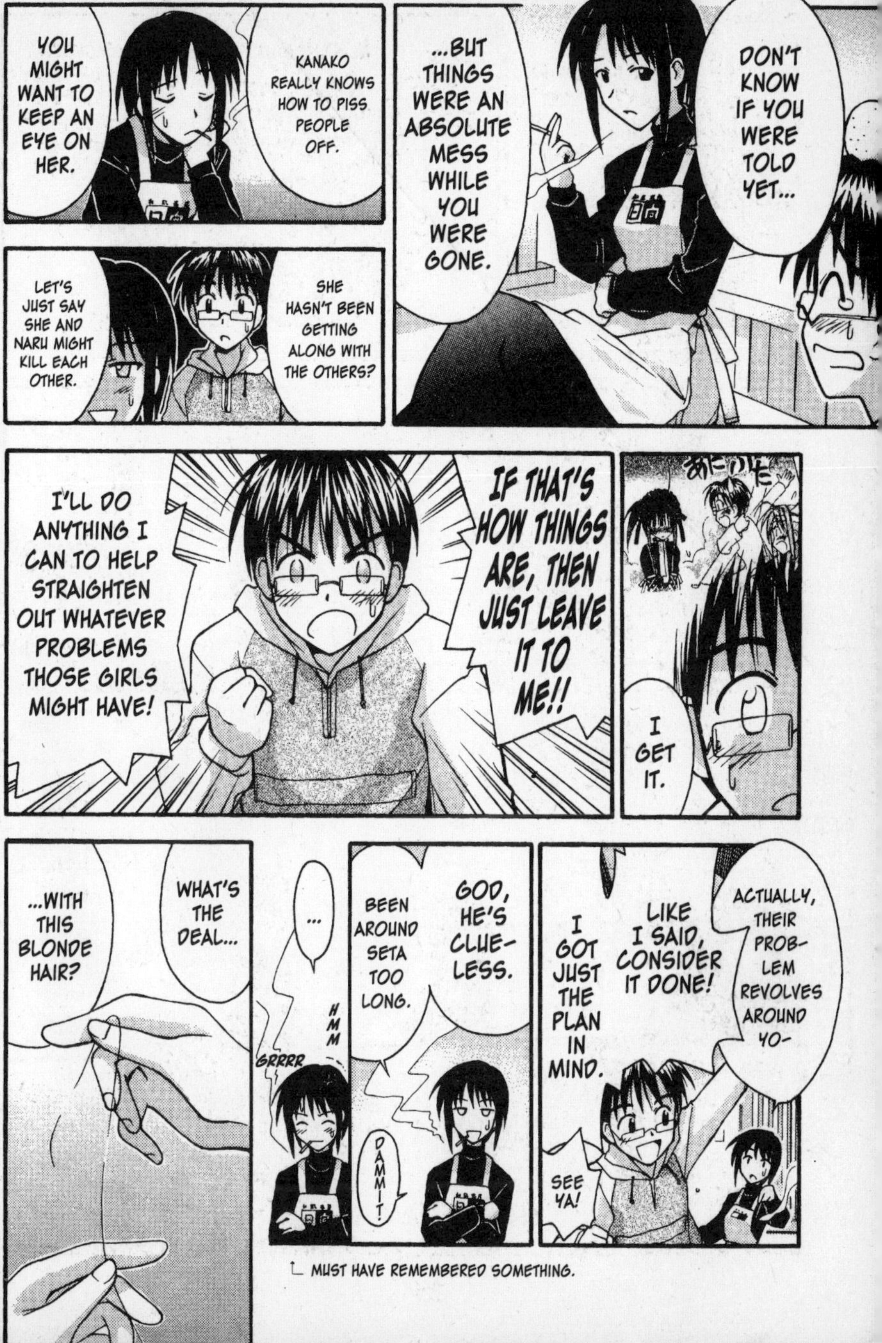
DON'T KNOW IF YOU WERE TOLD YET...
...BUT THINGS WERE AN ABSOLUTE MESS WHILE YOU WERE GONE.
KANAKO REALLY KNOWS HOW TO PISS PEOPLE OFF.
YOU MIGHT WANT TO KEEP AN EYE ON HER.
SHE HASN'T BEEN GETTING ALONG WITH THE OTHERS?
LET'S JUST SAY SHE AND NARU MIGHT KILL EACH OTHER.
I GET IT.
IF THAT'S HOW THINGS ARE, THEN JUST LEAVE IT TO ME!!
I'LL DO ANYTHING I CAN TO HELP STRAIGHTEN OUT WHATEVER PROBLEMS THOSE GIRLS MIGHT HAVE!
ACTUALLY, THEIR PROB-LEM REVOLVES AROUND YO-
LIKE I SAID, CONSIDER IT DONE!
I GOT JUST THE PLAN IN MIND.
SEE YA!
GOD, HE'S CLUE-LESS.
BEEN AROUND SETA TOO LONG.
...
HMM
GRRRR
DAMMIT!
WHAT'S THE DEAL...
...WITH THIS BLONDE HAIR?
MUST HAVE REMEMBERED SOMETHING.

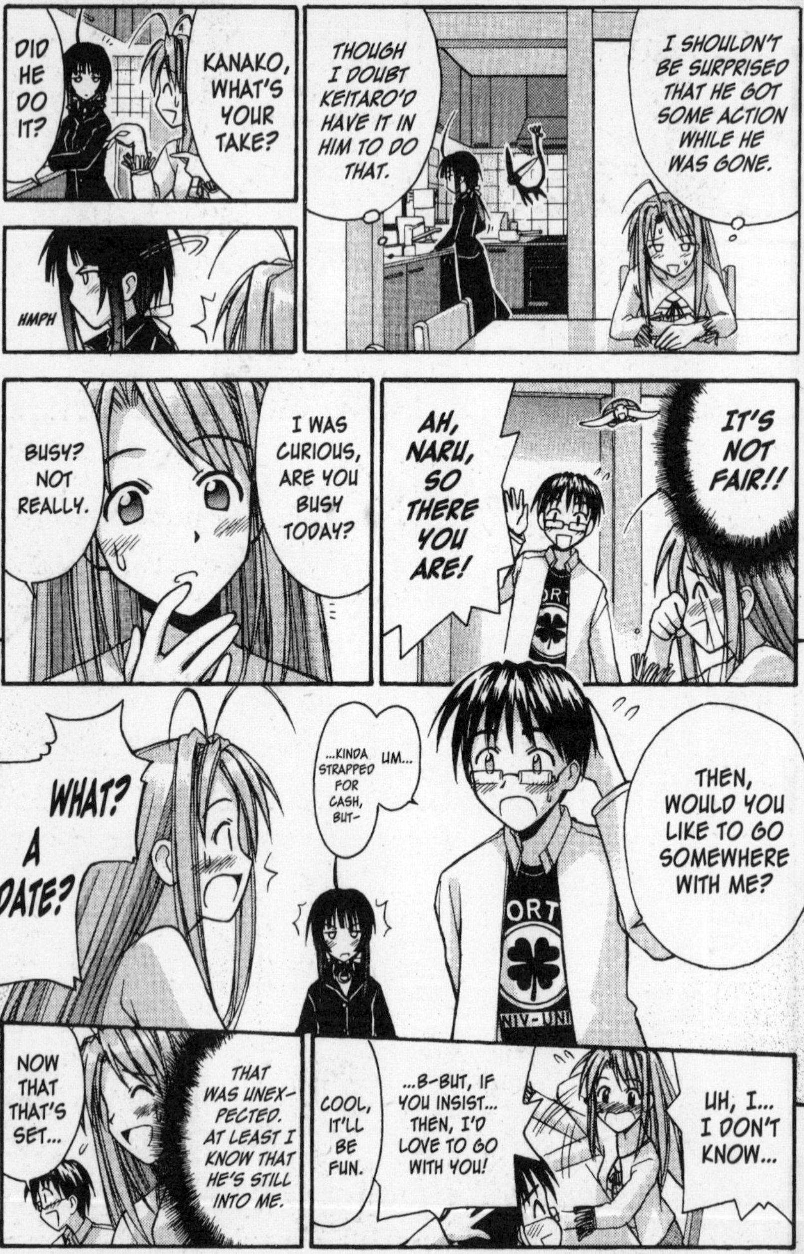
I SHOULDN'T BE SURPRISED THAT HE GOT SOME ACTION WHILE HE WAS GONE.
THOUGH I DOUBT KEITARO'D HAVE IT IN HIM TO DO THAT.
KANAKO, WHAT'S YOUR TAKE?
DID HE DO IT?
HMPH
IT'S NOT FAIR!!
AH, NARU, SO THERE YOU ARE!
I WAS CURIOUS, ARE YOU BUSY TODAY?
BUSY? NOT REALLY.
THEN, WOULD YOU LIKE TO GO SOMEWHERE WITH ME?
UM...
...KINDA STRAPPED FOR CASH, BUT-
WHAT? A DATE?
UH, I... I DON'T KNOW...
...B-BUT, IF YOU INSIST... THEN, I'D LOVE TO GO WITH YOU!
COOL, IT'LL BE FUN.
THAT WAS UNEXPECTED. AT LEAST I KNOW THAT HE'S STILL INTO ME.
NOW THAT THAT'S SET...

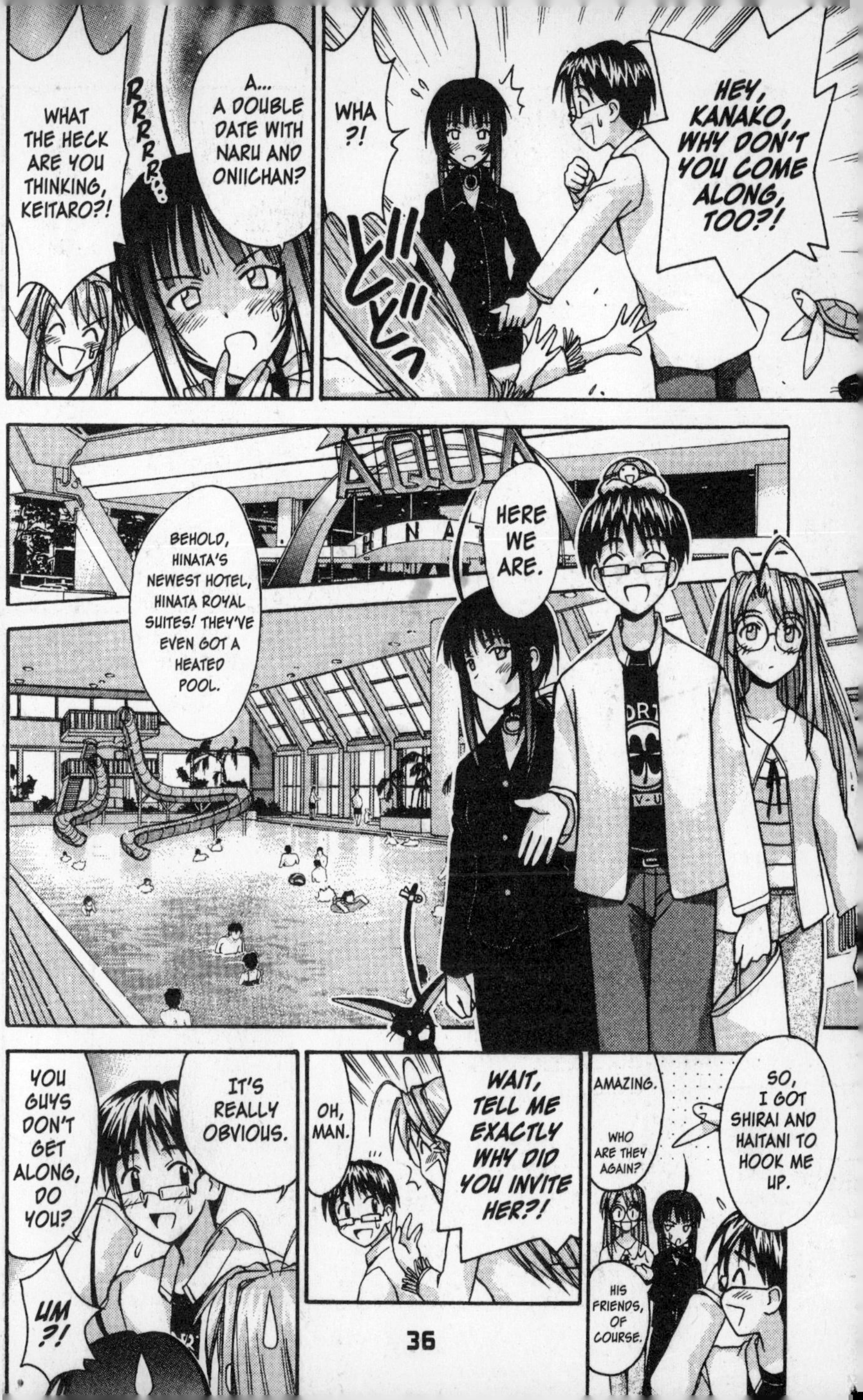
HEY, KANAKO, WHY DON'T YOU COME ALONG, TOO?!
WHA ?!
A... A DOUBLE DATE WITH NARU AND ONIICHAN?
RRRRR
WHAT THE HECK ARE YOU THINKING, KEITARO?!
HERE WE ARE.
BEHOLD, HINATA'S NEWEST HOTEL, HINATA ROYAL SUITES! THEY'VE EVEN GOT A HEATED POOL.
AQUA
SO, I GOT SHIRAI AND HAITANI TO HOOK ME UP.
AMAZING.
WHO ARE THEY AGAIN?
HIS FRIENDS, OF COURSE.
WAIT, TELL ME EXACTLY WHY DID YOU INVITE HER?!
OH, MAN.
IT'S REALLY OBVIOUS.
YOU GUYS DON'T GET ALONG, DO YOU?
UM ?!

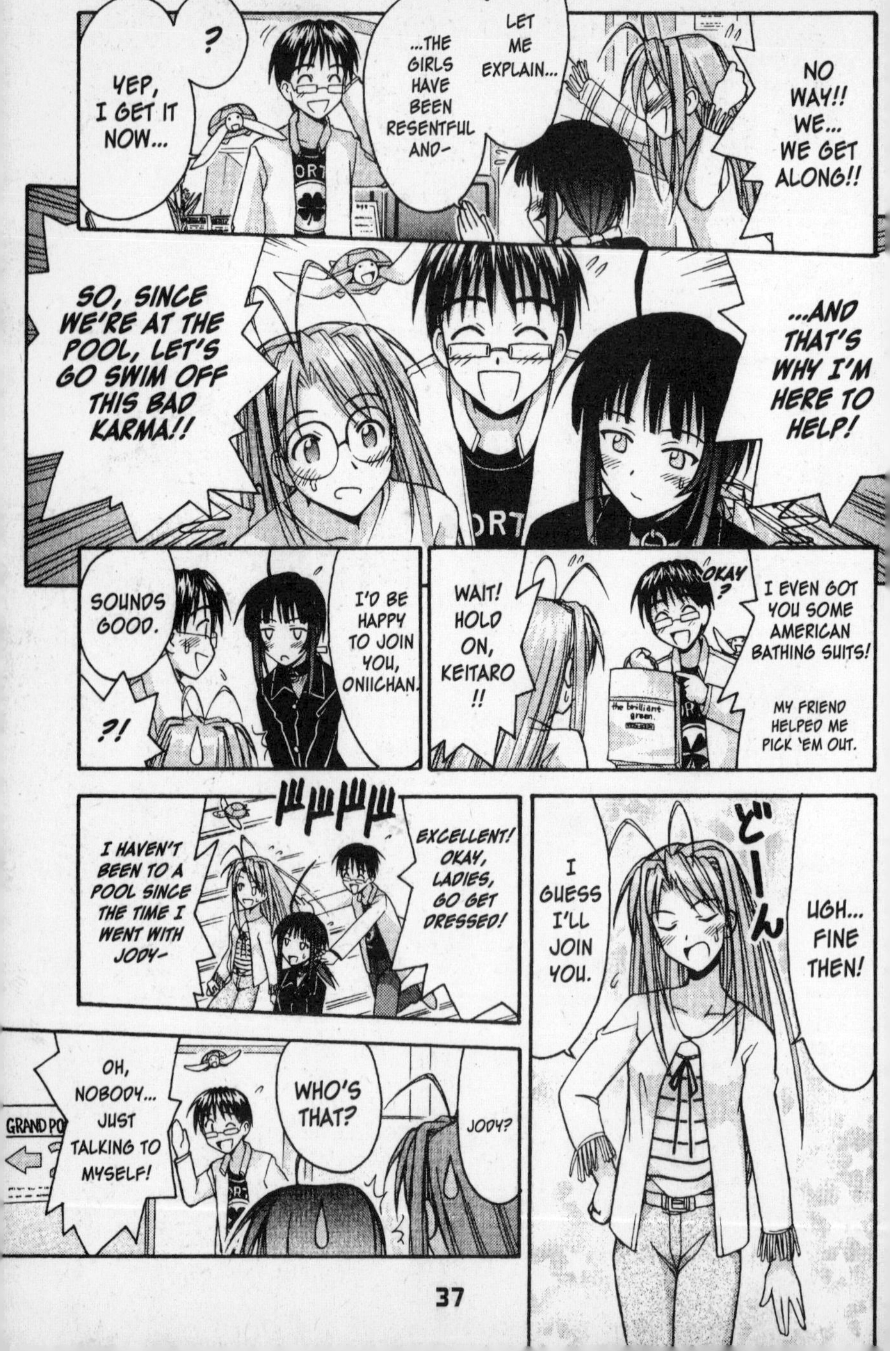

NO WAY!! WE... WE GET ALONG!!
LET ME EXPLAIN...
...THE GIRLS HAVE BEEN RESENTFUL AND-
?
YEP, I GET IT NOW...
...AND THAT'S WHY I'M HERE TO HELP!
SO, SINCE WE'RE AT THE POOL, LET'S GO SWIM OFF THIS BAD KARMA!!
I EVEN GOT YOU SOME AMERICAN BATHING SUITS!
OKAY?
MY FRIEND HELPED ME PICK 'EM OUT.
the brilliant green.
WAIT! HOLD ON, KEITARO!!
I'D BE HAPPY TO JOIN YOU, ONIICHAN.
SOUNDS GOOD.
?!
UGH... FINE THEN!
どーん
I GUESS I'LL JOIN YOU.
EXCELLENT! OKAY, LADIES, GO GET DRESSED!
I HAVEN'T BEEN TO A POOL SINCE THE TIME I WENT WITH JODY-
JODY?
WHO'S THAT?
OH, NOBODY... JUST TALKING TO MYSELF!
GRAND PO

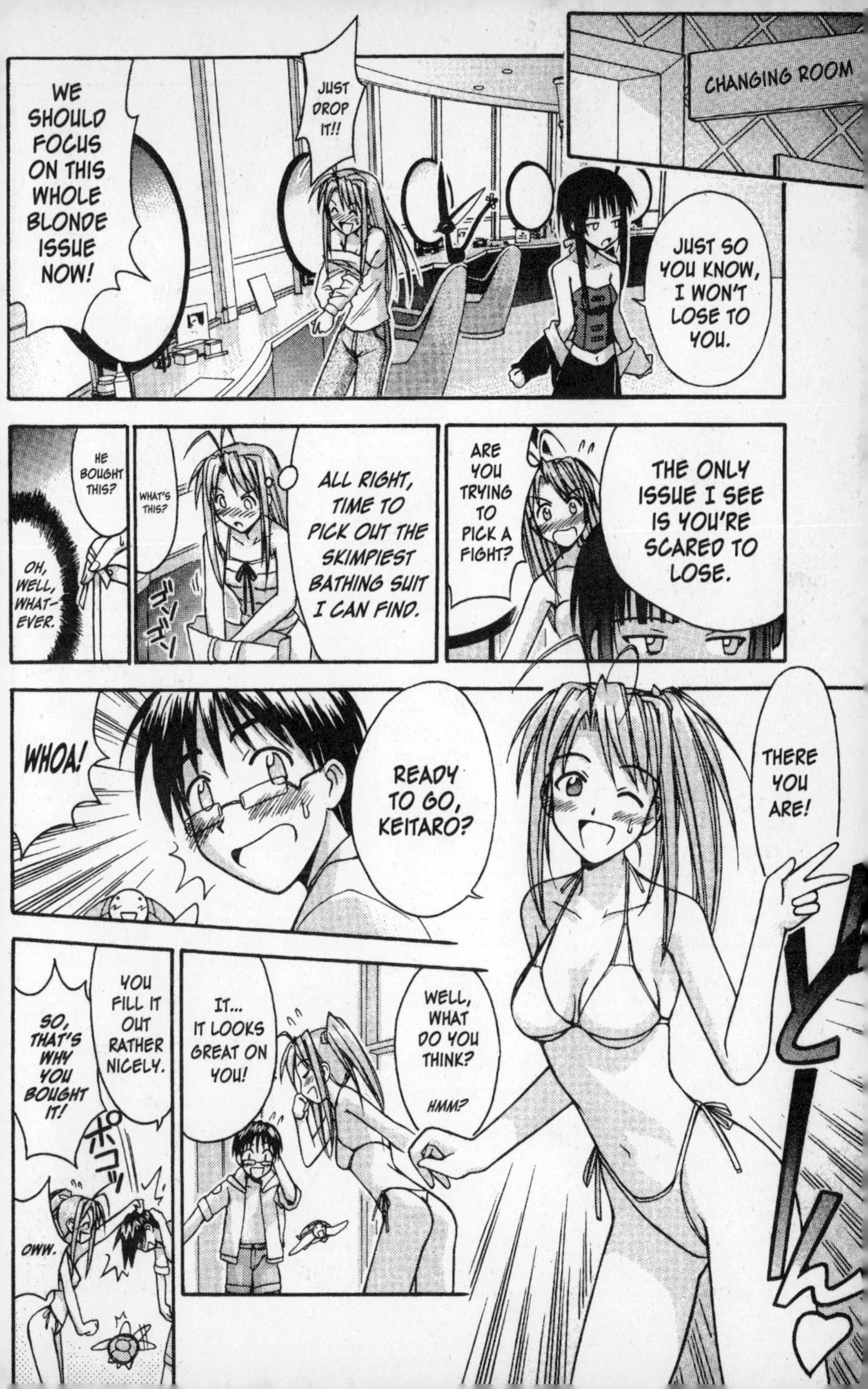
CHANGING ROOM
JUST SO YOU KNOW, I WON'T LOSE TO YOU.
JUST DROP IT!!
WE SHOULD FOCUS ON THIS WHOLE BLONDE ISSUE NOW!
THE ONLY ISSUE I SEE IS YOU'RE SCARED TO LOSE.
ARE YOU TRYING TO PICK A FIGHT?
ALL RIGHT, TIME TO PICK OUT THE SKIMPIEST BATHING SUIT I CAN FIND.
WHAT'S THIS?
HE BOUGHT THIS?
OH, WELL, WHATEVER.
THERE YOU ARE!
READY TO GO, KEITARO?
WHOA!
WELL, WHAT DO YOU THINK?
HMM?
IT... IT LOOKS GREAT ON YOU!
YOU FILL IT OUT RATHER NICELY.
SO, THAT'S WHY YOU BOUGHT IT!
ポコッ
OWW.

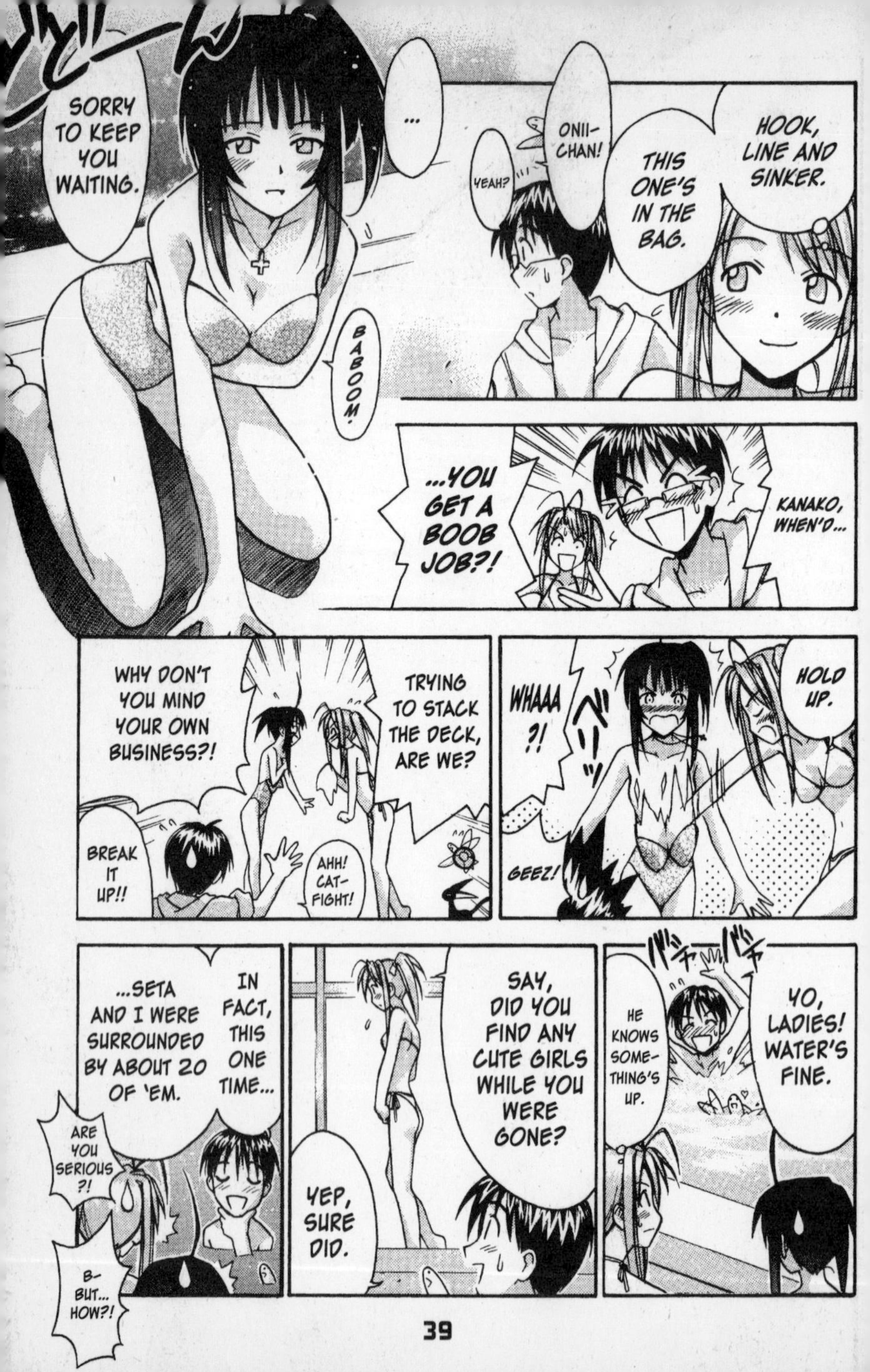
HOOK, LINE AND SINKER.
THIS ONE'S IN THE BAG.
ONII-CHAN!
YEAH?
KANAKO, WHEN'D...
...YOU GET A BOOB JOB?!
...
SORRY TO KEEP YOU WAITING.
BABOOM!
HOLD UP.
WHAAA?!
GEEZ!
TRYING TO STACK THE DECK, ARE WE?
WHY DON'T YOU MIND YOUR OWN BUSINESS?!
AHH! CAT-FIGHT!
BREAK IT UP!!
YO, LADIES! WATER'S FINE.
HE KNOWS SOME-THING'S UP.
SAY, DID YOU FIND ANY CUTE GIRLS WHILE YOU WERE GONE?
YEP, SURE DID.
IN FACT, THIS ONE TIME...
...SETA AND I WERE SURROUNDED BY ABOUT 20 OF 'EM.
ARE YOU SERIOUS?!
B-BUT... HOW?!

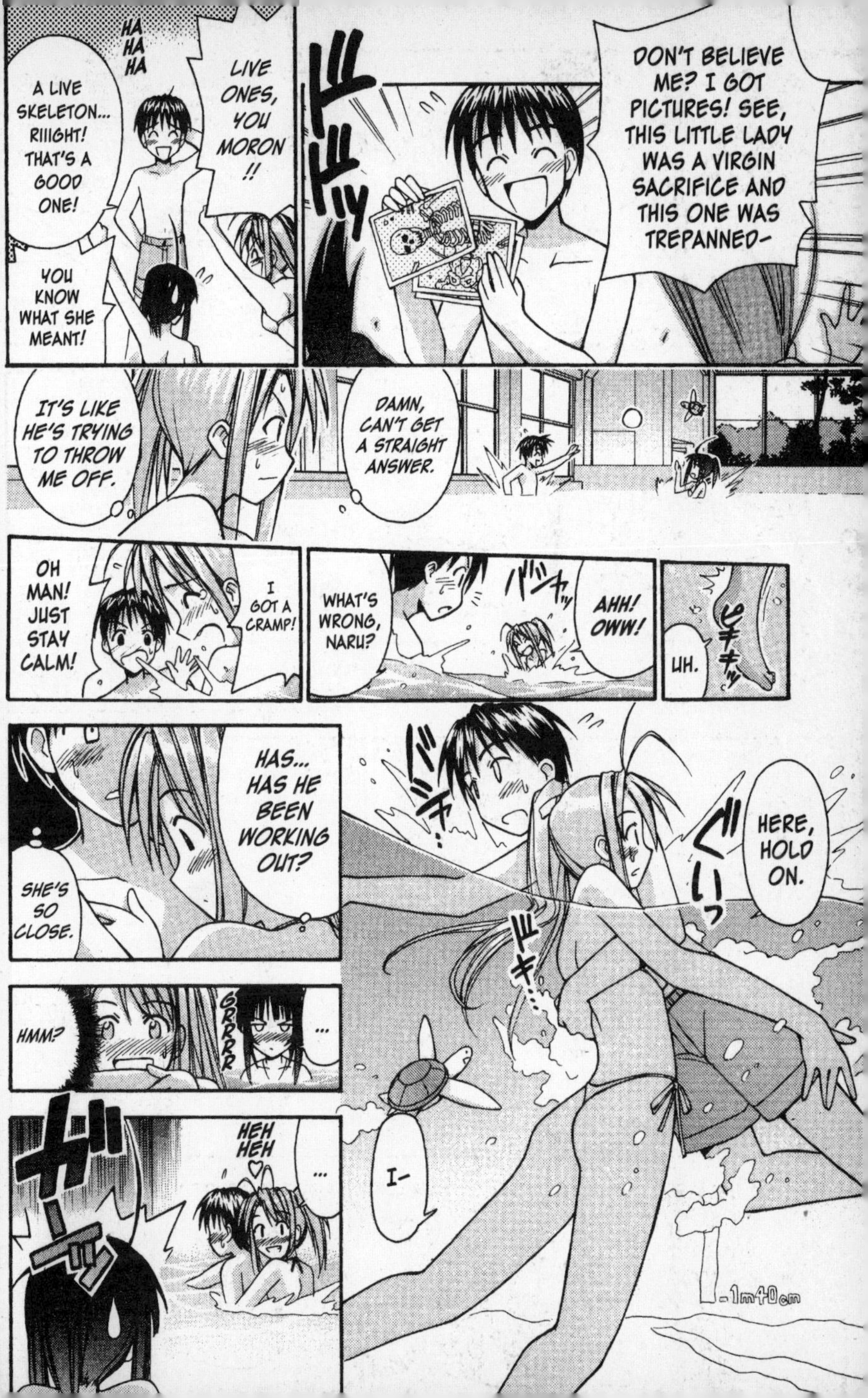
DON'T BELIEVE ME? I GOT PICTURES! SEE, THIS LITTLE LADY WAS A VIRGIN SACRIFICE AND THIS ONE WAS TREPANNED-
HA HA HA
LIVE ONES, YOU MORON!!
A LIVE SKELETON... RIIIGHT! THAT'S A GOOD ONE!
YOU KNOW WHAT SHE MEANT!
DAMN, CAN'T GET A STRAIGHT ANSWER.
IT'S LIKE HE'S TRYING TO THROW ME OFF.
UH.
AHH! OWW!
WHAT'S WRONG, NARU?
I GOT A CRAMP!
OH MAN! JUST STAY CALM!
HERE, HOLD ON.
I-
1m40cm
HAS... HAS HE BEEN WORKING OUT?
SHE'S SO CLOSE.
...
GRRRR
HMM?
HEH HEH ♡
...

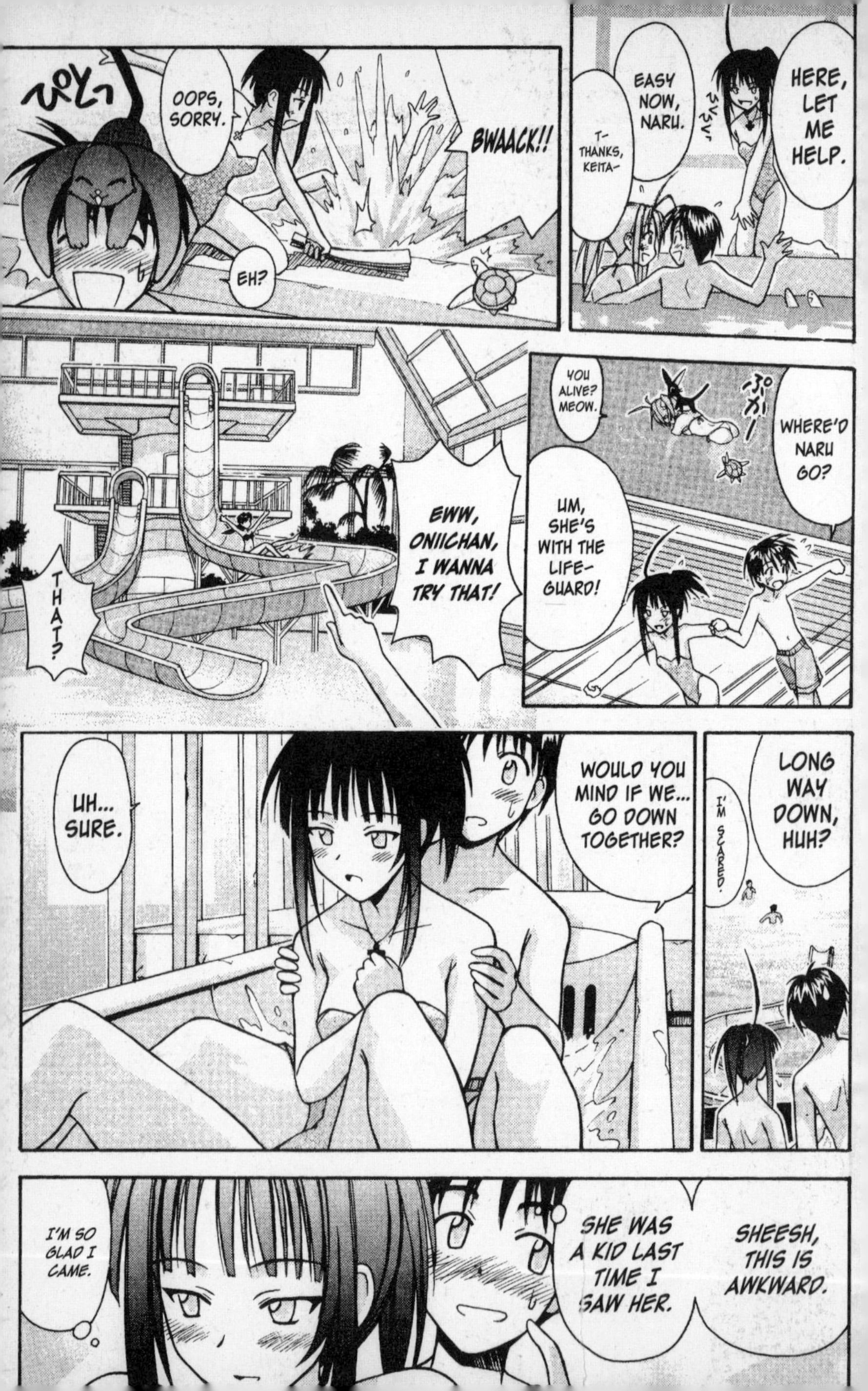
HERE, LET ME HELP.
EASY NOW, NARU.
T-THANKS, KEITA-
OOPS, SORRY.
BWAACK!!
EH?
WHERE'D NARU GO?
ぷかー
YOU ALIVE? MEOW.
UM, SHE'S WITH THE LIFE-GUARD!
EWW, ONIICHAN, I WANNA TRY THAT!
THAT?
LONG WAY DOWN, HUH?
I'M SCARED.
WOULD YOU MIND IF WE... GO DOWN TOGETHER?
UH... SURE.
SHEESH, THIS IS AWKWARD.
SHE WAS A KID LAST TIME I SAW HER.
I'M SO GLAD I CAME.

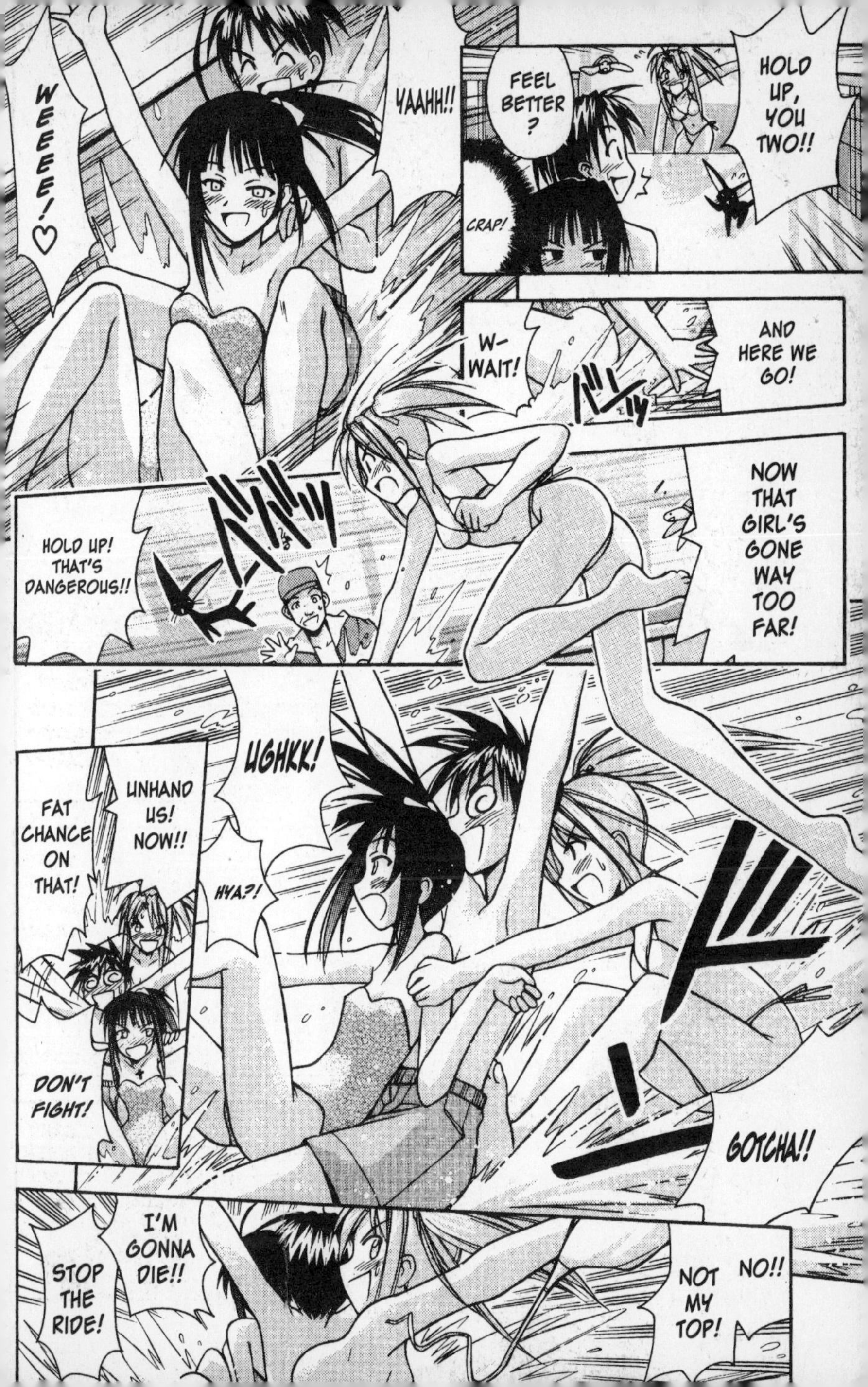
HOLD UP, YOU TWO!!
FEEL BETTER?
CRAP!
AND HERE WE GO!
W-WAIT!
YAAHH!!
WEEEE!♡
NOW THAT GIRL'S GONE WAY TOO FAR!
HOLD UP! THAT'S DANGEROUS!!
GOTCHA!!
UGHKK!
HYA?!
UNHAND US! NOW!!
FAT CHANCE ON THAT!
DON'T FIGHT!
NO!!
NOT MY TOP!
I'M GONNA DIE!!
STOP THE RIDE!

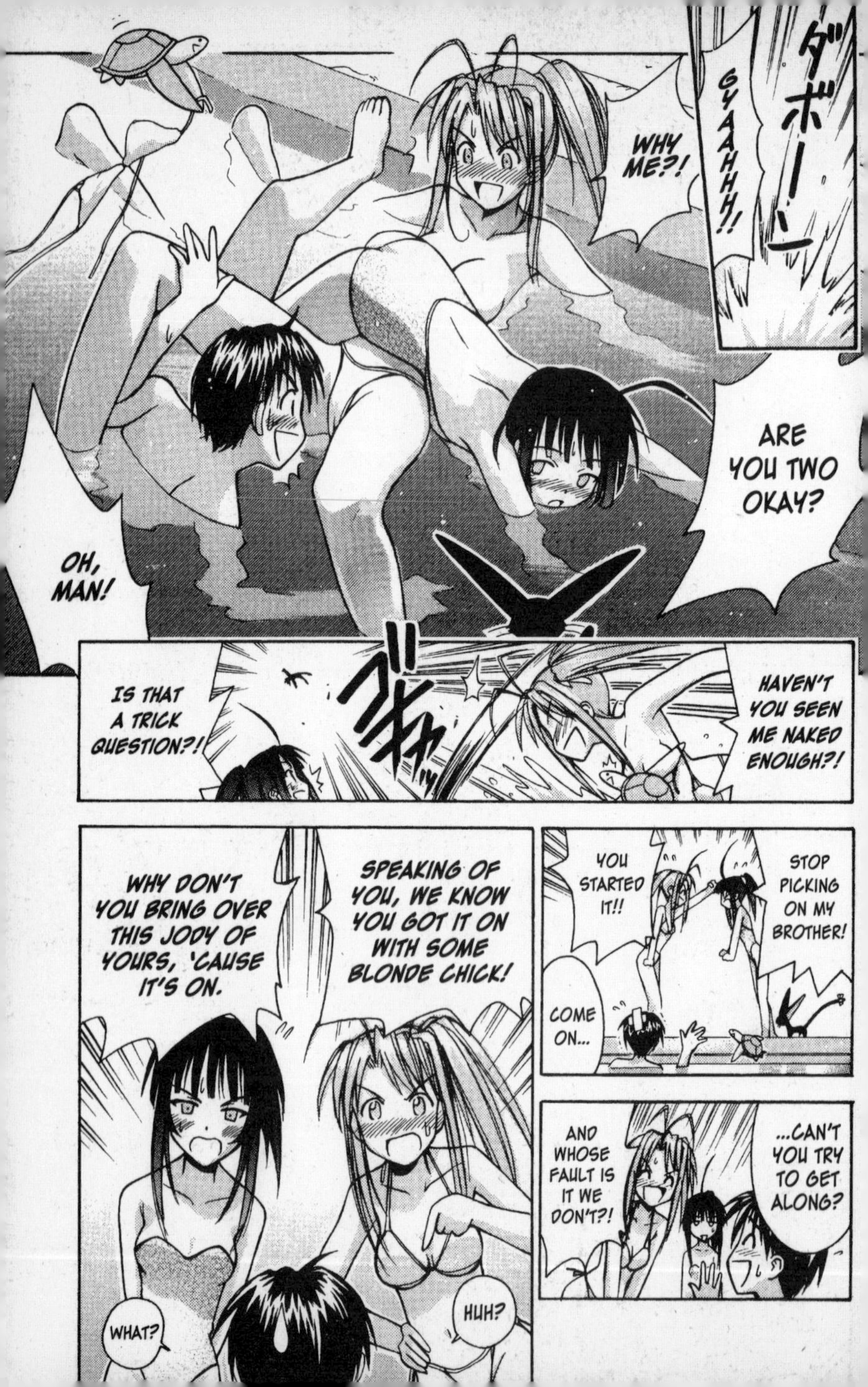
ダボーン
GYAAHHH!!
WHY ME?!
ARE YOU TWO OKAY?
OH, MAN!
HAVEN'T YOU SEEN ME NAKED ENOUGH?!
IS THAT A TRICK QUESTION?!
STOP PICKING ON MY BROTHER!
YOU STARTED IT!!
COME ON...
...CAN'T YOU TRY TO GET ALONG?
AND WHOSE FAULT IS IT WE DON'T?!
SPEAKING OF YOU, WE KNOW YOU GOT IT ON WITH SOME BLONDE CHICK!
WHY DON'T YOU BRING OVER THIS JODY OF YOURS, 'CAUSE IT'S ON.
HUH?
WHAT?

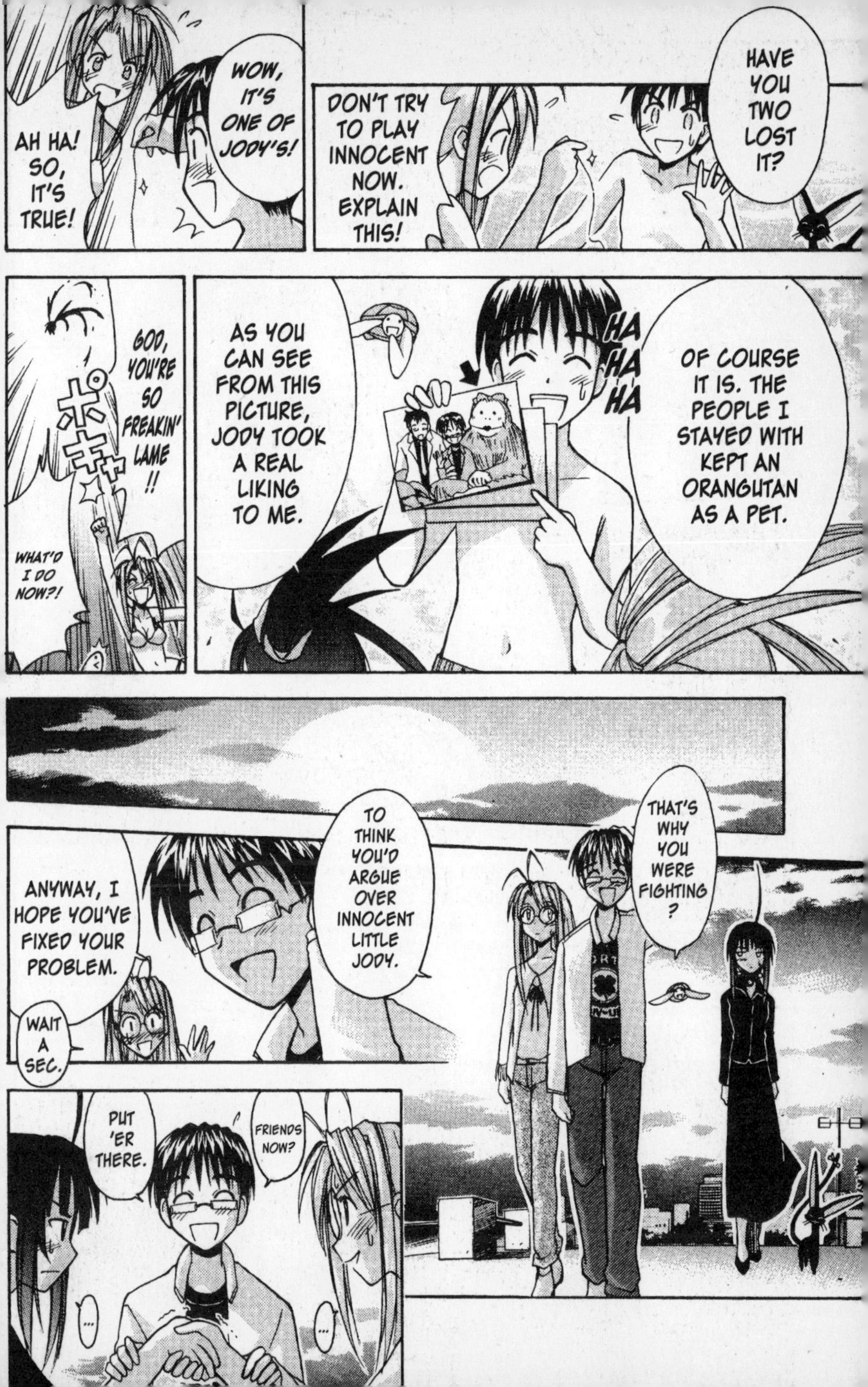
HAVE YOU TWO LOST IT?
DON'T TRY TO PLAY INNOCENT NOW. EXPLAIN THIS!
WOW, IT'S ONE OF JODY'S!
AH HA! SO, IT'S TRUE!
HA HA HA
OF COURSE IT IS. THE PEOPLE I STAYED WITH KEPT AN ORANGUTAN AS A PET.
AS YOU CAN SEE FROM THIS PICTURE, JODY TOOK A REAL LIKING TO ME.
GOD, YOU'RE SO FREAKIN' LAME!!
ポキャ
WHAT'D I DO NOW?!
THAT'S WHY YOU WERE FIGHTING?
TO THINK YOU'D ARGUE OVER INNOCENT LITTLE JODY.
ANYWAY, I HOPE YOU'VE FIXED YOUR PROBLEM.
WAIT A SEC.
FRIENDS NOW?
PUT 'ER THERE.
...
...

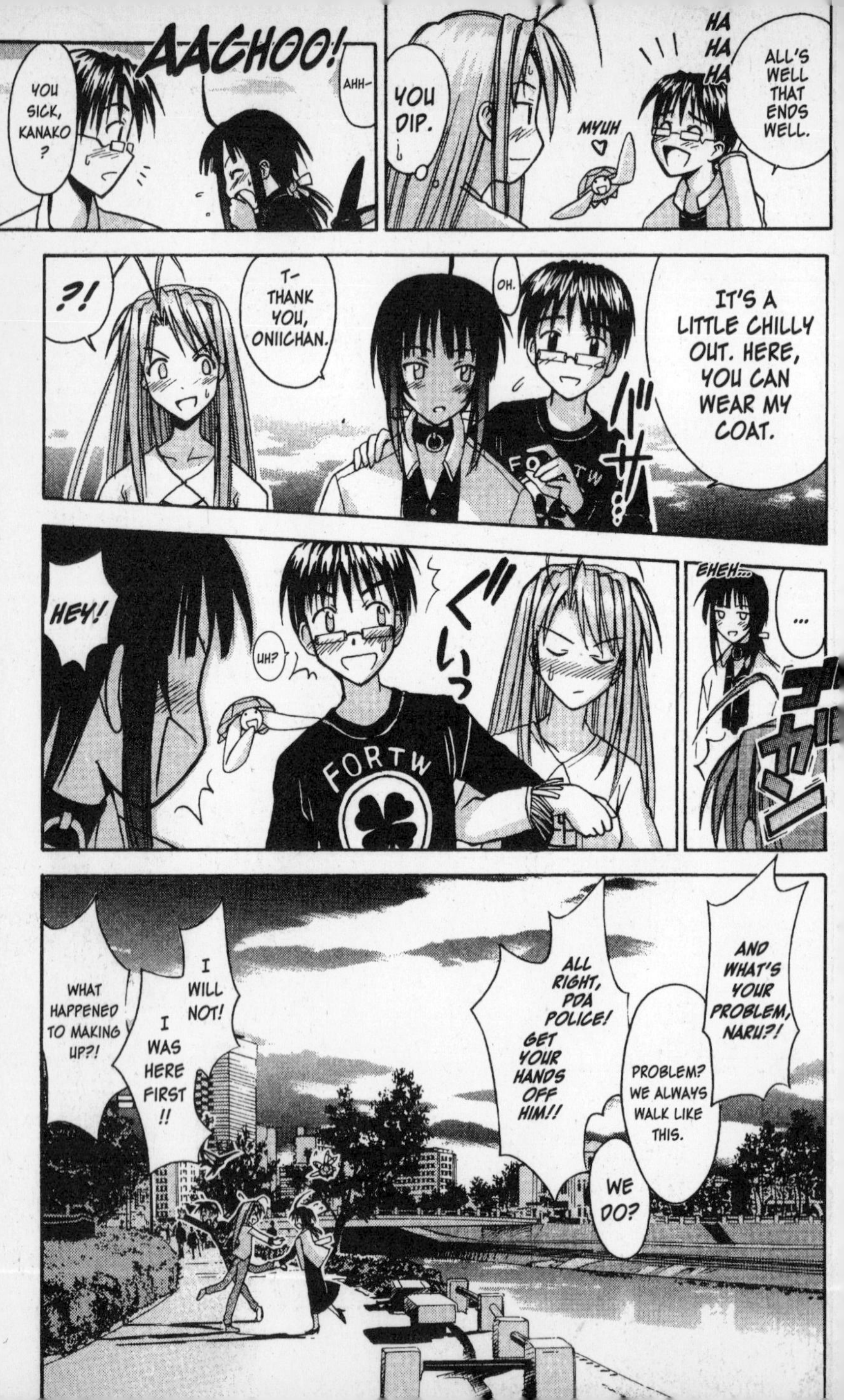
ALL'S WELL THAT ENDS WELL.
HA HA HA
MYUH ♥
YOU DIP. ¿
AHH-
AACHOO!
YOU SICK, KANAKO?
IT'S A LITTLE CHILLY OUT. HERE, YOU CAN WEAR MY COAT.
OH.
T-THANK YOU, ONIICHAN.
?!
EHEH...
...
UH?
HEY!
AND WHAT'S YOUR PROBLEM, NARU?!
PROBLEM? WE ALWAYS WALK LIKE THIS.
ALL RIGHT, PDA POLICE! GET YOUR HANDS OFF HIM!!
WE DO?
I WILL NOT! I WAS HERE FIRST!!
WHAT HAPPENED TO MAKING UP?!

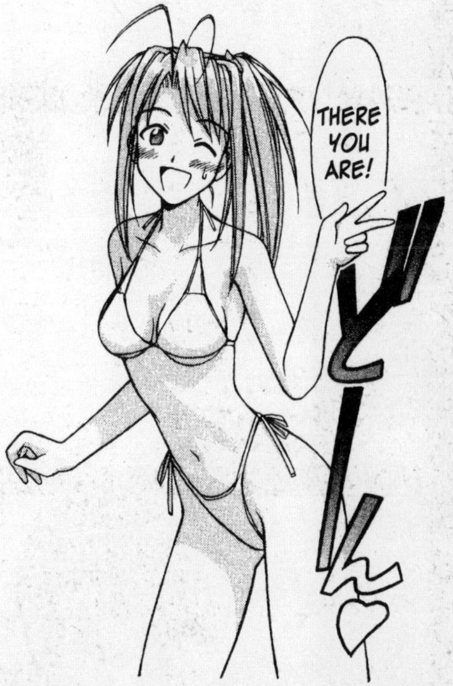
THERE YOU ARE!

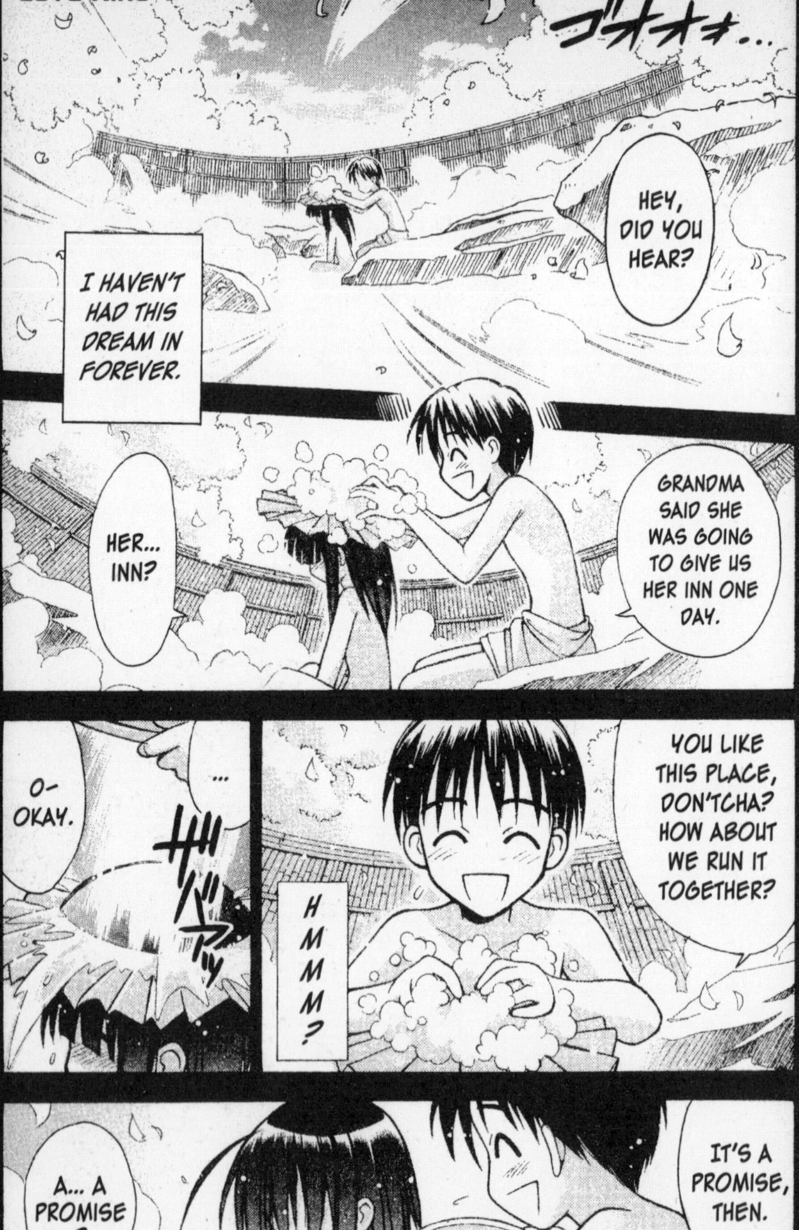
ゴオオオ…
HEY, DID YOU HEAR?
I HAVEN'T HAD THIS DREAM IN FOREVER.
GRANDMA SAID SHE WAS GOING TO GIVE US HER INN ONE DAY.
HER... INN?
YOU LIKE THIS PLACE, DON'TCHA? HOW ABOUT WE RUN IT TOGETHER?
HMMMM?
...
ザバァッ
O-OKAY.
IT'S A PROMISE, THEN.
A... A PROMISE?

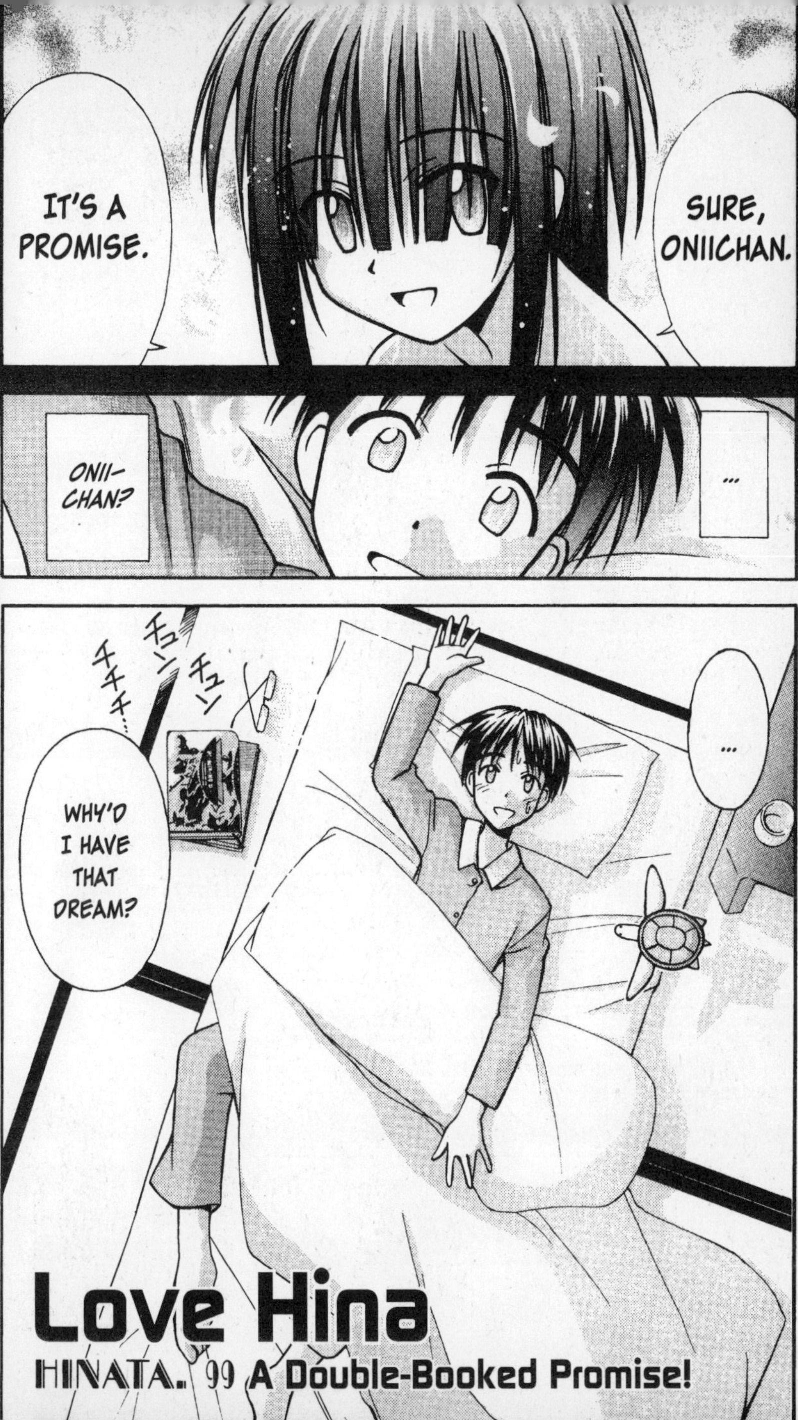
SURE, ONIICHAN.
IT'S A PROMISE.
...
ONII-CHAN?
チュン チュン
チチチ…
...
WHY'D I HAVE THAT DREAM?
Love Hina
HINATA. 99 A Double-Booked Promise!

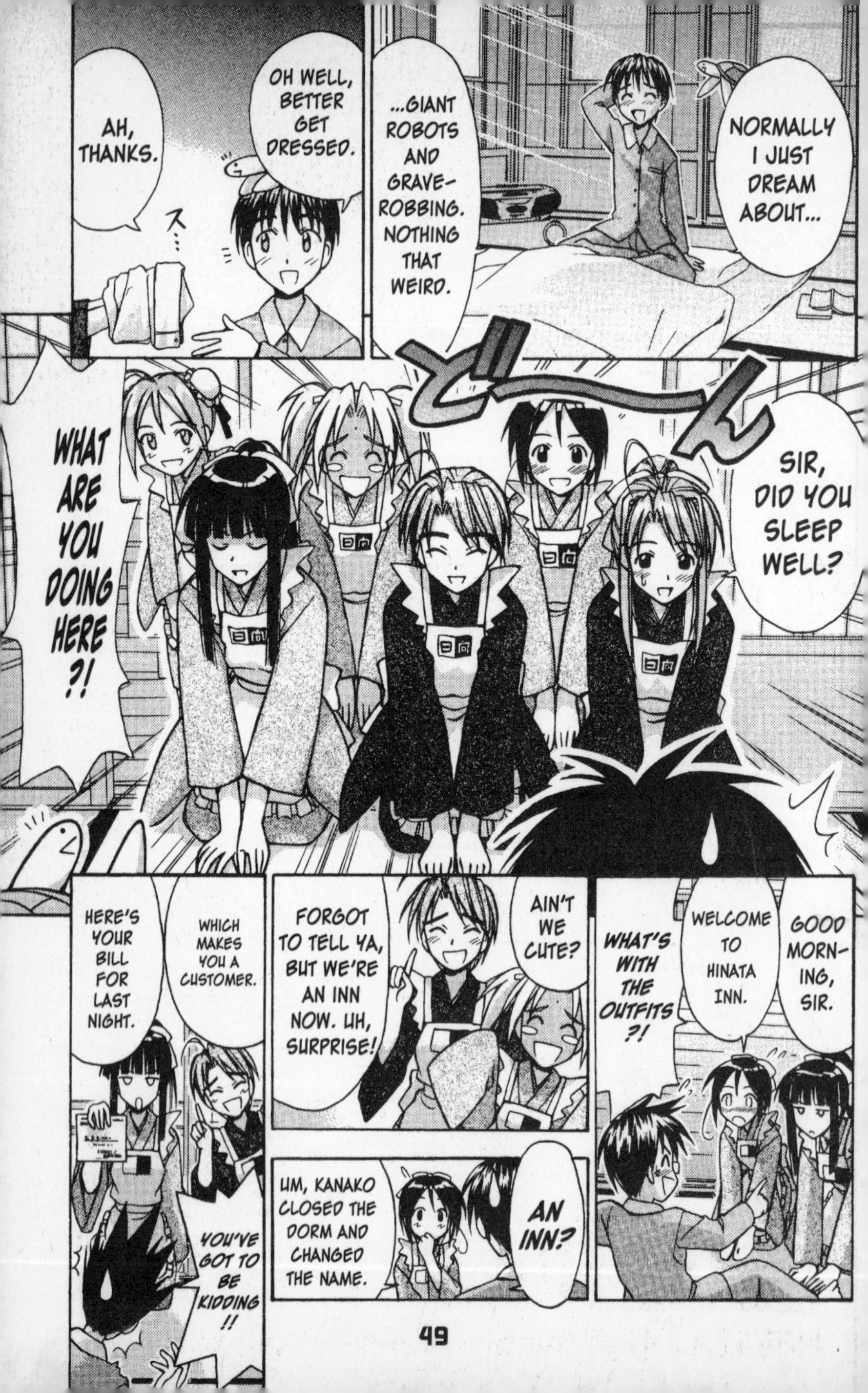
NORMALLY I JUST DREAM ABOUT...
...GIANT ROBOTS AND GRAVE-ROBBING. NOTHING THAT WEIRD.
OH WELL, BETTER GET DRESSED.
ス...
AH, THANKS.
どーん
SIR, DID YOU SLEEP WELL?
WHAT ARE YOU DOING HERE?!
GOOD MORNING, SIR.
WELCOME TO HINATA INN.
WHAT'S WITH THE OUTFITS?!
AIN'T WE CUTE?
FORGOT TO TELL YA, BUT WE'RE AN INN NOW. UH, SURPRISE!
AN INN?
UM, KANAKO CLOSED THE DORM AND CHANGED THE NAME.
WHICH MAKES YOU A CUSTOMER.
HERE'S YOUR BILL FOR LAST NIGHT.
YOU'VE GOT TO BE KIDDING!!

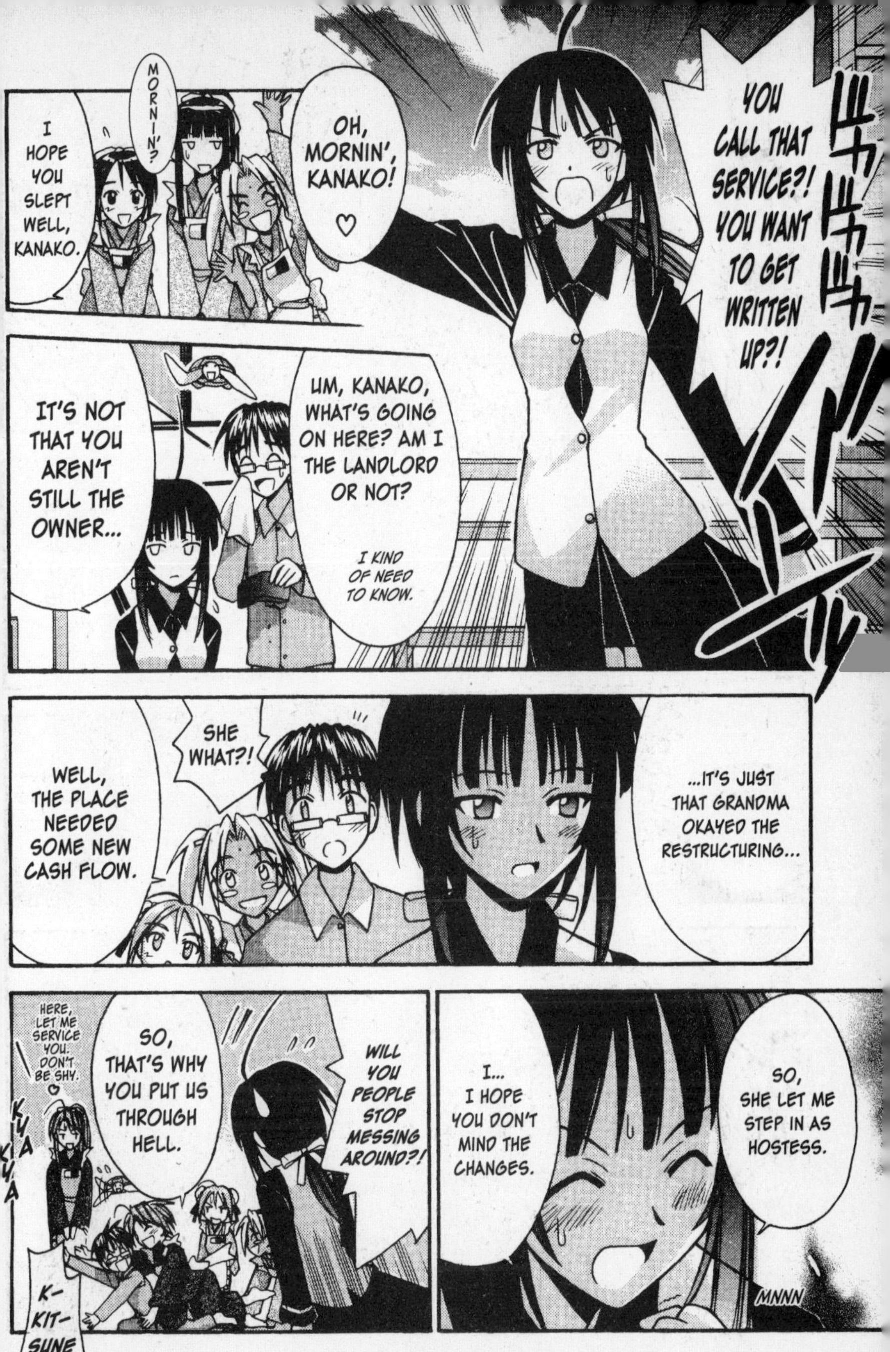
YOU CALL THAT SERVICE?! YOU WANT TO GET WRITTEN UP?!
OH, MORNIN', KANAKO! ♡
MORNIN'?
I HOPE YOU SLEPT WELL, KANAKO.
UM, KANAKO, WHAT'S GOING ON HERE? AM I THE LANDLORD OR NOT?
I KIND OF NEED TO KNOW.
IT'S NOT THAT YOU AREN'T STILL THE OWNER...
...IT'S JUST THAT GRANDMA OKAYED THE RESTRUCTURING...
SHE WHAT?!
WELL, THE PLACE NEEDED SOME NEW CASH FLOW.
SO, SHE LET ME STEP IN AS HOSTESS.
I... I HOPE YOU DON'T MIND THE CHANGES.
MNNN
WILL YOU PEOPLE STOP MESSING AROUND?!
SO, THAT'S WHY YOU PUT US THROUGH HELL.
HERE, LET ME SERVICE YOU. DON'T BE SHY. ♡
KYA KYA
K-KIT-SUNE?!

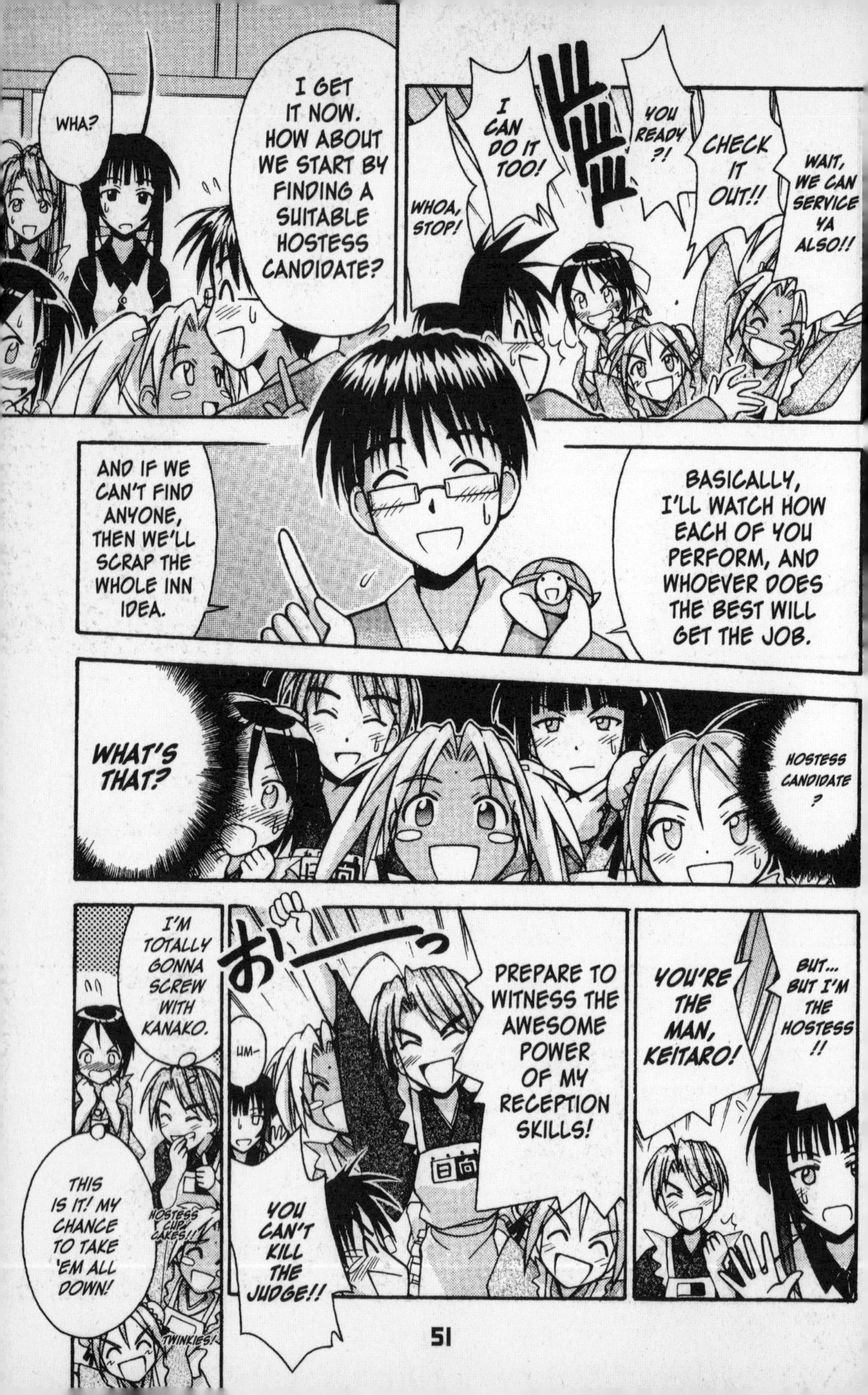
WAIT, WE CAN SERVICE YA ALSO!!
CHECK IT OUT!!
YOU READY ?!
I CAN DO IT TOO!
WHOA, STOP!
I GET IT NOW. HOW ABOUT WE START BY FINDING A SUITABLE HOSTESS CANDIDATE?
WHA?
BASICALLY, I'LL WATCH HOW EACH OF YOU PERFORM, AND WHOEVER DOES THE BEST WILL GET THE JOB.
AND IF WE CAN'T FIND ANYONE, THEN WE'LL SCRAP THE WHOLE INN IDEA.
HOSTESS CANDIDATE ?
WHAT'S THAT?
BUT... BUT I'M THE HOSTESS !!
YOU'RE THE MAN, KEITARO!
PREPARE TO WITNESS THE AWESOME POWER OF MY RECEPTION SKILLS!
お━━っ
UM—
YOU CAN'T KILL THE JUDGE!!
I'M TOTALLY GONNA SCREW WITH KANAKO.
HOSTESS CUP CAKES!!
THIS IS IT! MY CHANCE TO TAKE 'EM ALL DOWN!
TWINKIES!

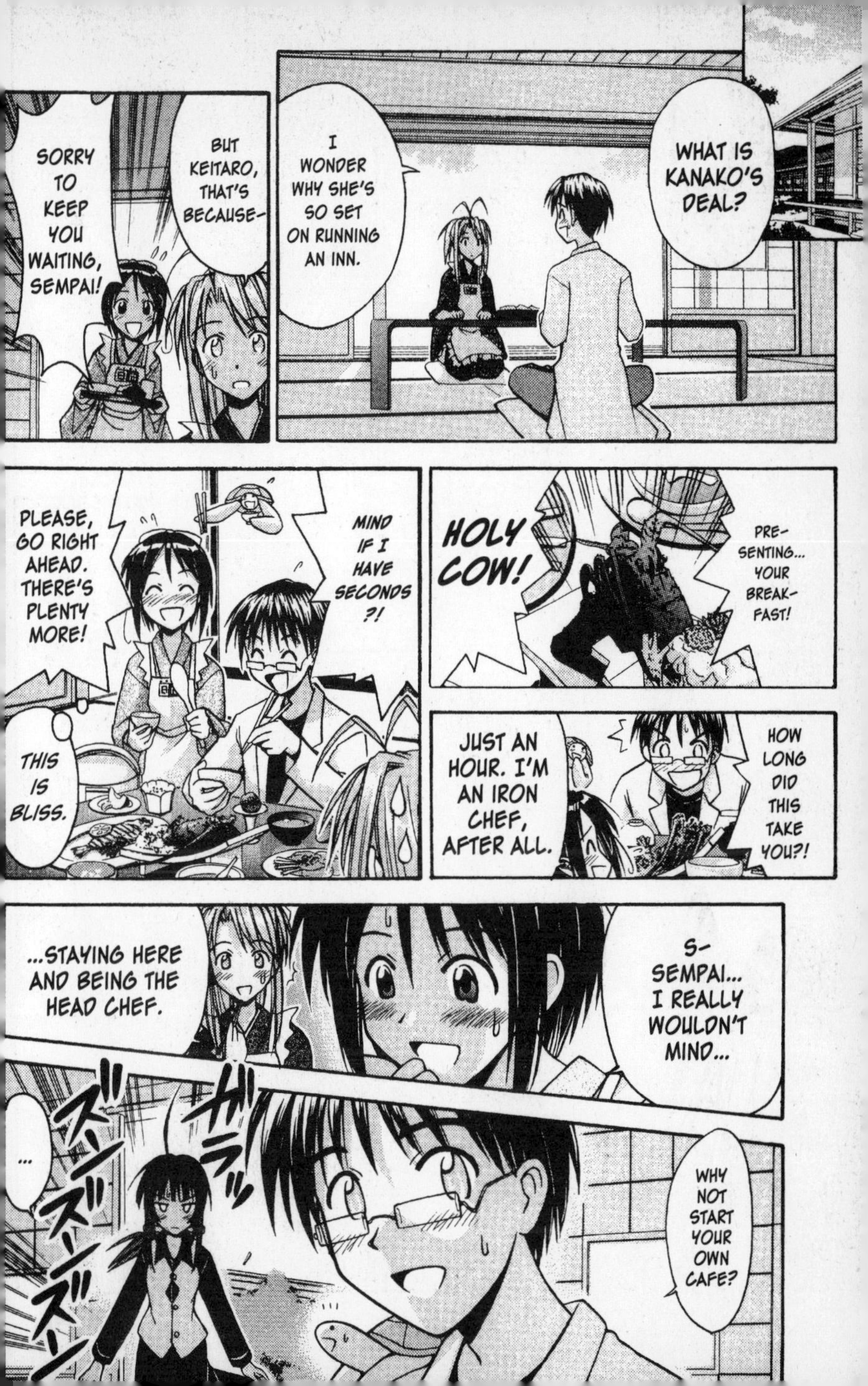
WHAT IS KANAKO'S DEAL?
I WONDER WHY SHE'S SO SET ON RUNNING AN INN.
BUT KEITARO, THAT'S BECAUSE-
SORRY TO KEEP YOU WAITING, SEMPAI!
PRE-SENTING... YOUR BREAK-FAST!
HOLY COW!
HOW LONG DID THIS TAKE YOU?!
JUST AN HOUR. I'M AN IRON CHEF, AFTER ALL.
MIND IF I HAVE SECONDS ?!
PLEASE, GO RIGHT AHEAD. THERE'S PLENTY MORE!
THIS IS BLISS.
S-SEMPAI... I REALLY WOULDN'T MIND...
...STAYING HERE AND BEING THE HEAD CHEF.
WHY NOT START YOUR OWN CAFE?
...

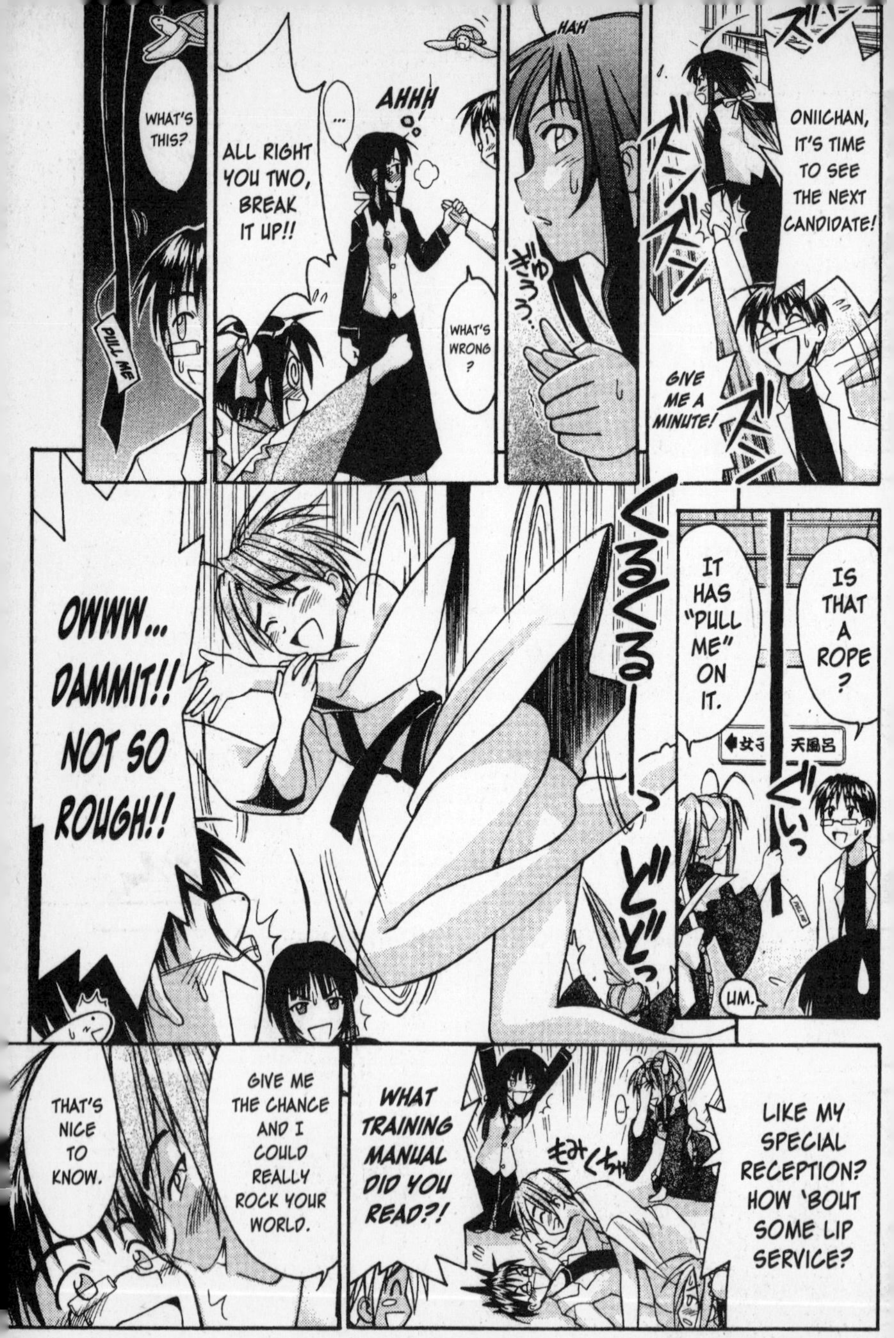
ONIICHAN, IT'S TIME TO SEE THE NEXT CANDIDATE!
GIVE ME A MINUTE!
HAH
AHHH
...
ALL RIGHT YOU TWO, BREAK IT UP!!
WHAT'S WRONG?
WHAT'S THIS?
PULL ME
IS THAT A ROPE?
IT HAS "PULL ME" ON IT.
UM.
くるくるー
どどっ
OWWW... DAMMIT!! NOT SO ROUGH!!
LIKE MY SPECIAL RECEPTION? HOW 'BOUT SOME LIP SERVICE?
もみくちゃ
WHAT TRAINING MANUAL DID YOU READ?!
GIVE ME THE CHANCE AND I COULD REALLY ROCK YOUR WORLD.
THAT'S NICE TO KNOW.

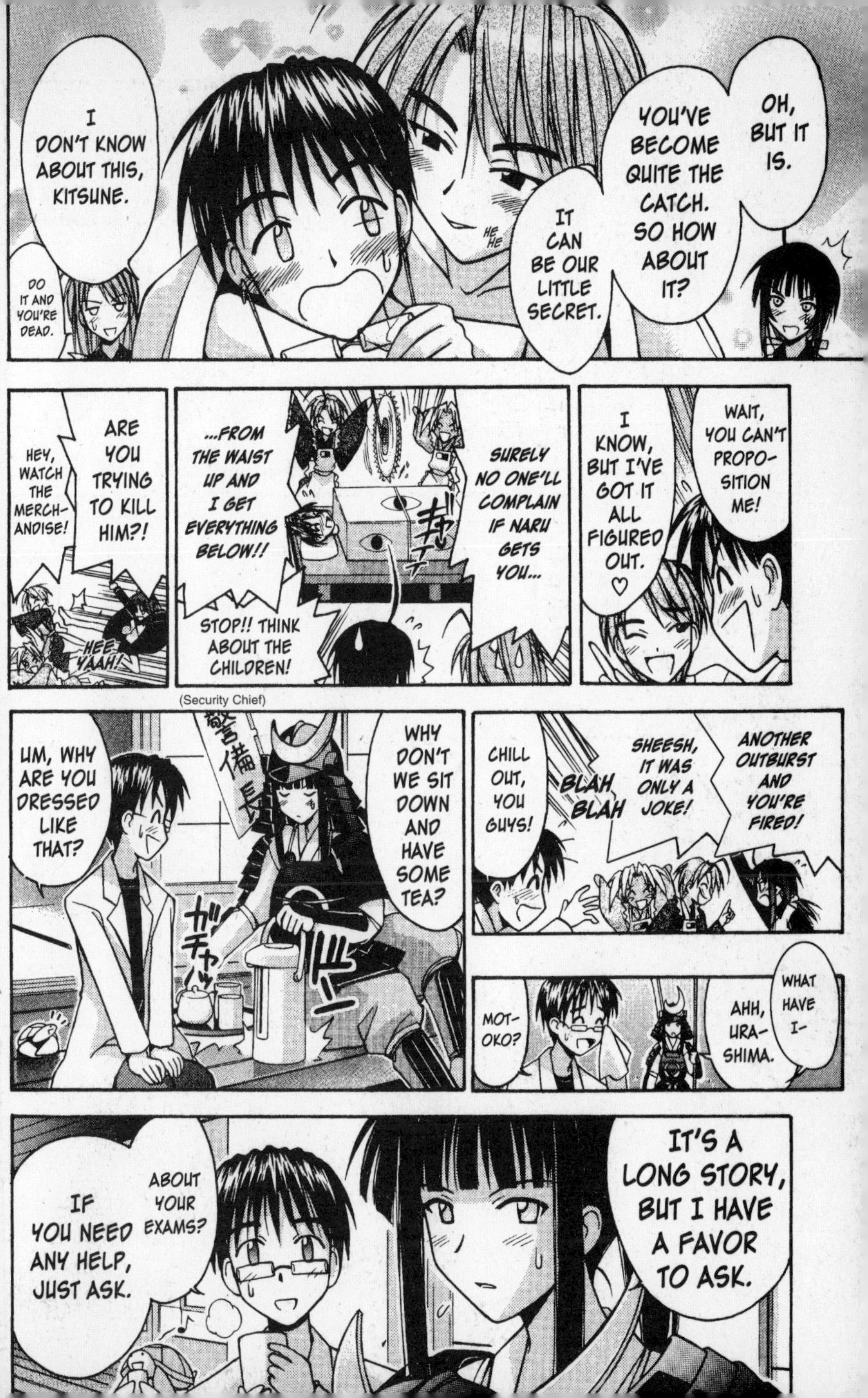
OH, BUT IT IS.
YOU'VE BECOME QUITE THE CATCH. SO HOW ABOUT IT?
IT CAN BE OUR LITTLE SECRET.
HE HE
I DON'T KNOW ABOUT THIS, KITSUNE.
DO IT AND YOU'RE DEAD.
WAIT, YOU CAN'T PROPO-SITION ME!
I KNOW, BUT I'VE GOT IT ALL FIGURED OUT. ♡
SURELY NO ONE'LL COMPLAIN IF NARU GETS YOU...
...FROM THE WAIST UP AND I GET EVERYTHING BELOW!!
STOP!! THINK ABOUT THE CHILDREN!
ARE YOU TRYING TO KILL HIM?!
HEY, WATCH THE MERCH-ANDISE!
HEE YAAH!
ANOTHER OUTBURST AND YOU'RE FIRED!
SHEESH, IT WAS ONLY A JOKE!
BLAH BLAH
CHILL OUT, YOU GUYS!
WHAT HAVE I-
AHH, URA-SHIMA.
MOT-OKO?
(Security Chief)
WHY DON'T WE SIT DOWN AND HAVE SOME TEA?
UM, WHY ARE YOU DRESSED LIKE THAT?
IT'S A LONG STORY, BUT I HAVE A FAVOR TO ASK.
ABOUT YOUR EXAMS?
IF YOU NEED ANY HELP, JUST ASK.

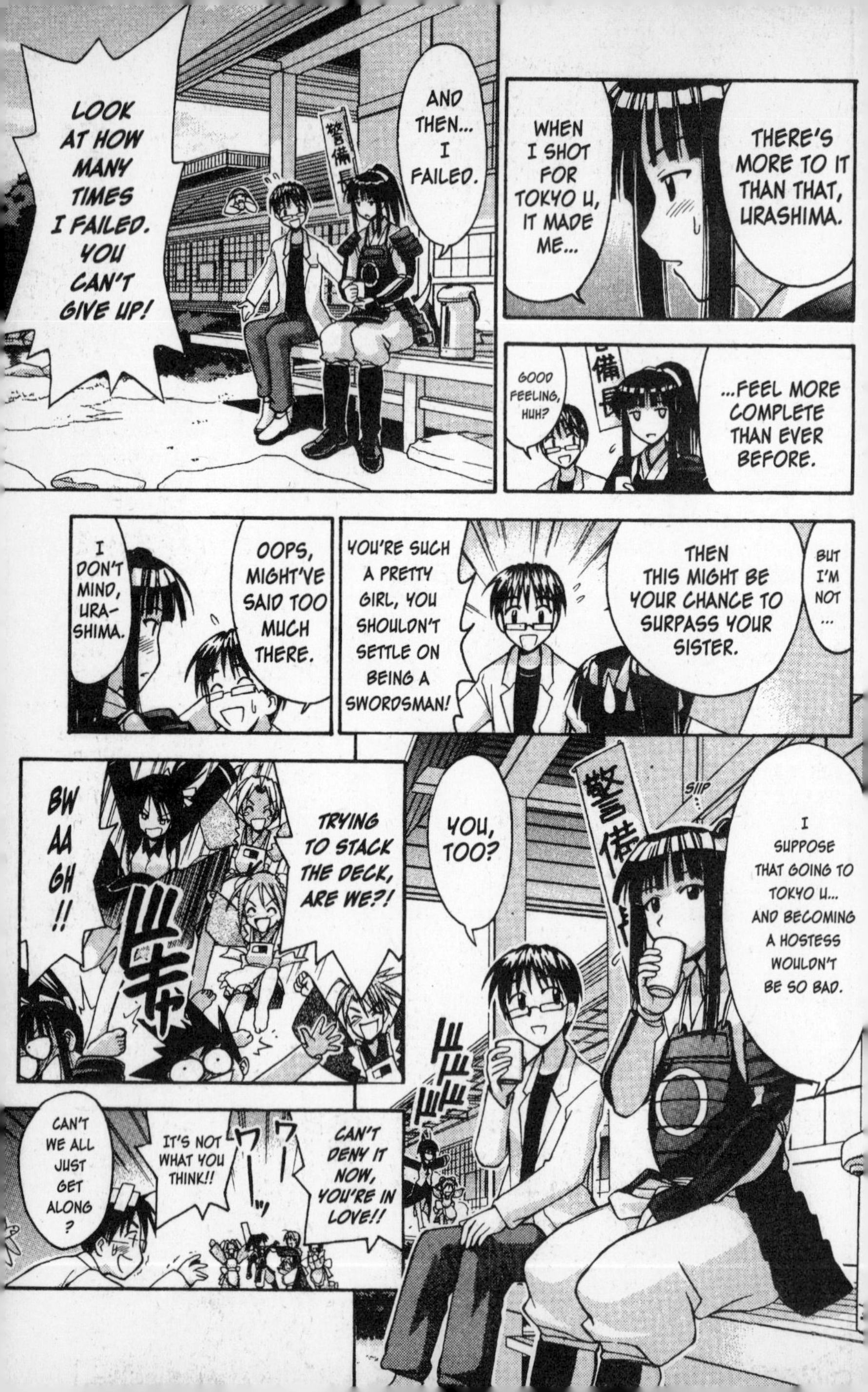
THERE'S MORE TO IT THAN THAT, URASHIMA.
WHEN I SHOT FOR TOKYO U, IT MADE ME...
...FEEL MORE COMPLETE THAN EVER BEFORE.
GOOD FEELING, HUH?
AND THEN... I FAILED.
LOOK AT HOW MANY TIMES I FAILED. YOU CAN'T GIVE UP!
BUT I'M NOT ...
THEN THIS MIGHT BE YOUR CHANCE TO SURPASS YOUR SISTER.
YOU'RE SUCH A PRETTY GIRL, YOU SHOULDN'T SETTLE ON BEING A SWORDSMAN!
OOPS, MIGHT'VE SAID TOO MUCH THERE.
I DON'T MIND, URASHIMA.
SIIP
I SUPPOSE THAT GOING TO TOKYO U... AND BECOMING A HOSTESS WOULDN'T BE SO BAD.
YOU, TOO?
TRYING TO STACK THE DECK, ARE WE?!
BWAAGH!!
CAN'T DENY IT NOW, YOU'RE IN LOVE!!
IT'S NOT WHAT YOU THINK!!
CAN'T WE ALL JUST GET ALONG?

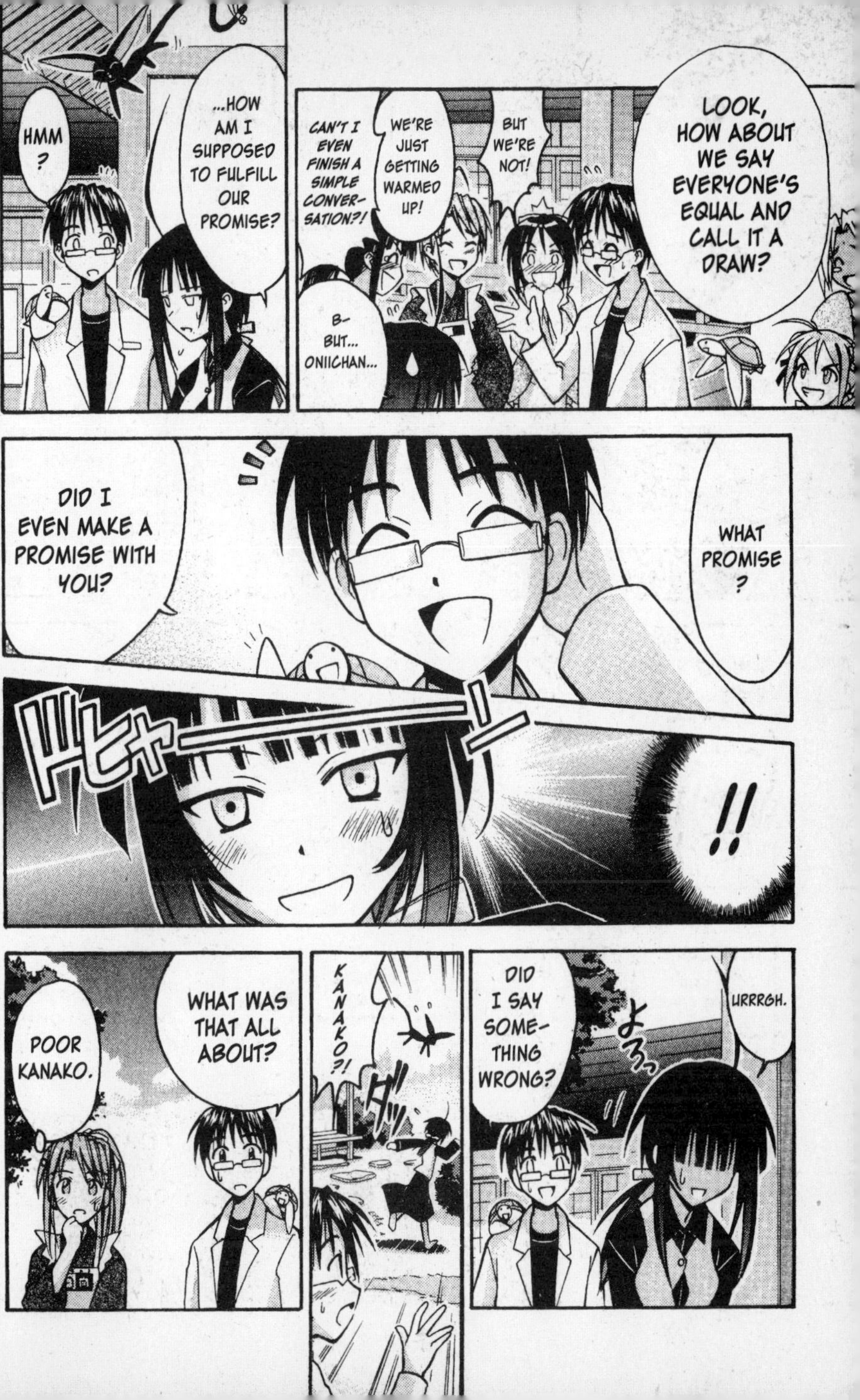
LOOK, HOW ABOUT WE SAY EVERYONE'S EQUAL AND CALL IT A DRAW?
BUT WE'RE NOT!
WE'RE JUST GETTING WARMED UP!
CAN'T I EVEN FINISH A SIMPLE CONVER-SATION?!
B-BUT... ONIICHAN...
...HOW AM I SUPPOSED TO FULFILL OUR PROMISE?
HMM?
WHAT PROMISE?
DID I EVEN MAKE A PROMISE WITH YOU?
ドヒャーー
!!
URRRGH.
よろっ
DID I SAY SOME-THING WRONG?
KANAKO?!
ダッ
WHAT WAS THAT ALL ABOUT?
POOR KANAKO.

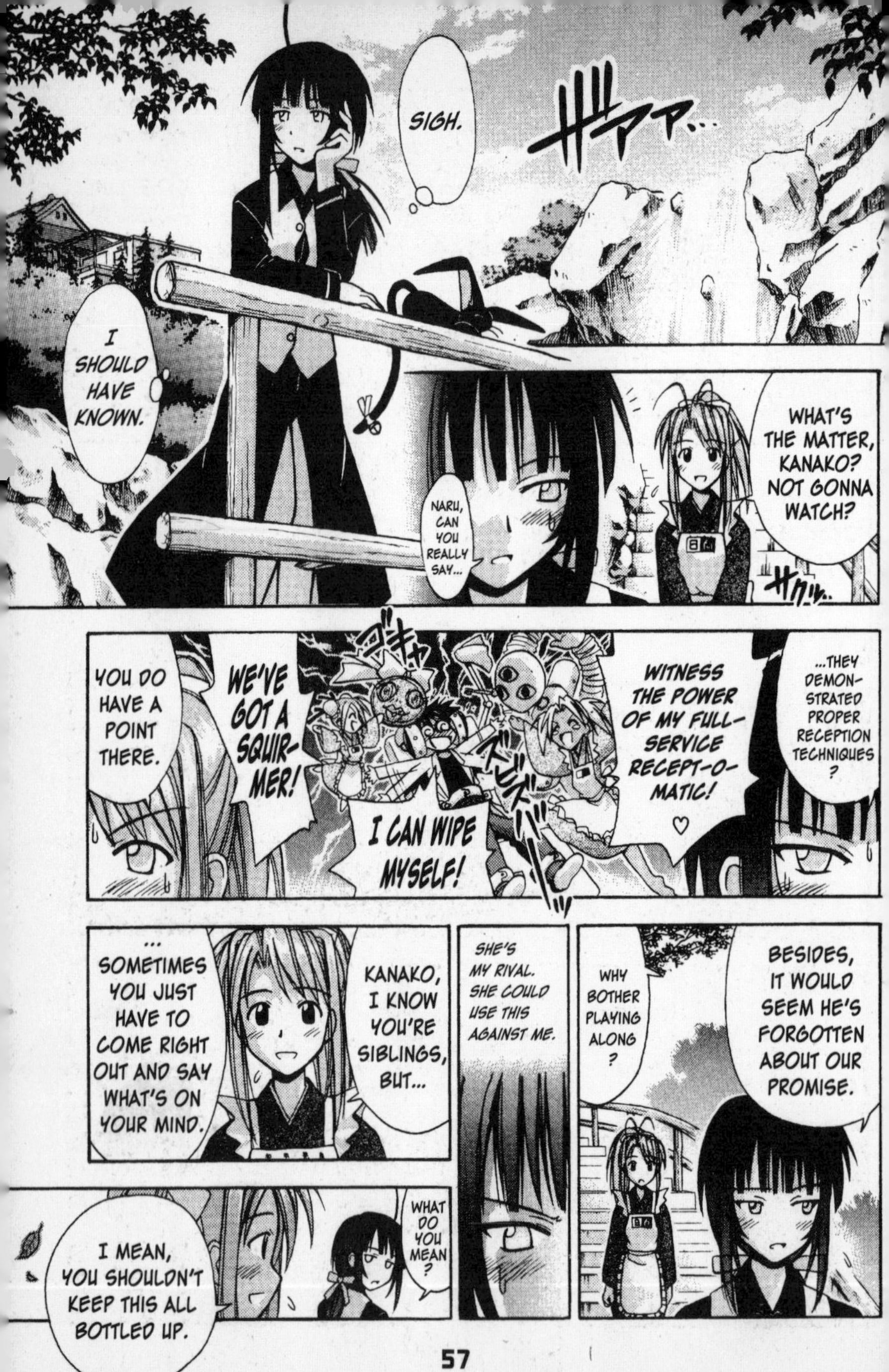
SIGH.
I SHOULD HAVE KNOWN.
WHAT'S THE MATTER, KANAKO? NOT GONNA WATCH?
NARU, CAN YOU REALLY SAY...
...THEY DEMONSTRATED PROPER RECEPTION TECHNIQUES?
WITNESS THE POWER OF MY FULL-SERVICE RECEPT-O-MATIC!
I CAN WIPE MYSELF!
WE'VE GOT A SQUIRMER!
YOU DO HAVE A POINT THERE.
BESIDES, IT WOULD SEEM HE'S FORGOTTEN ABOUT OUR PROMISE.
WHY BOTHER PLAYING ALONG?
SHE'S MY RIVAL. SHE COULD USE THIS AGAINST ME.
KANAKO, I KNOW YOU'RE SIBLINGS, BUT...
... SOMETIMES YOU JUST HAVE TO COME RIGHT OUT AND SAY WHAT'S ON YOUR MIND.
WHAT DO YOU MEAN?
I MEAN, YOU SHOULDN'T KEEP THIS ALL BOTTLED UP.

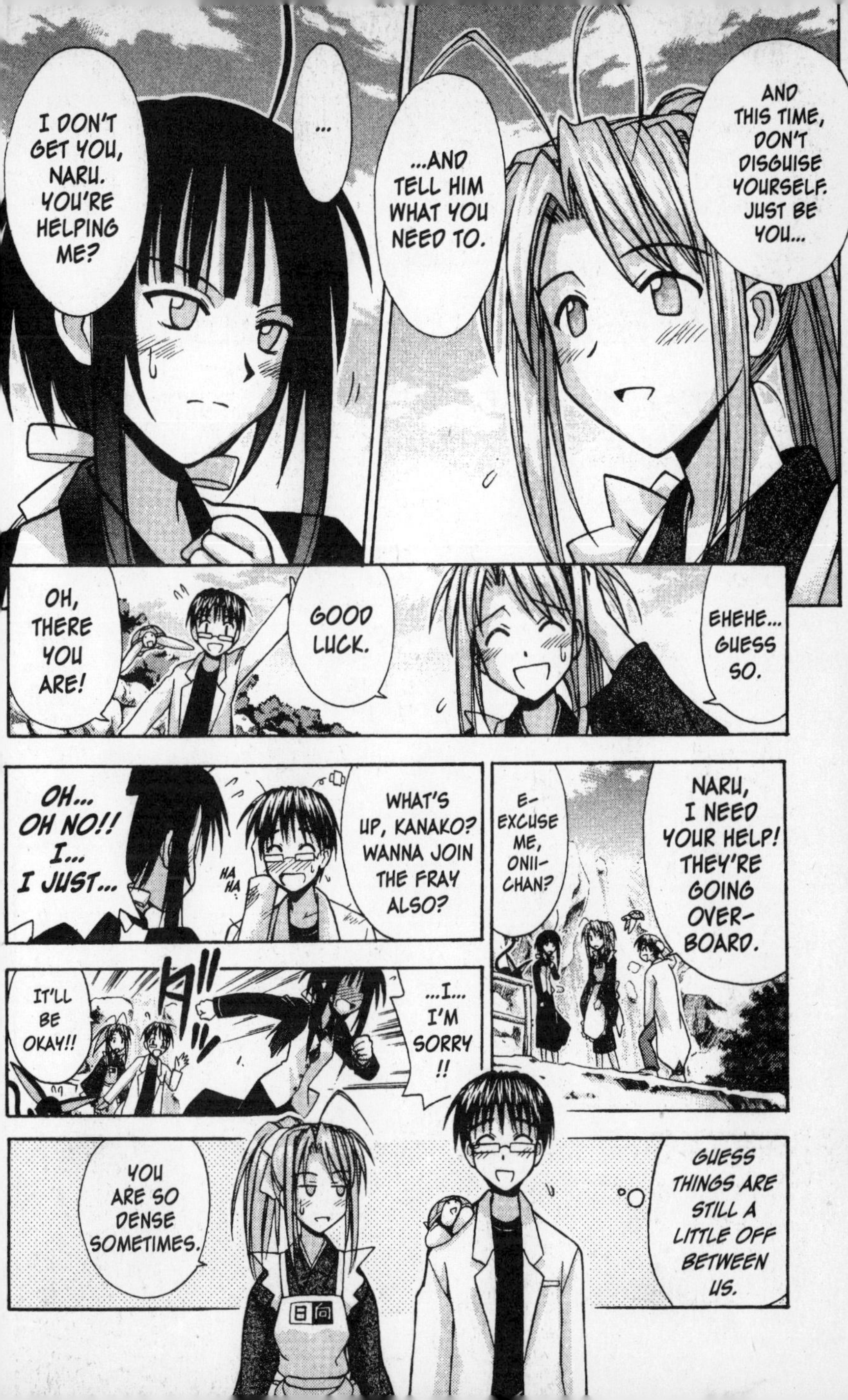
AND THIS TIME, DON'T DISGUISE YOURSELF. JUST BE YOU...
...AND TELL HIM WHAT YOU NEED TO.
...
I DON'T GET YOU, NARU. YOU'RE HELPING ME?
EHEHE... GUESS SO.
GOOD LUCK.
OH, THERE YOU ARE!
NARU, I NEED YOUR HELP! THEY'RE GOING OVER-BOARD.
E-EXCUSE ME, ONII-CHAN?
WHAT'S UP, KANAKO? WANNA JOIN THE FRAY ALSO?
HA HA
OH... OH NO!! I... I JUST...
...I... I'M SORRY !!
IT'LL BE OKAY!!
GUESS THINGS ARE STILL A LITTLE OFF BETWEEN US.
YOU ARE SO DENSE SOMETIMES.

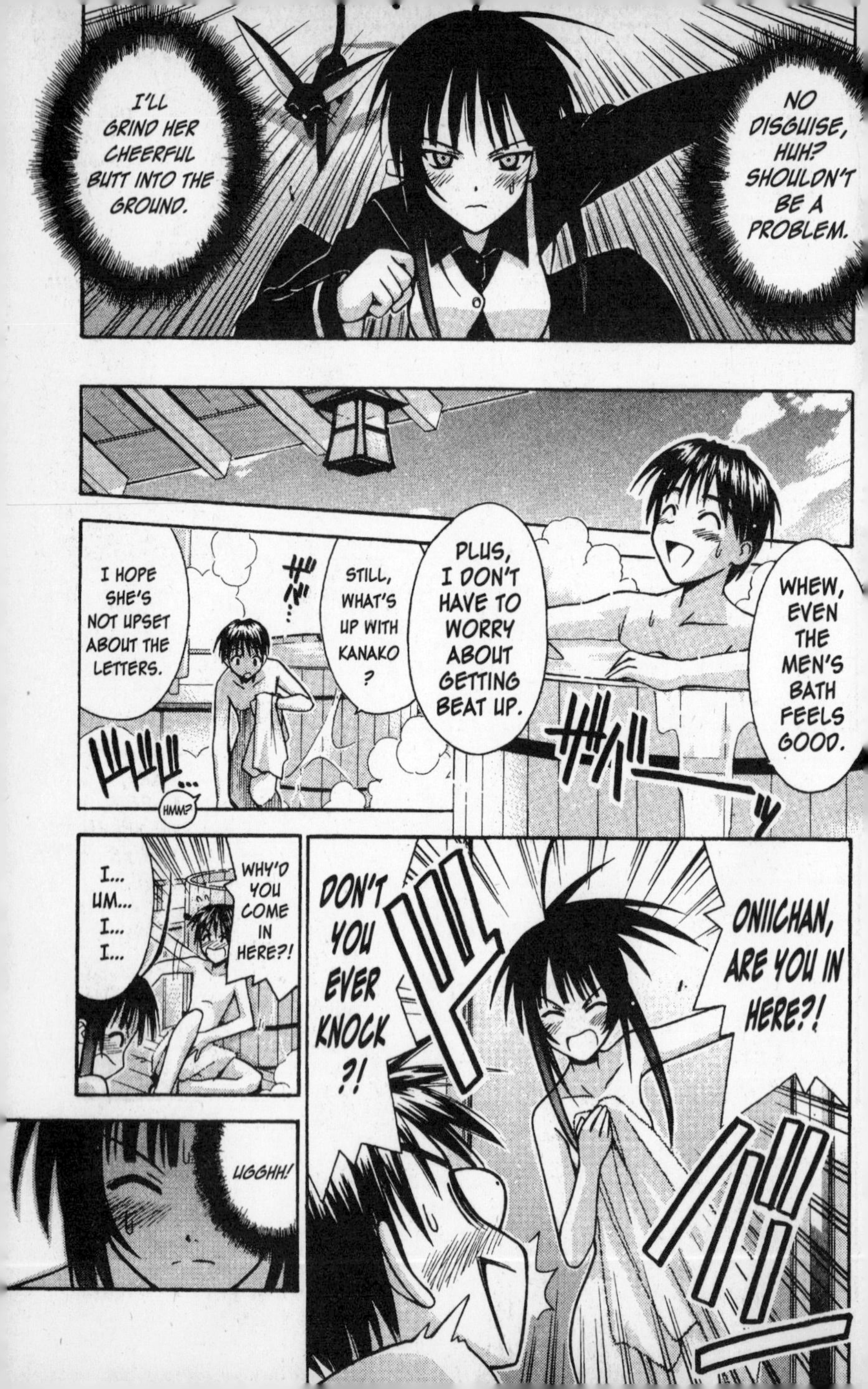
NO DISGUISE, HUH? SHOULDN'T BE A PROBLEM.
I'LL GRIND HER CHEERFUL BUTT INTO THE GROUND.
WHEW, EVEN THE MEN'S BATH FEELS GOOD.
PLUS, I DON'T HAVE TO WORRY ABOUT GETTING BEAT UP.
STILL, WHAT'S UP WITH KANAKO?
I HOPE SHE'S NOT UPSET ABOUT THE LETTERS.
HMM?
ONIICHAN, ARE YOU IN HERE?!
DON'T YOU EVER KNOCK?!
WHY'D YOU COME IN HERE?!
I... UM... I... I...
UGGHH!

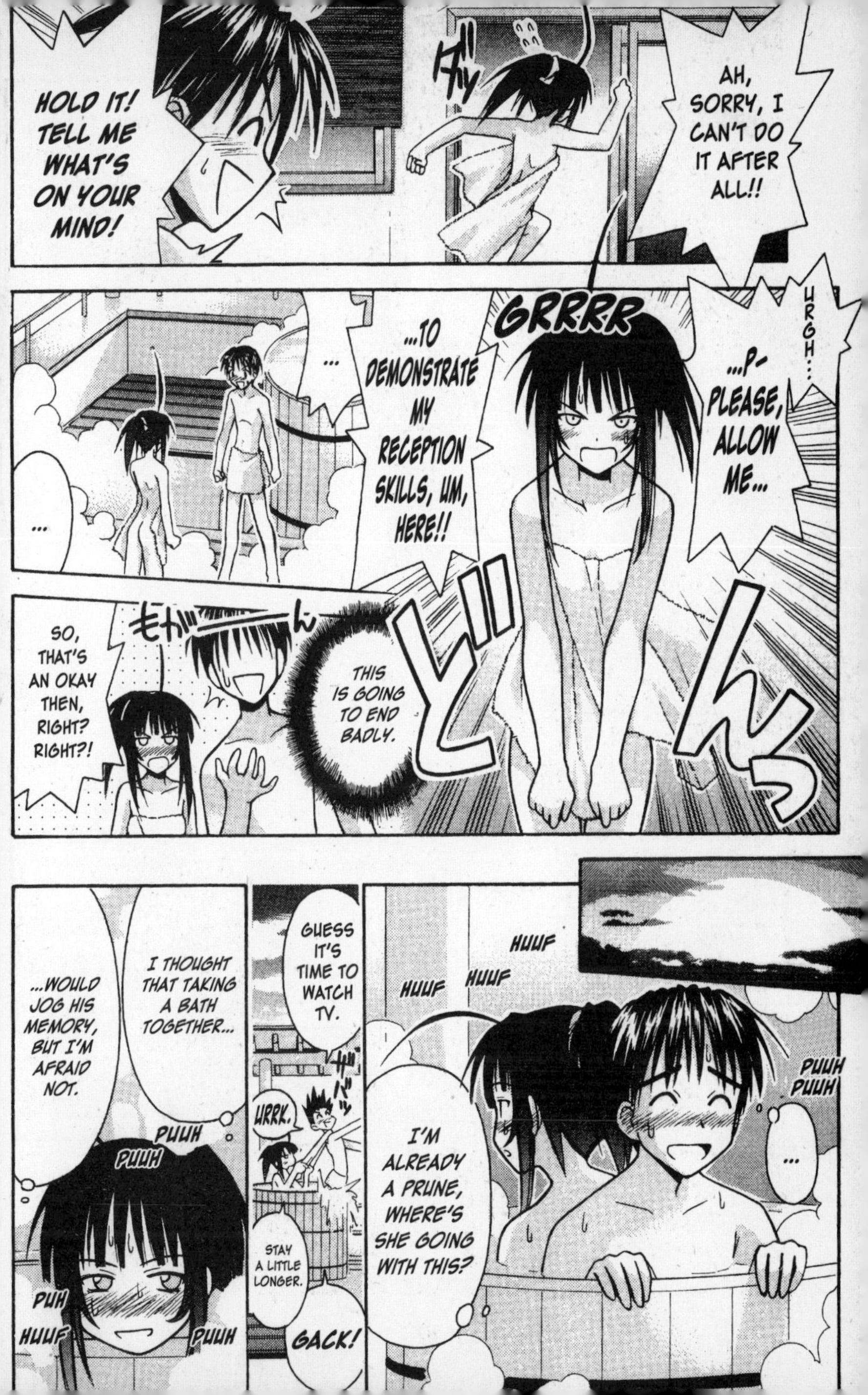
AH, SORRY, I CAN'T DO IT AFTER ALL!!
HOLD IT! TELL ME WHAT'S ON YOUR MIND!
URGH...
...P-PLEASE, ALLOW ME...
GRRRR
...TO DEMONSTRATE MY RECEPTION SKILLS, UM, HERE!!
...
...
THIS IS GOING TO END BADLY.
SO, THAT'S AN OKAY THEN, RIGHT? RIGHT?!
HUUF
HUUF
HUUF
PUUH PUUH
...
I'M ALREADY A PRUNE, WHERE'S SHE GOING WITH THIS?
GUESS IT'S TIME TO WATCH TV.
URRK.
STAY A LITTLE LONGER.
GACK!
I THOUGHT THAT TAKING A BATH TOGETHER...
...WOULD JOG HIS MEMORY, BUT I'M AFRAID NOT.
PUUH
PUUH
PUH
HUUF
PUUH

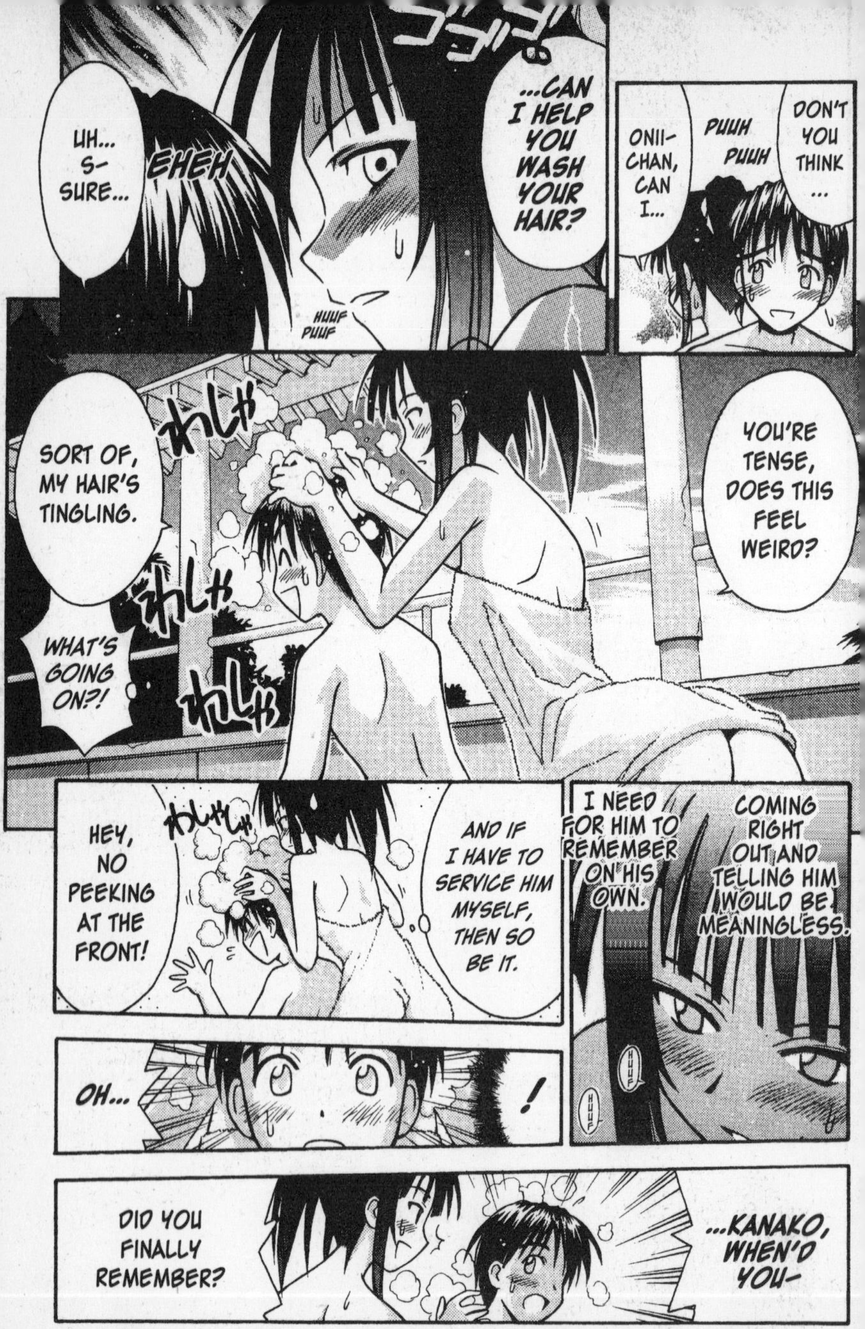
DON'T YOU THINK ...
PUUH PUUH
ONII-CHAN, CAN I...
...CAN I HELP YOU WASH YOUR HAIR?
UH... S-SURE...
EHEH
HUUF PUUF
YOU'RE TENSE, DOES THIS FEEL WEIRD?
SORT OF, MY HAIR'S TINGLING.
WHAT'S GOING ON?!
COMING RIGHT OUT AND TELLING HIM WOULD BE MEANINGLESS.
I NEED FOR HIM TO REMEMBER ON HIS OWN.
HUUF
HUUF
AND IF I HAVE TO SERVICE HIM MYSELF, THEN SO BE IT.
HEY, NO PEEKING AT THE FRONT!
!
OH...
...KANAKO, WHEN'D YOU-
DID YOU FINALLY REMEMBER?

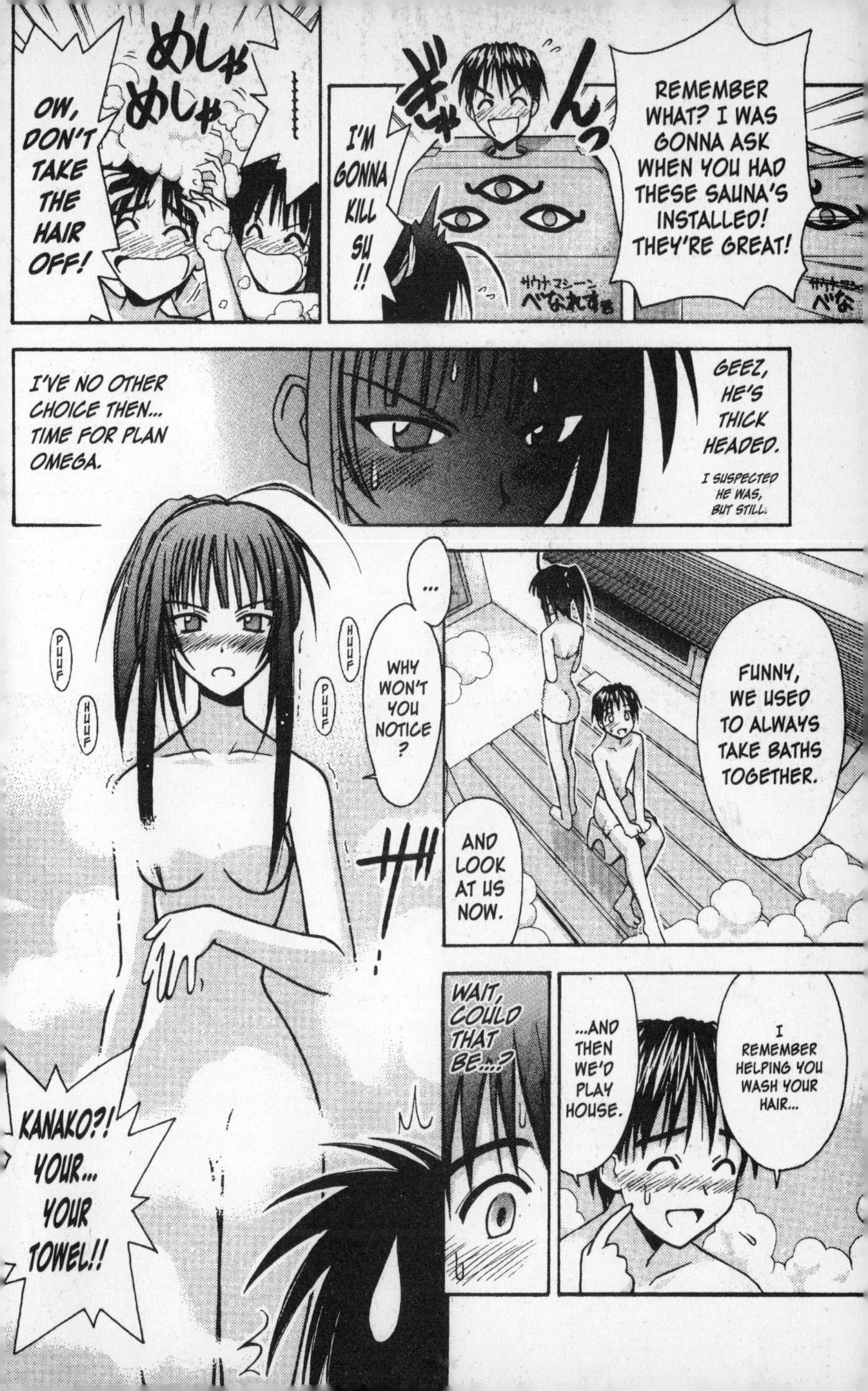
REMEMBER WHAT? I WAS GONNA ASK WHEN YOU HAD THESE SAUNA'S INSTALLED! THEY'RE GREAT!
ぎゃんっ
I'M GONNA KILL SU!!
めしゃめしゃ
OW, DON'T TAKE THE HAIR OFF!
GEEZ, HE'S THICK HEADED.
I SUSPECTED HE WAS, BUT STILL.
I'VE NO OTHER CHOICE THEN... TIME FOR PLAN OMEGA.
FUNNY, WE USED TO ALWAYS TAKE BATHS TOGETHER.
AND LOOK AT US NOW.
I REMEMBER HELPING YOU WASH YOUR HAIR...
...AND THEN WE'D PLAY HOUSE.
WAIT, COULD THAT BE...?
...
WHY WON'T YOU NOTICE?
HUUF
PUUF
HUUF
PUUF
KANAKO?! YOUR... YOUR TOWEL!!

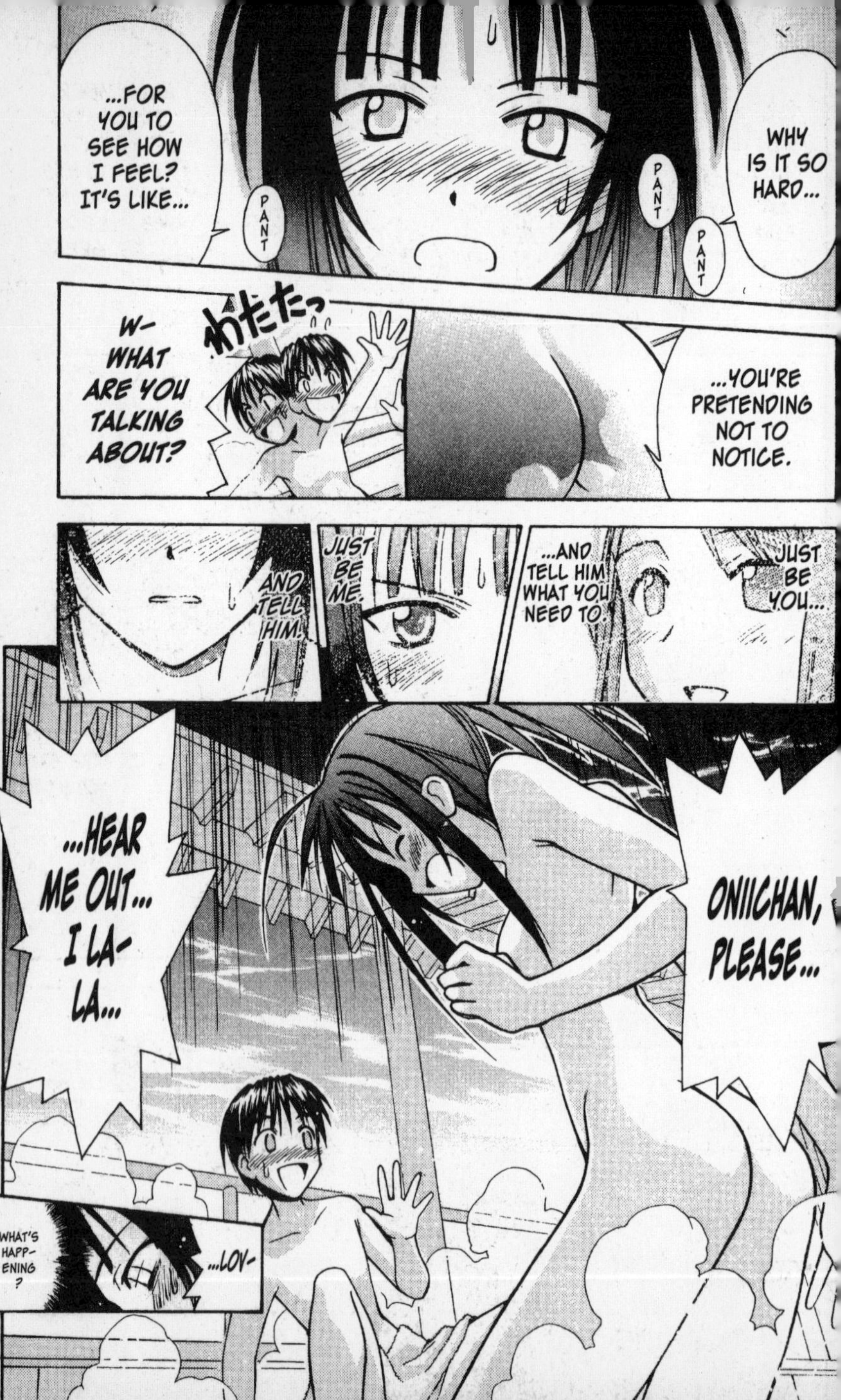
WHY IS IT SO HARD...
PANT
PANT
...FOR YOU TO SEE HOW I FEEL? IT'S LIKE...
PANT
...YOU'RE PRETENDING NOT TO NOTICE.
わたたっ
W-WHAT ARE YOU TALKING ABOUT?
JUST BE YOU...
...AND TELL HIM WHAT YOU NEED TO.
JUST BE ME.
AND TELL HIM.
ONIICHAN, PLEASE...
...HEAR ME OUT... I LA-LA...
...LOV-
WHAT'S HAPP-ENING?

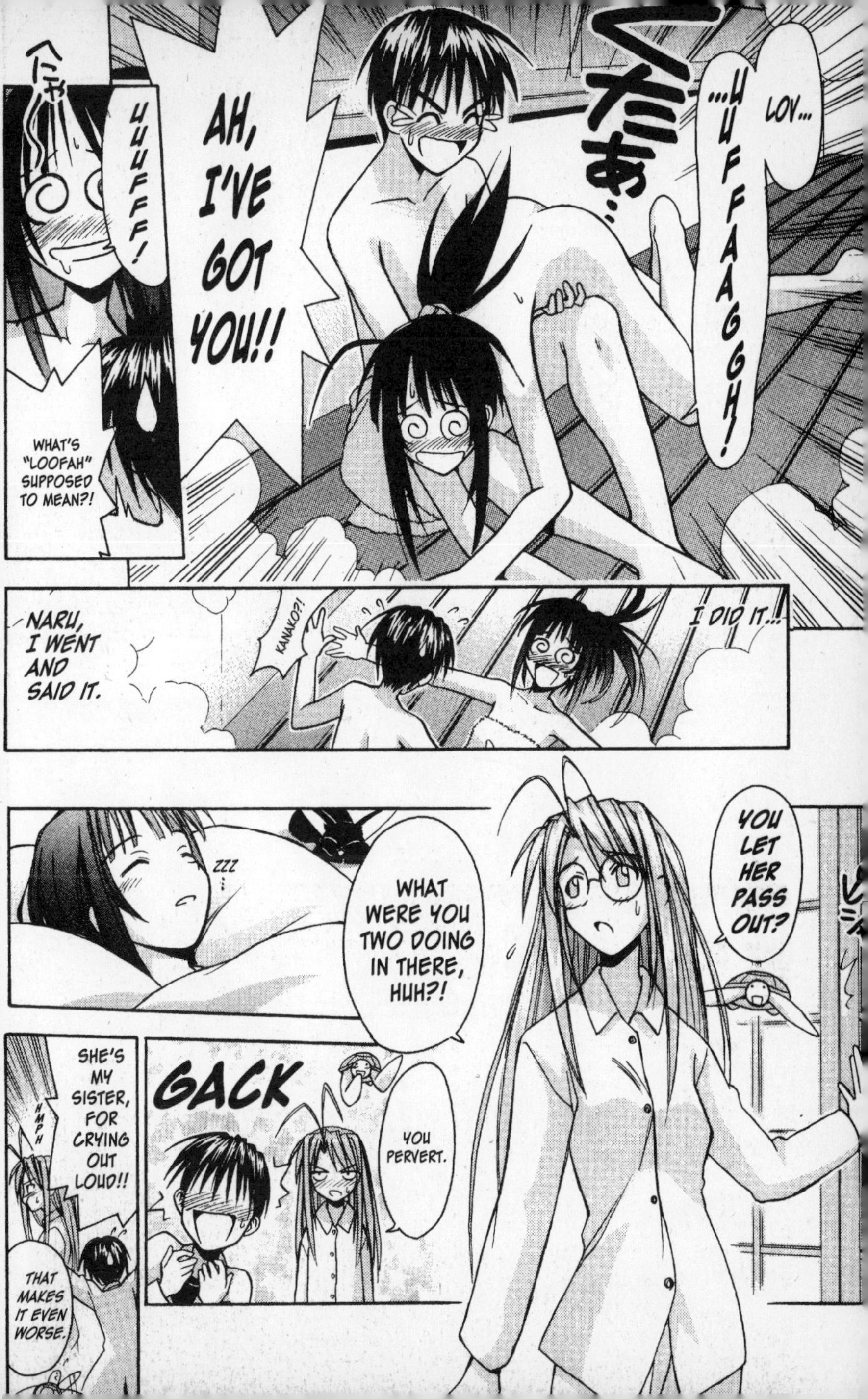
くたぁ…
LOV...
...UUFFAAGGH!
AH, I'VE GOT YOU!!
UUUFFF!
WHAT'S "LOOFAH" SUPPOSED TO MEAN?!
I DID IT...
KANAKO?!
NARU, I WENT AND SAID IT.
YOU LET HER PASS OUT?
WHAT WERE YOU TWO DOING IN THERE, HUH?!
ZZZ...
GACK
YOU PERVERT.
SHE'S MY SISTER, FOR CRYING OUT LOUD!!
HMPH
THAT MAKES IT EVEN WORSE.

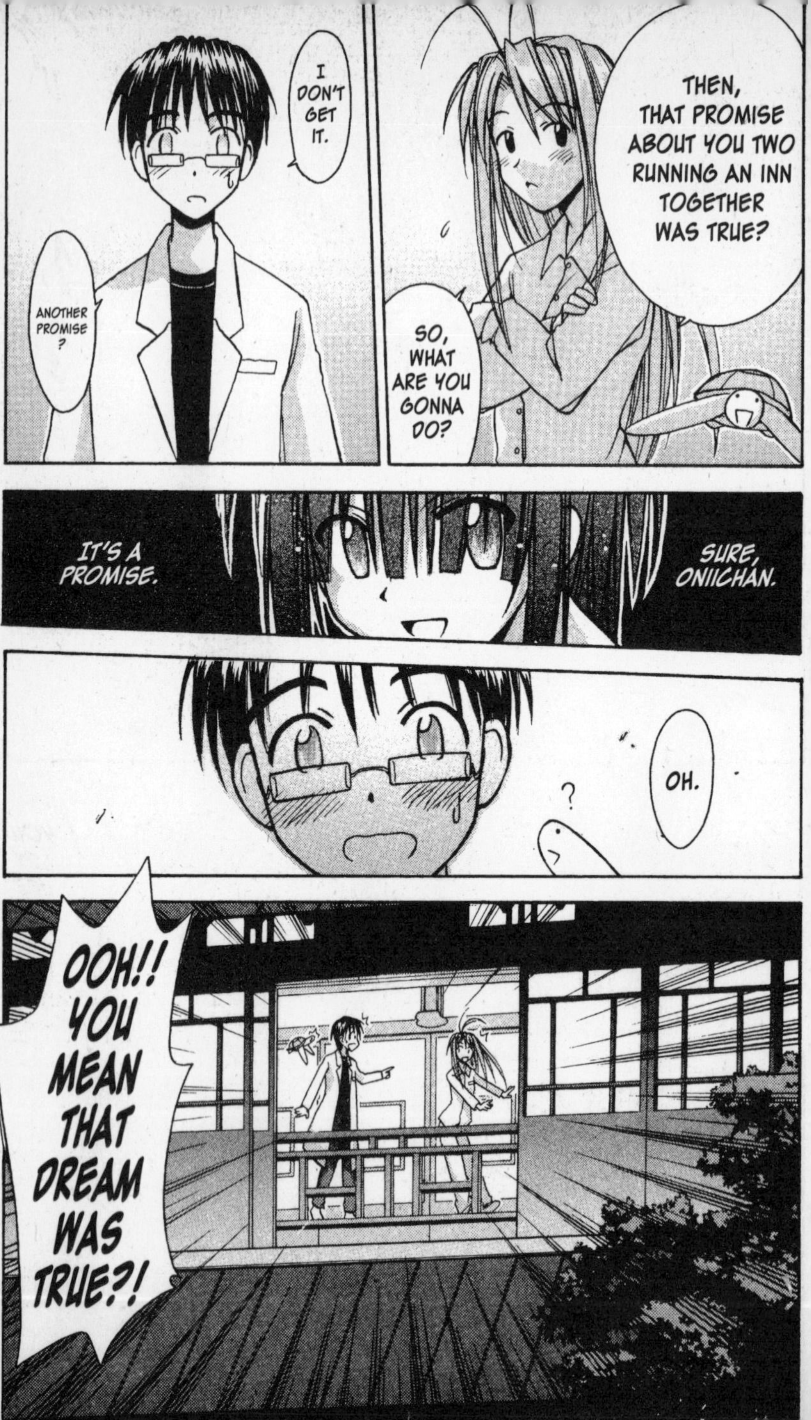
THEN, THAT PROMISE ABOUT YOU TWO RUNNING AN INN TOGETHER WAS TRUE?
SO, WHAT ARE YOU GONNA DO?
I DON'T GET IT.
ANOTHER PROMISE ?
SURE, ONIICHAN.
IT'S A PROMISE.
OH.
?
OOH!! YOU MEAN THAT DREAM WAS TRUE?!

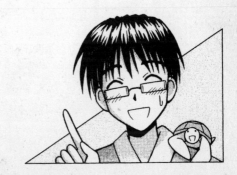

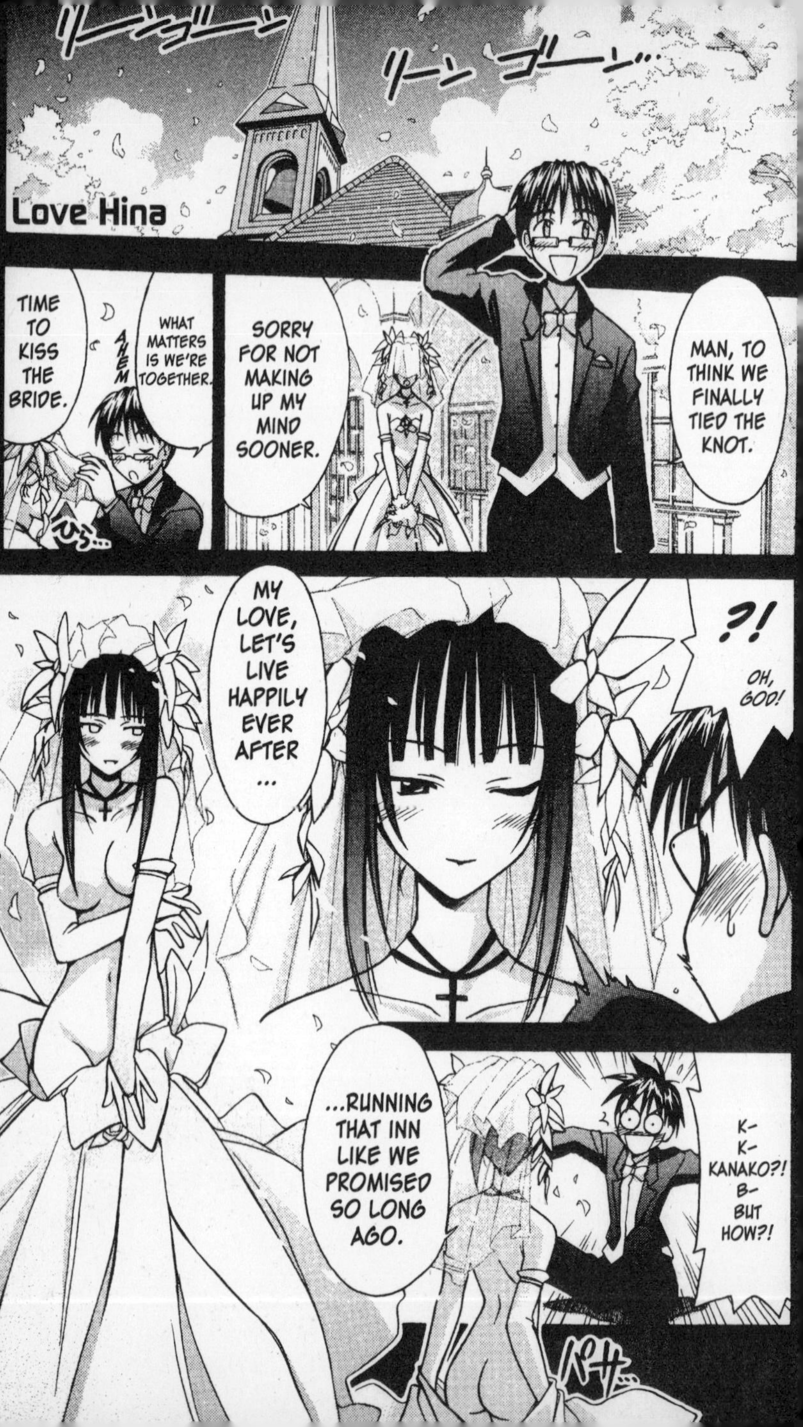
リーンゴーン
リーンゴーン…
Love Hina
MAN, TO THINK WE FINALLY TIED THE KNOT.
SORRY FOR NOT MAKING UP MY MIND SOONER.
WHAT MATTERS IS WE'RE TOGETHER.
AHEM
TIME TO KISS THE BRIDE.
ひら…
?!
OH, GOD!
MY LOVE, LET'S LIVE HAPPILY EVER AFTER ...
K-K-KANAKO?! B-BUT HOW?!
...RUNNING THAT INN LIKE WE PROMISED SO LONG AGO.
パサ…
しゅる…

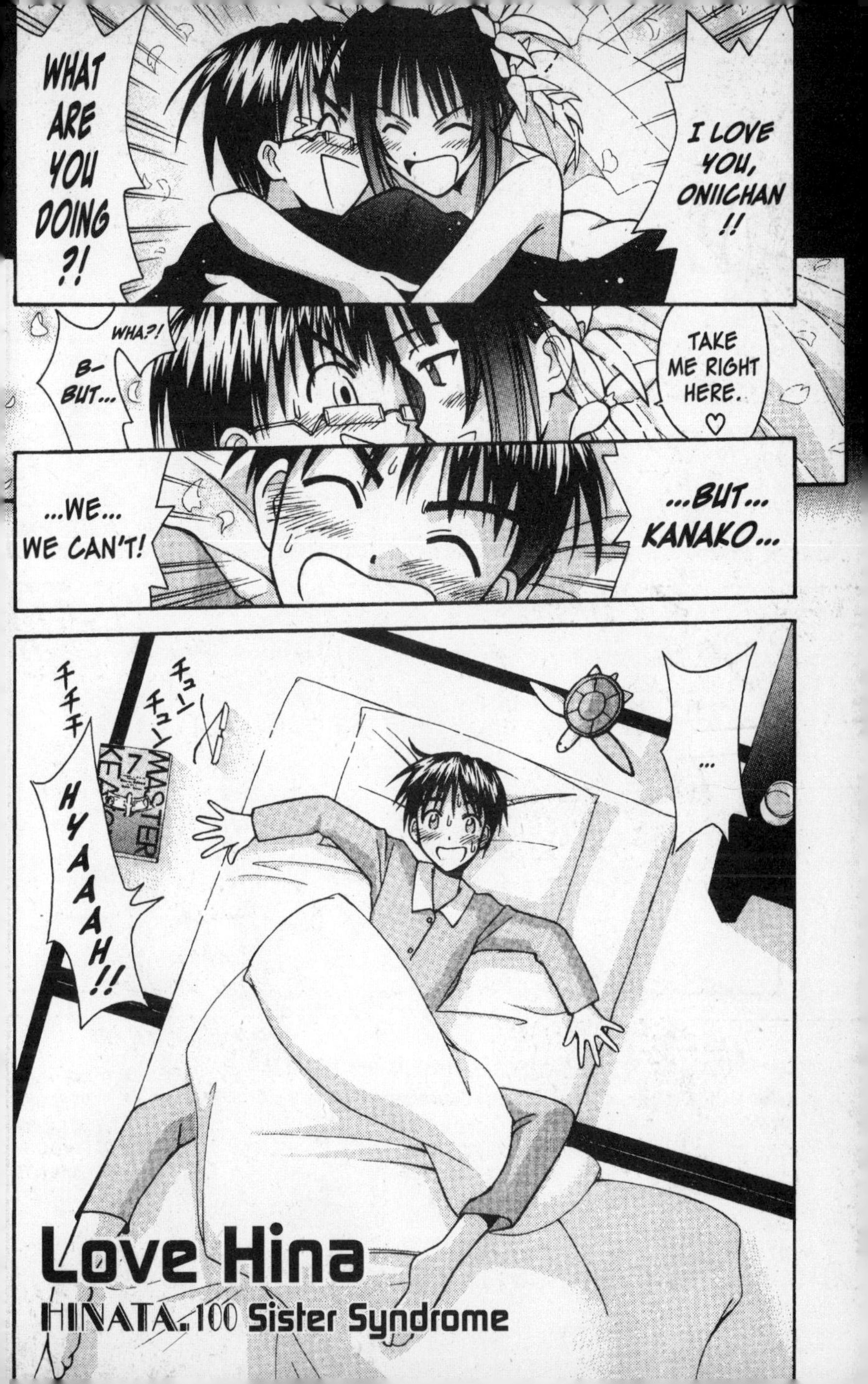

I LOVE YOU, ONIICHAN!!
WHAT ARE YOU DOING?!
TAKE ME RIGHT HERE. ♡
WHA?!
B-BUT...
...BUT... KANAKO...
...WE... WE CAN'T!
...
チュンチュン
チチチ
HYAAAAH!!
Love Hina
HINATA.100 Sister Syndrome

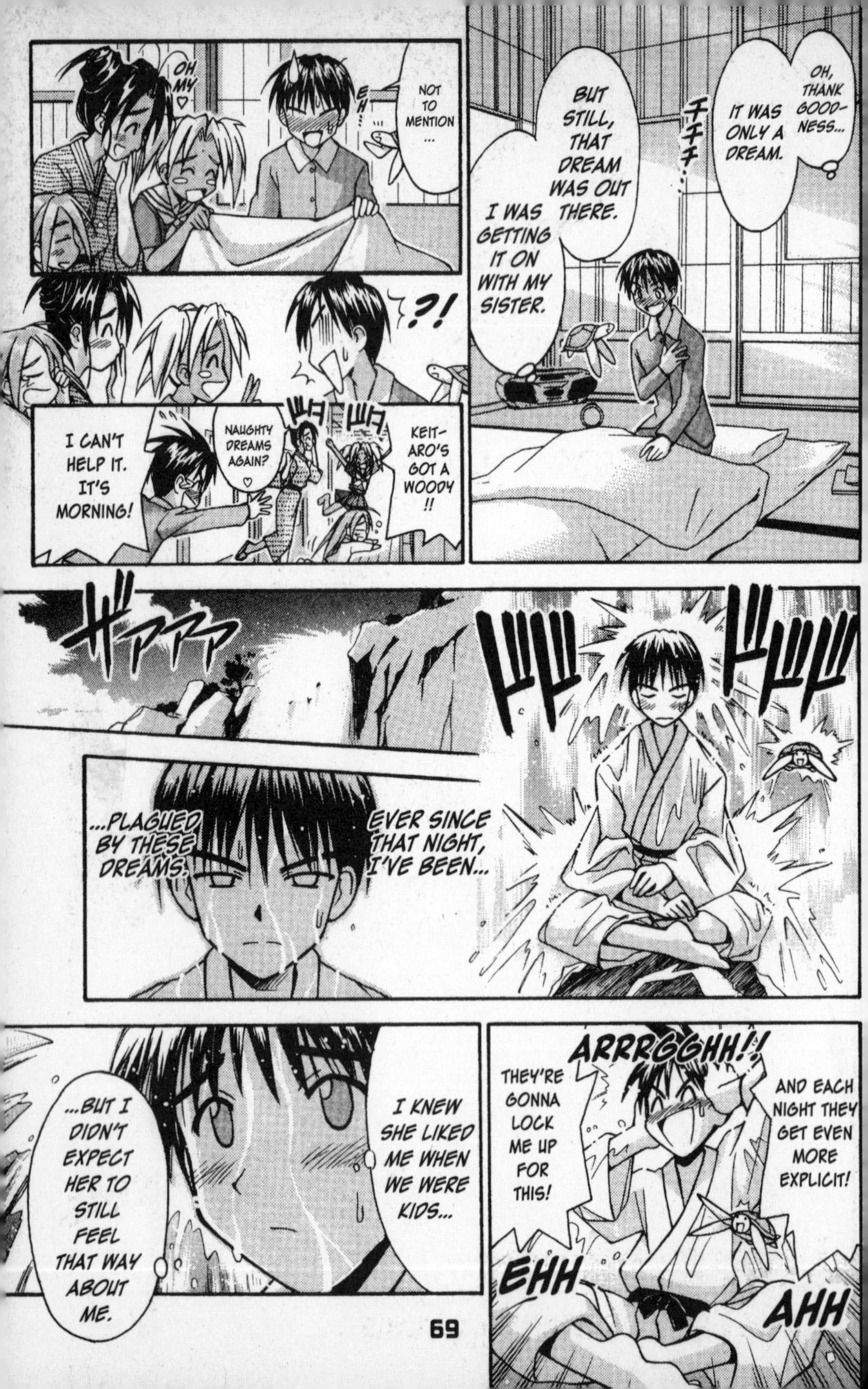
OH, THANK GOOD-NESS...
IT WAS ONLY A DREAM.
チチチ...
BUT STILL, THAT DREAM WAS OUT THERE.
I WAS GETTING IT ON WITH MY SISTER.
NOT TO MENTION ...
EH...!!
OH MY ♡
?!
KEIT-ARO'S GOT A WOODY !!
NAUGHTY DREAMS AGAIN? ♡
I CAN'T HELP IT. IT'S MORNING!
ザァアア
EVER SINCE THAT NIGHT, I'VE BEEN...
...PLAGUED BY THESE DREAMS.
AND EACH NIGHT THEY GET EVEN MORE EXPLICIT!
ARRRGGHH!!
THEY'RE GONNA LOCK ME UP FOR THIS!
EHH
AHH
I KNEW SHE LIKED ME WHEN WE WERE KIDS...
...BUT I DIDN'T EXPECT HER TO STILL FEEL THAT WAY ABOUT ME.

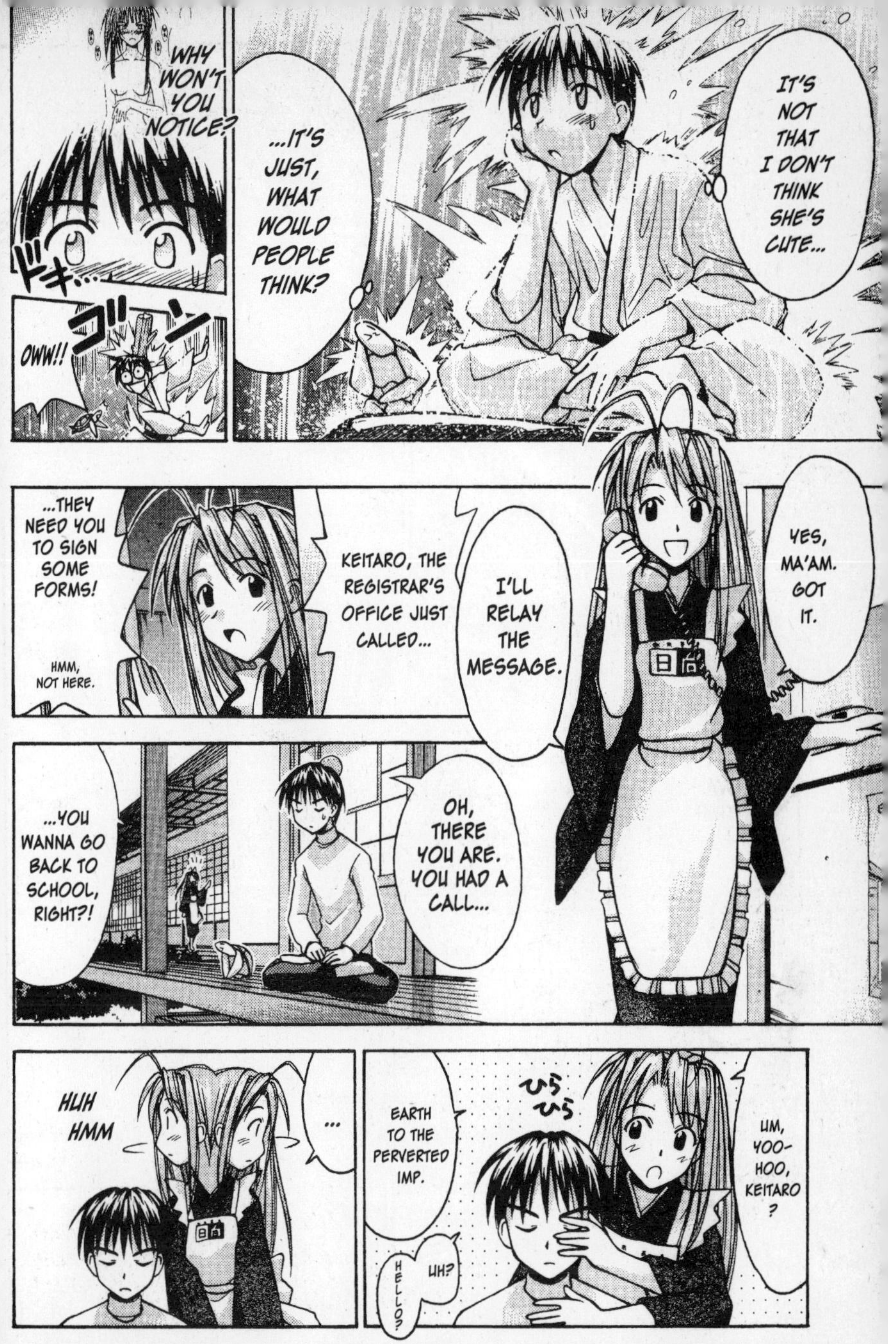
IT'S NOT THAT I DON'T THINK SHE'S CUTE...
...IT'S JUST, WHAT WOULD PEOPLE THINK?
WHY WON'T YOU NOTICE?
ドキ…
ゴーン
OWW!!
YES, MA'AM. GOT IT.
I'LL RELAY THE MESSAGE.
KEITARO, THE REGISTRAR'S OFFICE JUST CALLED...
...THEY NEED YOU TO SIGN SOME FORMS!
HMM, NOT HERE.
OH, THERE YOU ARE. YOU HAD A CALL...
...YOU WANNA GO BACK TO SCHOOL, RIGHT?!
UM, YOO-HOO, KEITARO?
ひら ひら
EARTH TO THE PERVERTED IMP.
UH?
HELLO?
...
HUH HMM

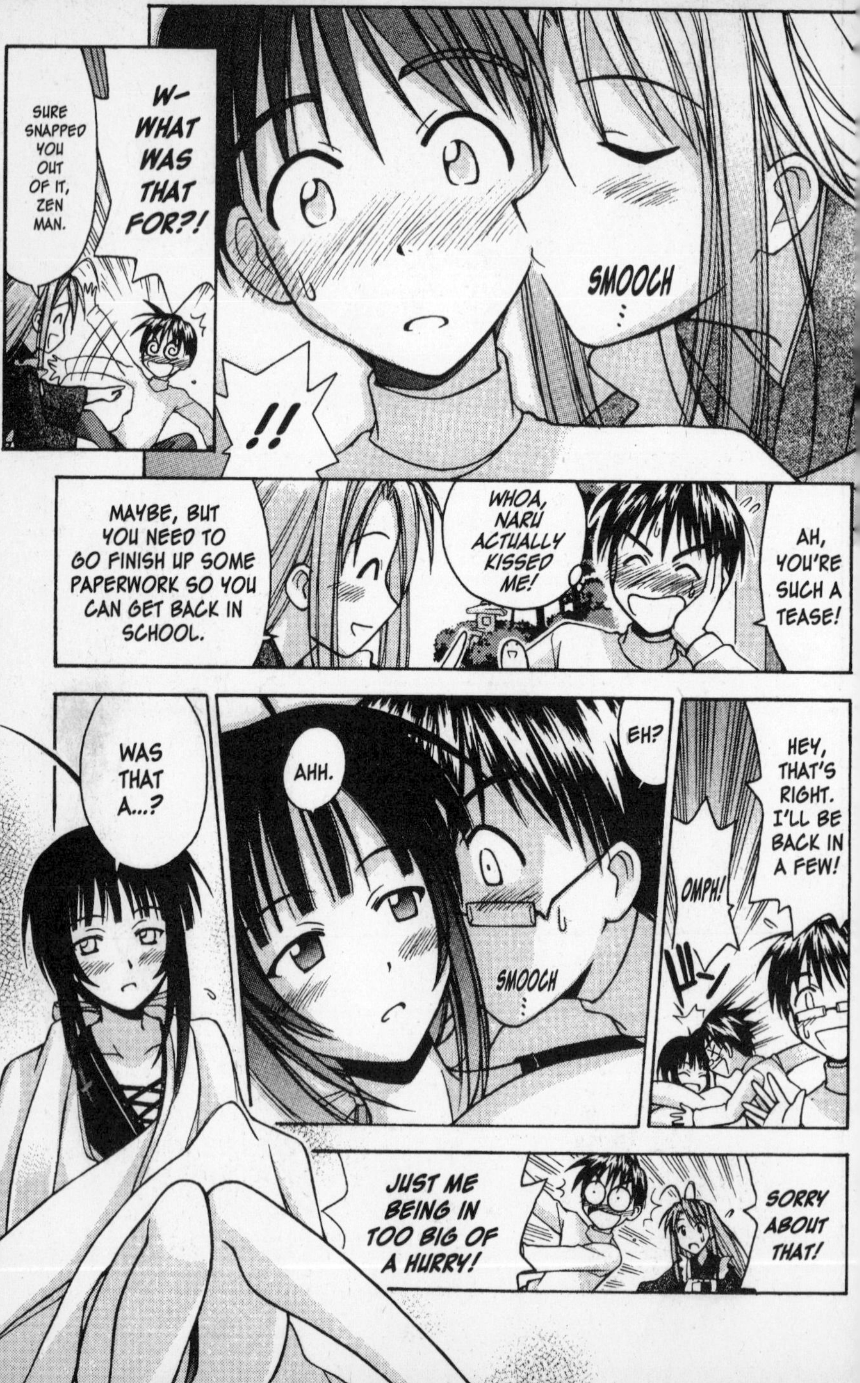
SMOOCH...
!!
W-WHAT WAS THAT FOR?!
SURE SNAPPED YOU OUT OF IT, ZEN MAN.
AH, YOU'RE SUCH A TEASE!
WHOA, NARU ACTUALLY KISSED ME!
MAYBE, BUT YOU NEED TO GO FINISH UP SOME PAPERWORK SO YOU CAN GET BACK IN SCHOOL.
HEY, THAT'S RIGHT. I'LL BE BACK IN A FEW!
OMPH!
EH?
AHH.
SMOOCH...
WAS THAT A...?
SORRY ABOUT THAT!
JUST ME BEING IN TOO BIG OF A HURRY!

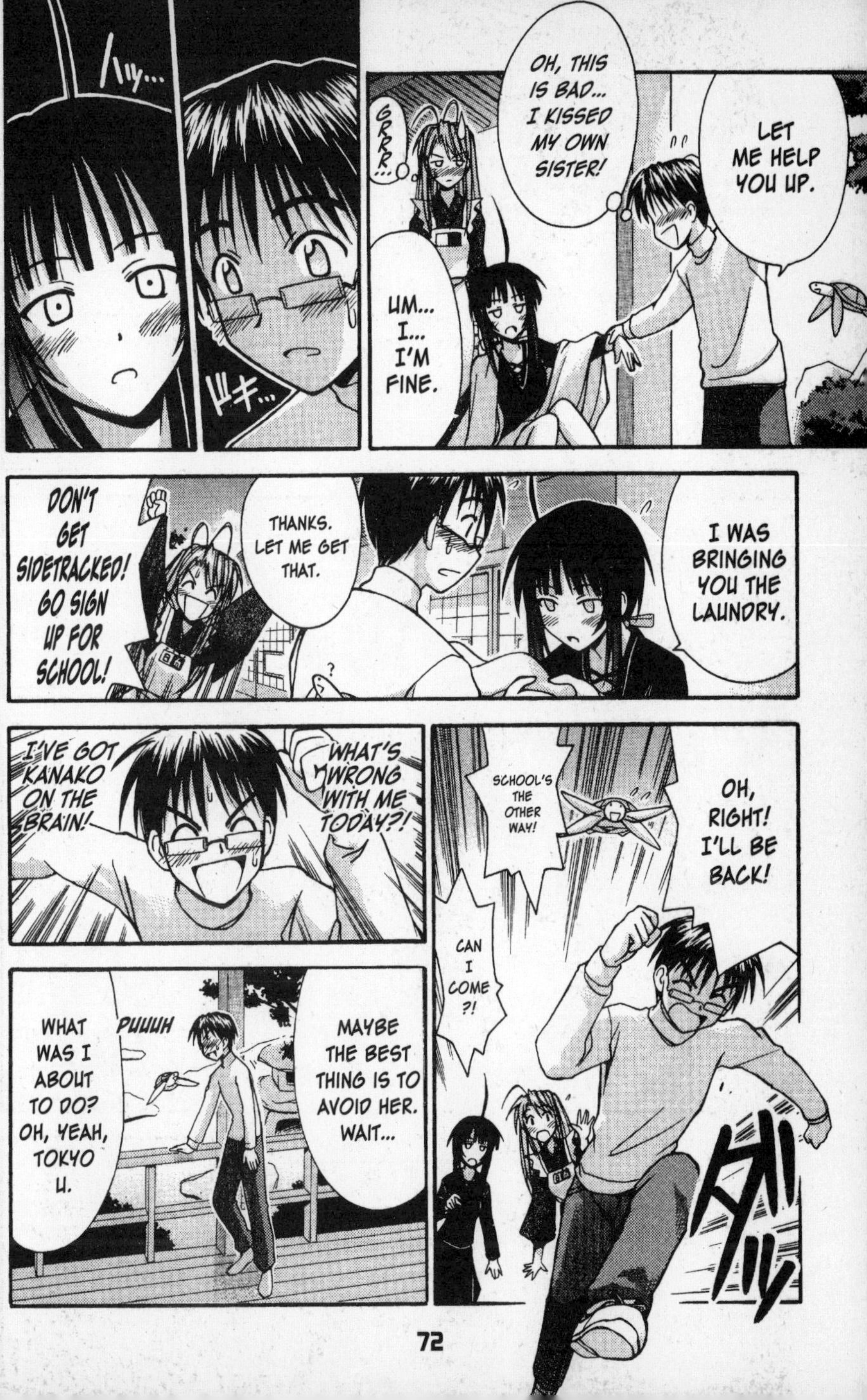
LET ME HELP YOU UP.
OH, THIS IS BAD... I KISSED MY OWN SISTER!
GRRR...
UM... I... I'M FINE.
ドキ...
ハッ...
I WAS BRINGING YOU THE LAUNDRY.
THANKS. LET ME GET THAT.
DON'T GET SIDETRACKED! GO SIGN UP FOR SCHOOL!
OH, RIGHT! I'LL BE BACK!
SCHOOL'S THE OTHER WAY!
CAN I COME?!
WHAT'S WRONG WITH ME TODAY?!
I'VE GOT KANAKO ON THE BRAIN!
MAYBE THE BEST THING IS TO AVOID HER. WAIT...
PUUUH
WHAT WAS I ABOUT TO DO? OH, YEAH, TOKYO U.

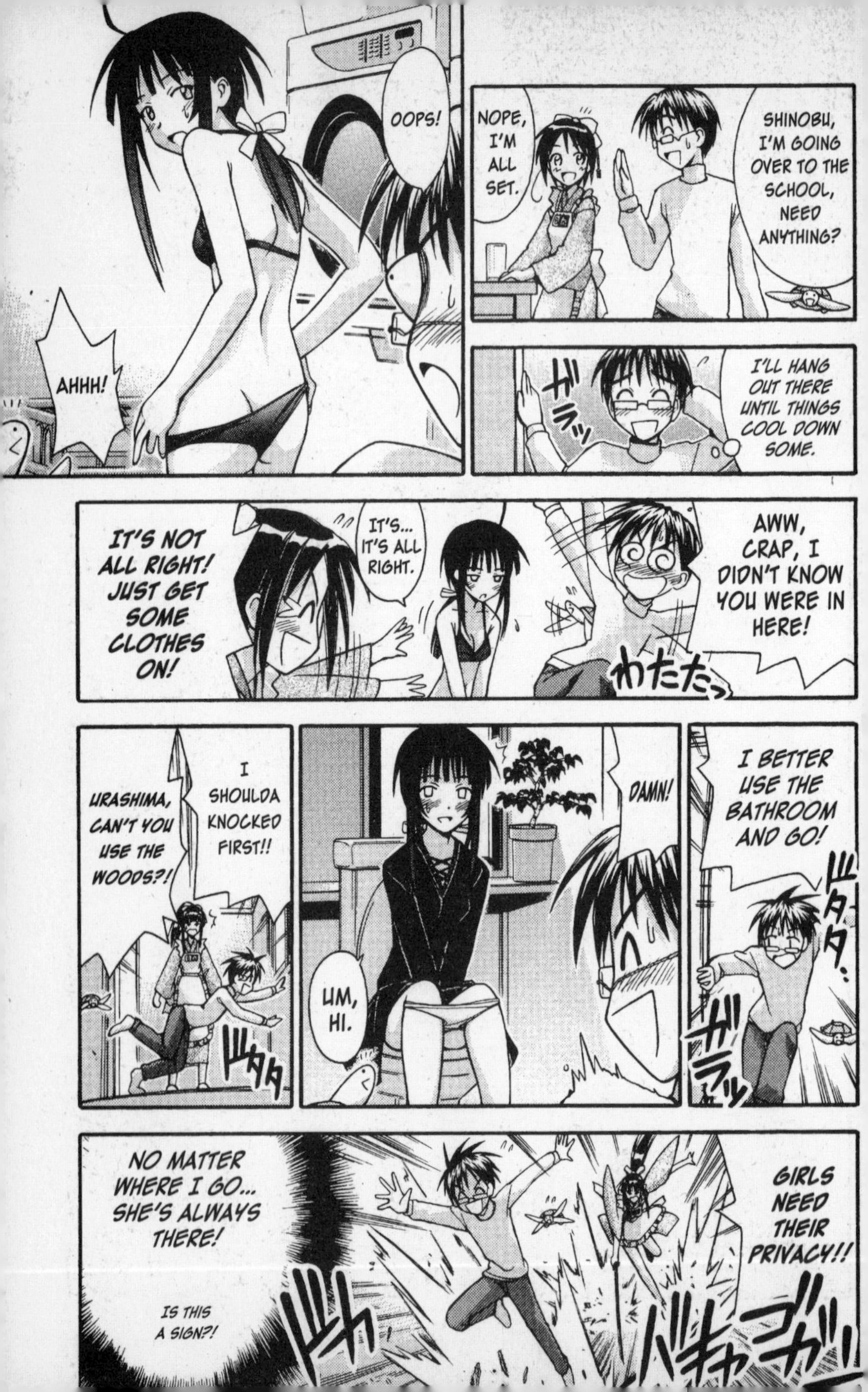
SHINOBU, I'M GOING OVER TO THE SCHOOL, NEED ANYTHING?
NOPE, I'M ALL SET.
I'LL HANG OUT THERE UNTIL THINGS COOL DOWN SOME.
ガラッ
OOPS!
AHHH!
AWW, CRAP, I DIDN'T KNOW YOU WERE IN HERE!
わたたっ
IT'S... IT'S ALL RIGHT.
IT'S NOT ALL RIGHT! JUST GET SOME CLOTHES ON!
I BETTER USE THE BATHROOM AND GO!
ダタタ..
ガラッ
DAMN!
UM, HI.
I SHOULDA KNOCKED FIRST!!
URASHIMA, CAN'T YOU USE THE WOODS?!
ドタタ
GIRLS NEED THEIR PRIVACY!!
NO MATTER WHERE I GO... SHE'S ALWAYS THERE!
IS THIS A SIGN?!
ドカ

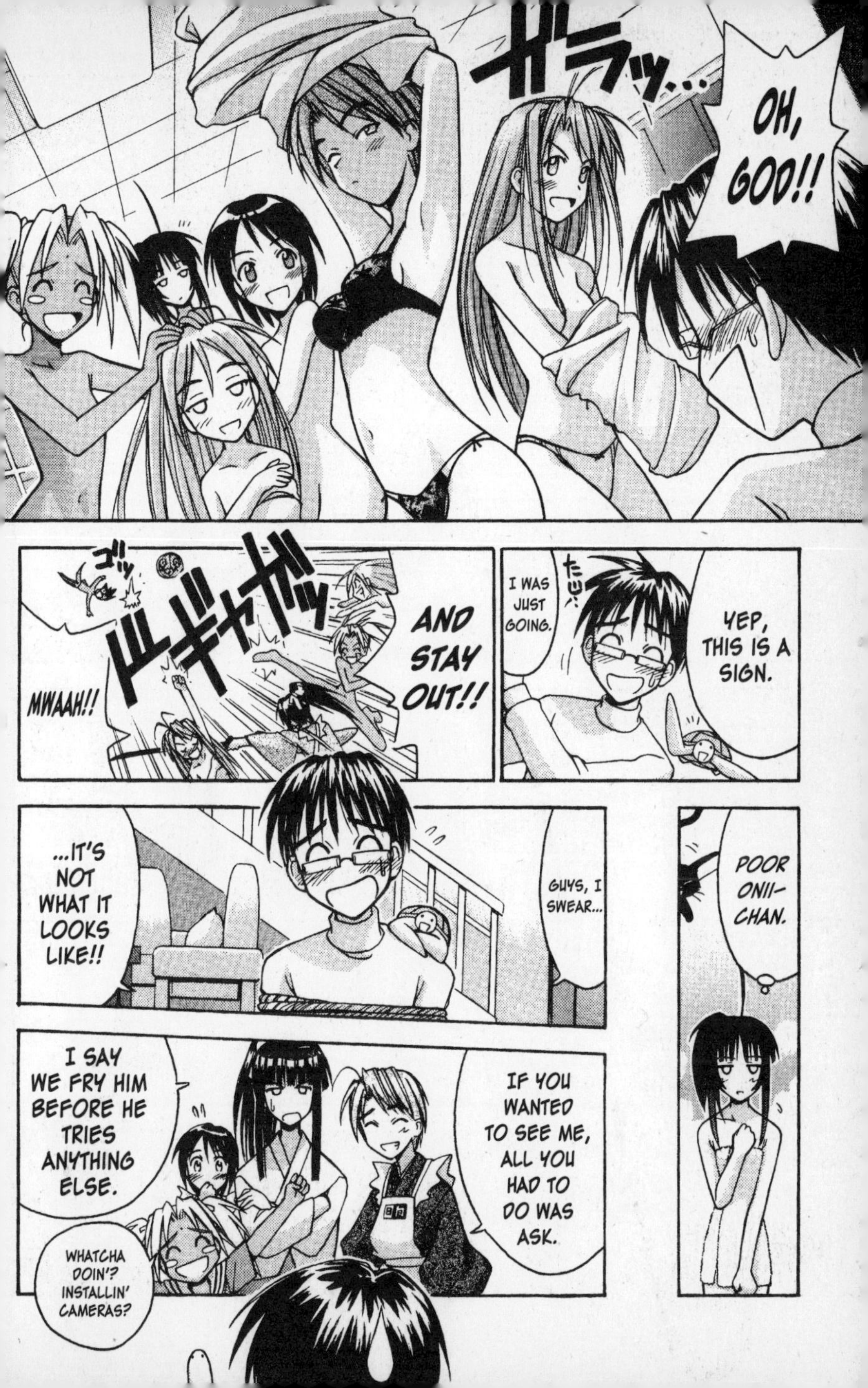

ガラッ...
OH, GOD!!
YEP, THIS IS A SIGN.
I WAS JUST GOING.
AND STAY OUT!!
ドギャガッ
MWAAH!!
POOR ONII-CHAN.
GUYS, I SWEAR...
...IT'S NOT WHAT IT LOOKS LIKE!!
IF YOU WANTED TO SEE ME, ALL YOU HAD TO DO WAS ASK.
I SAY WE FRY HIM BEFORE HE TRIES ANYTHING ELSE.
WHATCHA DOIN'? INSTALLIN' CAMERAS?

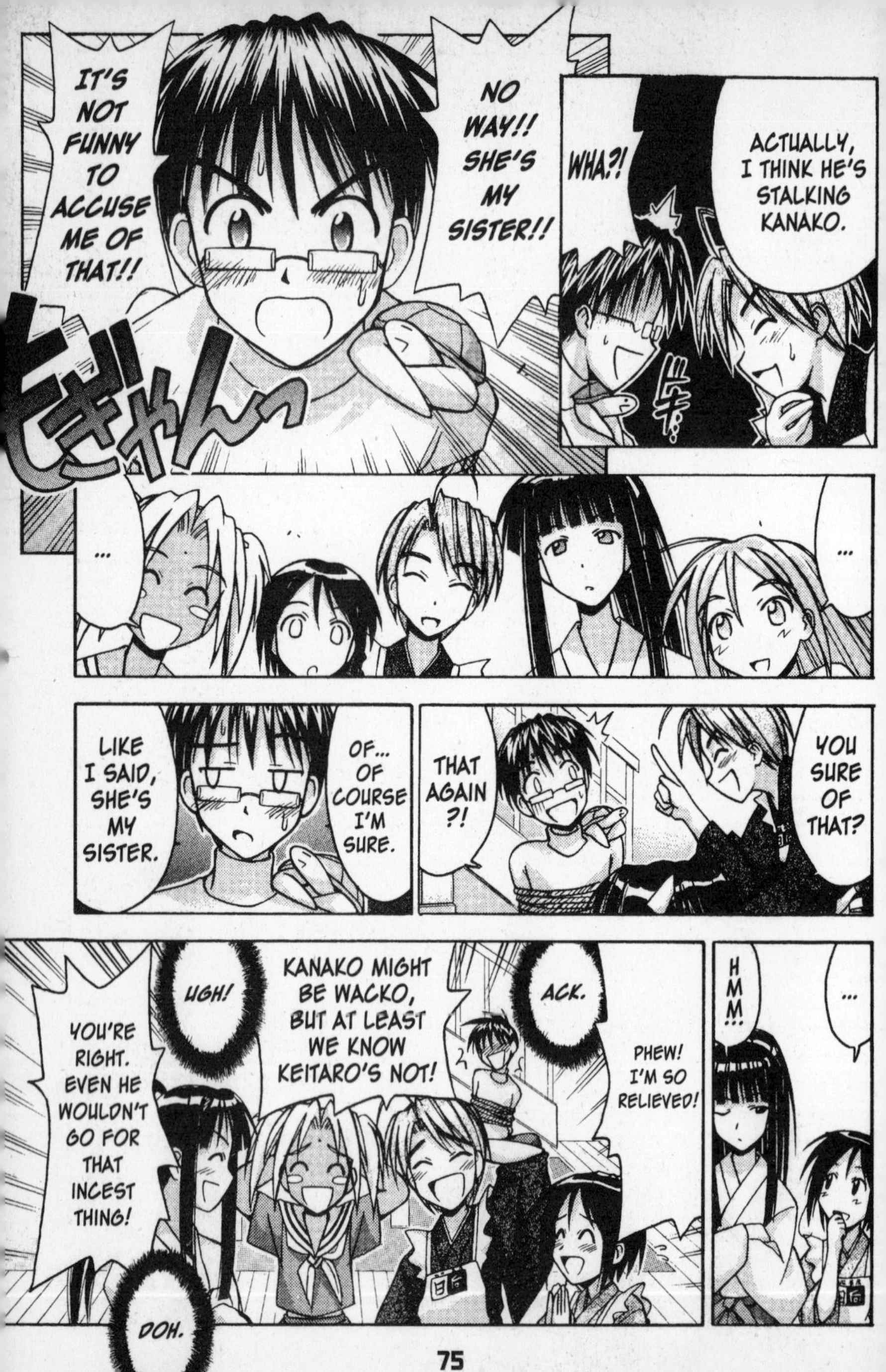

ACTUALLY, I THINK HE'S STALKING KANAKO.
WHA?!
NO WAY!! SHE'S MY SISTER!!
IT'S NOT FUNNY TO ACCUSE ME OF THAT!!
...
...
YOU SURE OF THAT?
THAT AGAIN ?!
OF... OF COURSE I'M SURE.
LIKE I SAID, SHE'S MY SISTER.
...
HMM...
ACK.
KANAKO MIGHT BE WACKO, BUT AT LEAST WE KNOW KEITARO'S NOT!
UGH!
PHEW! I'M SO RELIEVED!
YOU'RE RIGHT. EVEN HE WOULDN'T GO FOR THAT INCEST THING!
DOH.

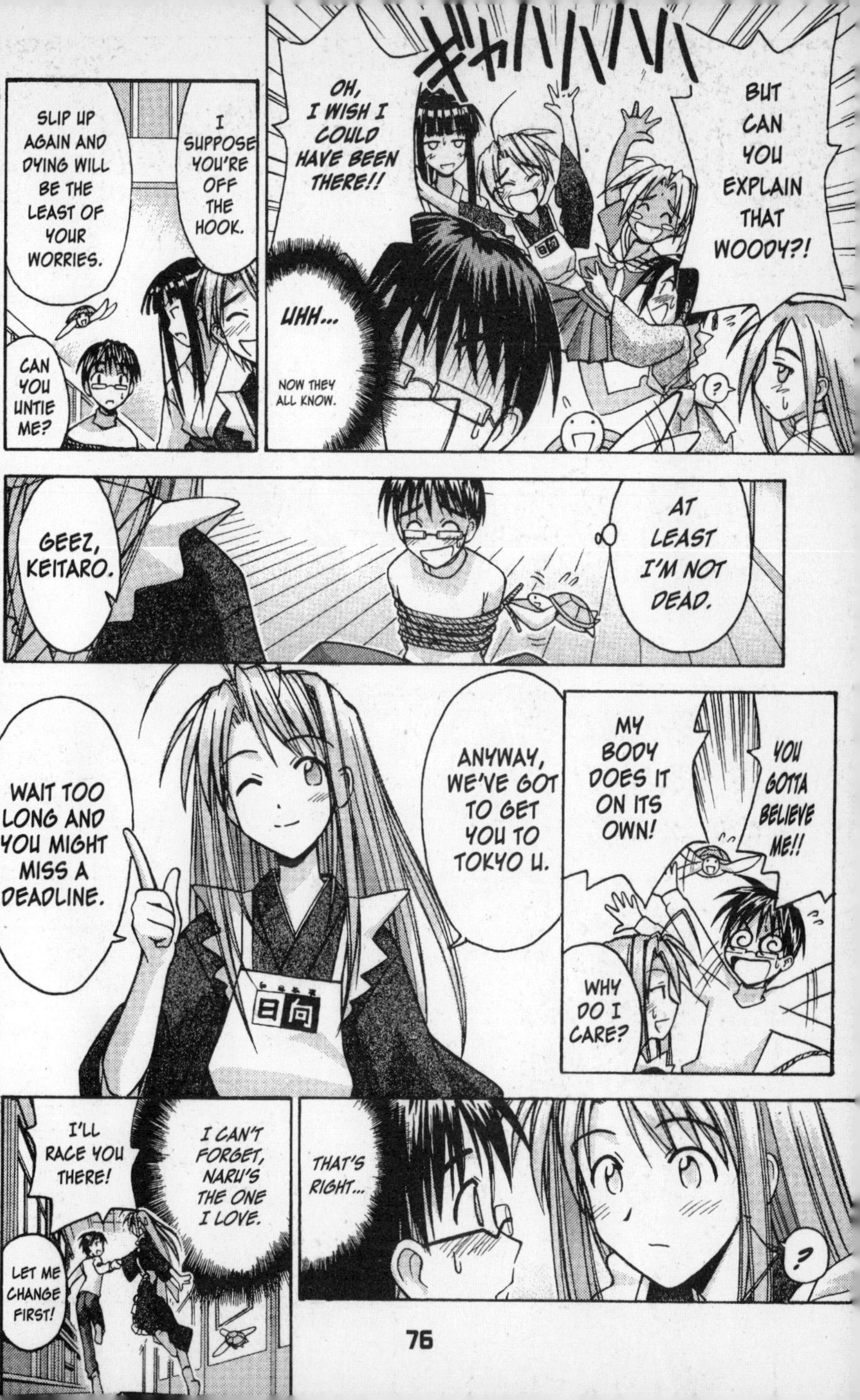
ギャハハハハ
BUT CAN YOU EXPLAIN THAT WOODY?!
OH, I WISH I COULD HAVE BEEN THERE!!
?
UHH...
NOW THEY ALL KNOW.
I SUPPOSE YOU'RE OFF THE HOOK.
SLIP UP AGAIN AND DYING WILL BE THE LEAST OF YOUR WORRIES.
CAN YOU UNTIE ME?
AT LEAST I'M NOT DEAD.
GEEZ, KEITARO.
YOU GOTTA BELIEVE ME!!
MY BODY DOES IT ON ITS OWN!
WHY DO I CARE?
ANYWAY, WE'VE GOT TO GET YOU TO TOKYO U.
WAIT TOO LONG AND YOU MIGHT MISS A DEADLINE.
?
THAT'S RIGHT...
I CAN'T FORGET, NARU'S THE ONE I LOVE.
I'LL RACE YOU THERE!
LET ME CHANGE FIRST!

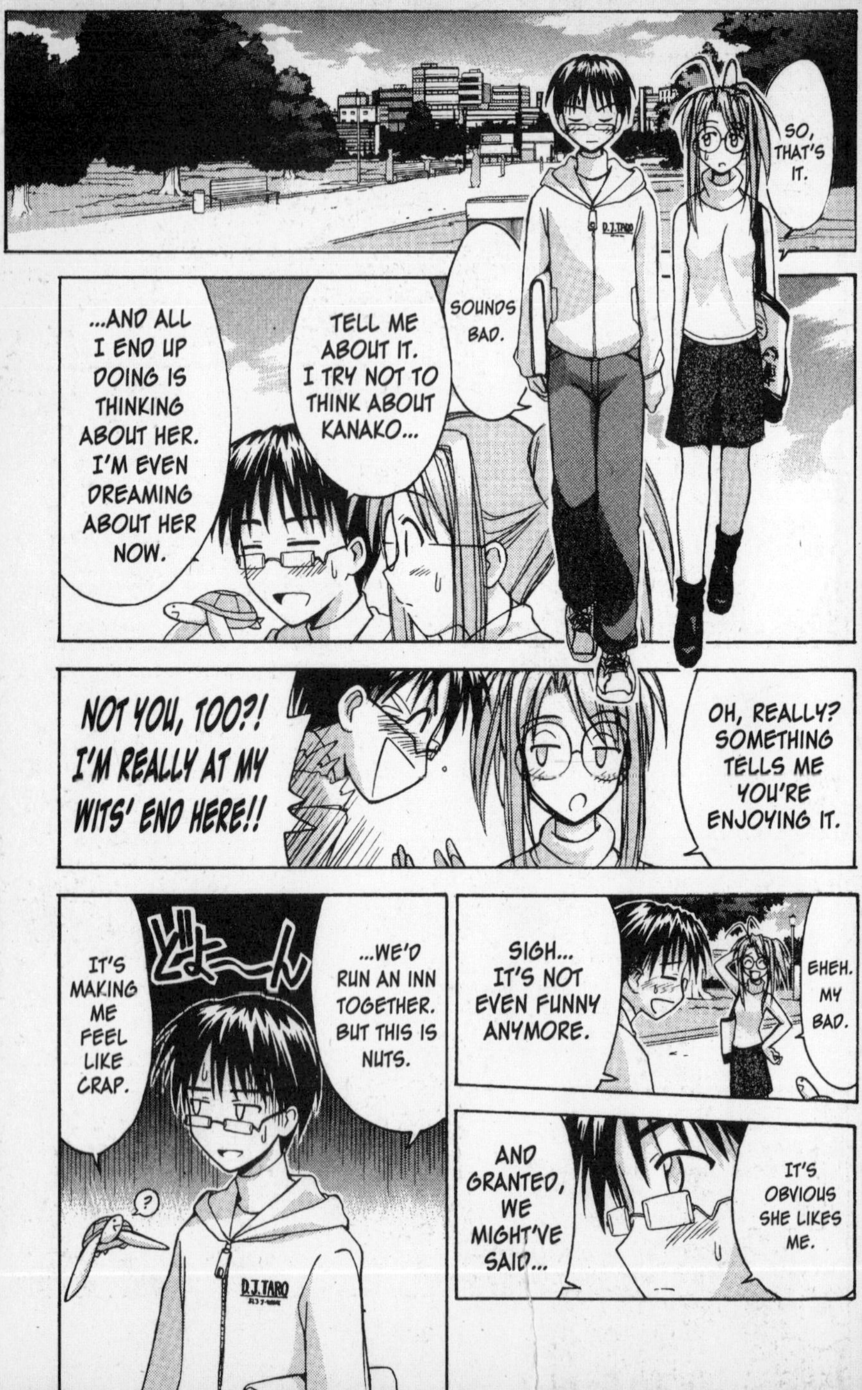
SO, THAT'S IT.
SOUNDS BAD.
TELL ME ABOUT IT. I TRY NOT TO THINK ABOUT KANAKO...
...AND ALL I END UP DOING IS THINKING ABOUT HER. I'M EVEN DREAMING ABOUT HER NOW.
OH, REALLY? SOMETHING TELLS ME YOU'RE ENJOYING IT.
NOT YOU, TOO?! I'M REALLY AT MY WITS' END HERE!!
EHEH. MY BAD.
SIGH... IT'S NOT EVEN FUNNY ANYMORE.
IT'S OBVIOUS SHE LIKES ME.
AND GRANTED, WE MIGHT'VE SAID...
どよ〜ん
...WE'D RUN AN INN TOGETHER. BUT THIS IS NUTS.
IT'S MAKING ME FEEL LIKE CRAP.
?

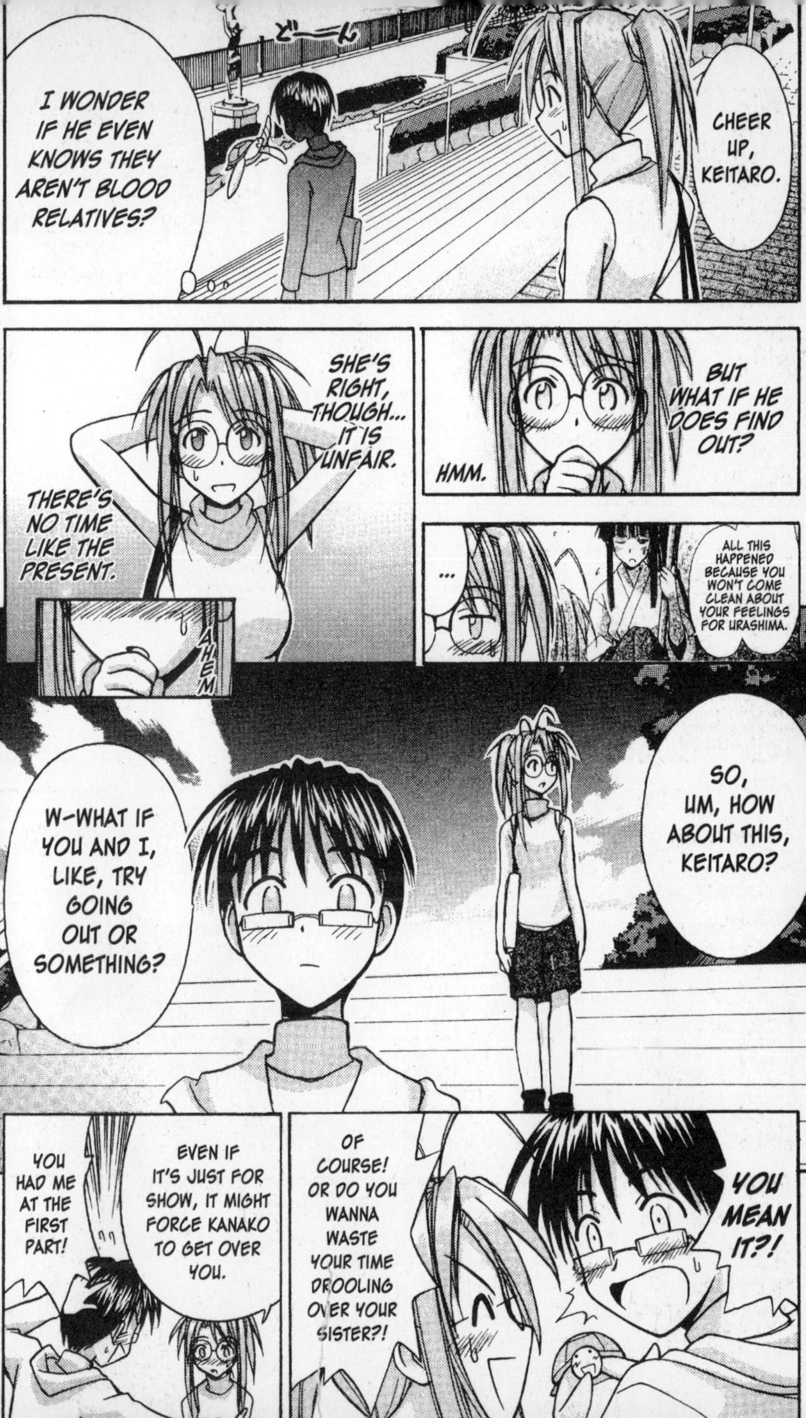
どーーん
CHEER UP, KEITARO.
I WONDER IF HE EVEN KNOWS THEY AREN'T BLOOD RELATIVES?
BUT WHAT IF HE DOES FIND OUT?
HMM.
ALL THIS HAPPENED BECAUSE YOU WON'T COME CLEAN ABOUT YOUR FEELINGS FOR URASHIMA.
...
SHE'S RIGHT, THOUGH... IT IS UNFAIR.
THERE'S NO TIME LIKE THE PRESENT.
AHEM
SO, UM, HOW ABOUT THIS, KEITARO?
W-WHAT IF YOU AND I, LIKE, TRY GOING OUT OR SOMETHING?
YOU MEAN IT?!
OF COURSE! OR DO YOU WANNA WASTE YOUR TIME DROOLING OVER YOUR SISTER?!
EVEN IF IT'S JUST FOR SHOW, IT MIGHT FORCE KANAKO TO GET OVER YOU.
YOU HAD ME AT THE FIRST PART!

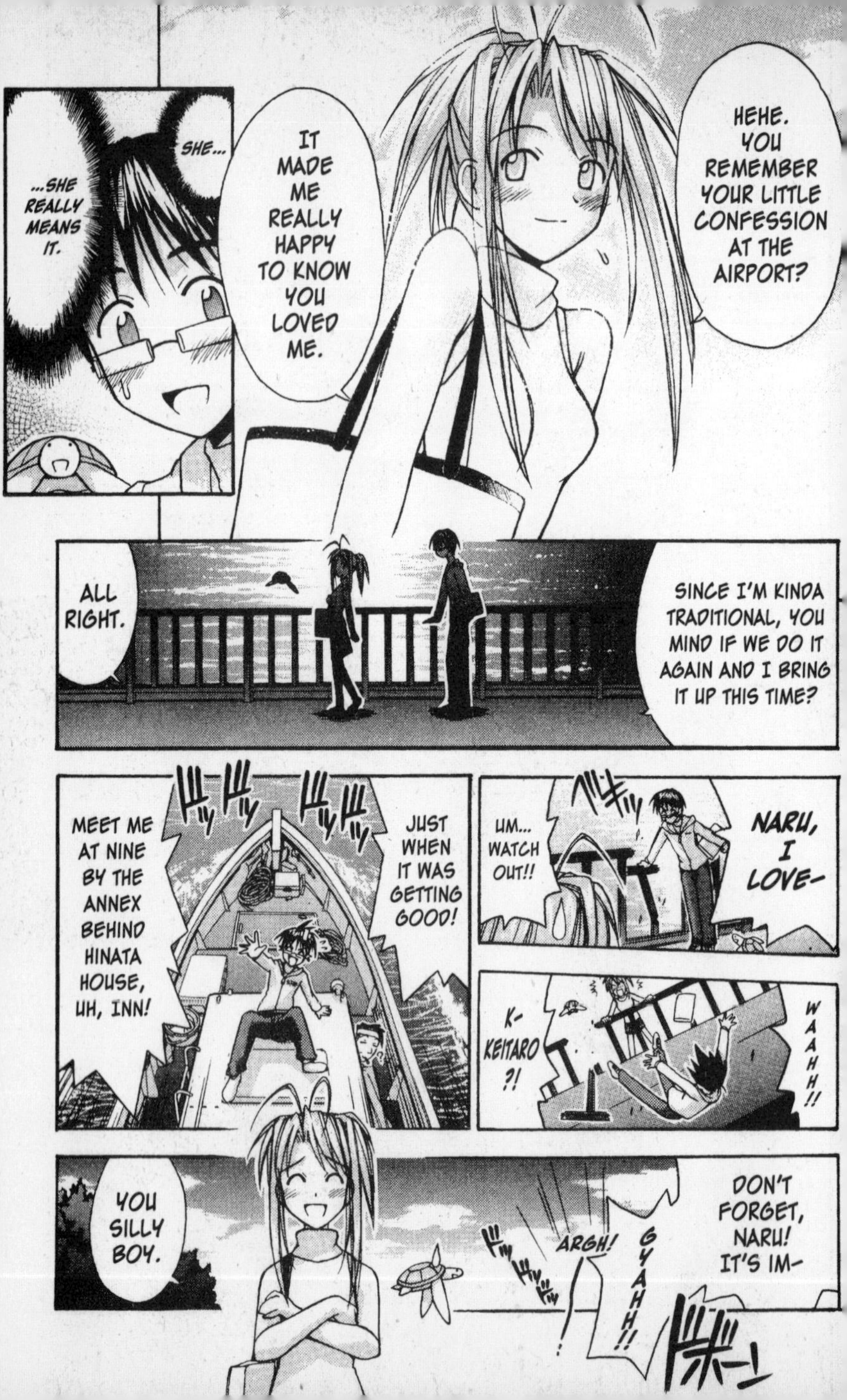
HEHE. YOU REMEMBER YOUR LITTLE CONFESSION AT THE AIRPORT?
IT MADE ME REALLY HAPPY TO KNOW YOU LOVED ME.
SHE...
...SHE REALLY MEANS IT.
SINCE I'M KINDA TRADITIONAL, YOU MIND IF WE DO IT AGAIN AND I BRING IT UP THIS TIME?
ALL RIGHT.
NARU, I LOVE-
UM... WATCH OUT!!
WAAHH!!
K-KEITARO?!
JUST WHEN IT WAS GETTING GOOD!
MEET ME AT NINE BY THE ANNEX BEHIND HINATA HOUSE, UH, INN!
DON'T FORGET, NARU! IT'S IM-
GYAHHH!!
ARGH!
YOU SILLY BOY.

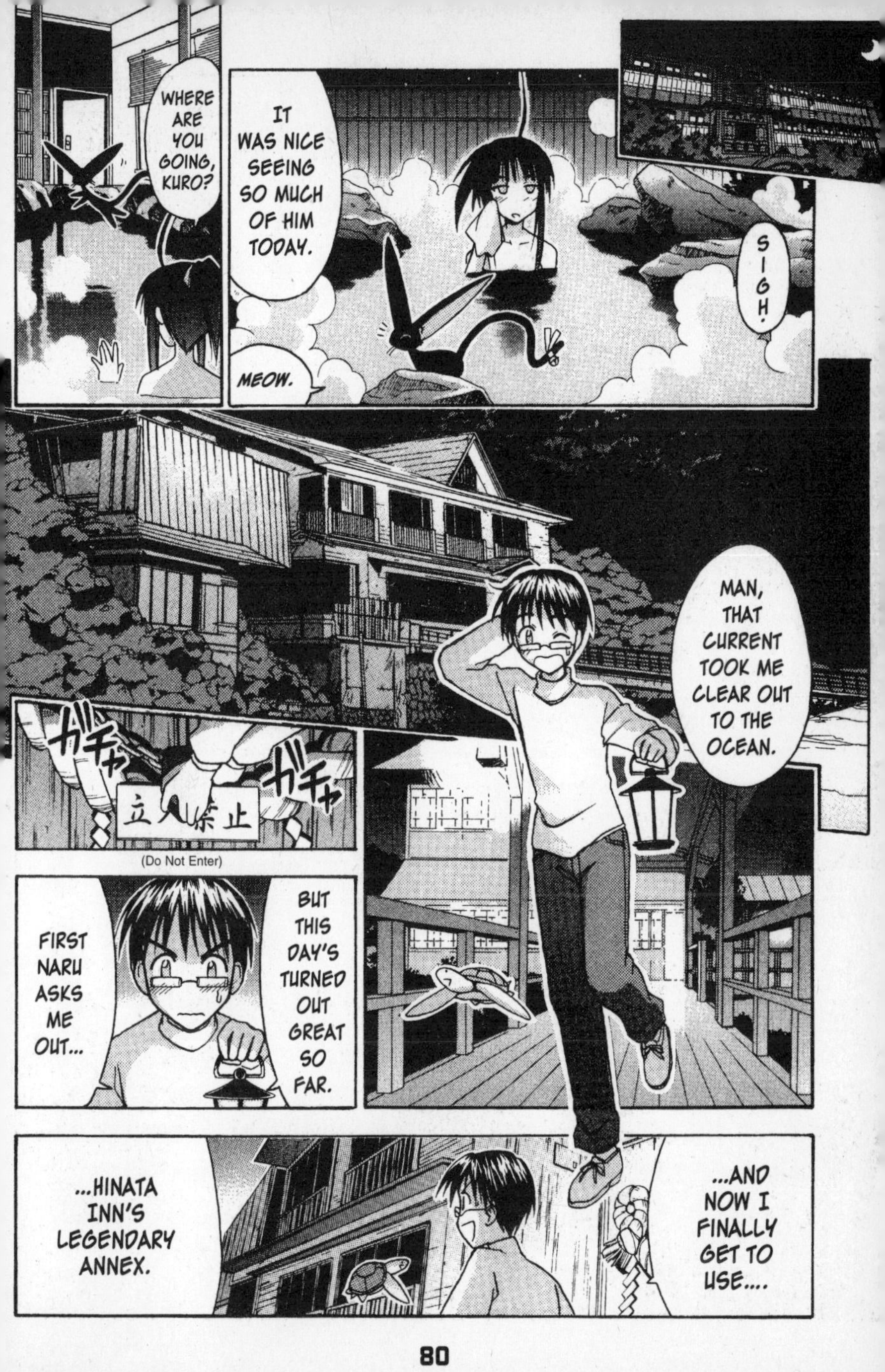
SIGH!
IT WAS NICE SEEING SO MUCH OF HIM TODAY.
MEOW.
WHERE ARE YOU GOING, KURO?
MAN, THAT CURRENT TOOK ME CLEAR OUT TO THE OCEAN.
ガチャ
ガチャ
立入禁止
(Do Not Enter)
BUT THIS DAY'S TURNED OUT GREAT SO FAR.
FIRST NARU ASKS ME OUT...
...AND NOW I FINALLY GET TO USE....
...HINATA INN'S LEGENDARY ANNEX.

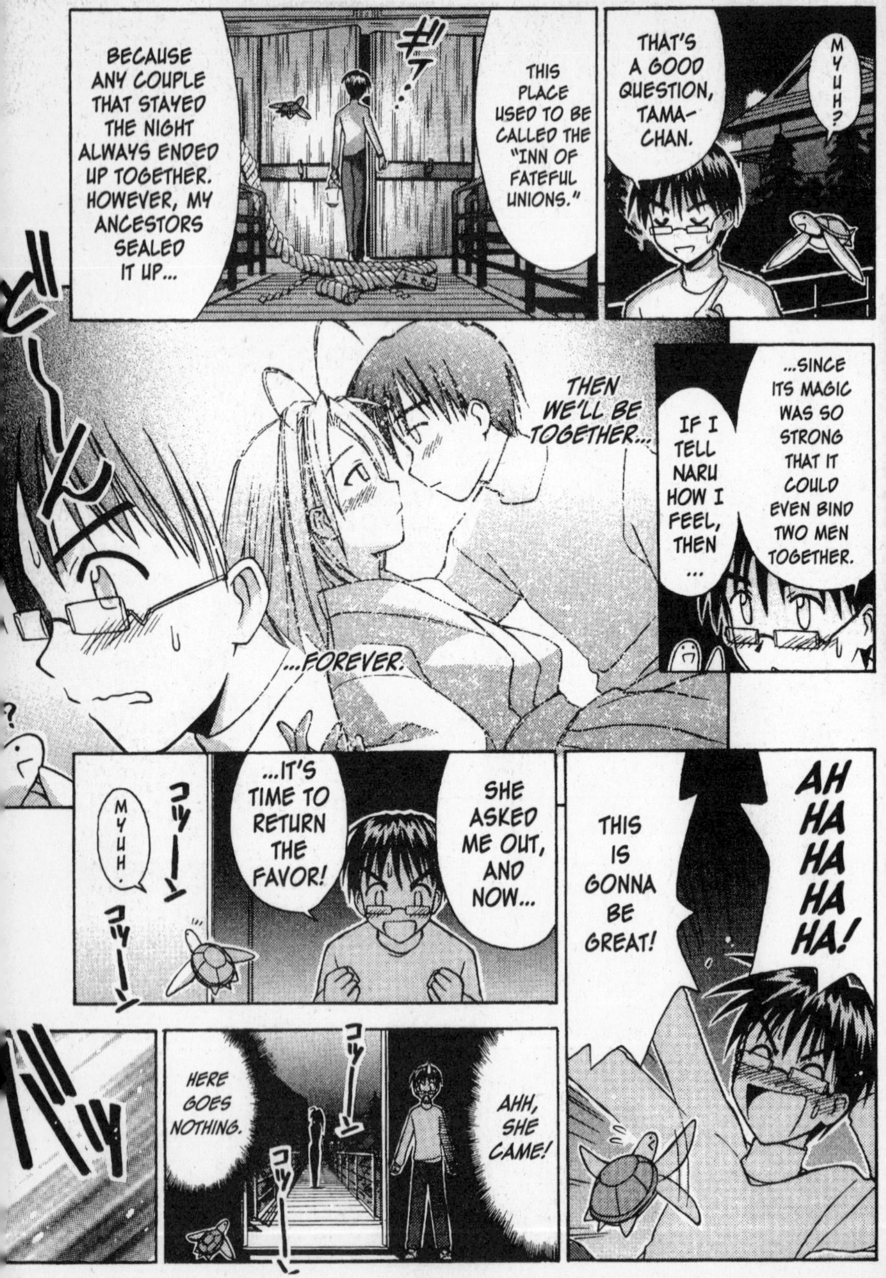
THAT'S A GOOD QUESTION, TAMA-CHAN.
MYUH?
THIS PLACE USED TO BE CALLED THE "INN OF FATEFUL UNIONS."
BECAUSE ANY COUPLE THAT STAYED THE NIGHT ALWAYS ENDED UP TOGETHER. HOWEVER, MY ANCESTORS SEALED IT UP...
...SINCE ITS MAGIC WAS SO STRONG THAT IT COULD EVEN BIND TWO MEN TOGETHER.
IF I TELL NARU HOW I FEEL, THEN ...
THEN WE'LL BE TOGETHER...
...FOREVER.
AH HA HA HA HA HA!
THIS IS GONNA BE GREAT!
SHE ASKED ME OUT, AND NOW...
...IT'S TIME TO RETURN THE FAVOR!
MYUH.
AHH, SHE CAME!
HERE GOES NOTHING.

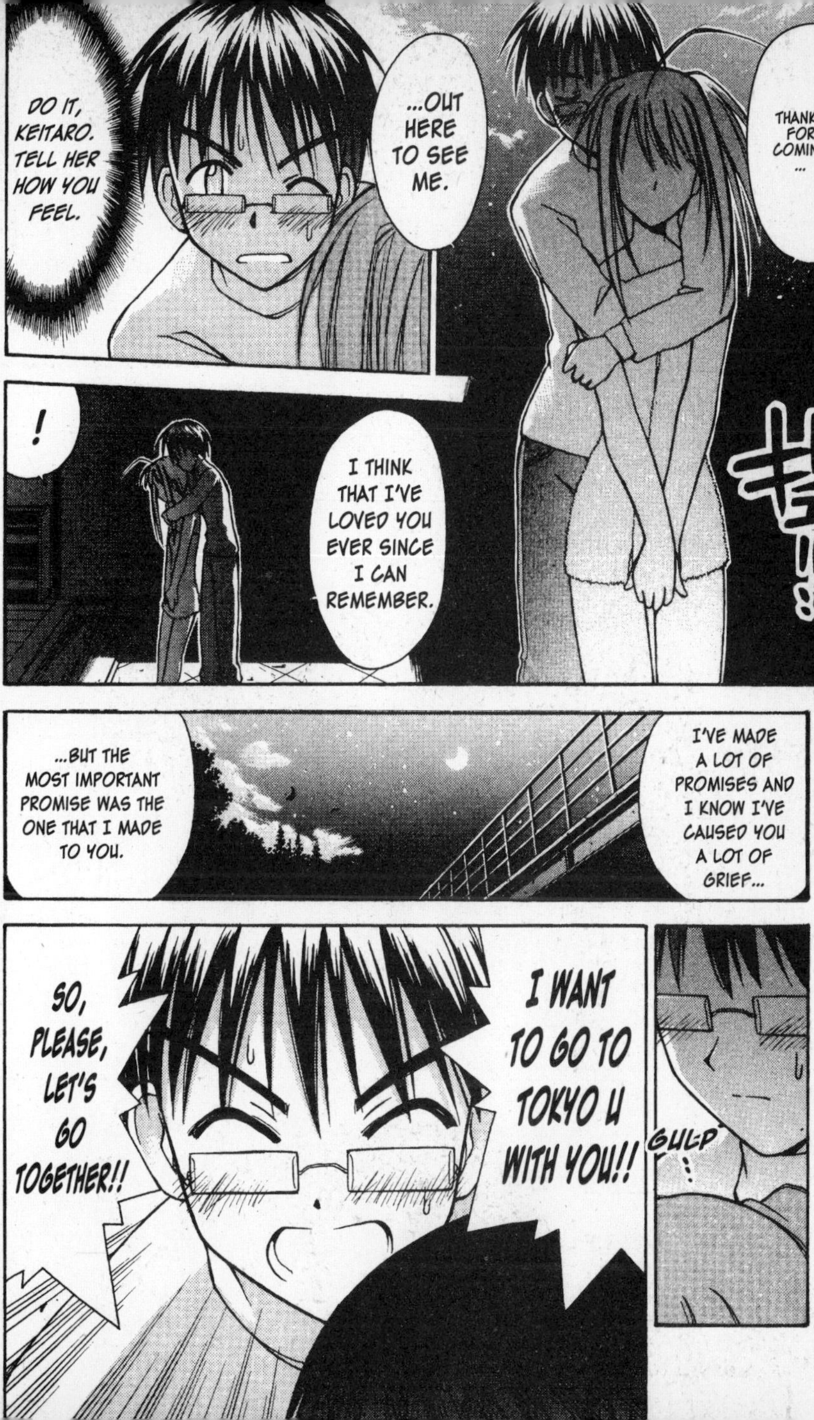
THANKS FOR COMING ...
ギュッ!!
...OUT HERE TO SEE ME.
DO IT, KEITARO. TELL HER HOW YOU FEEL.
I THINK THAT I'VE LOVED YOU EVER SINCE I CAN REMEMBER.
!
I'VE MADE A LOT OF PROMISES AND I KNOW I'VE CAUSED YOU A LOT OF GRIEF...
...BUT THE MOST IMPORTANT PROMISE WAS THE ONE THAT I MADE TO YOU.
GULP
I WANT TO GO TO TOKYO U WITH YOU!!
SO, PLEASE, LET'S GO TOGETHER!!

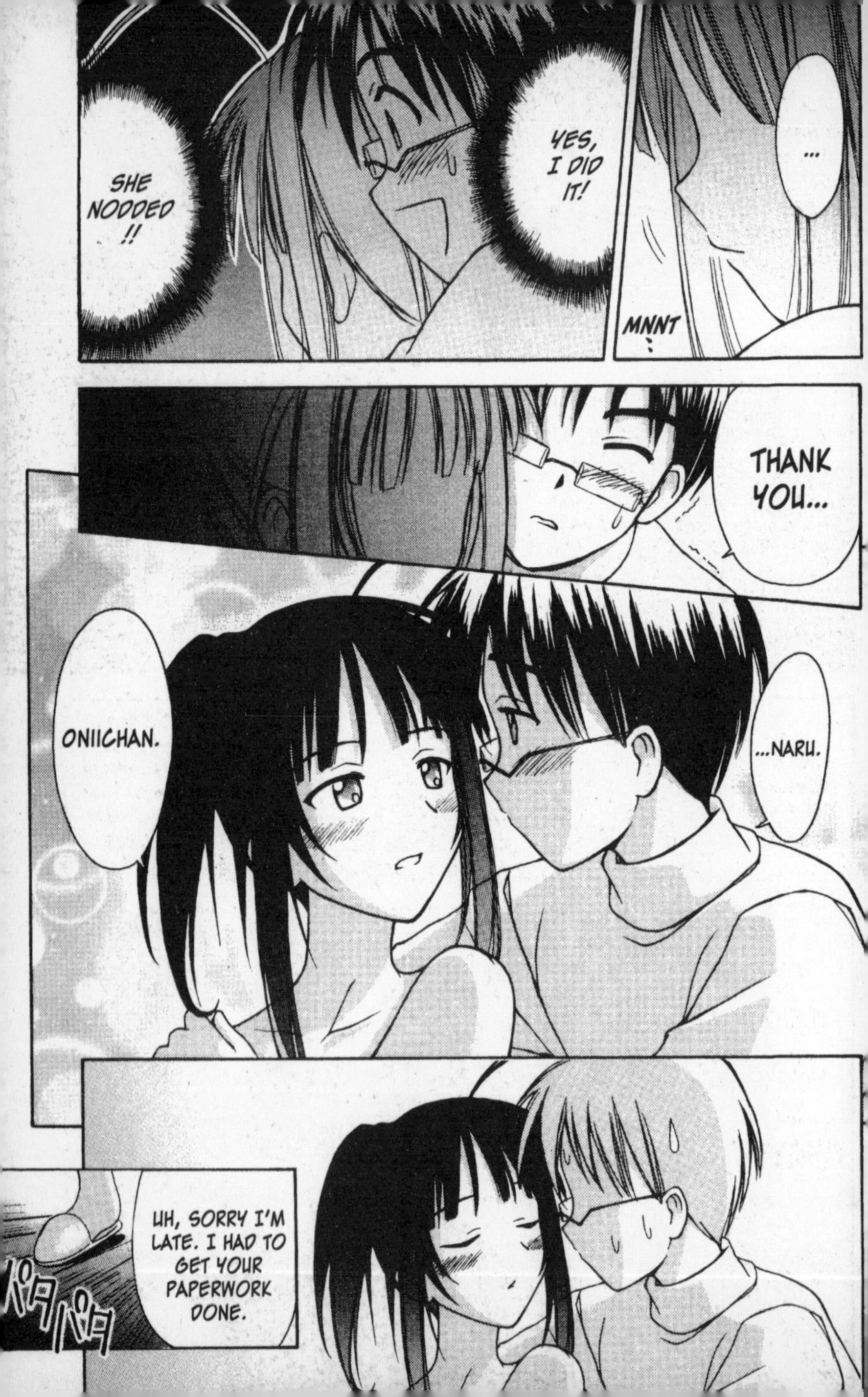
...
MNNT
YES, I DID IT!
SHE NODDED !!
THANK YOU...
...NARU.
ONIICHAN.
UH, SORRY I'M LATE. I HAD TO GET YOUR PAPERWORK DONE.
パタ パタ

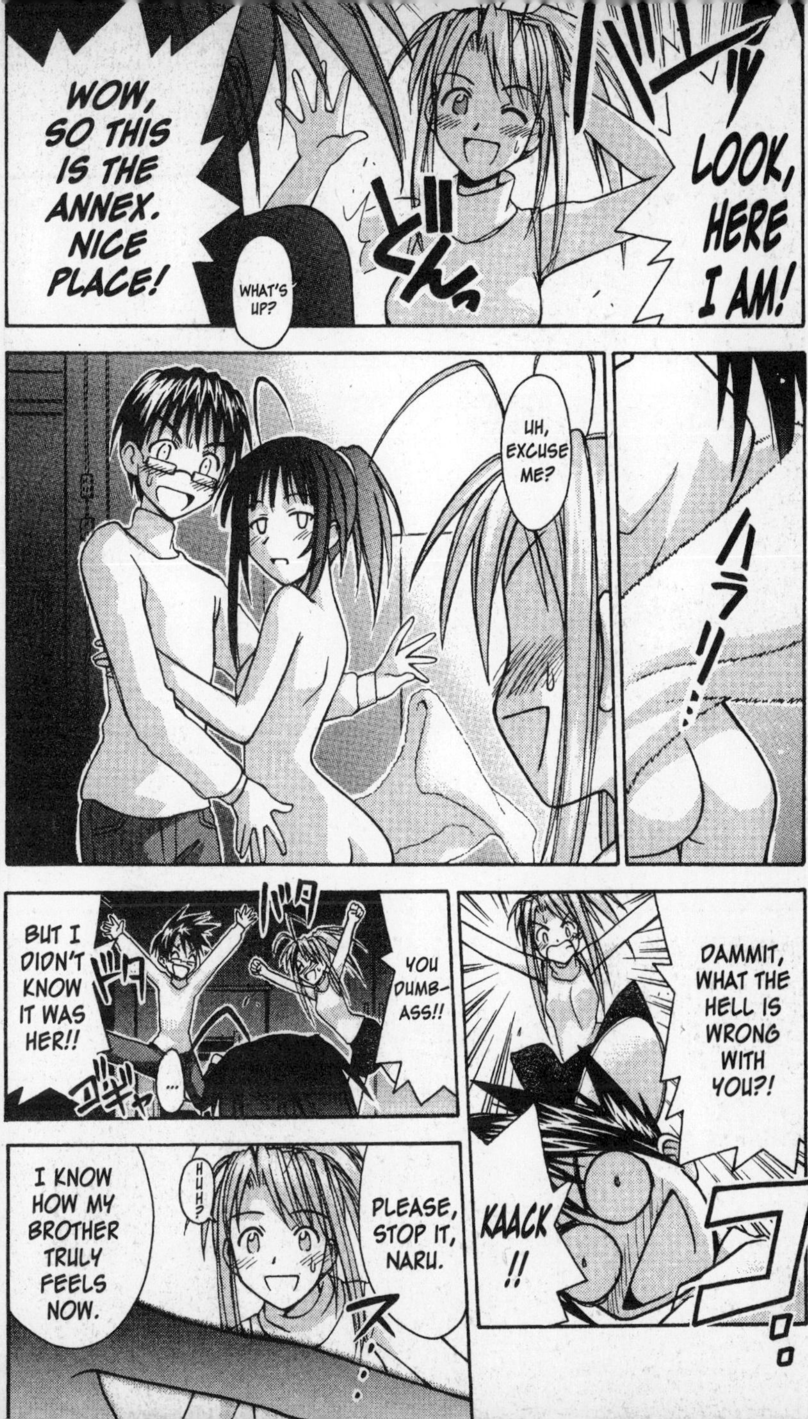
LOOK, HERE I AM!
WOW, SO THIS IS THE ANNEX. NICE PLACE!
WHAT'S UP?
UH, EXCUSE ME?
DAMMIT, WHAT THE HELL IS WRONG WITH YOU?!
YOU DUMB-ASS!!
BUT I DIDN'T KNOW IT WAS HER!!
...
KAACK!!
PLEASE, STOP IT, NARU.
HUH?
I KNOW HOW MY BROTHER TRULY FEELS NOW.

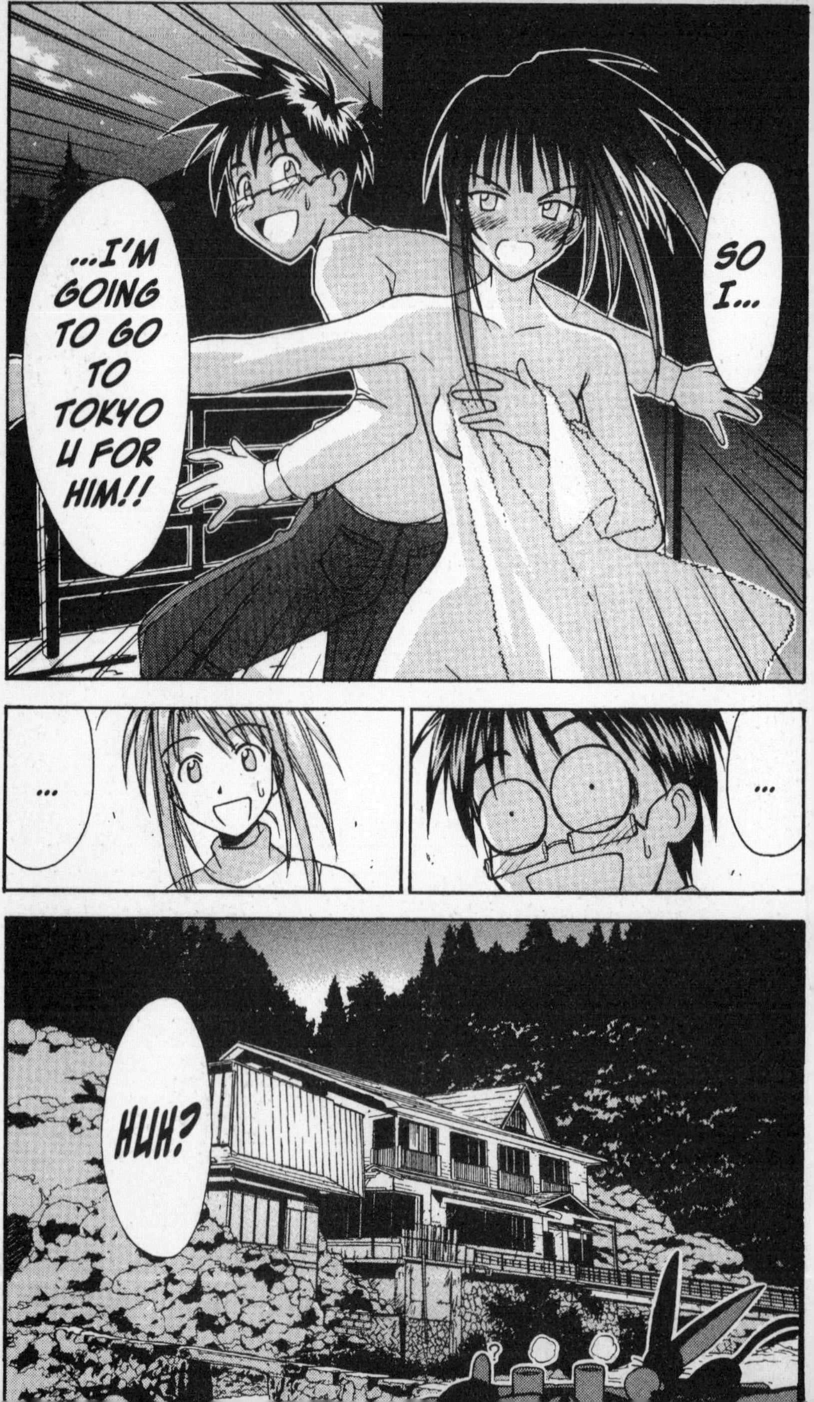
SO I...
...I'M GOING TO GO TO TOKYO U FOR HIM!!
...
...
HUH?

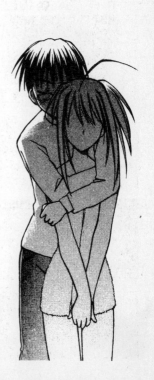

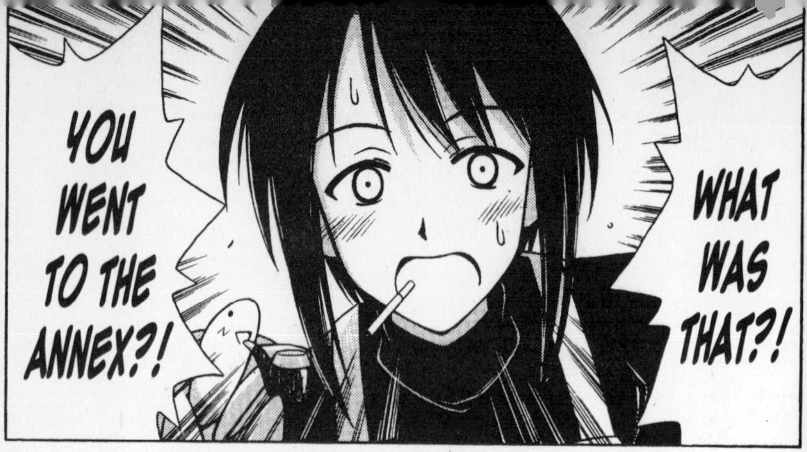
WHAT WAS THAT?!
YOU WENT TO THE ANNEX?!

Love Hina

HINATA. 101 A Future Overflowing With Magic

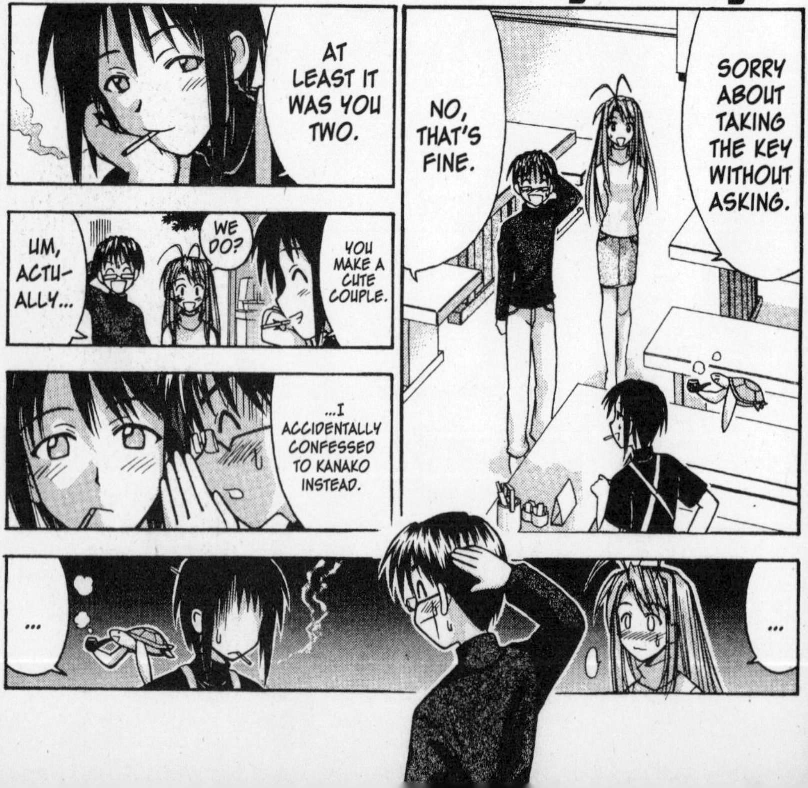
SORRY ABOUT TAKING THE KEY WITHOUT ASKING.
NO, THAT'S FINE.
AT LEAST IT WAS YOU TWO.
YOU MAKE A CUTE COUPLE.
WE DO?
UM, ACTU-ALLY...
...I ACCIDENTALLY CONFESSED TO KANAKO INSTEAD.
...
...

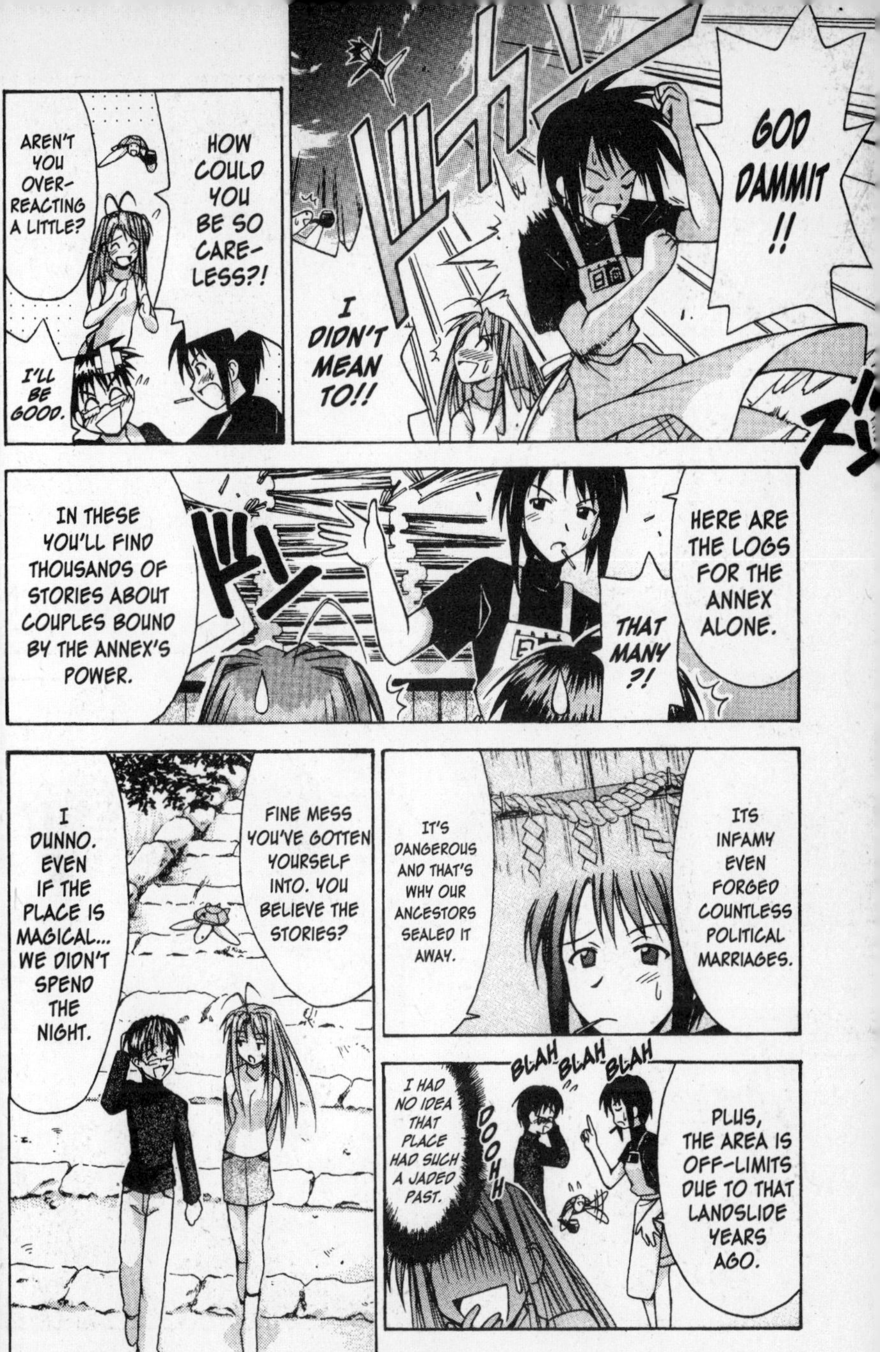
GOD DAMMIT!!
I DIDN'T MEAN TO!!
HOW COULD YOU BE SO CARELESS?!
AREN'T YOU OVER-REACTING A LITTLE?
I'LL BE GOOD.
HERE ARE THE LOGS FOR THE ANNEX ALONE.
THAT MANY?!
IN THESE YOU'LL FIND THOUSANDS OF STORIES ABOUT COUPLES BOUND BY THE ANNEX'S POWER.
ITS INFAMY EVEN FORGED COUNTLESS POLITICAL MARRIAGES.
IT'S DANGEROUS AND THAT'S WHY OUR ANCESTORS SEALED IT AWAY.
PLUS, THE AREA IS OFF-LIMITS DUE TO THAT LANDSLIDE YEARS AGO.
BLAH BLAH BLAH
DOOHH
I HAD NO IDEA THAT PLACE HAD SUCH A JADED PAST.
FINE MESS YOU'VE GOTTEN YOURSELF INTO. YOU BELIEVE THE STORIES?
I DUNNO. EVEN IF THE PLACE IS MAGICAL... WE DIDN'T SPEND THE NIGHT.

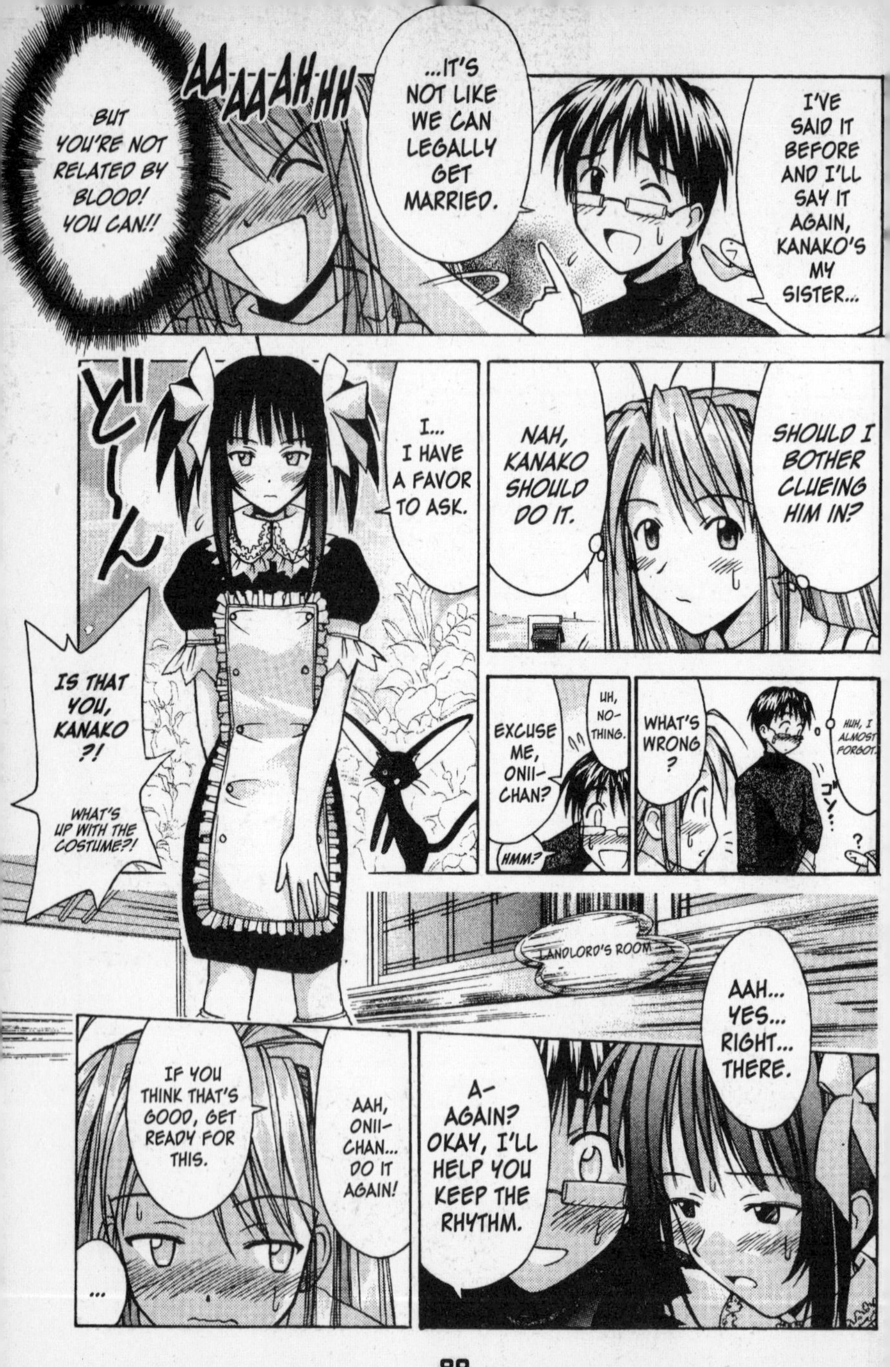
I'VE SAID IT BEFORE AND I'LL SAY IT AGAIN, KANAKO'S MY SISTER...
...IT'S NOT LIKE WE CAN LEGALLY GET MARRIED.
AA-A-AAAH HH
BUT YOU'RE NOT RELATED BY BLOOD! YOU CAN!!
SHOULD I BOTHER CLUEING HIM IN?
NAH, KANAKO SHOULD DO IT.
HUH, I ALMOST FORGOT.
WHAT'S WRONG?
?
UH, NO-THING.
EXCUSE ME, ONII-CHAN?
HMM?
I... I HAVE A FAVOR TO ASK.
どーん
IS THAT YOU, KANAKO?!
WHAT'S UP WITH THE COSTUME?!
LANDLORD'S ROOM
AAH... YES... RIGHT... THERE.
A- AGAIN? OKAY, I'LL HELP YOU KEEP THE RHYTHM.
AAH, ONII-CHAN... DO IT AGAIN!
IF YOU THINK THAT'S GOOD, GET READY FOR THIS.
...

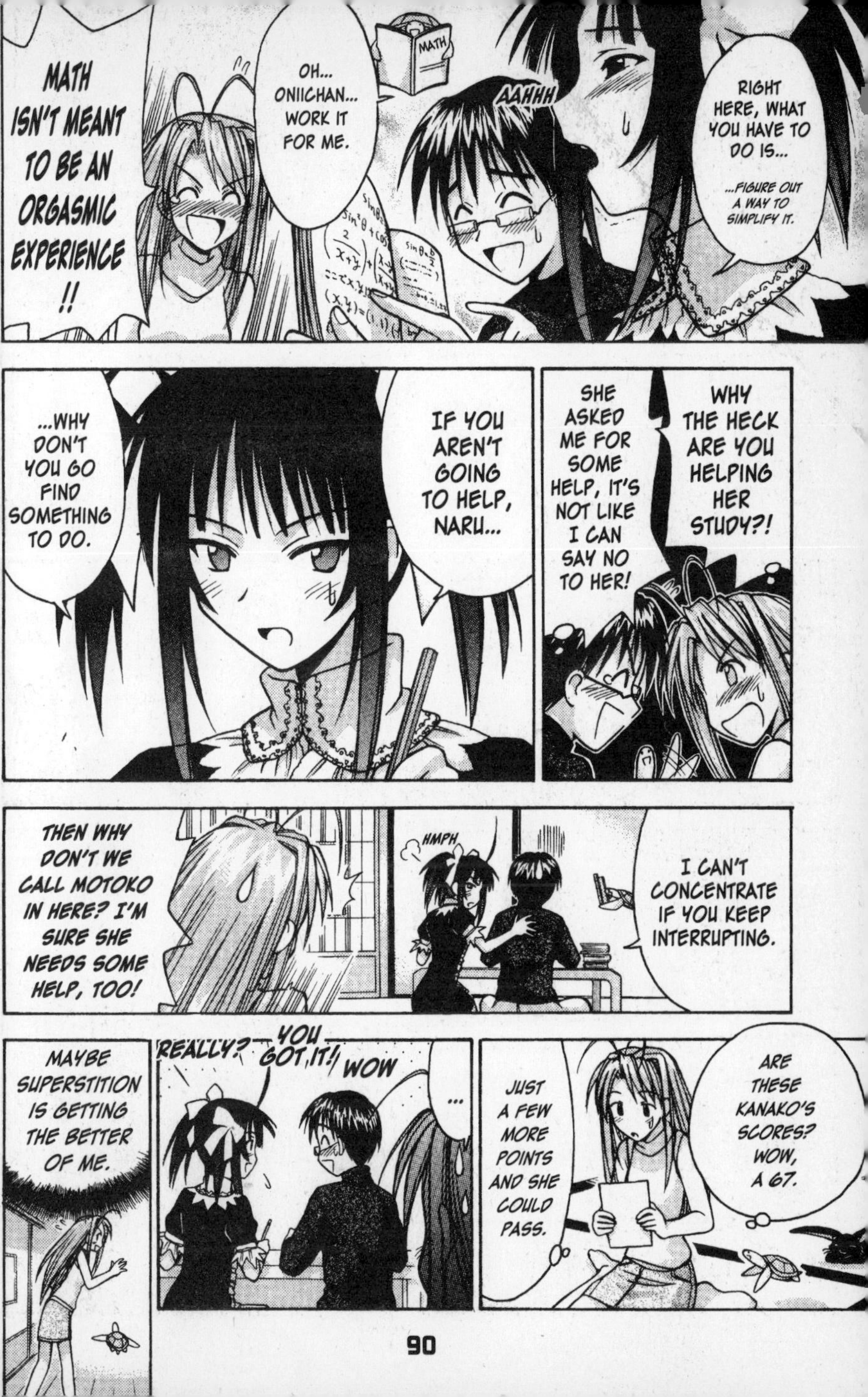
RIGHT HERE, WHAT YOU HAVE TO DO IS...
...FIGURE OUT A WAY TO SIMPLIFY IT.
AAHHH
MATH
OH... ONIICHAN... WORK IT FOR ME.
MATH ISN'T MEANT TO BE AN ORGASMIC EXPERIENCE !!
WHY THE HECK ARE YOU HELPING HER STUDY?!
SHE ASKED ME FOR SOME HELP, IT'S NOT LIKE I CAN SAY NO TO HER!
IF YOU AREN'T GOING TO HELP, NARU...
...WHY DON'T YOU GO FIND SOMETHING TO DO.
I CAN'T CONCENTRATE IF YOU KEEP INTERRUPTING.
HMPH
THEN WHY DON'T WE CALL MOTOKO IN HERE? I'M SURE SHE NEEDS SOME HELP, TOO!
ARE THESE KANAKO'S SCORES? WOW, A 67.
JUST A FEW MORE POINTS AND SHE COULD PASS.
...
WOW
YOU GOT IT!
REALLY?
MAYBE SUPERSTITION IS GETTING THE BETTER OF ME.

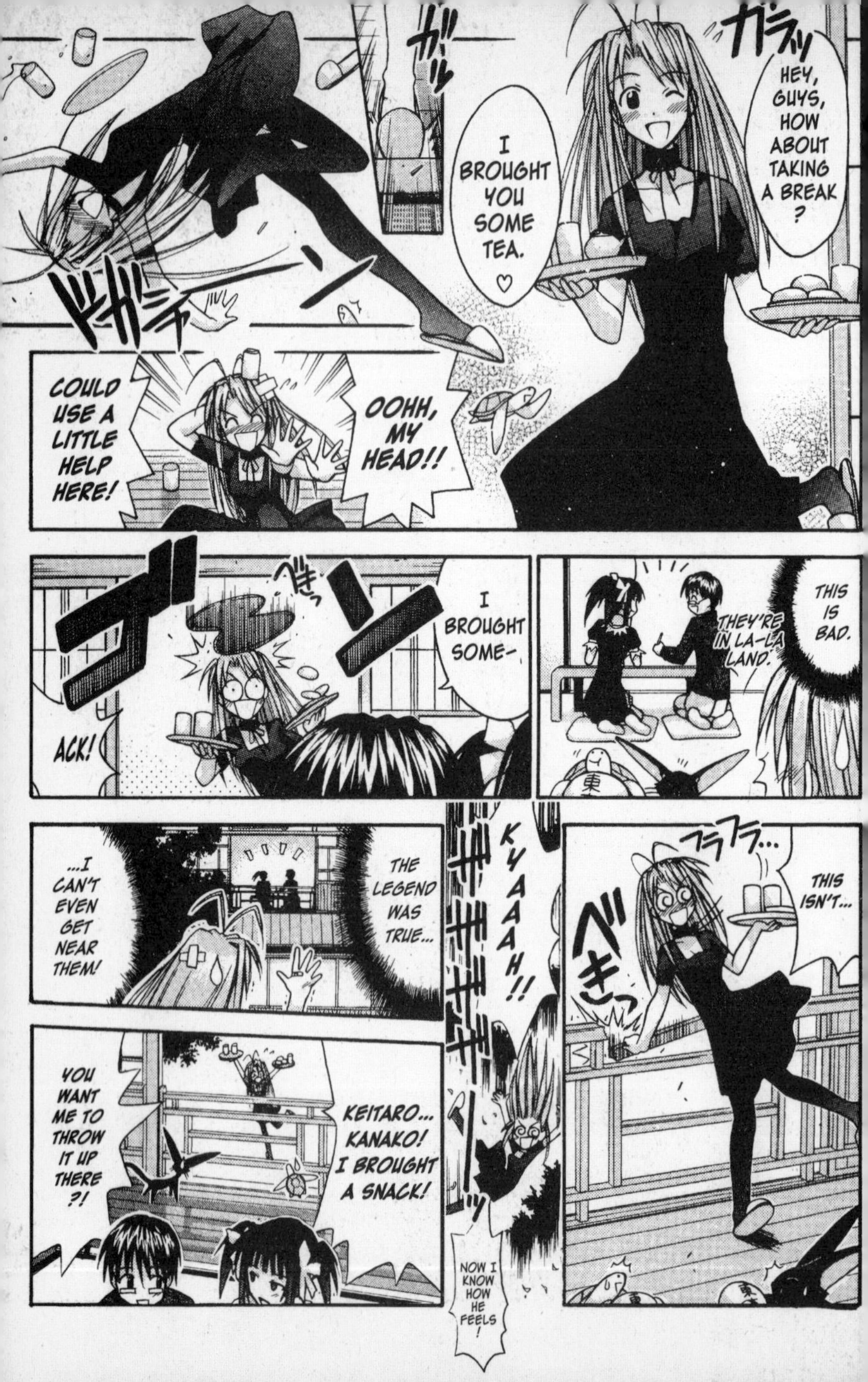
ガラッ
HEY, GUYS, HOW ABOUT TAKING A BREAK?
I BROUGHT YOU SOME TEA. ♡
ガッ
ドガシャ
OOHH, MY HEAD!!
COULD USE A LITTLE HELP HERE!
THIS IS BAD.
THEY'RE IN LA-LA LAND.
I BROUGHT SOME-
べきっ
ゴン
ACK!
フラフラ...
THIS ISN'T...
べきっ
KYAAAAH!!
NOW I KNOW HOW HE FEELS!
THE LEGEND WAS TRUE...
...I CAN'T EVEN GET NEAR THEM!
KEITARO... KANAKO! I BROUGHT A SNACK!
YOU WANT ME TO THROW IT UP THERE?!

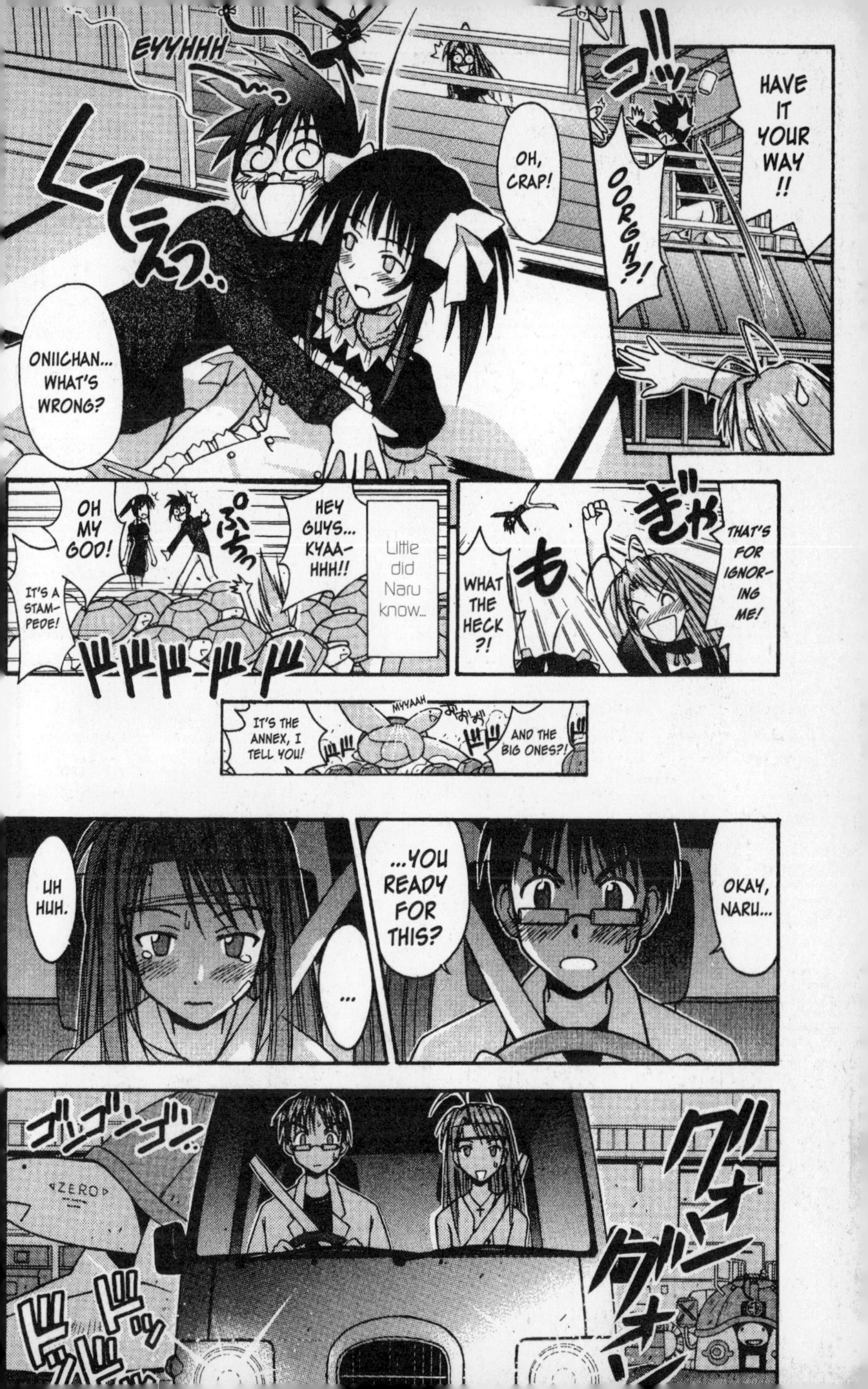
HAVE IT YOUR WAY!!
ゴッ
OORGH?!
OH, CRAP!
EYYHHH
ONIICHAN... WHAT'S WRONG?
THAT'S FOR IGNORING ME!
ぎゃ
も
WHAT THE HECK?!
Little did Naru know...
HEY GUYS... KYAA-HHH!!
ぷちっ
OH MY GOD!
IT'S A STAMPEDE!
AND THE BIG ONES?!
MYYAAH
IT'S THE ANNEX, I TELL YOU!
OKAY, NARU...
...YOU READY FOR THIS?
...
UH HUH.
ZERO

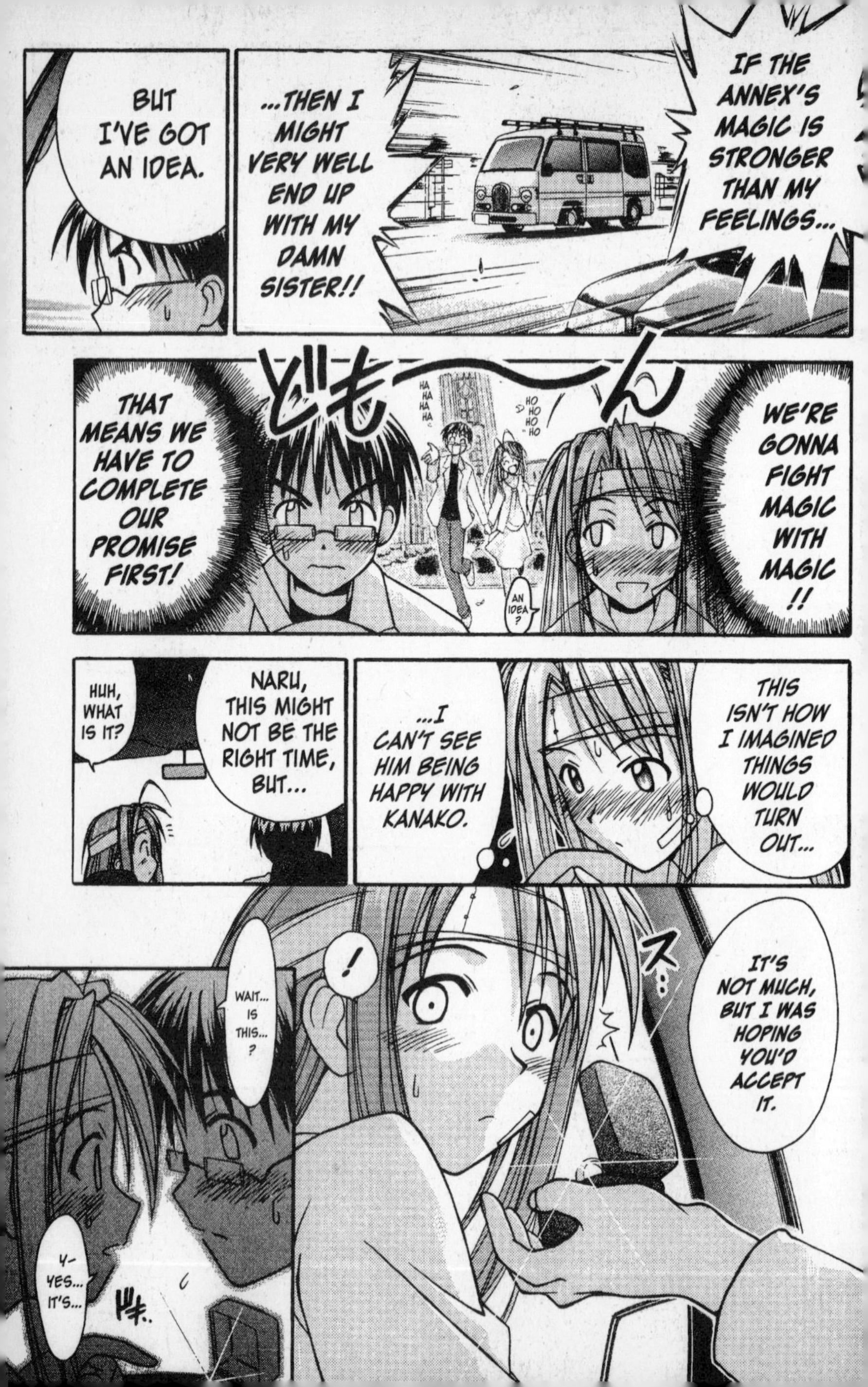
IF THE ANNEX'S MAGIC IS STRONGER THAN MY FEELINGS...
...THEN I MIGHT VERY WELL END UP WITH MY DAMN SISTER!!
BUT I'VE GOT AN IDEA.
ども〜〜ん
WE'RE GONNA FIGHT MAGIC WITH MAGIC!!
HO HO HO HO HO
HA HA HA HA
AN IDEA?
THAT MEANS WE HAVE TO COMPLETE OUR PROMISE FIRST!
THIS ISN'T HOW I IMAGINED THINGS WOULD TURN OUT...
...I CAN'T SEE HIM BEING HAPPY WITH KANAKO.
NARU, THIS MIGHT NOT BE THE RIGHT TIME, BUT...
HUH, WHAT IS IT?
IT'S NOT MUCH, BUT I WAS HOPING YOU'D ACCEPT IT.
!
WAIT... IS THIS...?
Y-YES... IT'S...

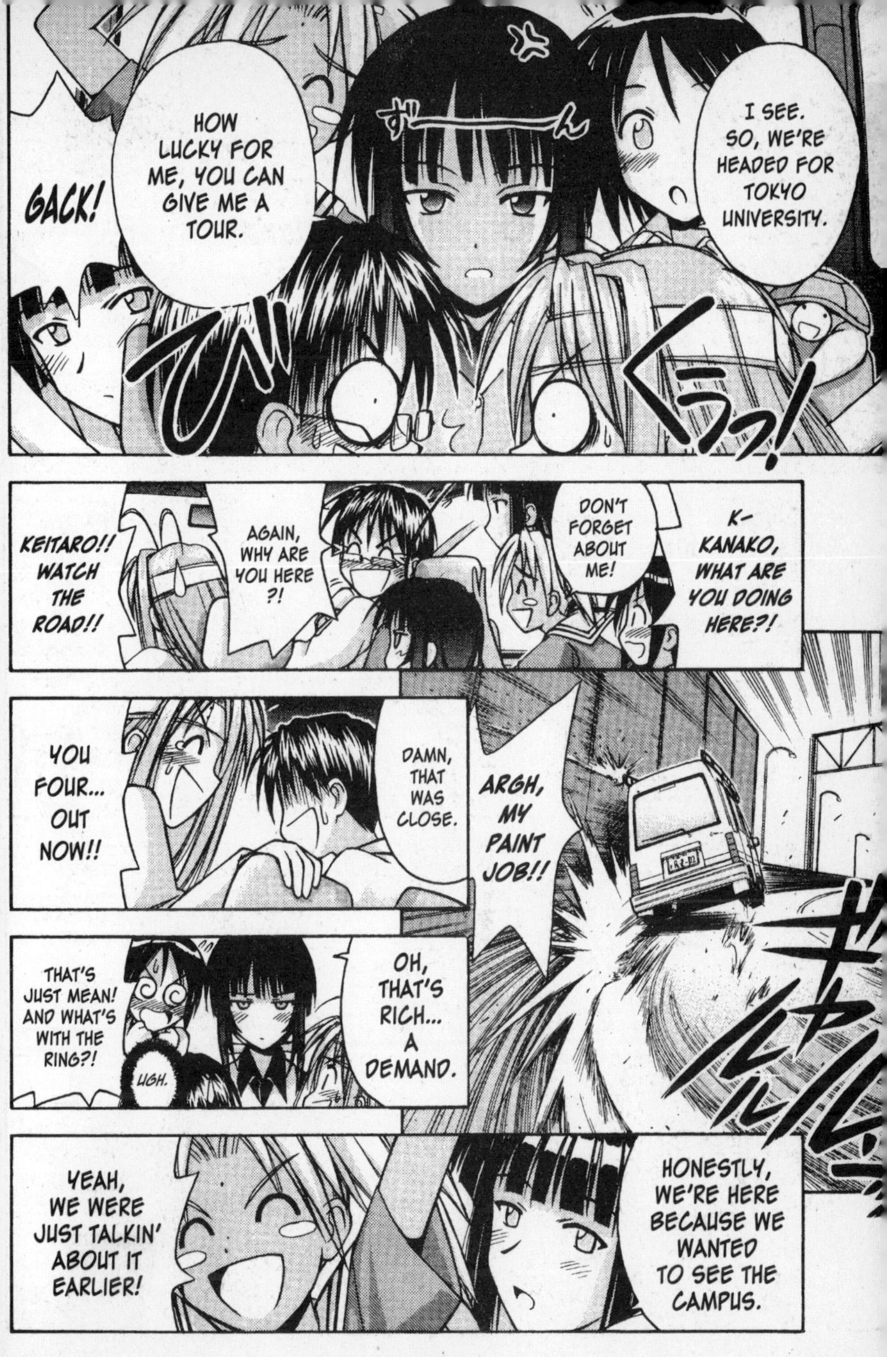
I SEE. SO, WE'RE HEADED FOR TOKYO UNIVERSITY.
HOW LUCKY FOR ME, YOU CAN GIVE ME A TOUR.
GACK!
K-KANAKO, WHAT ARE YOU DOING HERE?!
DON'T FORGET ABOUT ME!
AGAIN, WHY ARE YOU HERE ?!
KEITARO!! WATCH THE ROAD!!
ARGH, MY PAINT JOB!!
DAMN, THAT WAS CLOSE.
YOU FOUR... OUT NOW!!
OH, THAT'S RICH... A DEMAND.
THAT'S JUST MEAN! AND WHAT'S WITH THE RING?!
UGH.
HONESTLY, WE'RE HERE BECAUSE WE WANTED TO SEE THE CAMPUS.
YEAH, WE WERE JUST TALKIN' ABOUT IT EARLIER!

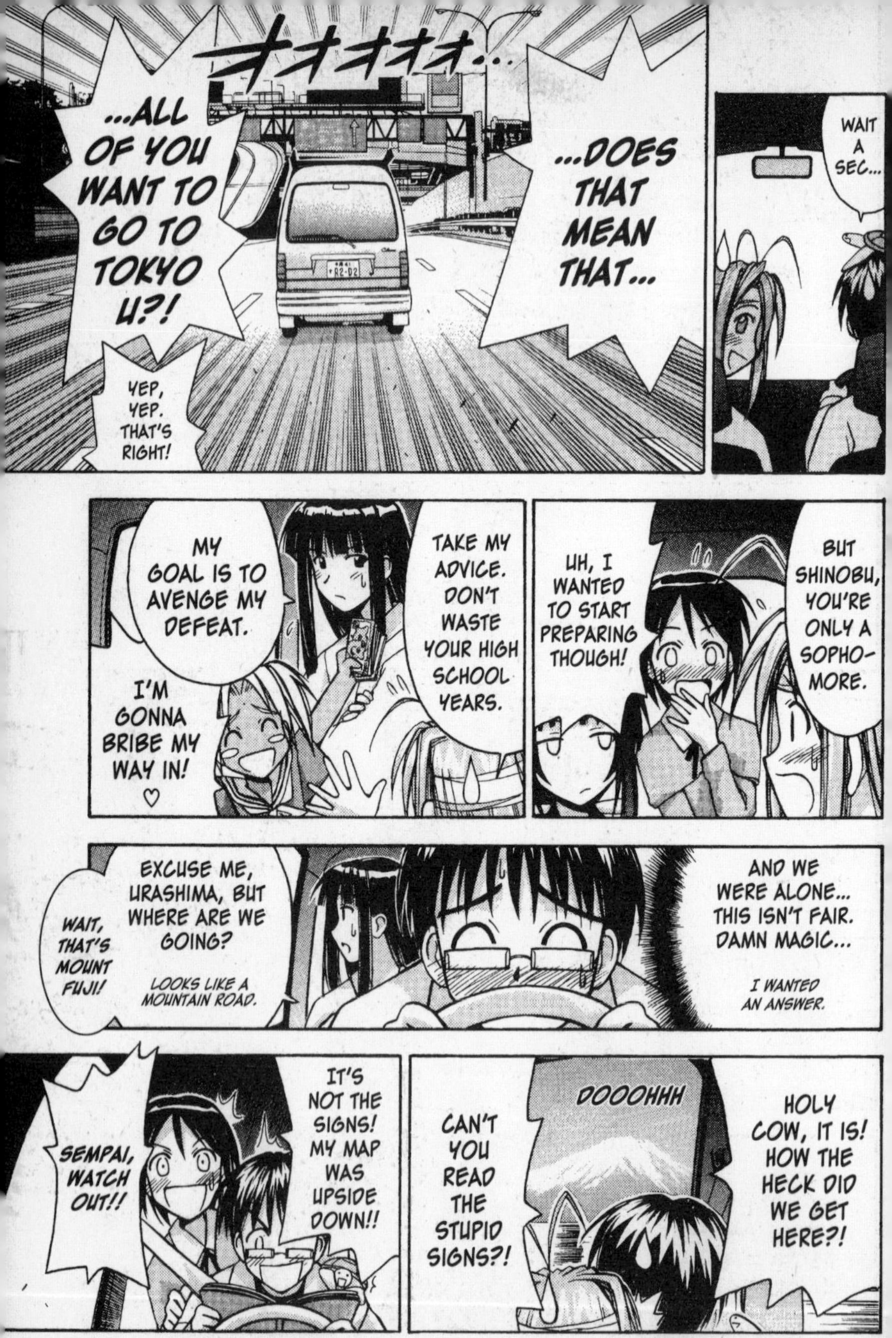
WAIT A SEC...
オオオオオ...
...DOES THAT MEAN THAT...
...ALL OF YOU WANT TO GO TO TOKYO U?!
YEP, YEP. THAT'S RIGHT!
BUT SHINOBU, YOU'RE ONLY A SOPHOMORE.
UH, I WANTED TO START PREPARING THOUGH!
TAKE MY ADVICE. DON'T WASTE YOUR HIGH SCHOOL YEARS.
MY GOAL IS TO AVENGE MY DEFEAT.
I'M GONNA BRIBE MY WAY IN! ♡
AND WE WERE ALONE... THIS ISN'T FAIR. DAMN MAGIC...
I WANTED AN ANSWER.
EXCUSE ME, URASHIMA, BUT WHERE ARE WE GOING?
LOOKS LIKE A MOUNTAIN ROAD.
WAIT, THAT'S MOUNT FUJI!
DOOOHHH
HOLY COW, IT IS! HOW THE HECK DID WE GET HERE?!
CAN'T YOU READ THE STUPID SIGNS?!
IT'S NOT THE SIGNS! MY MAP WAS UPSIDE DOWN!!
SEMPAI, WATCH OUT!!

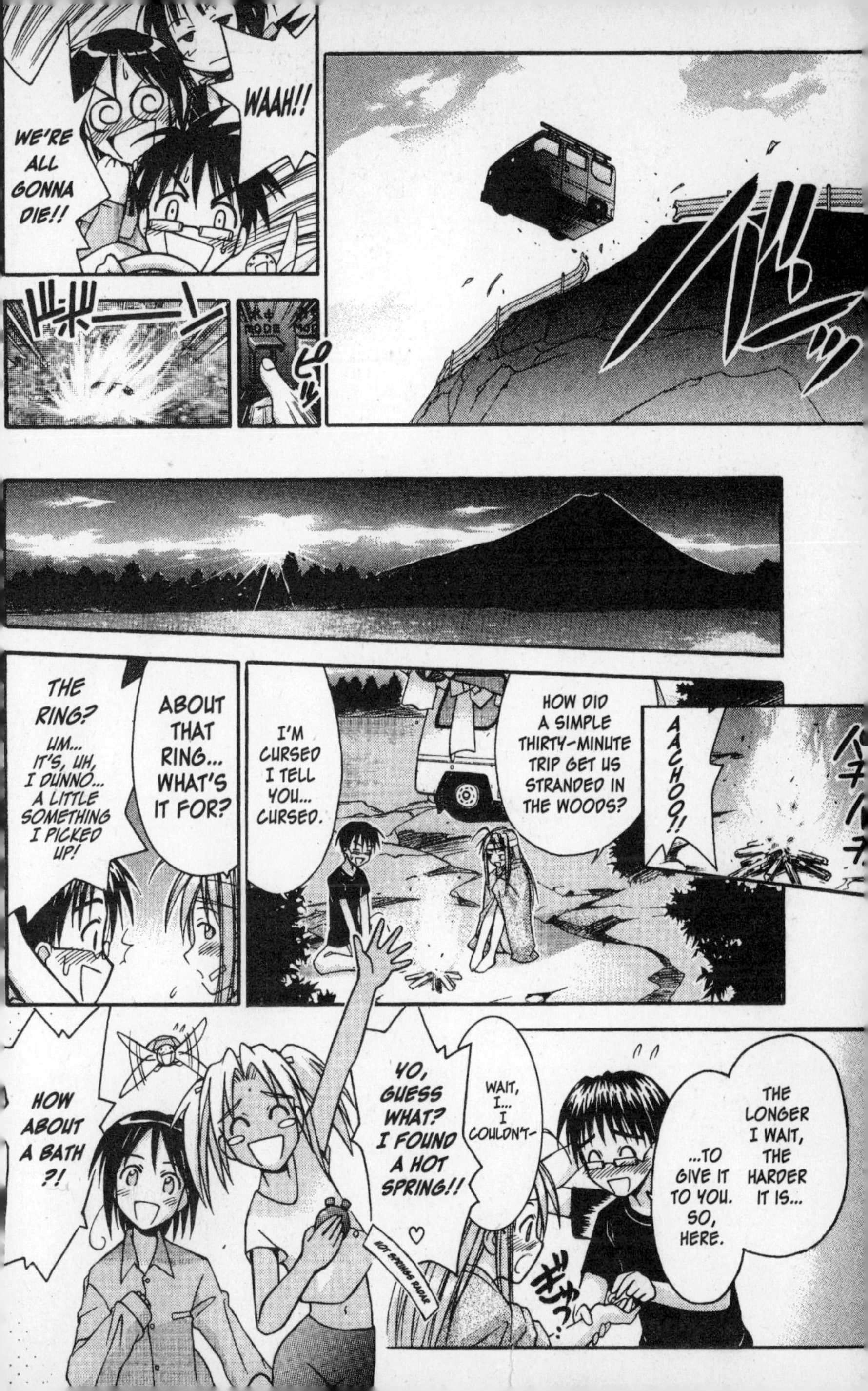
WAAH!!
WE'RE ALL GONNA DIE!!
AACHOO!!
HOW DID A SIMPLE THIRTY-MINUTE TRIP GET US STRANDED IN THE WOODS?
I'M CURSED I TELL YOU... CURSED.
ABOUT THAT RING... WHAT'S IT FOR?
THE RING? UM... IT'S, UH, I DUNNO... A LITTLE SOMETHING I PICKED UP!
THE LONGER I WAIT, THE HARDER IT IS...
...TO GIVE IT TO YOU. SO, HERE.
WAIT, I... I COULDN'T-
YO, GUESS WHAT? I FOUND A HOT SPRING!!
HOT SPRINGS RADAR
HOW ABOUT A BATH?!

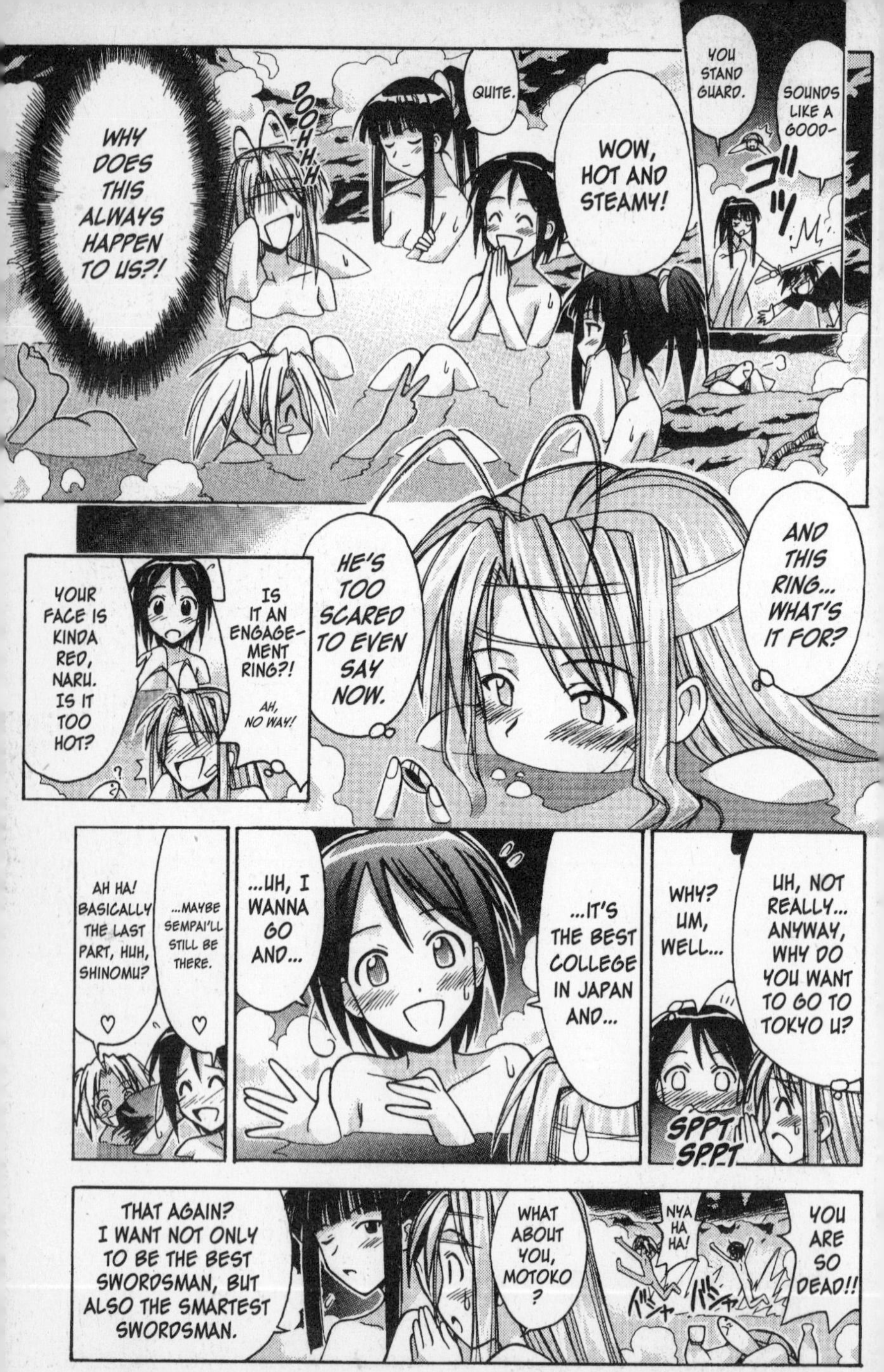
YOU STAND GUARD.
SOUNDS LIKE A GOOD-
WOW, HOT AND STEAMY!
QUITE.
DOOOHHHH
WHY DOES THIS ALWAYS HAPPEN TO US?!
AND THIS RING... WHAT'S IT FOR?
HE'S TOO SCARED TO EVEN SAY NOW.
IS IT AN ENGAGEMENT RING?!
AH, NO WAY!
YOUR FACE IS KINDA RED, NARU. IS IT TOO HOT?
UH, NOT REALLY... ANYWAY, WHY DO YOU WANT TO GO TO TOKYO U?
WHY? UM, WELL...
SPPT SPPT
...IT'S THE BEST COLLEGE IN JAPAN AND...
...UH, I WANNA GO AND...
...MAYBE SEMPAI'LL STILL BE THERE.
AH HA! BASICALLY THE LAST PART, HUH, SHINOMU?
YOU ARE SO DEAD!!
NYA HA HA!
WHAT ABOUT YOU, MOTOKO?
THAT AGAIN? I WANT NOT ONLY TO BE THE BEST SWORDSMAN, BUT ALSO THE SMARTEST SWORDSMAN.

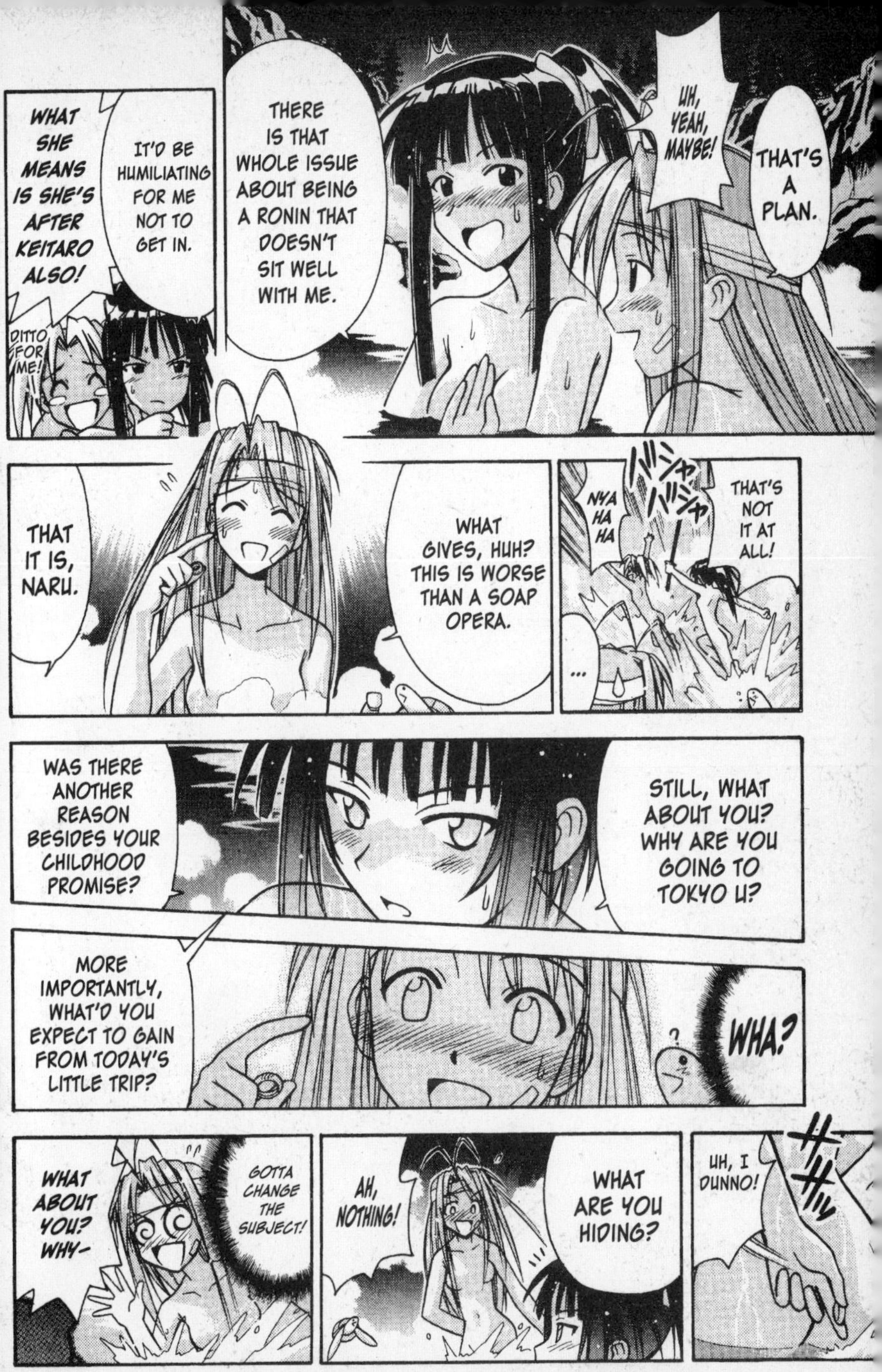
UH, YEAH, MAYBE!
THAT'S A PLAN.
THERE IS THAT WHOLE ISSUE ABOUT BEING A RONIN THAT DOESN'T SIT WELL WITH ME.
IT'D BE HUMILIATING FOR ME NOT TO GET IN.
WHAT SHE MEANS IS SHE'S AFTER KEITARO ALSO!
DITTO FOR ME!
THAT'S NOT IT AT ALL!
バシャバシャ
NYA HA HA
...
WHAT GIVES, HUH? THIS IS WORSE THAN A SOAP OPERA.
THAT IT IS, NARU.
STILL, WHAT ABOUT YOU? WHY ARE YOU GOING TO TOKYO U?
WAS THERE ANOTHER REASON BESIDES YOUR CHILDHOOD PROMISE?
WHA?
?
MORE IMPORTANTLY, WHAT'D YOU EXPECT TO GAIN FROM TODAY'S LITTLE TRIP?
UH, I DUNNO!
WHAT ARE YOU HIDING?
AH, NOTHING!
GOTTA CHANGE THE SUBJECT!
WHAT ABOUT YOU? WHY-

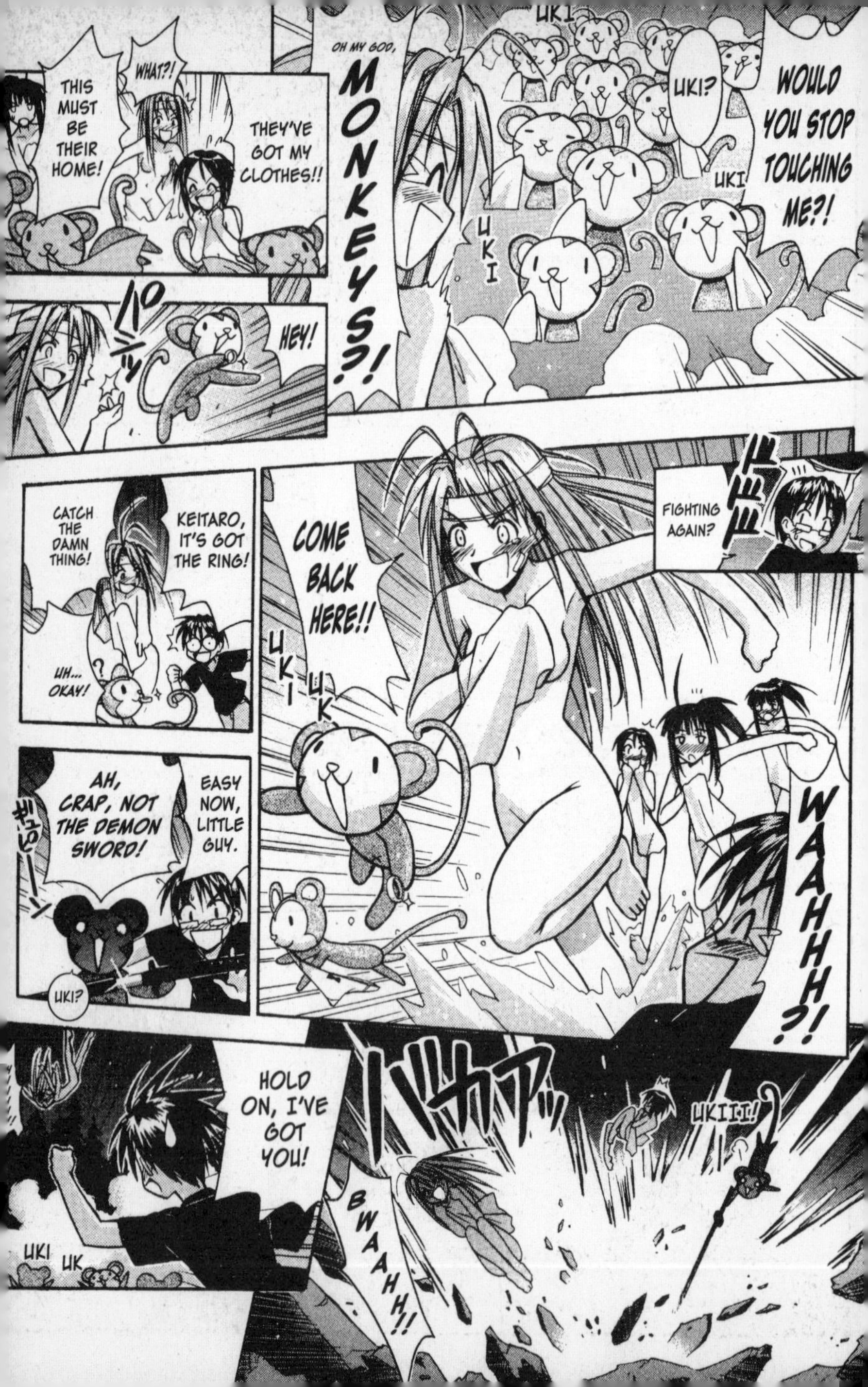

WOULD YOU STOP TOUCHING ME?!
UKI
UKI?
UKI
UKI
OH MY GOD, MONKEYS?!
WHAT?!
THEY'VE GOT MY CLOTHES!!
THIS MUST BE THEIR HOME!
HEY!
FIGHTING AGAIN?
WAAHHHH?!
COME BACK HERE!!
UK
UKI
KEITARO, IT'S GOT THE RING!
CATCH THE DAMN THING!
UH... OKAY!
EASY NOW, LITTLE GUY.
AH, CRAP, NOT THE DEMON SWORD!
UKI?
UKIII!
BWAAHH!!
HOLD ON, I'VE GOT YOU!
UKI
UK

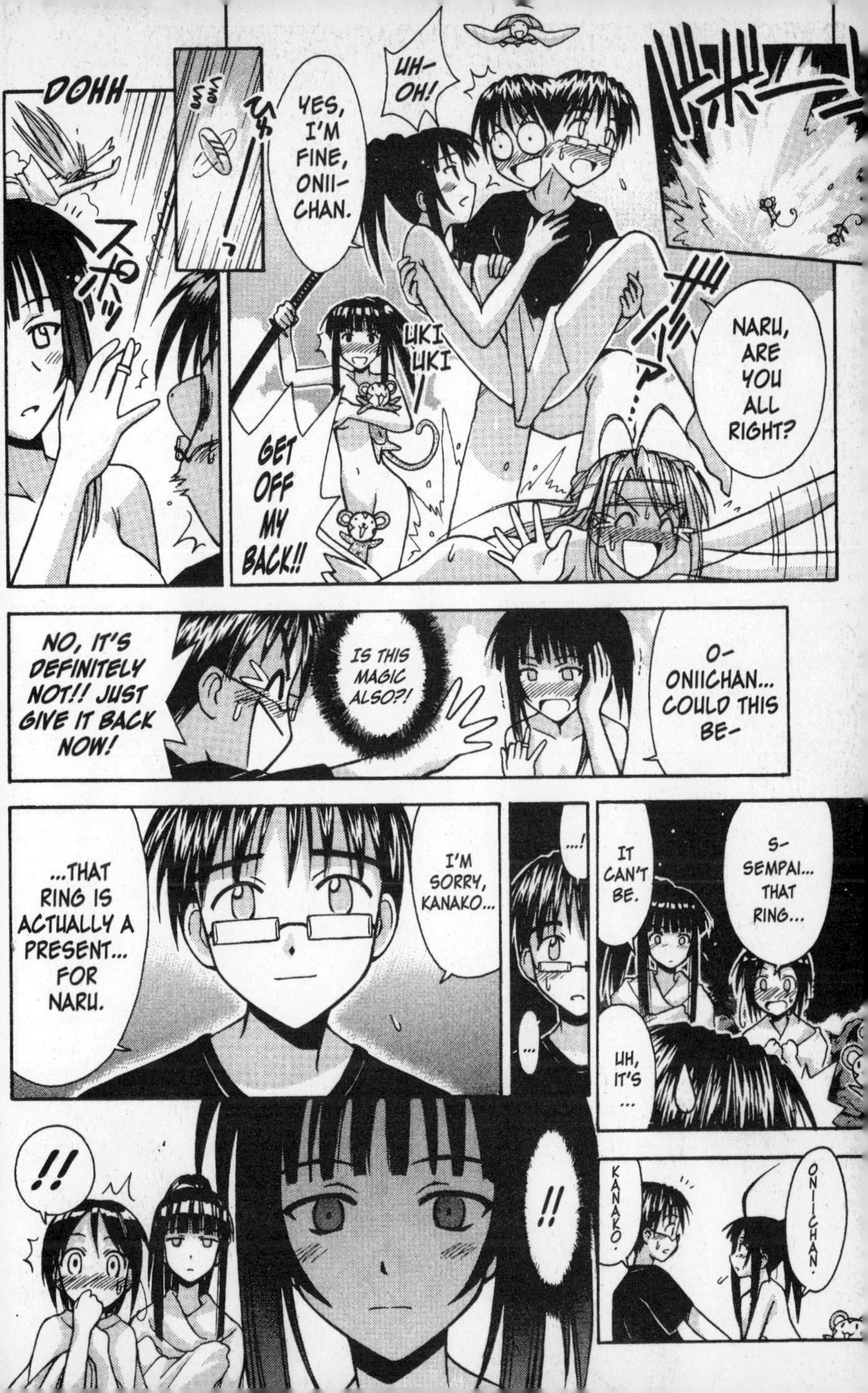
NARU, ARE YOU ALL RIGHT?
UH-OH!
YES, I'M FINE, ONII-CHAN.
UKI UKI
GET OFF MY BACK!!
DOHH
O-ONIICHAN... COULD THIS BE-
IS THIS MAGIC ALSO?!
NO, IT'S DEFINITELY NOT!! JUST GIVE IT BACK NOW!
S-SEMPAI... THAT RING...
IT CAN'T BE.
UH, IT'S ...
...!
...
I'M SORRY, KANAKO...
...THAT RING IS ACTUALLY A PRESENT... FOR NARU.
ONIICHAN.
KANAKO.
!!
!!

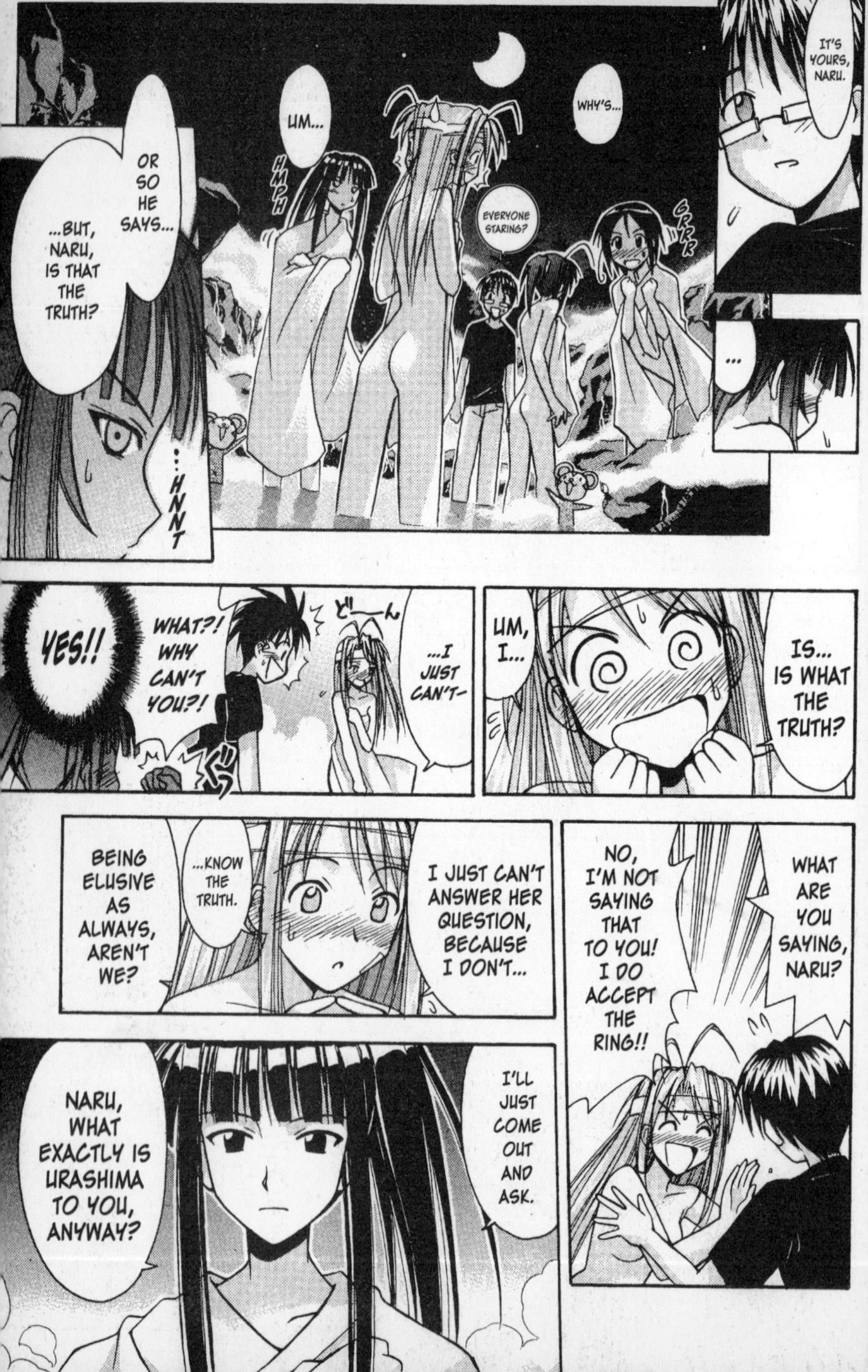
IT'S YOURS, NARU.
...
WHY'S...
EVERYONE STARING?
GRRR
UM...
HMPH
OR SO HE SAYS...
...BUT, NARU, IS THAT THE TRUTH?
...HNNT
IS... IS WHAT THE TRUTH?
UM, I...
...I JUST CAN'T-
どーん
WHAT?! WHY CAN'T YOU?!
YES!!
WHAT ARE YOU SAYING, NARU?
NO, I'M NOT SAYING THAT TO YOU! I DO ACCEPT THE RING!!
I JUST CAN'T ANSWER HER QUESTION, BECAUSE I DON'T...
...KNOW THE TRUTH.
BEING ELUSIVE AS ALWAYS, AREN'T WE?
I'LL JUST COME OUT AND ASK.
NARU, WHAT EXACTLY IS URASHIMA TO YOU, ANYWAY?

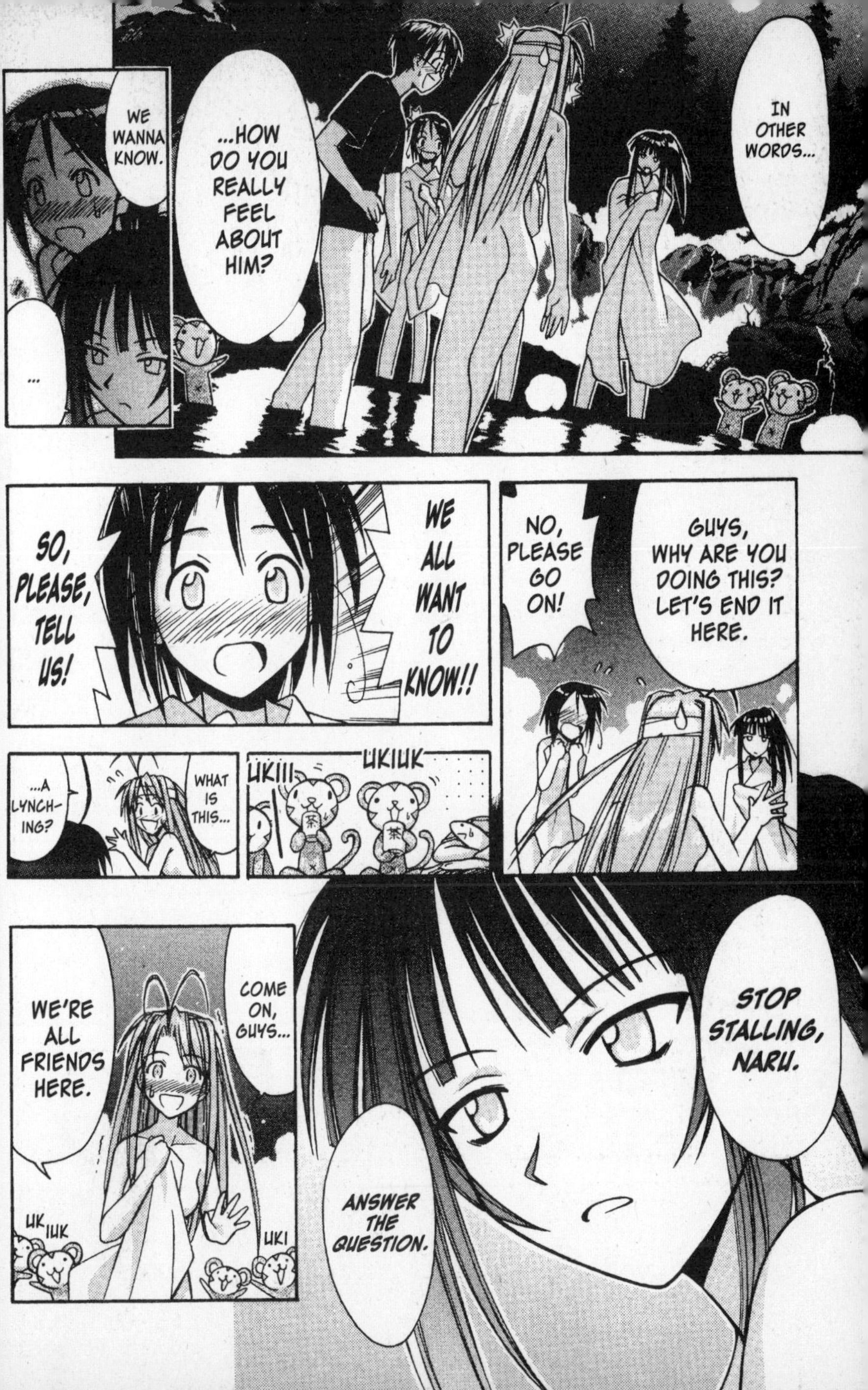
IN OTHER WORDS...
...HOW DO YOU REALLY FEEL ABOUT HIM?
WE WANNA KNOW.
...
GUYS, WHY ARE YOU DOING THIS? LET'S END IT HERE.
NO, PLEASE GO ON!
WE ALL WANT TO KNOW!!
SO, PLEASE, TELL US!
UKIUK
UKIII
WHAT IS THIS...
...A LYNCHING?
STOP STALLING, NARU.
ANSWER THE QUESTION.
COME ON, GUYS...
WE'RE ALL FRIENDS HERE.
UKI
UK IUK

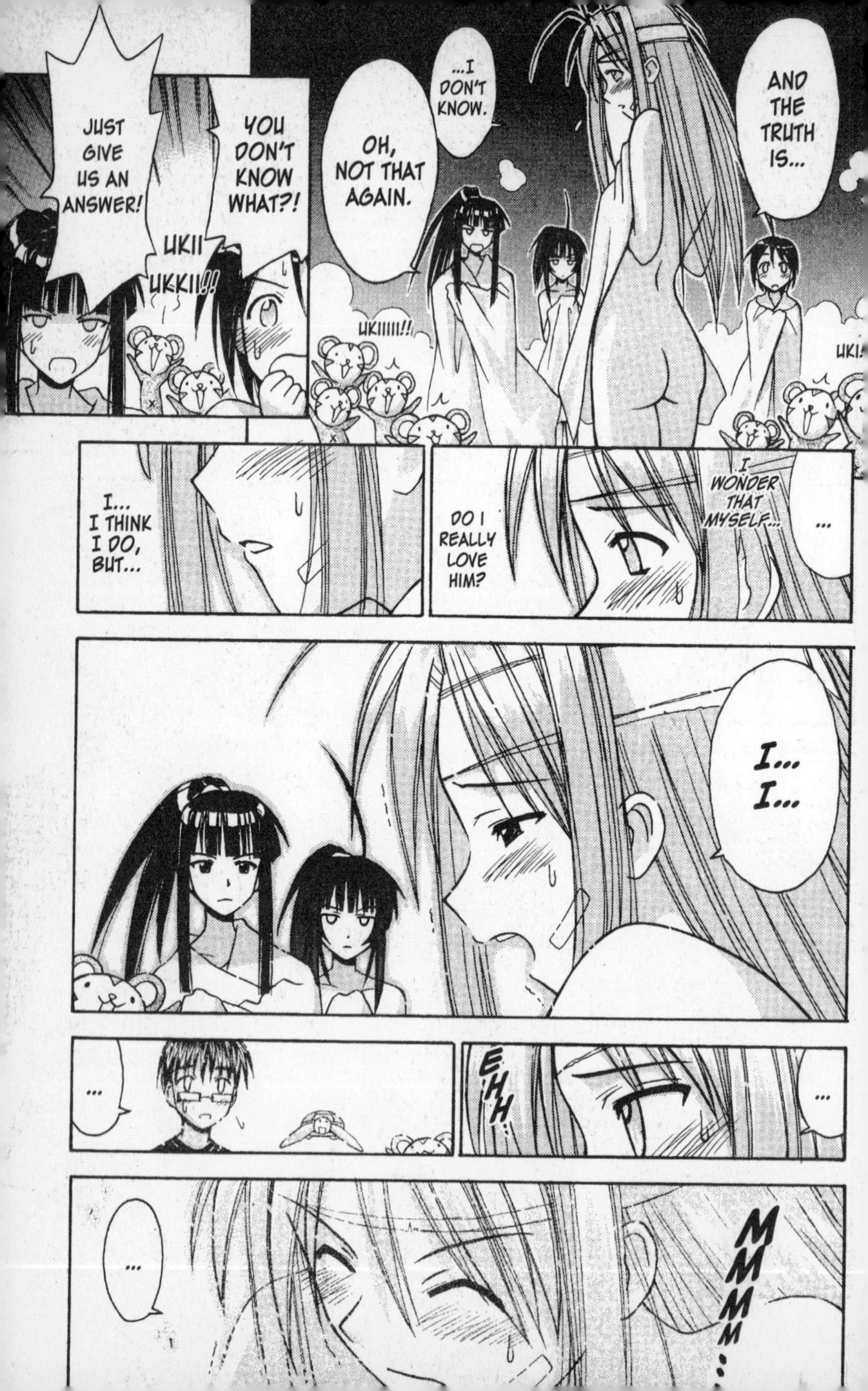
AND THE TRUTH IS...
...I DON'T KNOW.
OH, NOT THAT AGAIN.
UKI!
UKIIIII!!
YOU DON'T KNOW WHAT?!
UKII UKKII!!
JUST GIVE US AN ANSWER!
...
I WONDER THAT MYSELF...
DO I REALLY LOVE HIM?
I... I THINK I DO, BUT...
I... I...
...
EHH...
...
MMMM...
...

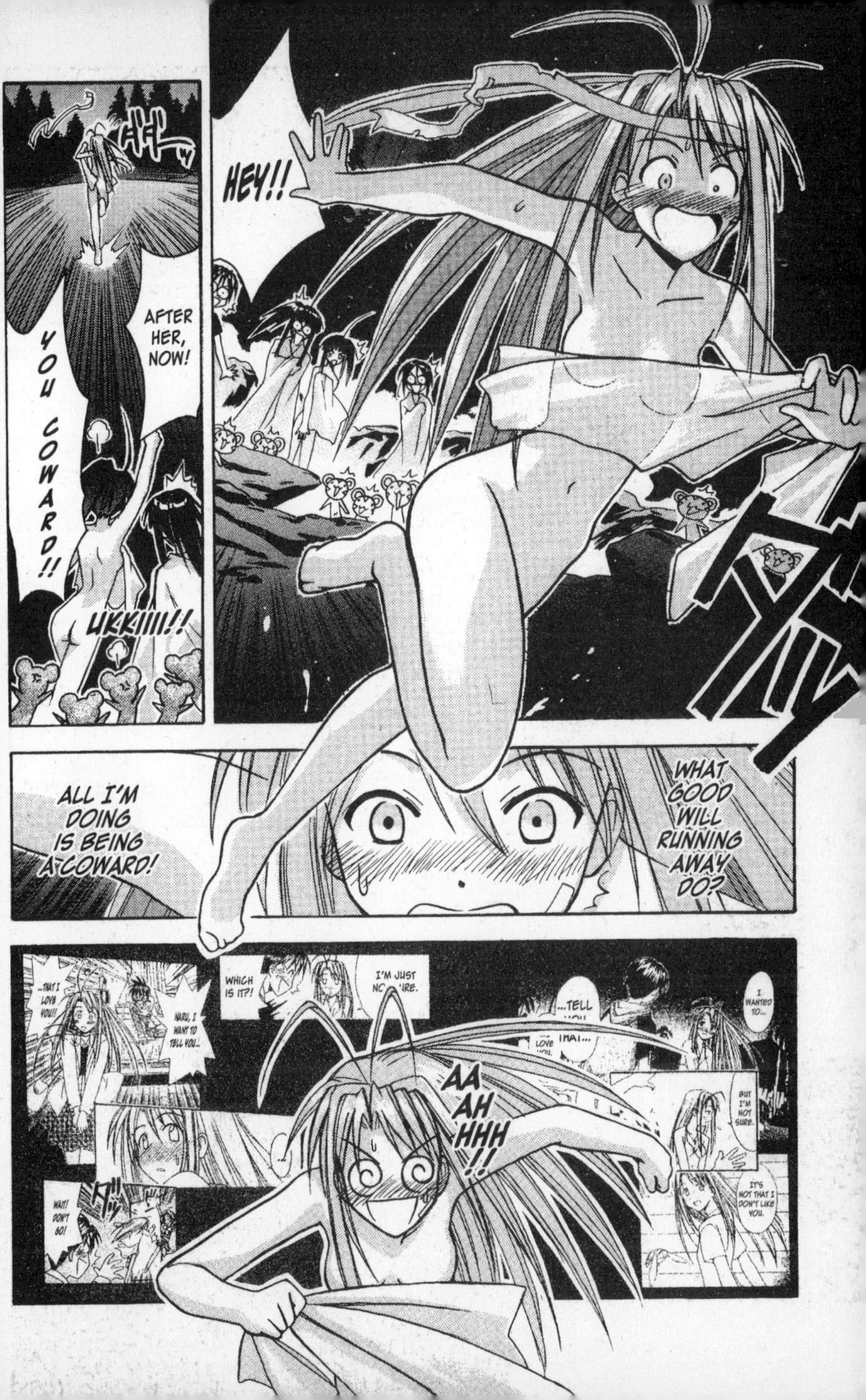
HEY!!
AFTER HER, NOW!
YOU COWARD!!
UKKIIII!!
WHAT GOOD WILL RUNNING AWAY DO?
ALL I'M DOING IS BEING A COWARD!
I WANTED TO...
...TELL
BUT I'M NOT SURE.
IT'S NOT THAT I DON'T LIKE YOU.
AAAHHHH!!
I'M JUST
WHICH IS IT?!
NARU, I WANT TO TELL YOU...
...THAT I LOVE YOU!!
WAIT! DON'T GO!

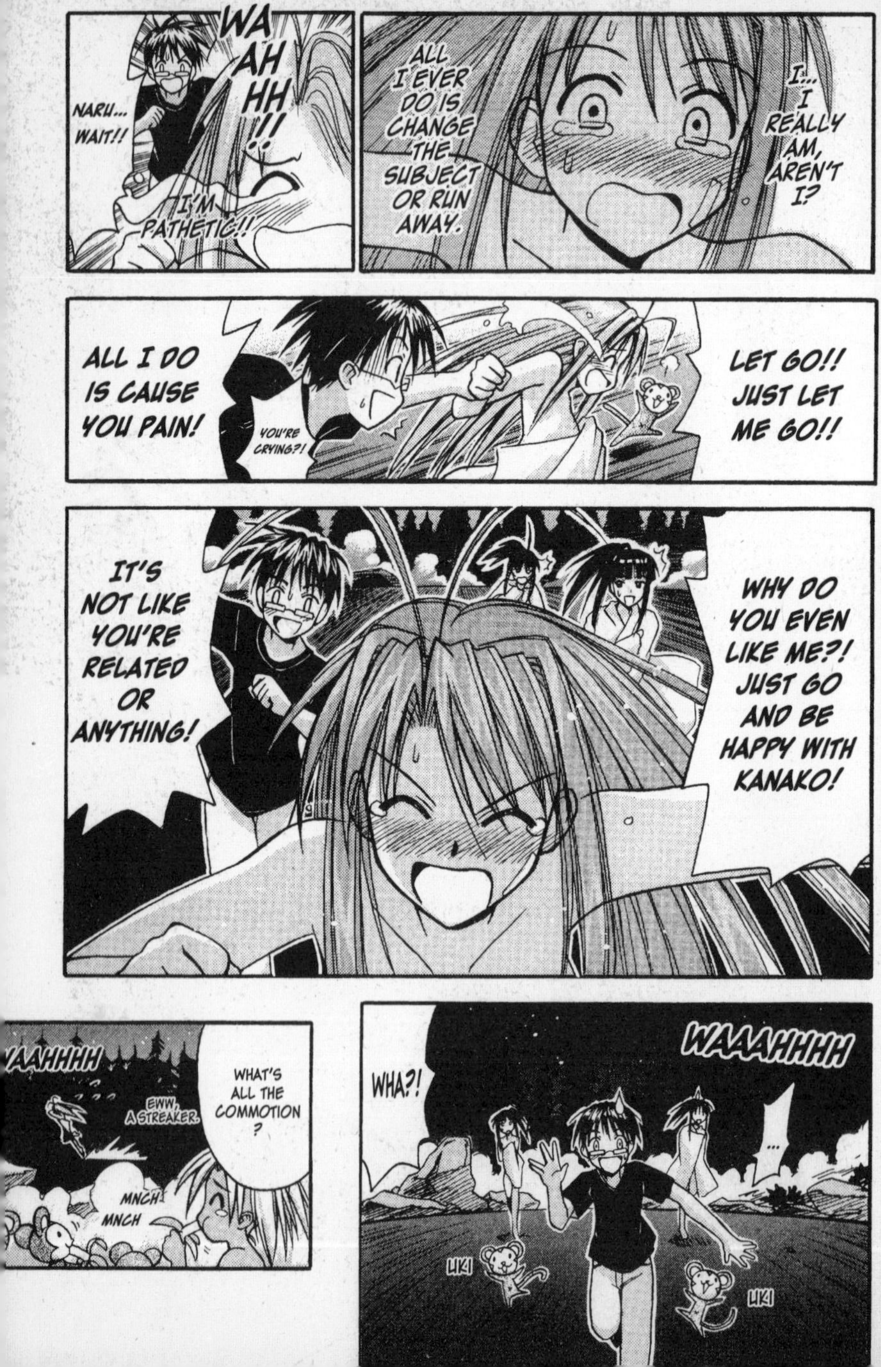
I... I REALLY AM, AREN'T I?
ALL I EVER DO IS CHANGE THE SUBJECT OR RUN AWAY.
WAAHHH!!
I'M PATHETIC!!
NARU... WAIT!!
LET GO!! JUST LET ME GO!!
ALL I DO IS CAUSE YOU PAIN!
YOU'RE CRYING?!
WHY DO YOU EVEN LIKE ME?! JUST GO AND BE HAPPY WITH KANAKO!
IT'S NOT LIKE YOU'RE RELATED OR ANYTHING!
WAAAHHHH
!
...
WHA?!
UKI
UKI
WHAT'S ALL THE COMMOTION ?
EWW, A STREAKER.
MNCH MNCH

SHE EVEN HAD THE AUDACITY TO GO HOME IN THE SAME VEHICLE AFTERWARDS.

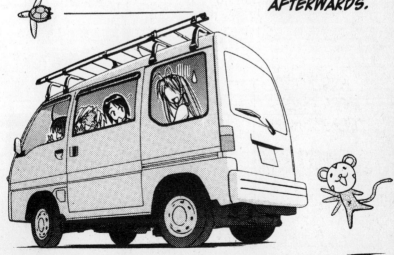

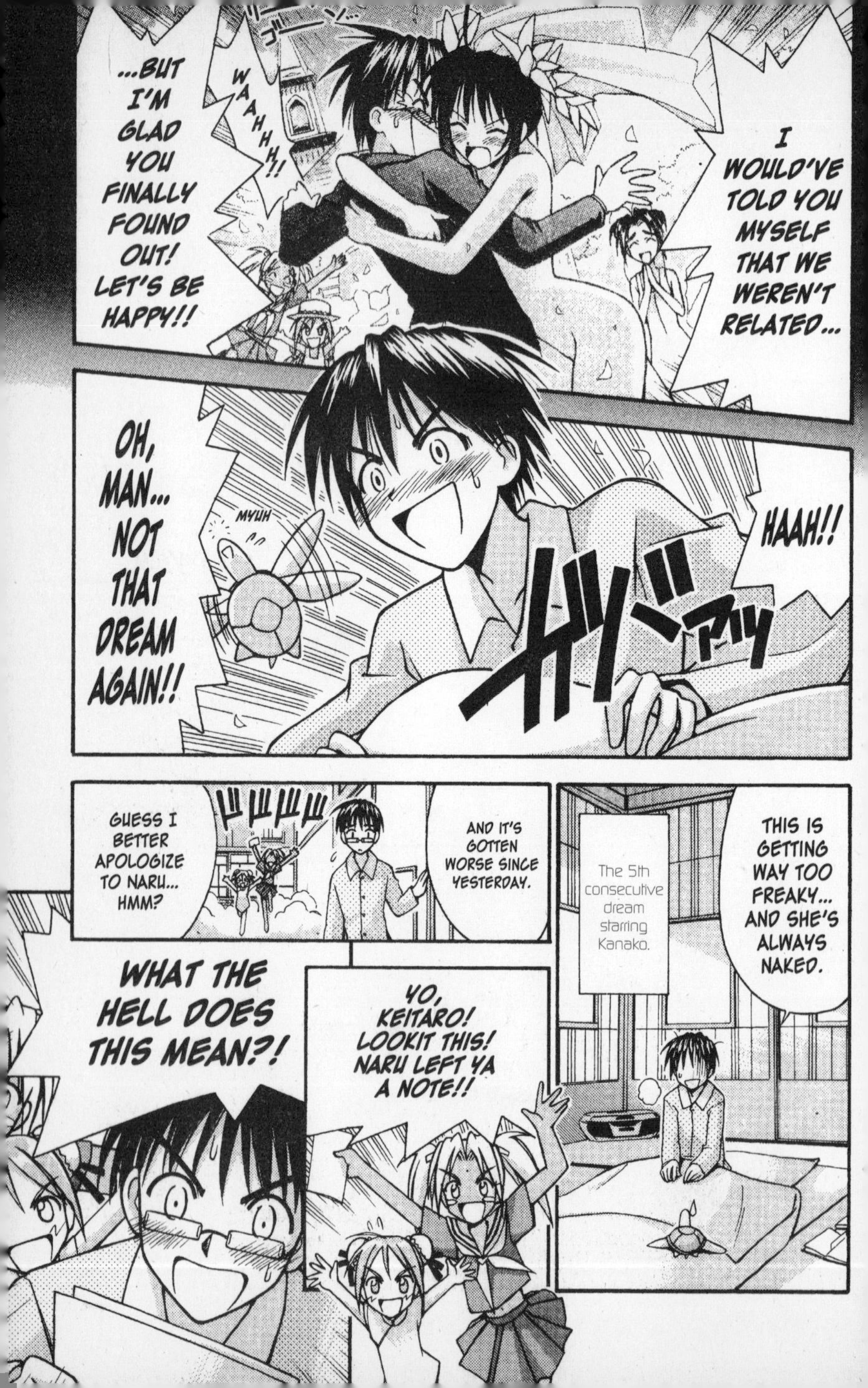
I WOULD'VE TOLD YOU MYSELF THAT WE WEREN'T RELATED...
WAAHHH!!
...BUT I'M GLAD YOU FINALLY FOUND OUT! LET'S BE HAPPY!!
HAAH!!
MYUH
OH, MAN... NOT THAT DREAM AGAIN!!
THIS IS GETTING WAY TOO FREAKY... AND SHE'S ALWAYS NAKED.
The 5th consecutive dream starring Kanako.
AND IT'S GOTTEN WORSE SINCE YESTERDAY.
GUESS I BETTER APOLOGIZE TO NARU... HMM?
YO, KEITARO! LOOKIT THIS! NARU LEFT YA A NOTE!!
WHAT THE HELL DOES THIS MEAN?!

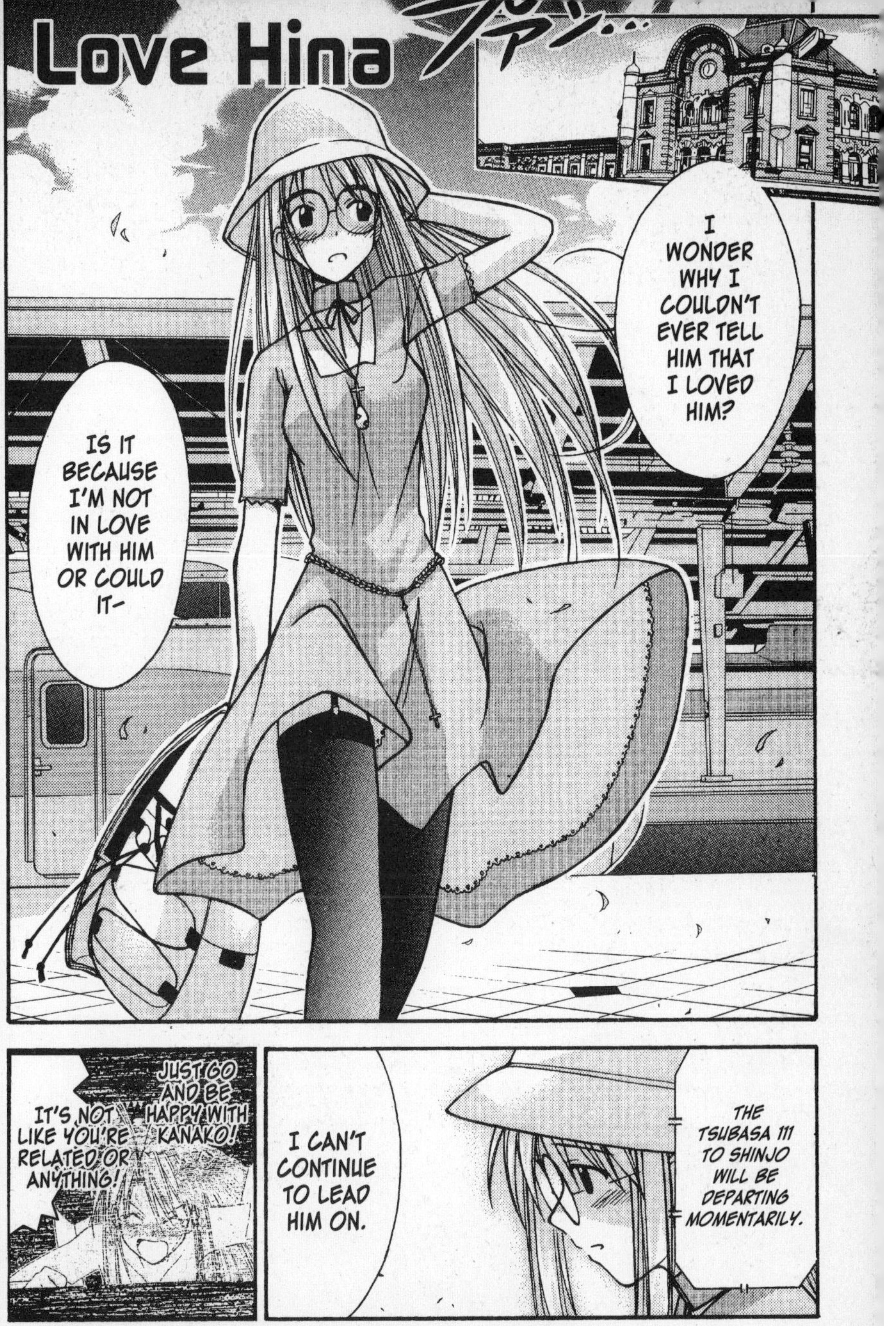
Love Hina
I WONDER WHY I COULDN'T EVER TELL HIM THAT I LOVED HIM?
IS IT BECAUSE I'M NOT IN LOVE WITH HIM OR COULD IT-
THE TSUBASA 111 TO SHINJO WILL BE DEPARTING MOMENTARILY.
I CAN'T CONTINUE TO LEAD HIM ON.
JUST GO AND BE HAPPY WITH KANAKO!
IT'S NOT LIKE YOU'RE RELATED OR ANYTHING!

HINATA. 102 Heart Break Crossing

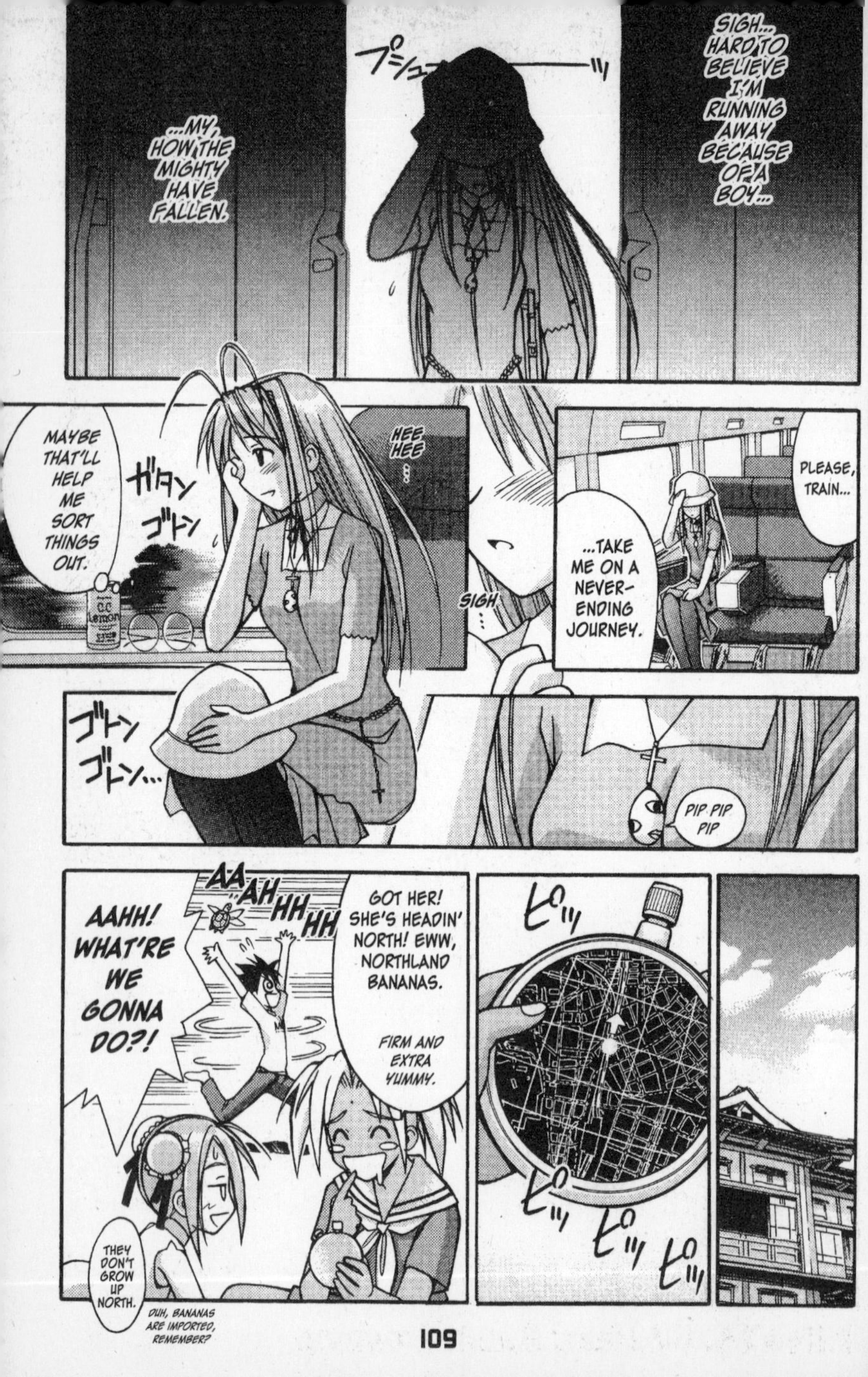
SIGH... HARD TO BELIEVE I'M RUNNING AWAY BECAUSE OF A BOY...
...MY, HOW THE MIGHTY HAVE FALLEN.
PLEASE, TRAIN...
...TAKE ME ON A NEVER-ENDING JOURNEY.
SIGH...
HEE HEE...
MAYBE THAT'LL HELP ME SORT THINGS OUT.
ガタン
ゴトン
C.C Lemon
PIP PIP PIP
ゴトン
ゴトン...
GOT HER! SHE'S HEADIN' NORTH! EWW, NORTHLAND BANANAS.
FIRM AND EXTRA YUMMY.
AAAHHHH
AAHH! WHAT'RE WE GONNA DO?!
THEY DON'T GROW UP NORTH.
DUH, BANANAS ARE IMPORTED, REMEMBER?

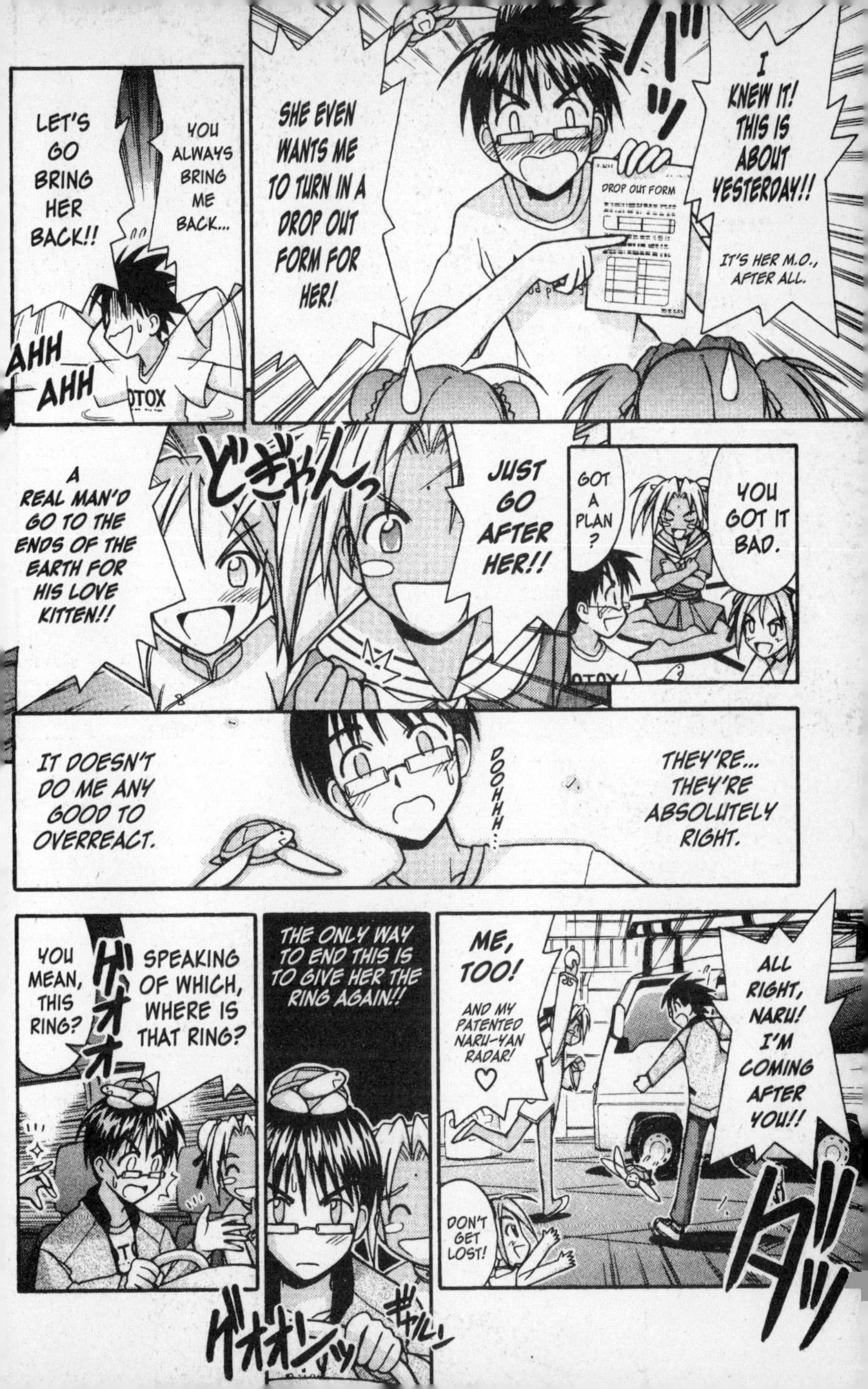
I KNEW IT! THIS IS ABOUT YESTERDAY!!
IT'S HER M.O., AFTER ALL.
DROP OUT FORM
SHE EVEN WANTS ME TO TURN IN A DROP OUT FORM FOR HER!
YOU ALWAYS BRING ME BACK...
LET'S GO BRING HER BACK!!
AHH AHH
YOU GOT IT BAD.
GOT A PLAN?
JUST GO AFTER HER!!
どぎゃんっ
A REAL MAN'D GO TO THE ENDS OF THE EARTH FOR HIS LOVE KITTEN!!
THEY'RE... THEY'RE ABSOLUTELY RIGHT.
DOOHHH...
IT DOESN'T DO ME ANY GOOD TO OVERREACT.
ALL RIGHT, NARU! I'M COMING AFTER YOU!!
ME, TOO!
AND MY PATENTED NARU-YAN RADAR! ♡
DON'T GET LOST!
THE ONLY WAY TO END THIS IS TO GIVE HER THE RING AGAIN!!
SPEAKING OF WHICH, WHERE IS THAT RING?
YOU MEAN, THIS RING?

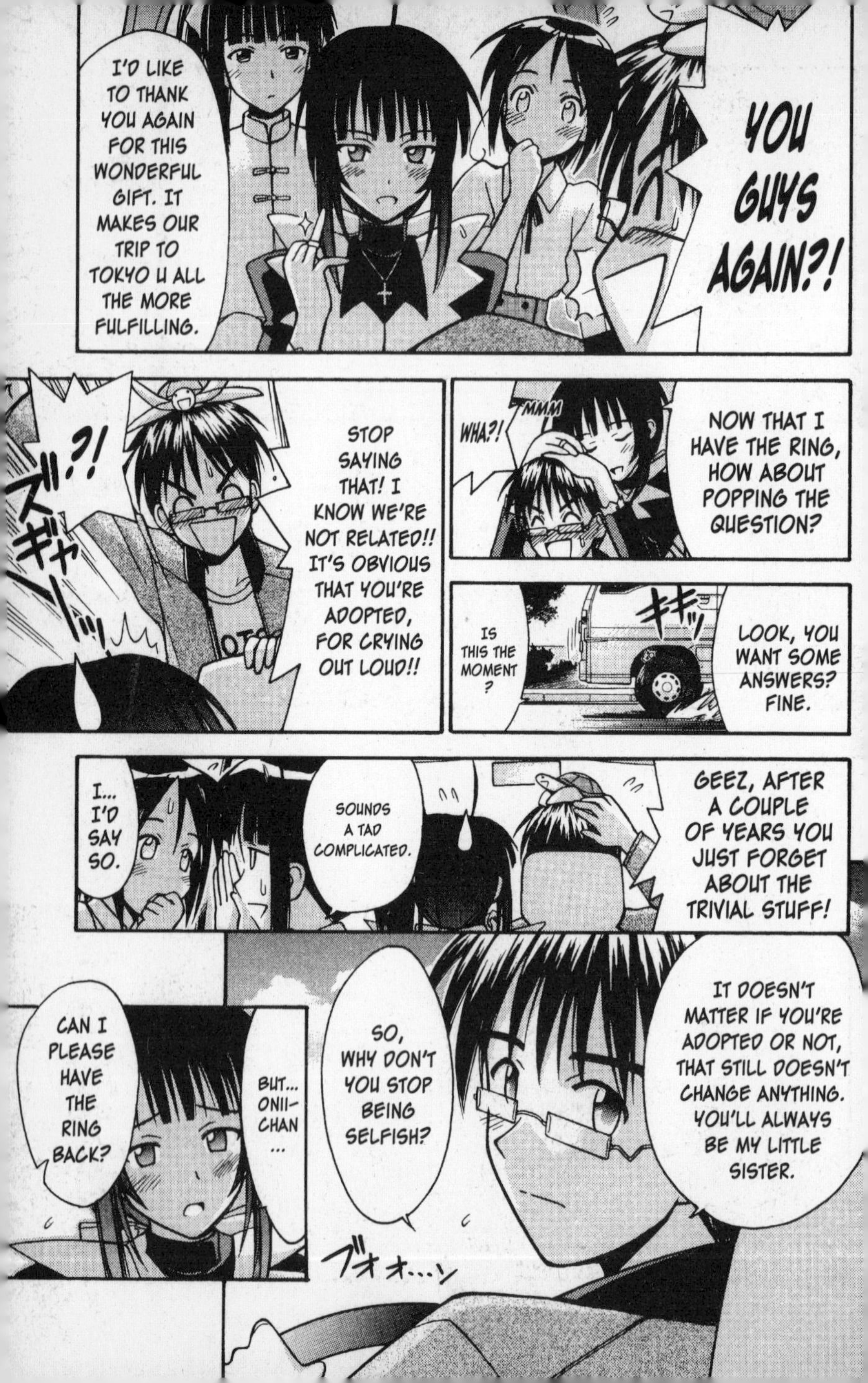
YOU GUYS AGAIN?!
I'D LIKE TO THANK YOU AGAIN FOR THIS WONDERFUL GIFT. IT MAKES OUR TRIP TO TOKYO U ALL THE MORE FULFILLING.
NOW THAT I HAVE THE RING, HOW ABOUT POPPING THE QUESTION?
MMM
WHA?!
LOOK, YOU WANT SOME ANSWERS? FINE.
キキッ
IS THIS THE MOMENT?
STOP SAYING THAT! I KNOW WE'RE NOT RELATED!! IT'S OBVIOUS THAT YOU'RE ADOPTED, FOR CRYING OUT LOUD!!
?!
ズギャーン
GEEZ, AFTER A COUPLE OF YEARS YOU JUST FORGET ABOUT THE TRIVIAL STUFF!
SOUNDS A TAD COMPLICATED.
I... I'D SAY SO.
IT DOESN'T MATTER IF YOU'RE ADOPTED OR NOT, THAT STILL DOESN'T CHANGE ANYTHING. YOU'LL ALWAYS BE MY LITTLE SISTER.
SO, WHY DON'T YOU STOP BEING SELFISH?
BUT... ONII-CHAN...
CAN I PLEASE HAVE THE RING BACK?
ブオオ…ン

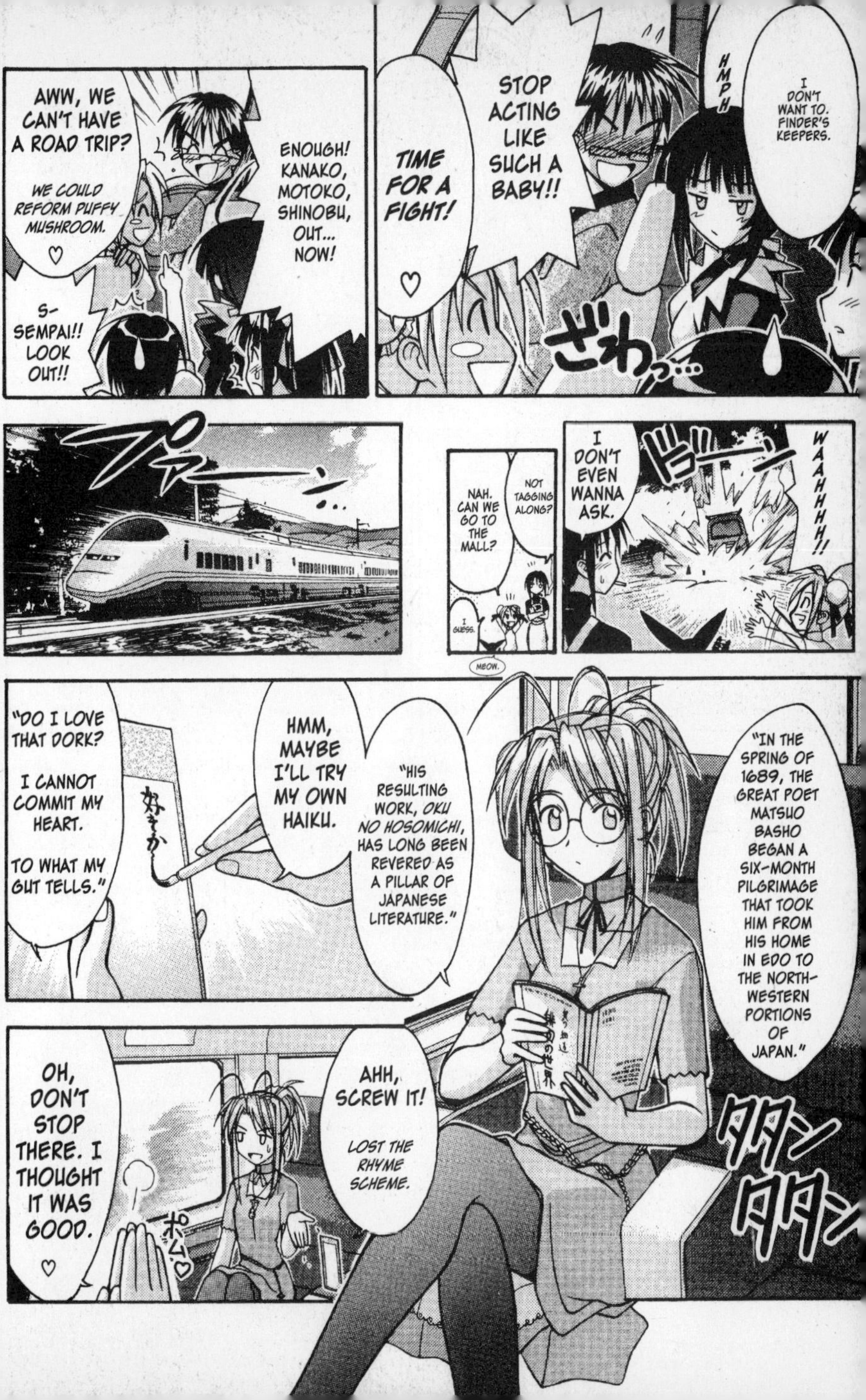
I DON'T WANT TO. FINDER'S KEEPERS.
HMPH
STOP ACTING LIKE SUCH A BABY!!
TIME FOR A FIGHT! ♡
ざわっ…
ENOUGH! KANAKO, MOTOKO, SHINOBU, OUT... NOW!
AWW, WE CAN'T HAVE A ROAD TRIP?
WE COULD REFORM PUFFY MUSHROOM. ♡
S-SEMPAI!! LOOK OUT!!
WAAHHHHH!!
I DON'T EVEN WANNA ASK.
NOT TAGGING ALONG?
NAH. CAN WE GO TO THE MALL?
I GUESS.
MEOW.
プァーン…
"IN THE SPRING OF 1689, THE GREAT POET MATSUO BASHO BEGAN A SIX-MONTH PILGRIMAGE THAT TOOK HIM FROM HIS HOME IN EDO TO THE NORTH-WESTERN PORTIONS OF JAPAN."
"HIS RESULTING WORK, OKU NO HOSOMICHI, HAS LONG BEEN REVERED AS A PILLAR OF JAPANESE LITERATURE."
HMM, MAYBE I'LL TRY MY OWN HAIKU.
"DO I LOVE THAT DORK?
I CANNOT COMMIT MY HEART.
TO WHAT MY GUT TELLS."
好きか
タタン
タタン
AHH, SCREW IT!
LOST THE RHYME SCHEME.
OH, DON'T STOP THERE. I THOUGHT IT WAS GOOD. ♡
ポム♡

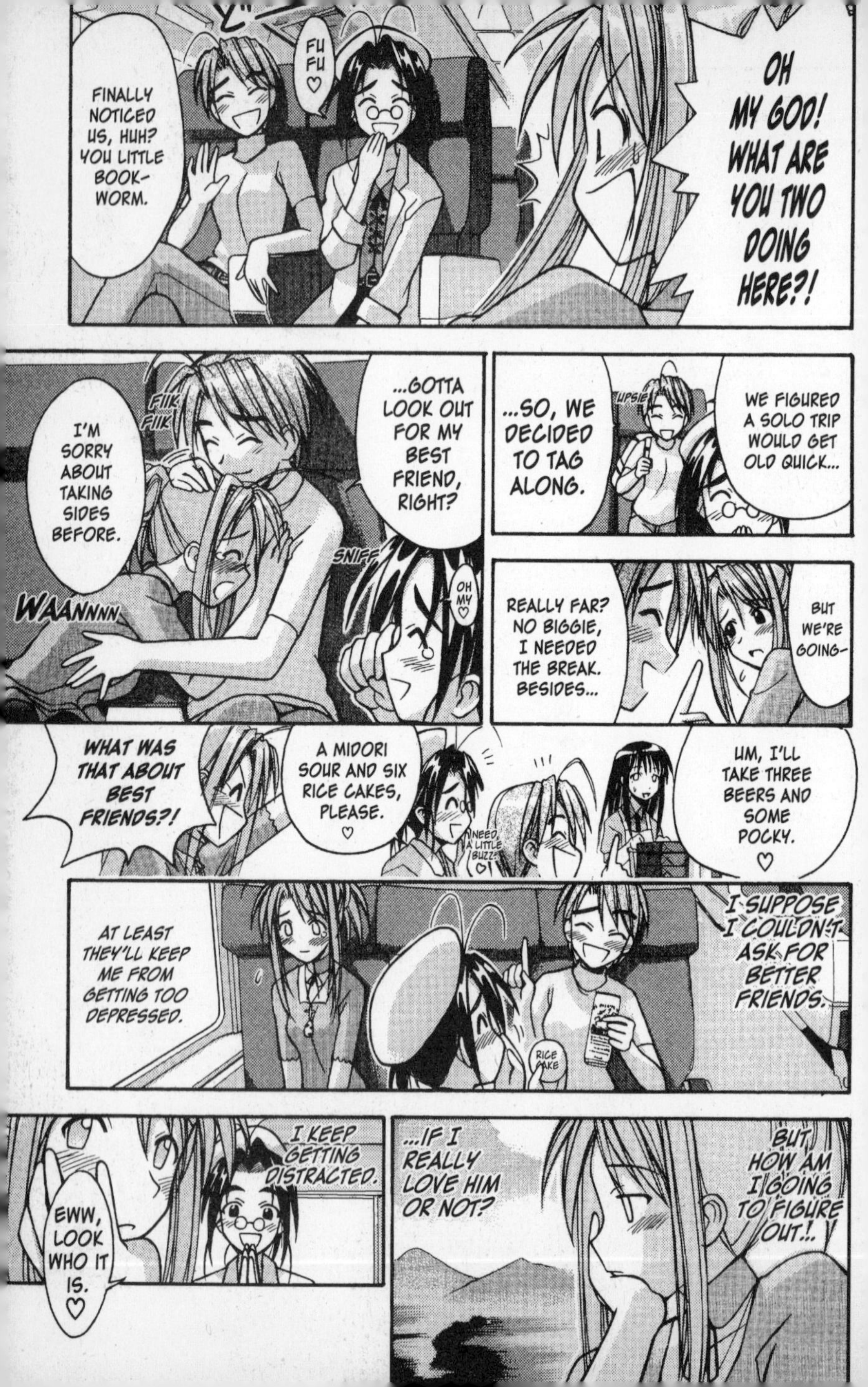

OH MY GOD! WHAT ARE YOU TWO DOING HERE?!
FU FU ♡
FINALLY NOTICED US, HUH? YOU LITTLE BOOK-WORM.
WE FIGURED A SOLO TRIP WOULD GET OLD QUICK...
UPSIE
...SO, WE DECIDED TO TAG ALONG.
BUT WE'RE GOING-
REALLY FAR? NO BIGGIE, I NEEDED THE BREAK. BESIDES...
...GOTTA LOOK OUT FOR MY BEST FRIEND, RIGHT?
OH MY ♡
SNIFF
FIIK FIIK
I'M SORRY ABOUT TAKING SIDES BEFORE.
WAANNNN
UM, I'LL TAKE THREE BEERS AND SOME POCKY. ♡
NEED A LITTLE BUZZ? ♡
A MIDORI SOUR AND SIX RICE CAKES, PLEASE. ♡
WHAT WAS THAT ABOUT BEST FRIENDS?!
I SUPPOSE I COULDN'T ASK FOR BETTER FRIENDS.
RICE CAKE
AT LEAST THEY'LL KEEP ME FROM GETTING TOO DEPRESSED.
BUT HOW AM I GOING TO FIGURE OUT...
...IF I REALLY LOVE HIM OR NOT?
I KEEP GETTING DISTRACTED.
EWW, LOOK WHO IT IS. ♡

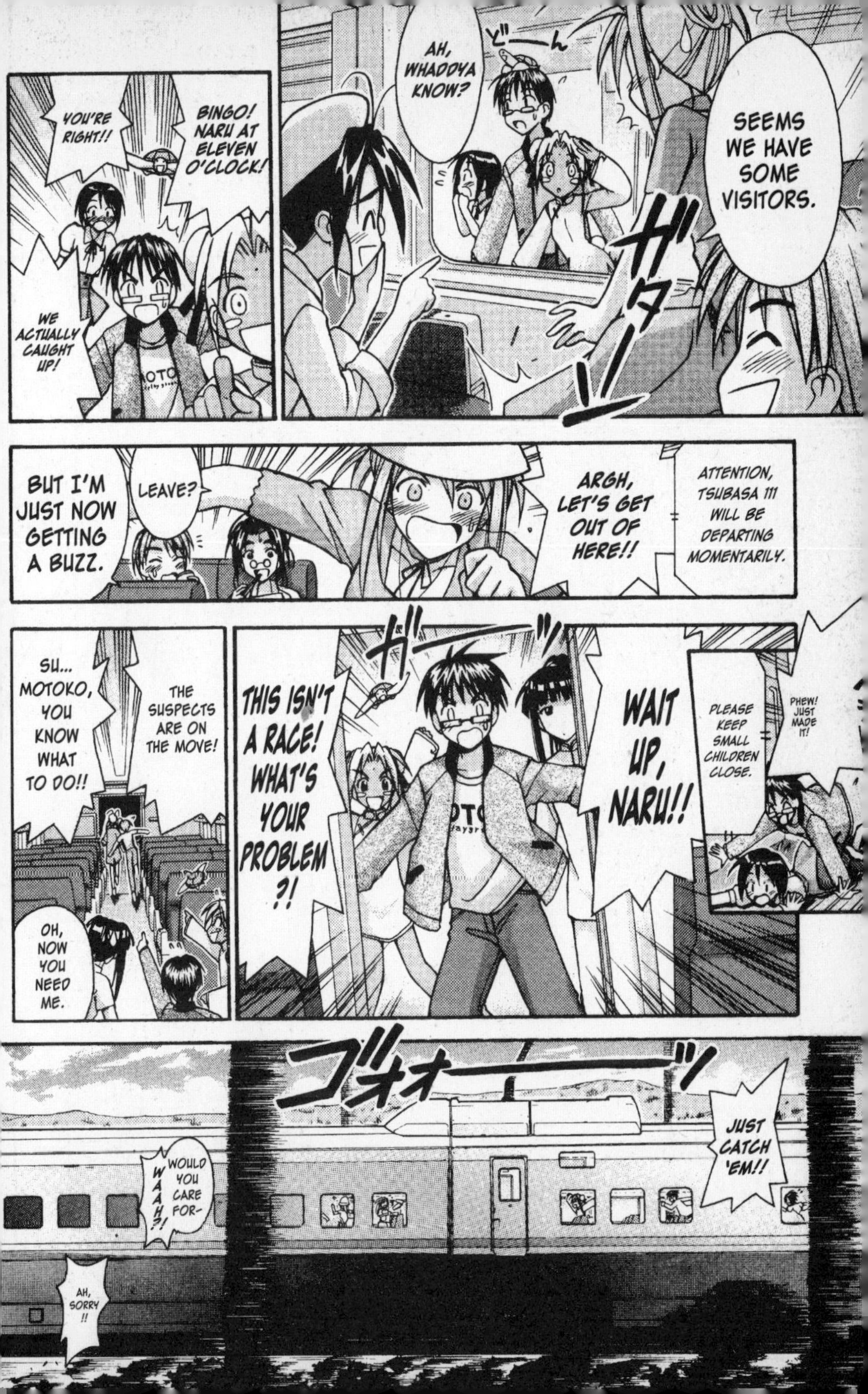
SEEMS WE HAVE SOME VISITORS.
ガターン
どーん
AH, WHADDYA KNOW?
BINGO! NARU AT ELEVEN O'CLOCK!
YOU'RE RIGHT!!
WE ACTUALLY CAUGHT UP!
ATTENTION, TSUBASA 111 WILL BE DEPARTING MOMENTARILY.
ARGH, LET'S GET OUT OF HERE!!
LEAVE?
BUT I'M JUST NOW GETTING A BUZZ.
PHEW! JUST MADE IT!
PLEASE KEEP SMALL CHILDREN CLOSE.
WAIT UP, NARU!!
ガーッ
THIS ISN'T A RACE! WHAT'S YOUR PROBLEM?!
THE SUSPECTS ARE ON THE MOVE!
SU... MOTOKO, YOU KNOW WHAT TO DO!!
OH, NOW YOU NEED ME.
ゴオーッ
JUST CATCH 'EM!!
WOULD YOU CARE FOR-
WAAAH?!
AH, SORRY!!

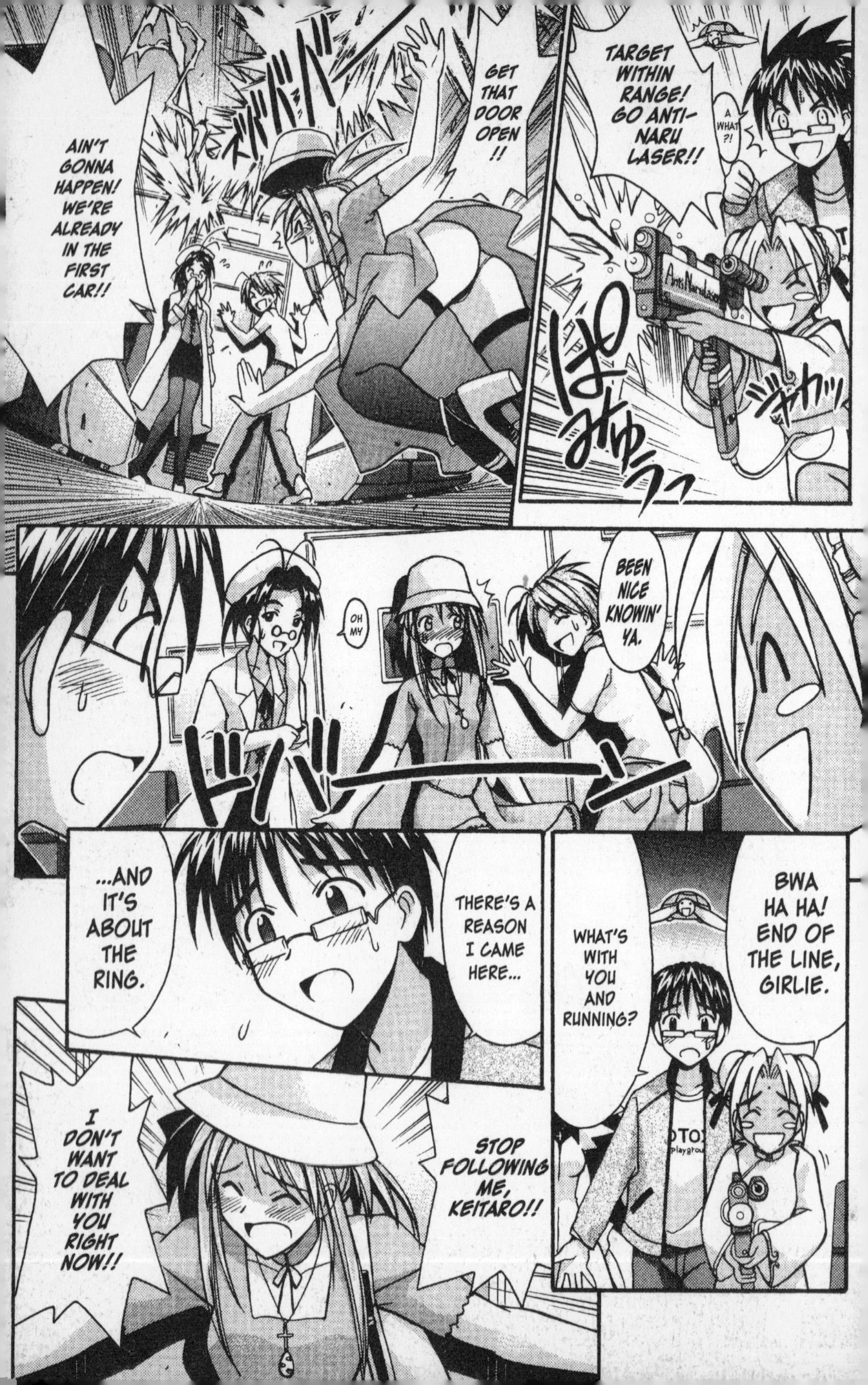
TARGET WITHIN RANGE! GO ANTI-NARU LASER!!
A WHAT?!
Anti Naru Laser
GET THAT DOOR OPEN!!
AIN'T GONNA HAPPEN! WE'RE ALREADY IN THE FIRST CAR!!
BEEN NICE KNOWIN' YA.
OH MY
BWA HA HA! END OF THE LINE, GIRLIE.
WHAT'S WITH YOU AND RUNNING?
THERE'S A REASON I CAME HERE...
...AND IT'S ABOUT THE RING.
STOP FOLLOWING ME, KEITARO!!
I DON'T WANT TO DEAL WITH YOU RIGHT NOW!!

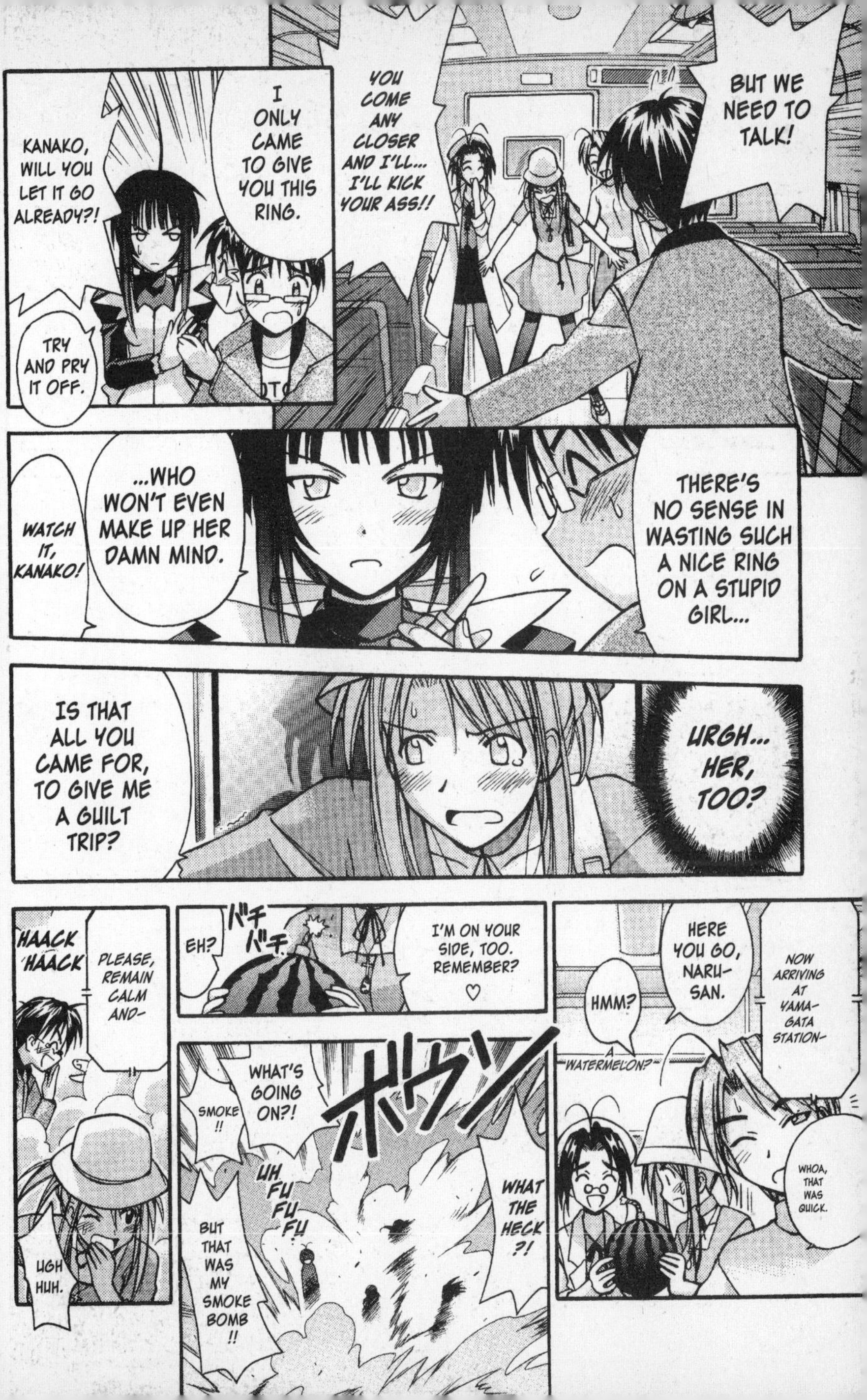
BUT WE NEED TO TALK!
YOU COME ANY CLOSER AND I'LL... I'LL KICK YOUR ASS!!
I ONLY CAME TO GIVE YOU THIS RING.
KANAKO, WILL YOU LET IT GO ALREADY?!
TRY AND PRY IT OFF.
THERE'S NO SENSE IN WASTING SUCH A NICE RING ON A STUPID GIRL...
...WHO WON'T EVEN MAKE UP HER DAMN MIND.
WATCH IT, KANAKO!
URGH... HER, TOO?
IS THAT ALL YOU CAME FOR, TO GIVE ME A GUILT TRIP?
NOW ARRIVING AT YAMA-GATA STATION-
HERE YOU GO, NARU-SAN.
HMM?
A WATERMELON?
WHOA, THAT WAS QUICK.
I'M ON YOUR SIDE, TOO. REMEMBER? ♡
バチ バチ
EH?
ボウン
WHAT'S GOING ON?!
SMOKE!!
WHAT THE HECK?!
UH FU FU FU
BUT THAT WAS MY SMOKE BOMB!!
PLEASE, REMAIN CALM AND-
HAACK HAACK
UGH HUH.

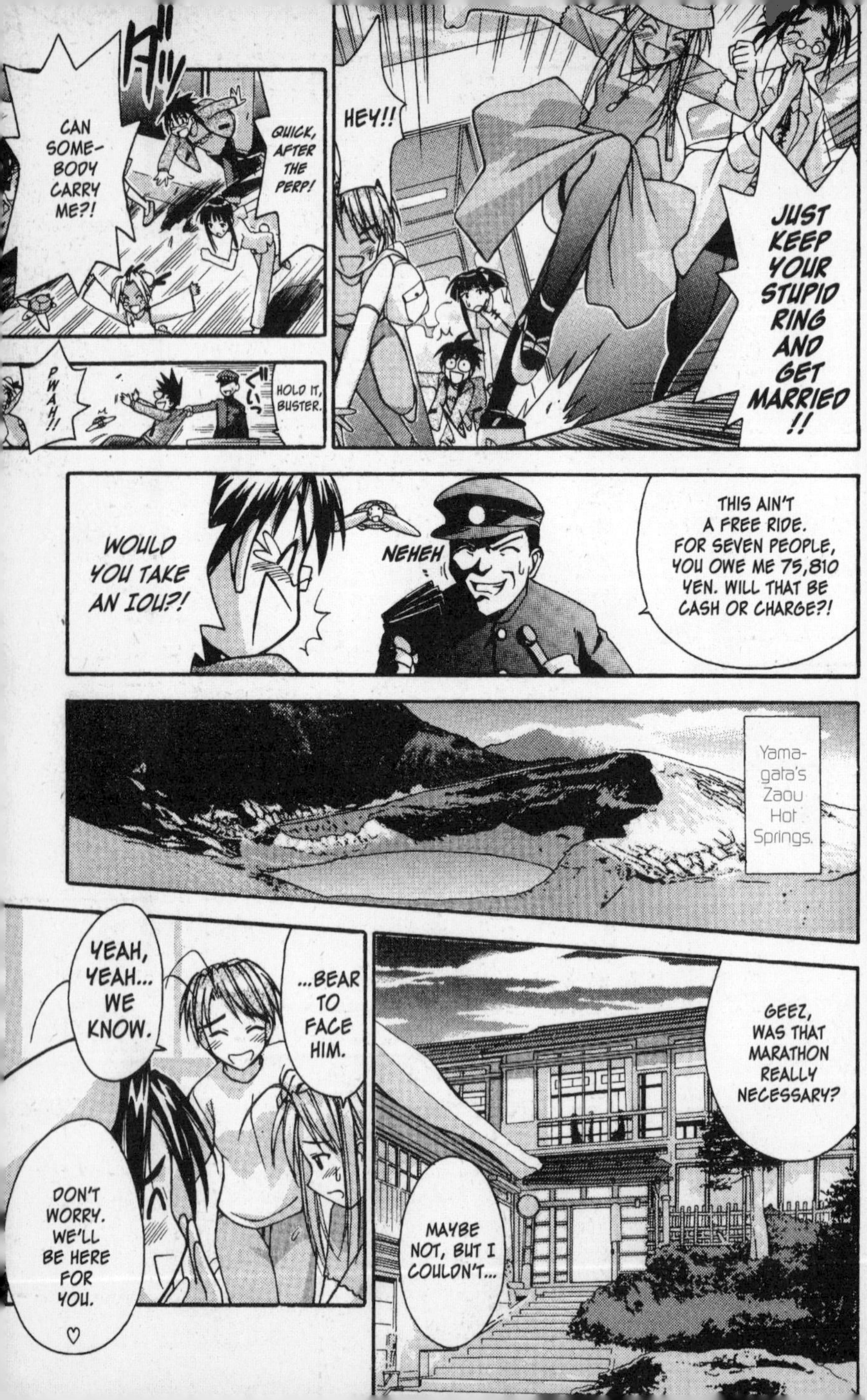
JUST KEEP YOUR STUPID RING AND GET MARRIED!!
HEY!!
QUICK, AFTER THE PERP!
CAN SOMEBODY CARRY ME?!
HOLD IT, BUSTER.
ぐいっ
PWAH!!
THIS AIN'T A FREE RIDE. FOR SEVEN PEOPLE, YOU OWE ME 75,810 YEN. WILL THAT BE CASH OR CHARGE?!
NEHEH
WOULD YOU TAKE AN IOU?!
Yamagata's Zaou Hot Springs.
GEEZ, WAS THAT MARATHON REALLY NECESSARY?
MAYBE NOT, BUT I COULDN'T...
...BEAR TO FACE HIM.
YEAH, YEAH... WE KNOW.
DON'T WORRY. WE'LL BE HERE FOR YOU. ♡

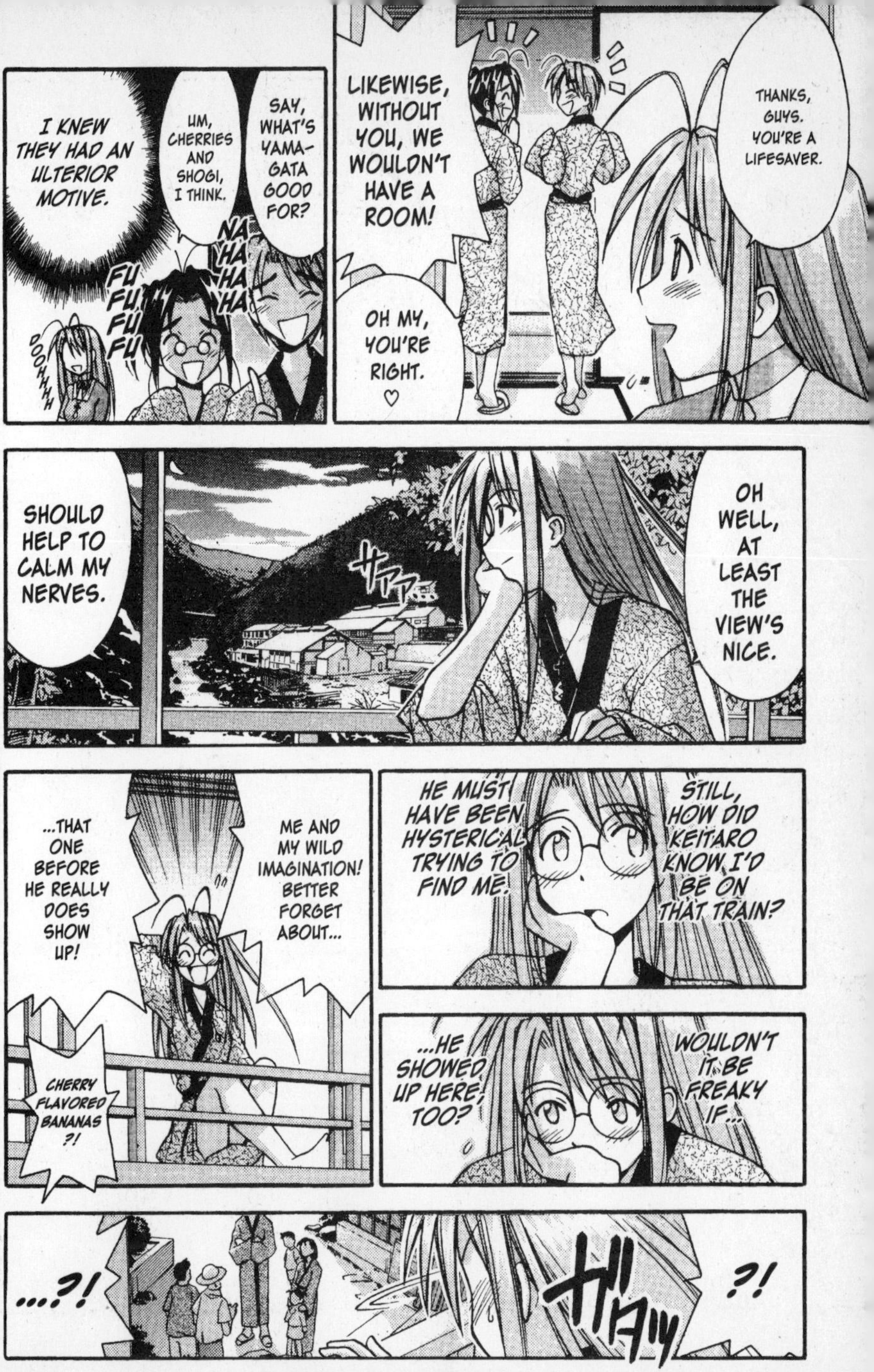
THANKS, GUYS. YOU'RE A LIFESAVER.
LIKEWISE, WITHOUT YOU, WE WOULDN'T HAVE A ROOM!
OH MY, YOU'RE RIGHT. ♡
SAY, WHAT'S YAMA-GATA GOOD FOR?
UM, CHERRIES AND SHOGI, I THINK.
NA HA HA HA HA
FU FU FU FU
I KNEW THEY HAD AN ULTERIOR MOTIVE.
DOOHHHH
OH WELL, AT LEAST THE VIEW'S NICE.
SHOULD HELP TO CALM MY NERVES.
STILL, HOW DID KEITARO KNOW I'D BE ON THAT TRAIN?
HE MUST HAVE BEEN HYSTERICAL TRYING TO FIND ME.
WOULDN'T IT BE FREAKY IF...
...HE SHOWED UP HERE, TOO?
ME AND MY WILD IMAGINATION! BETTER FORGET ABOUT...
...THAT ONE BEFORE HE REALLY DOES SHOW UP!
CHERRY FLAVORED BANANAS ?!
?!
...?!

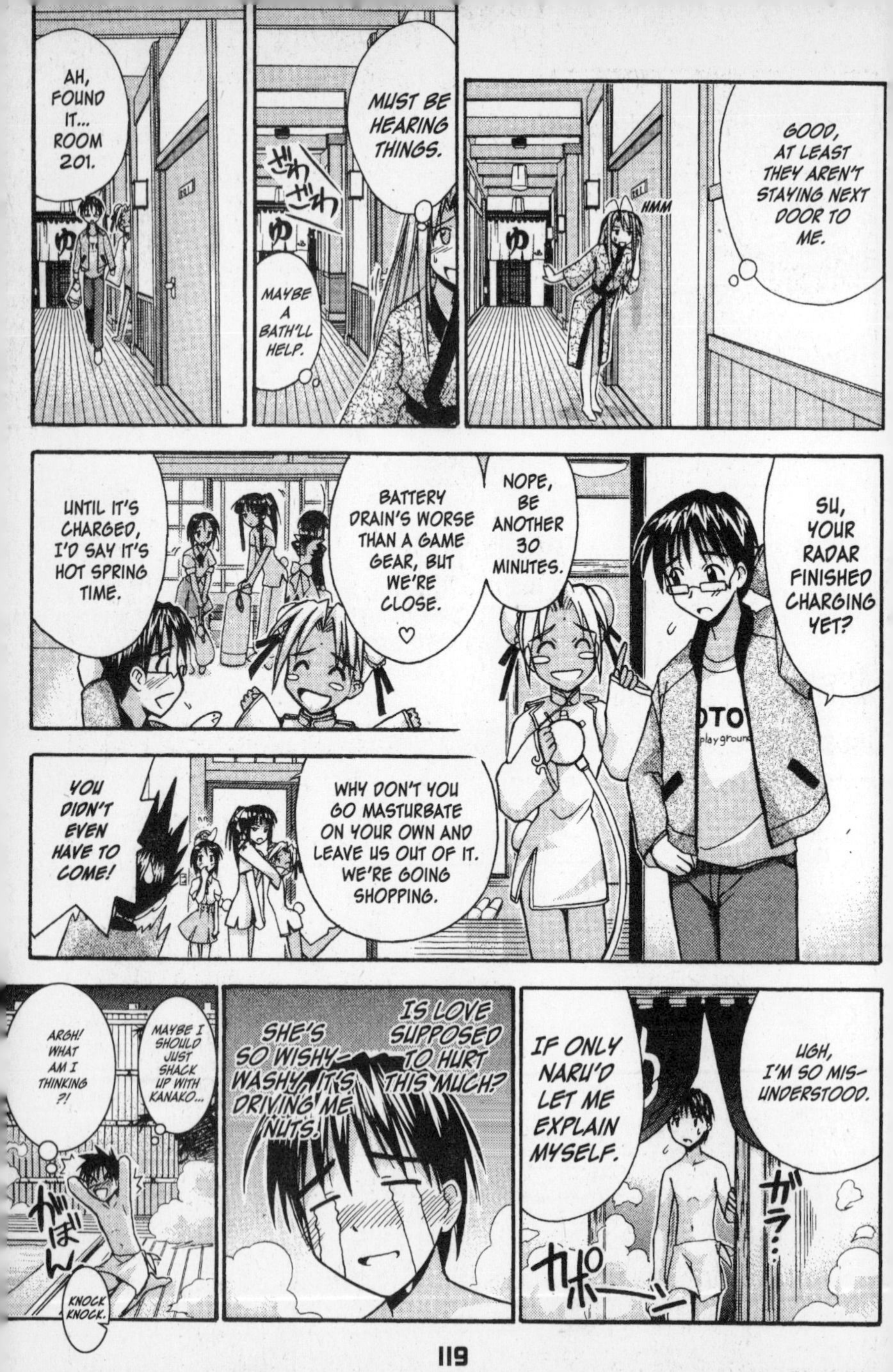
GOOD, AT LEAST THEY AREN'T STAYING NEXT DOOR TO ME.
HMM
MUST BE HEARING THINGS.
ざわざわ
MAYBE A BATH'LL HELP.
AH, FOUND IT... ROOM 201.
SU, YOUR RADAR FINISHED CHARGING YET?
NOPE, BE ANOTHER 30 MINUTES.
BATTERY DRAIN'S WORSE THAN A GAME GEAR, BUT WE'RE CLOSE. ♡
UNTIL IT'S CHARGED, I'D SAY IT'S HOT SPRING TIME.
WHY DON'T YOU GO MASTURBATE ON YOUR OWN AND LEAVE US OUT OF IT. WE'RE GOING SHOPPING.
YOU DIDN'T EVEN HAVE TO COME!
UGH, I'M SO MIS-UNDERSTOOD.
IF ONLY NARU'D LET ME EXPLAIN MYSELF.
ガラ…
カポーン
IS LOVE SUPPOSED TO HURT THIS MUCH?
SHE'S SO WISHY-WASHY, IT'S DRIVING ME NUTS.
MAYBE I SHOULD JUST SHACK UP WITH KANAKO...
ARGH! WHAT AM I THINKING ?!
がぼん
KNOCK KNOCK.

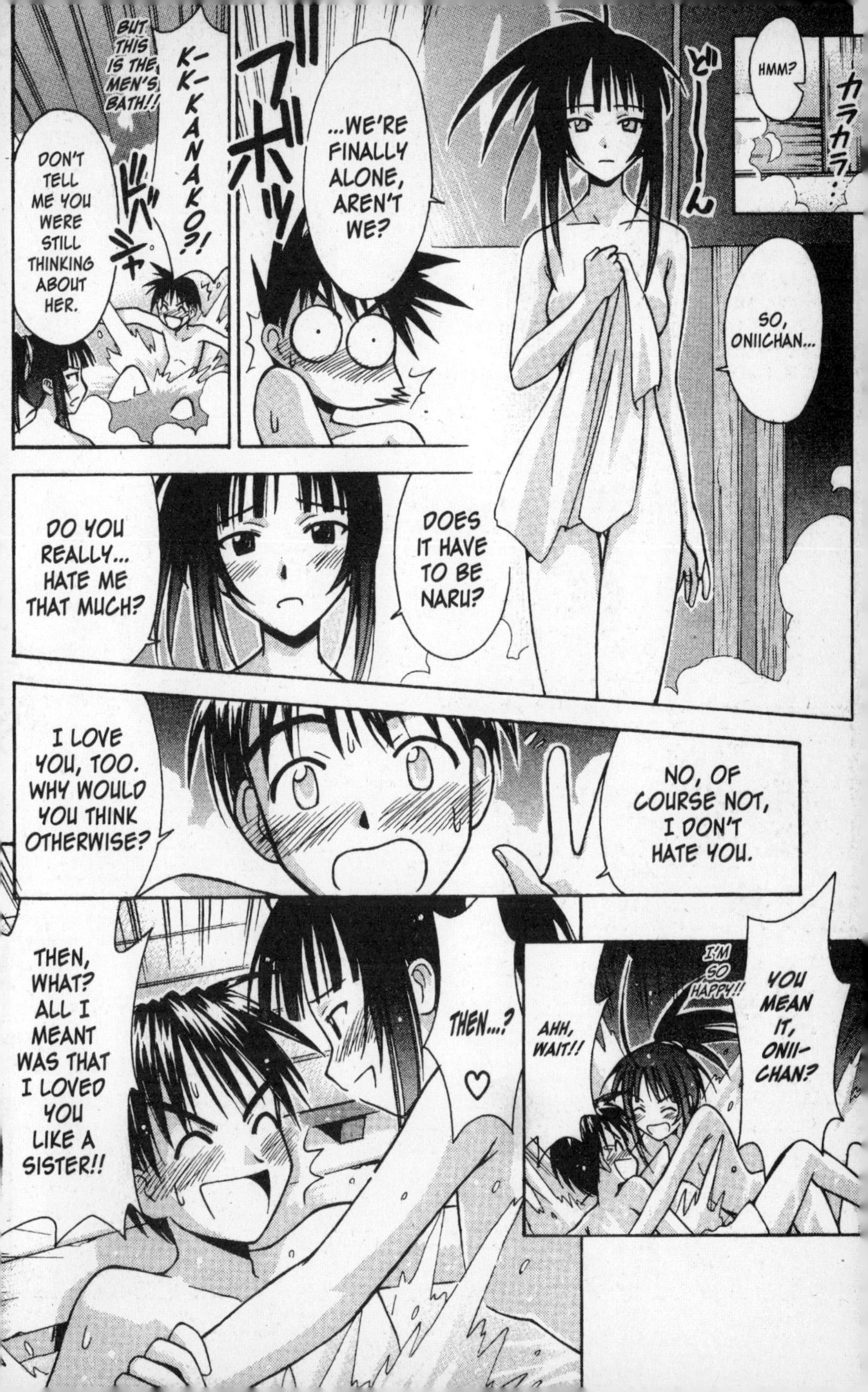
HMM?
カラカラ…
どーーん
...WE'RE FINALLY ALONE, AREN'T WE?
ブボッ
K-K-KANAKO?!
BUT THIS IS THE MEN'S BATH!!
DON'T TELL ME YOU WERE STILL THINKING ABOUT HER.
ドバ
ジャ
SO, ONIICHAN...
DOES IT HAVE TO BE NARU?
DO YOU REALLY... HATE ME THAT MUCH?
NO, OF COURSE NOT, I DON'T HATE YOU.
I LOVE YOU, TOO. WHY WOULD YOU THINK OTHERWISE?
YOU MEAN IT, ONII-CHAN?
I'M SO HAPPY!!
AHH, WAIT!!
THEN...?
THEN, WHAT? ALL I MEANT WAS THAT I LOVED YOU LIKE A SISTER!!

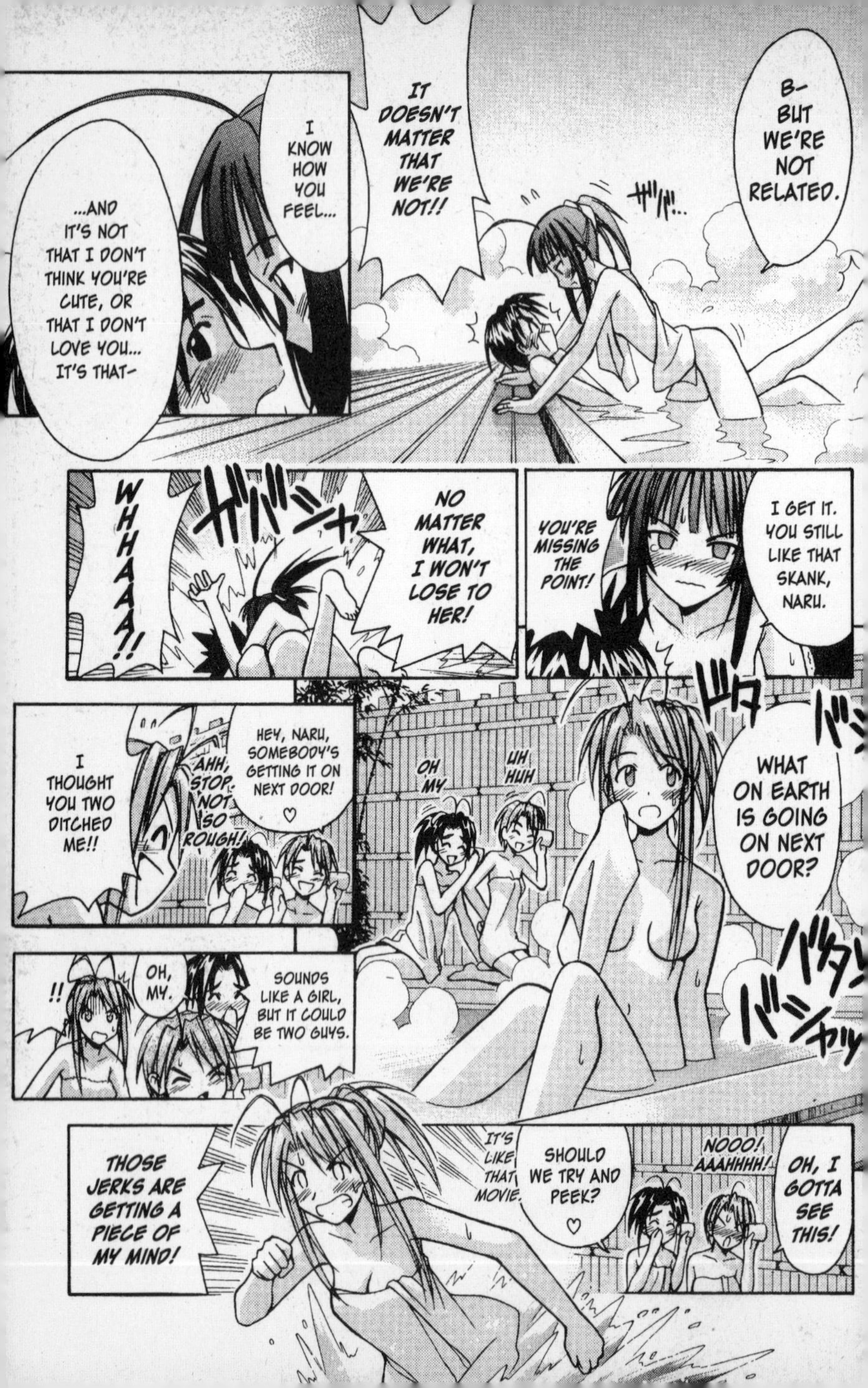
B-BUT WE'RE NOT RELATED.
IT DOESN'T MATTER THAT WE'RE NOT!!
I KNOW HOW YOU FEEL...
...AND IT'S NOT THAT I DON'T THINK YOU'RE CUTE, OR THAT I DON'T LOVE YOU... IT'S THAT-
I GET IT. YOU STILL LIKE THAT SKANK, NARU.
YOU'RE MISSING THE POINT!
NO MATTER WHAT, I WON'T LOSE TO HER!
WHHAAAA!!
WHAT ON EARTH IS GOING ON NEXT DOOR?
UH HUH
OH MY
HEY, NARU, SOMEBODY'S GETTING IT ON NEXT DOOR! ♡
AHH, STOP. NOT SO ROUGH!
I THOUGHT YOU TWO DITCHED ME!!
SOUNDS LIKE A GIRL, BUT IT COULD BE TWO GUYS.
OH, MY.
!!
OH, I GOTTA SEE THIS!
NOOO! AAAHHHH!
SHOULD WE TRY AND PEEK? ♡
IT'S LIKE THAT MOVIE.
THOSE JERKS ARE GETTING A PIECE OF MY MIND!

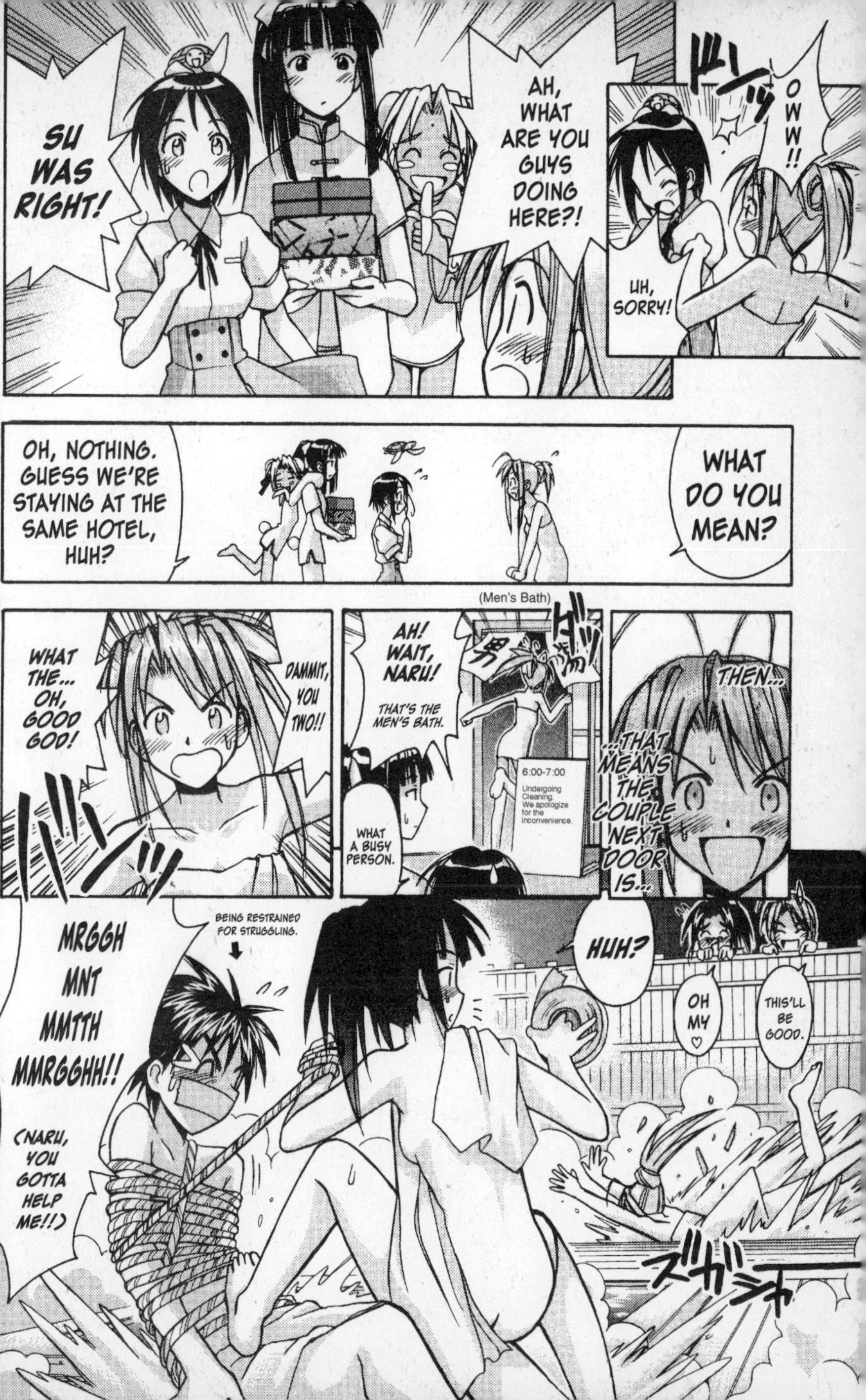
OWW!!
UH, SORRY!
AH, WHAT ARE YOU GUYS DOING HERE?!
SU WAS RIGHT!
WHAT DO YOU MEAN?
OH, NOTHING. GUESS WE'RE STAYING AT THE SAME HOTEL, HUH?
THEN...
...THAT MEANS THE COUPLE NEXT DOOR IS...
(Men's Bath)
AH! WAIT, NARU!
THAT'S THE MEN'S BATH.
6:00-7:00 Undergoing Cleaning. We apologize for the inconvenience.
WHAT A BUSY PERSON.
DAMMIT, YOU TWO!!
WHAT THE... OH, GOOD GOD!
HUH?
THIS'LL BE GOOD.
OH MY ♡
BEING RESTRAINED FOR STRUGGLING.
MRGGH MNT MMTTH MMRGGHH!!
(NARU, YOU GOTTA HELP ME!!)

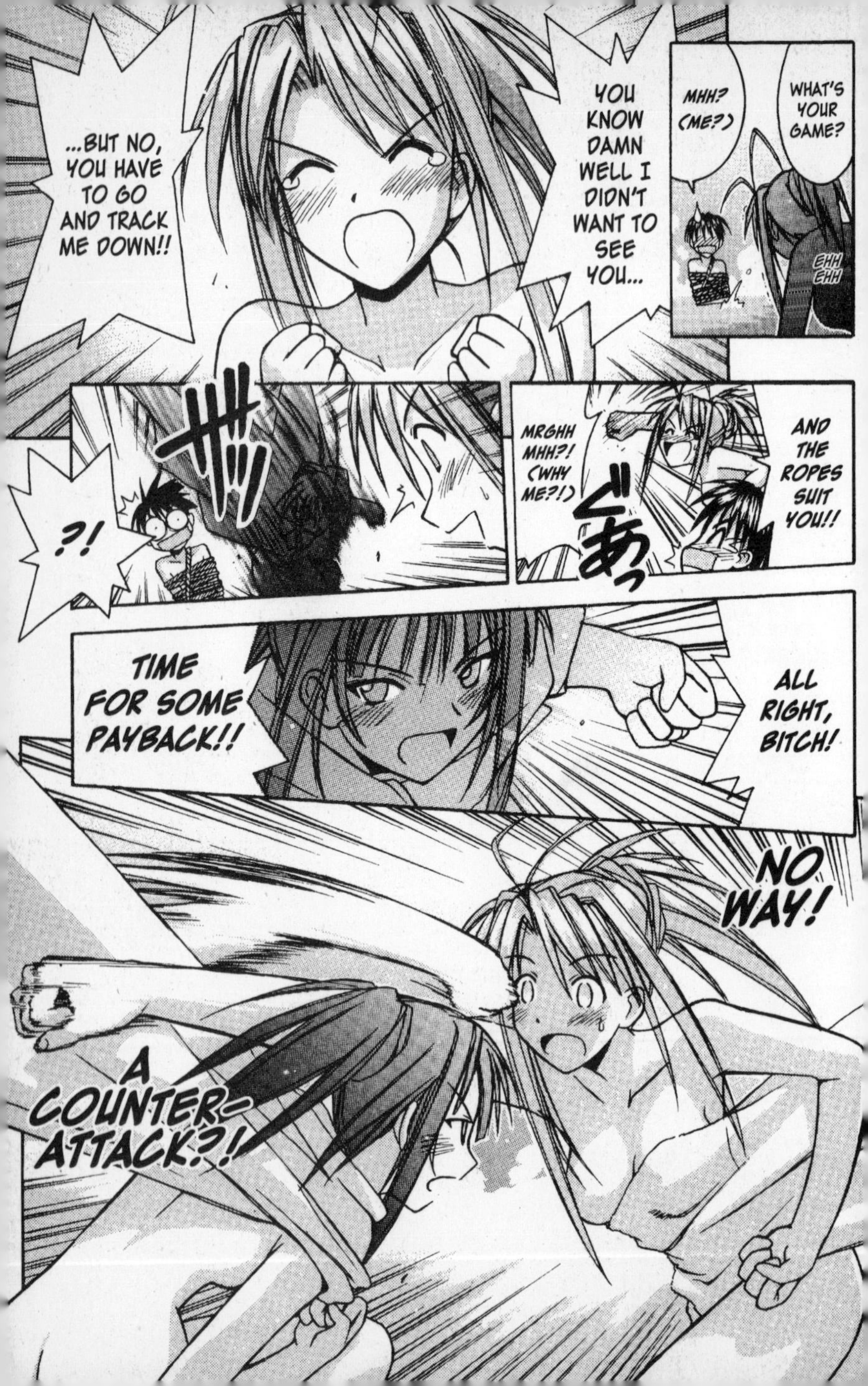
WHAT'S YOUR GAME?
MHH? (ME?)
EHH EHH
YOU KNOW DAMN WELL I DIDN'T WANT TO SEE YOU...
...BUT NO, YOU HAVE TO GO AND TRACK ME DOWN!!
AND THE ROPES SUIT YOU!!
MRGHH MHH?! (WHY ME?!)
ぐあっ
?!
ALL RIGHT, BITCH!
TIME FOR SOME PAYBACK!!
NO WAY!
A COUNTER-ATTACK?!

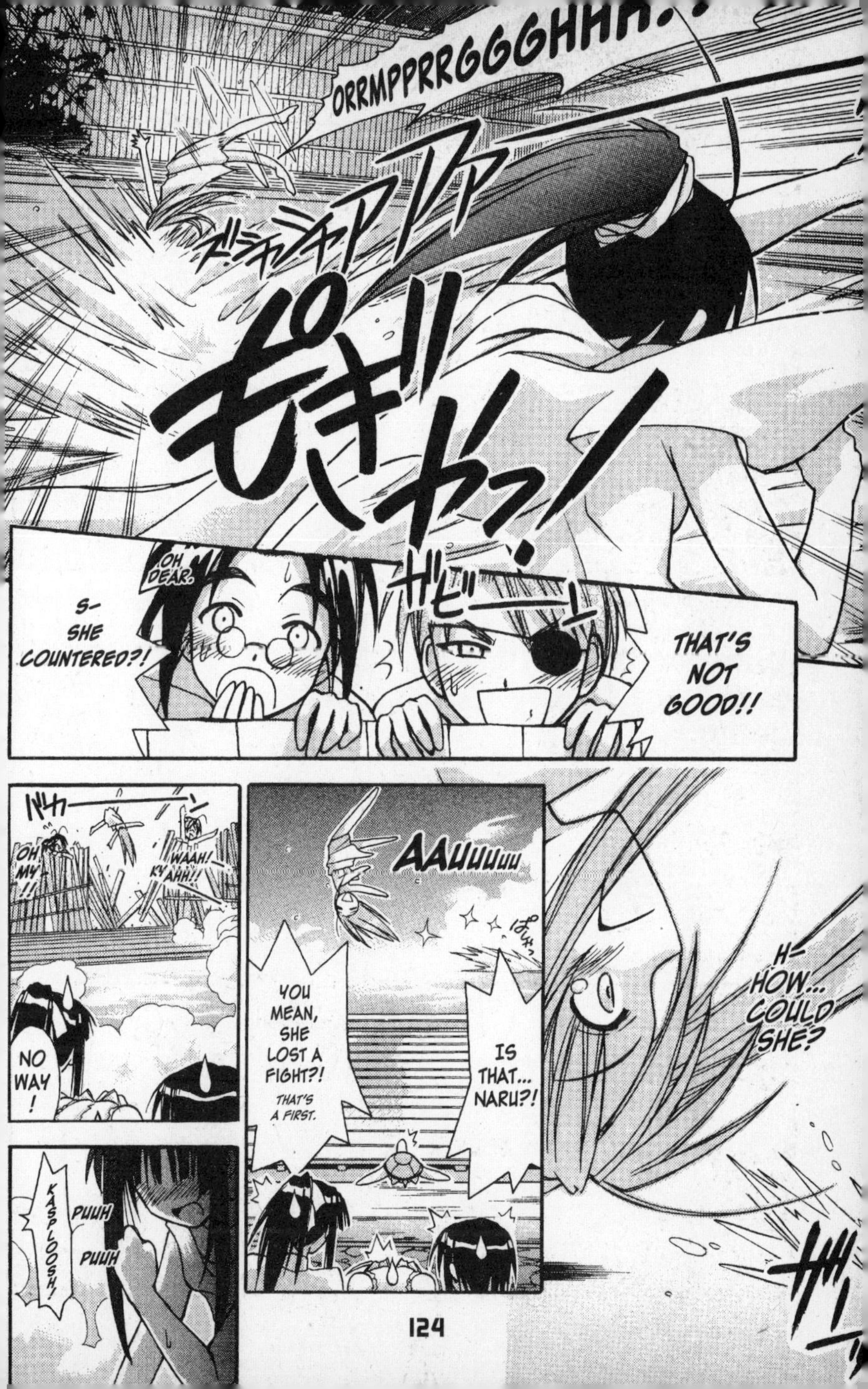
ORRMPPRRGGGGHHH...
ズシャアア
もぎゃっ!
ガビーン
THAT'S NOT GOOD!!
OH DEAR.
S-SHE COUNTERED?!
H-HOW... COULD SHE?
AAUUUUU
IS THAT... NARU?!
YOU MEAN, SHE LOST A FIGHT?!
THAT'S A FIRST.
WAAH! KYAHH!!
OH MY!!
NO WAY!
PUUH
PUUH
KASPLOOSH!

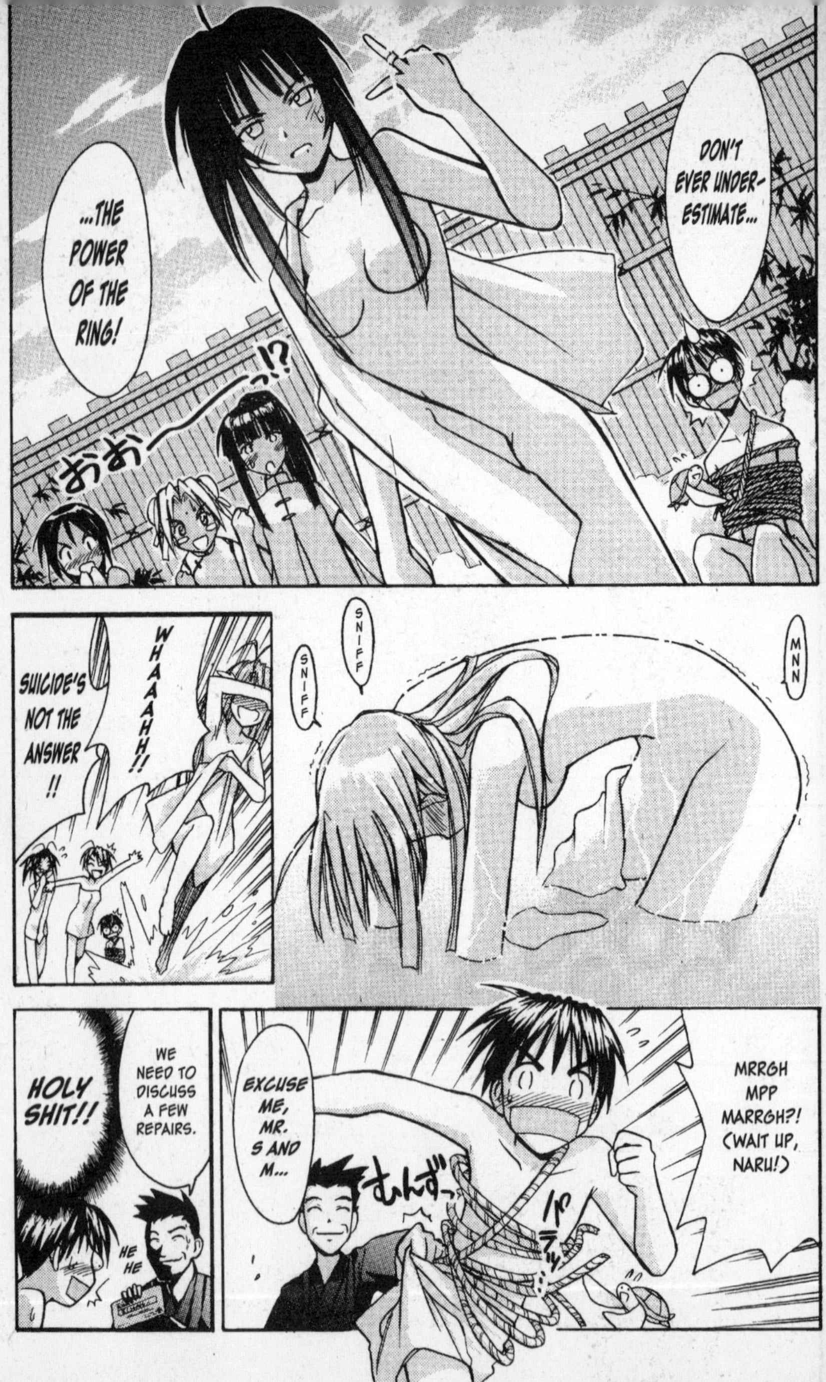
DON'T EVER UNDER-ESTIMATE...
...THE POWER OF THE RING!
おおーっ!?
MNN
SNIFF
SNIFF
WHAAAAHH!!
SUICIDE'S NOT THE ANSWER!!
MRRGH MPP MARRGH?! (WAIT UP, NARU!)
パラッ
むんずっ
EXCUSE ME, MR. S AND M...
WE NEED TO DISCUSS A FEW REPAIRS.
HOLY SHIT!!
HE HE

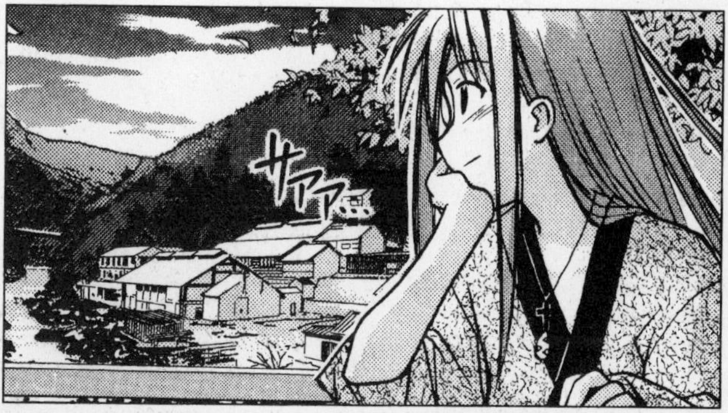
サァァ

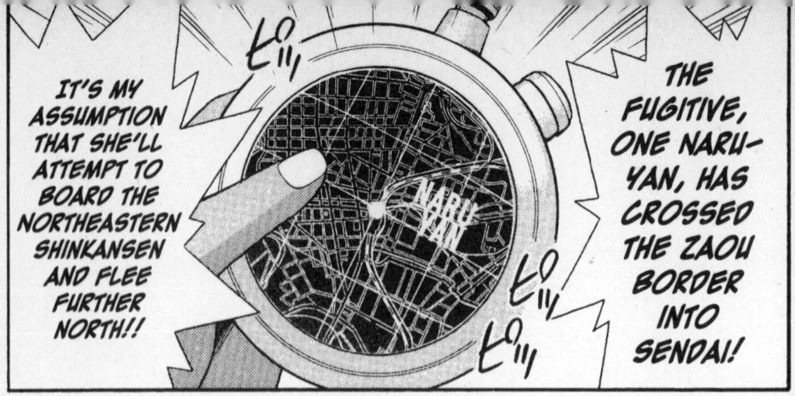
THE FUGITIVE, ONE NARU-YAN, HAS CROSSED THE ZAOU BORDER INTO SENDAI!
ピッ
ピッ
ピッ
NARU YAN
IT'S MY ASSUMPTION THAT SHE'LL ATTEMPT TO BOARD THE NORTHEASTERN SHINKANSEN AND FLEE FURTHER NORTH!!

Love Hina

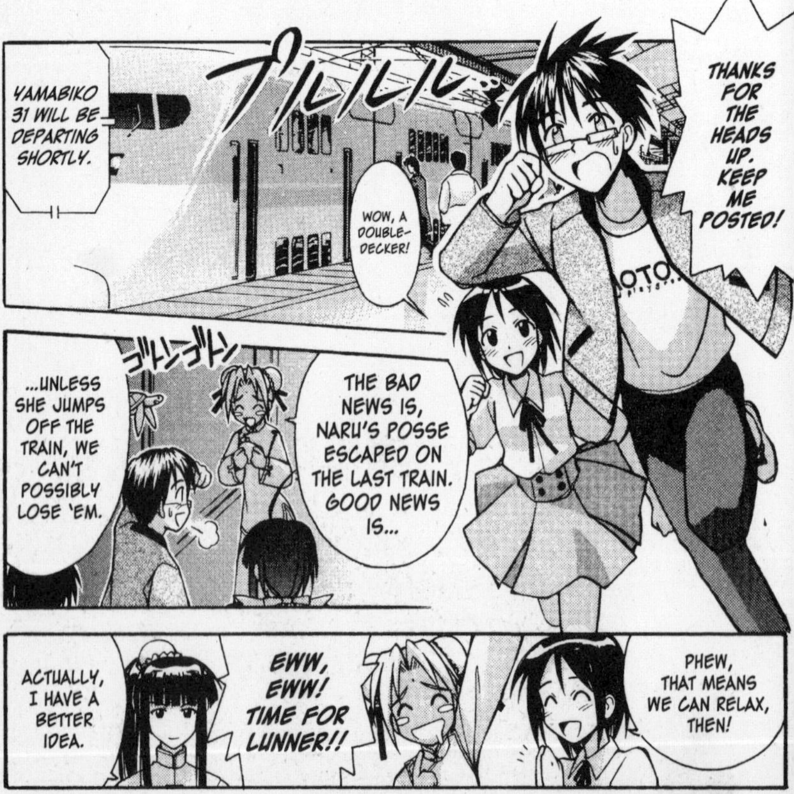
THANKS FOR THE HEADS UP. KEEP ME POSTED!
WOW, A DOUBLE-DECKER!
プルルル
YAMABIKO 31 WILL BE DEPARTING SHORTLY.
THE BAD NEWS IS, NARU'S POSSE ESCAPED ON THE LAST TRAIN. GOOD NEWS IS...
ゴトンゴトン
...UNLESS SHE JUMPS OFF THE TRAIN, WE CAN'T POSSIBLY LOSE 'EM.
PHEW, THAT MEANS WE CAN RELAX, THEN!
EWW, EWW! TIME FOR LUNNER!!
ACTUALLY, I HAVE A BETTER IDEA.

HINATA..103 Escape En Route With My Stalker

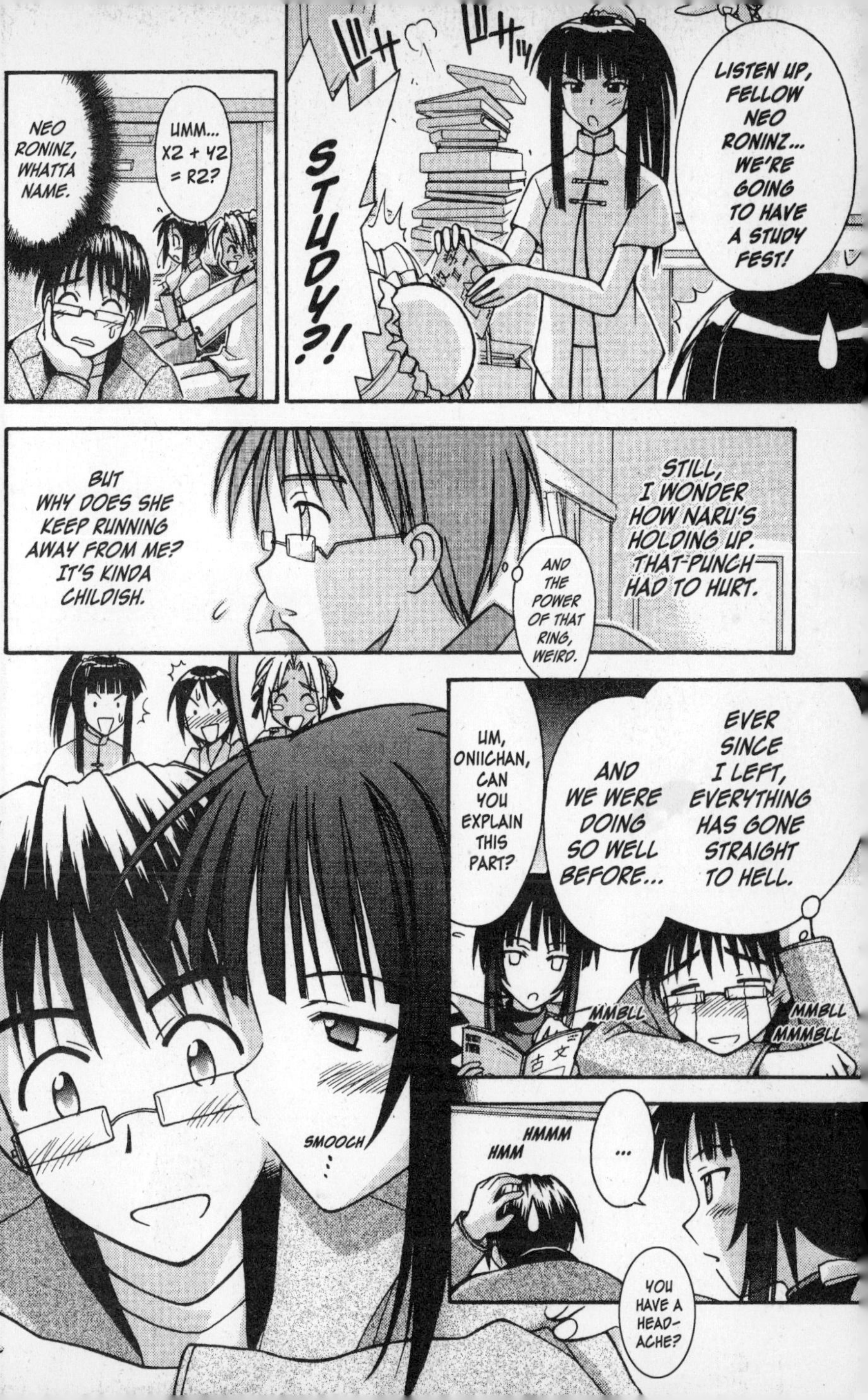
LISTEN UP, FELLOW NEO RONINZ... WE'RE GOING TO HAVE A STUDY FEST!
STUDY?!
UMM... X2 + Y2 = R2?
NEO RONINZ, WHATTA NAME.
STILL, I WONDER HOW NARU'S HOLDING UP. THAT PUNCH HAD TO HURT.
AND THE POWER OF THAT RING, WEIRD.
BUT WHY DOES SHE KEEP RUNNING AWAY FROM ME? IT'S KINDA CHILDISH.
EVER SINCE I LEFT, EVERYTHING HAS GONE STRAIGHT TO HELL.
AND WE WERE DOING SO WELL BEFORE...
UM, ONIICHAN, CAN YOU EXPLAIN THIS PART?
MMBLL
MMBLL MMMBLL
古文
...
HMMM HMM
YOU HAVE A HEADACHE?
SMOOCH

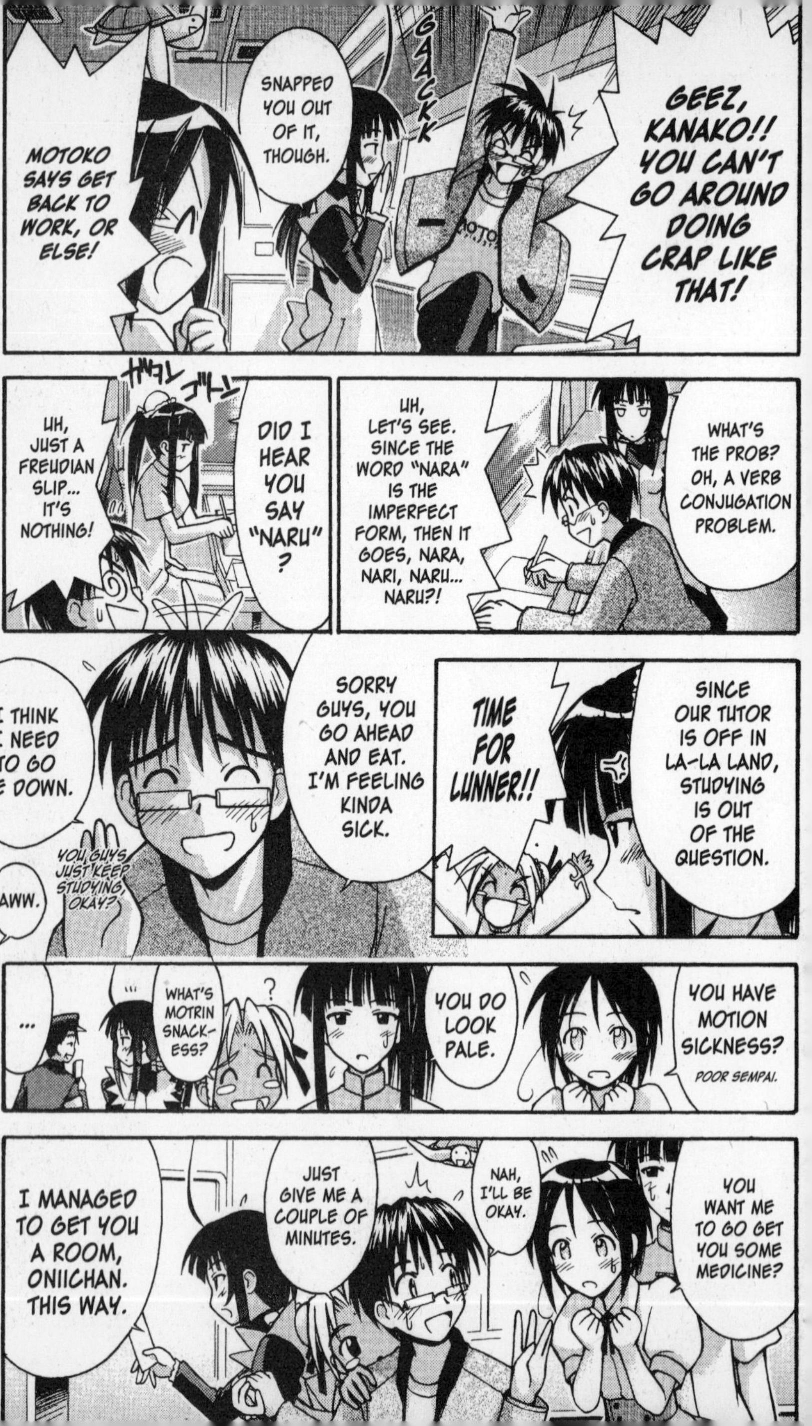

GEEZ, KANAKO!! YOU CAN'T GO AROUND DOING CRAP LIKE THAT!
GAACKK
SNAPPED YOU OUT OF IT, THOUGH.
MOTOKO SAYS GET BACK TO WORK, OR ELSE!
WHAT'S THE PROB? OH, A VERB CONJUGATION PROBLEM.
UH, LET'S SEE. SINCE THE WORD "NARA" IS THE IMPERFECT FORM, THEN IT GOES, NARA, NARI, NARU... NARU?!
ガタン ゴトン
DID I HEAR YOU SAY "NARU"?
UH, JUST A FREUDIAN SLIP... IT'S NOTHING!
SINCE OUR TUTOR IS OFF IN LA-LA LAND, STUDYING IS OUT OF THE QUESTION.
TIME FOR LUNNER!!
SORRY GUYS, YOU GO AHEAD AND EAT. I'M FEELING KINDA SICK.
I THINK I NEED TO GO LIE DOWN.
YOU GUYS JUST KEEP STUDYING, OKAY?
AWW.
YOU HAVE MOTION SICKNESS?
POOR SEMPAI.
YOU DO LOOK PALE.
?
WHAT'S MOTRIN SNACK-ESS?
...
...
YOU WANT ME TO GO GET YOU SOME MEDICINE?
NAH, I'LL BE OKAY.
JUST GIVE ME A COUPLE OF MINUTES.
I MANAGED TO GET YOU A ROOM, ONIICHAN. THIS WAY.

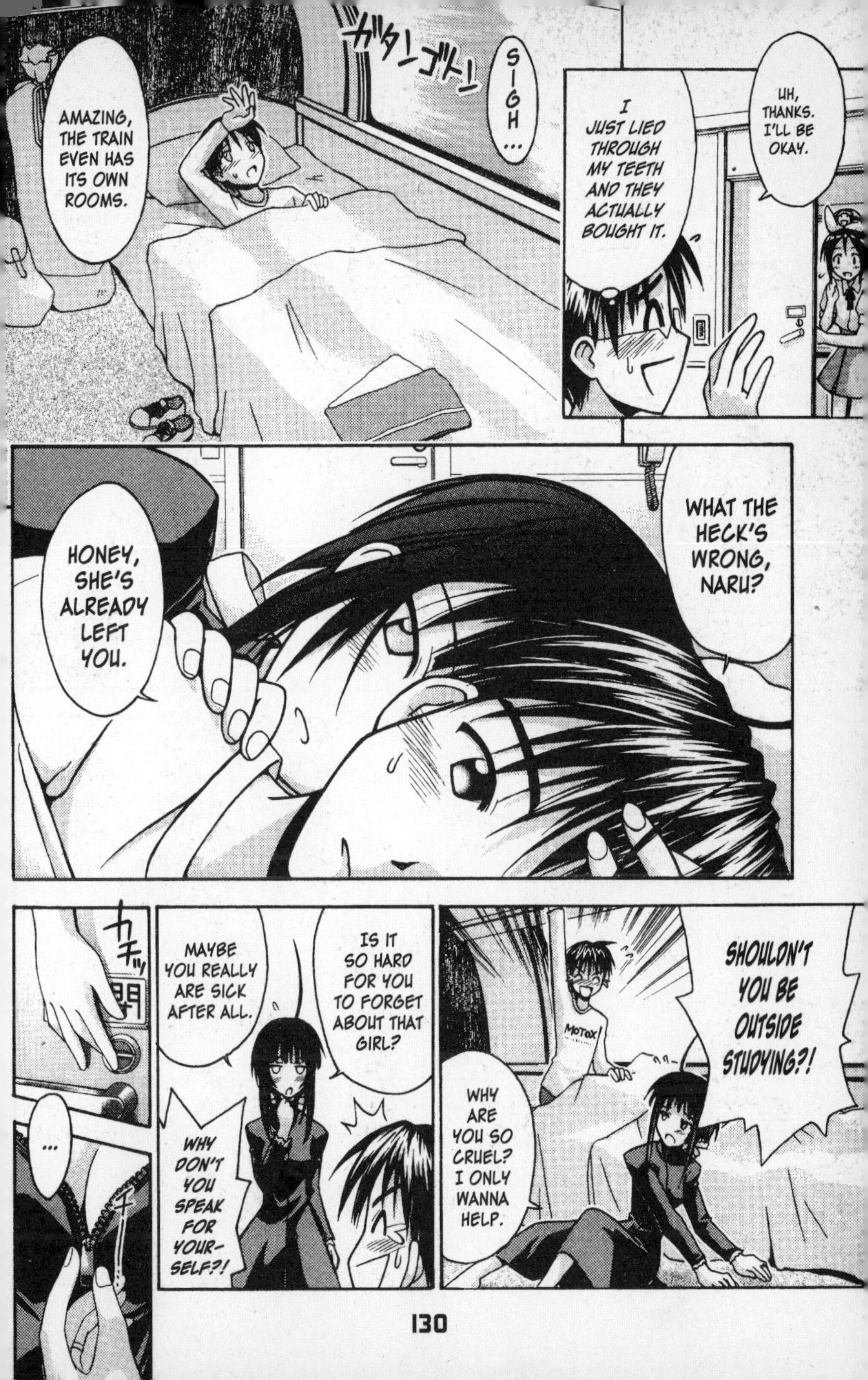
UH, THANKS. I'LL BE OKAY.
I JUST LIED THROUGH MY TEETH AND THEY ACTUALLY BOUGHT IT.
SIGH...
AMAZING, THE TRAIN EVEN HAS ITS OWN ROOMS.
WHAT THE HECK'S WRONG, NARU?
HONEY, SHE'S ALREADY LEFT YOU.
SHOULDN'T YOU BE OUTSIDE STUDYING?!
WHY ARE YOU SO CRUEL? I ONLY WANNA HELP.
IS IT SO HARD FOR YOU TO FORGET ABOUT THAT GIRL?
MAYBE YOU REALLY ARE SICK AFTER ALL.
WHY DON'T YOU SPEAK FOR YOUR-SELF?!
開
...

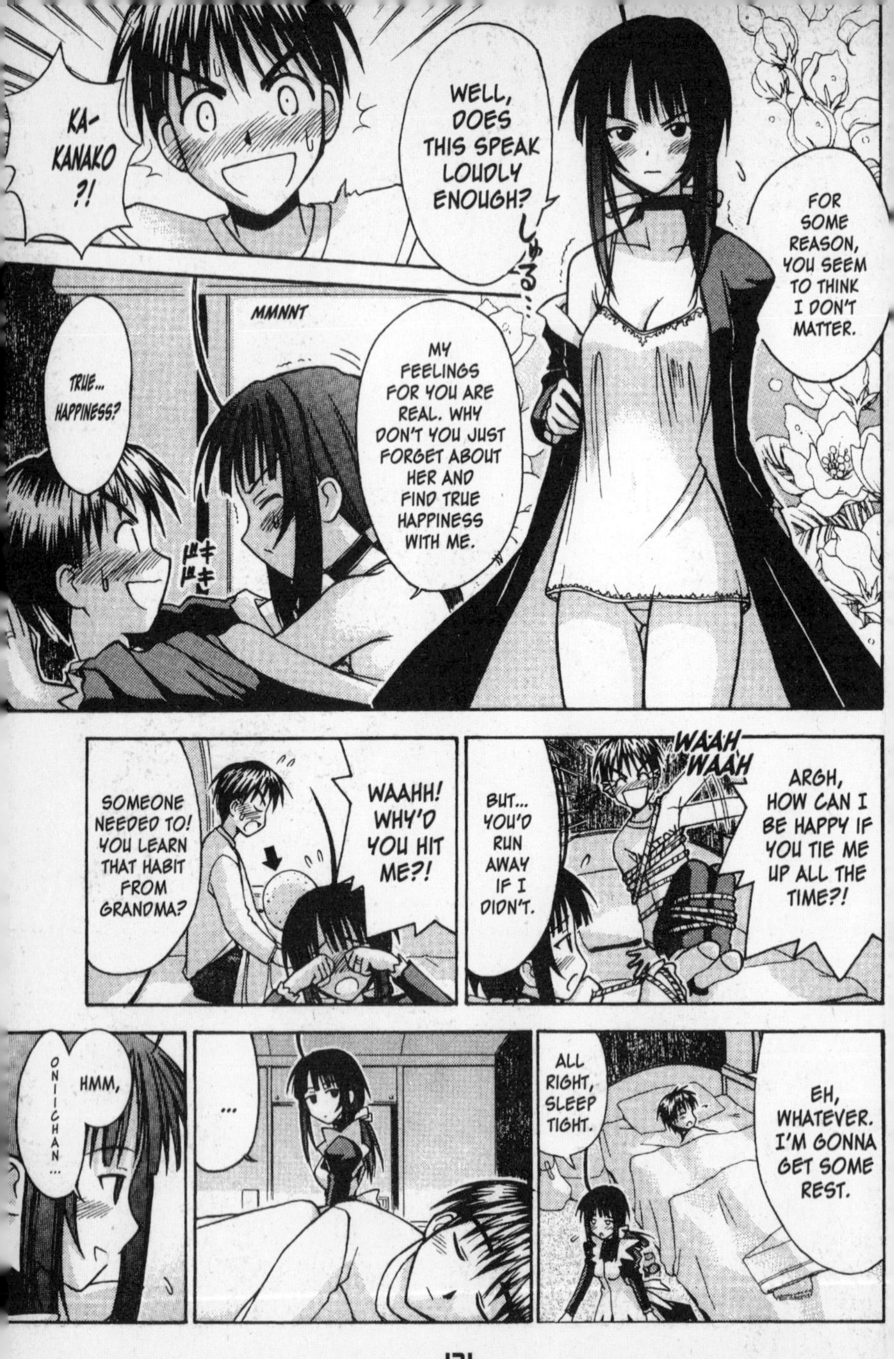
FOR SOME REASON, YOU SEEM TO THINK I DON'T MATTER.
WELL, DOES THIS SPEAK LOUDLY ENOUGH?
しゅる…
KA-KANAKO?!
MY FEELINGS FOR YOU ARE REAL. WHY DON'T YOU JUST FORGET ABOUT HER AND FIND TRUE HAPPINESS WITH ME.
MMNNT
ドキドキ
TRUE... HAPPINESS?
ARGH, HOW CAN I BE HAPPY IF YOU TIE ME UP ALL THE TIME?!
WAAH WAAH
BUT... YOU'D RUN AWAY IF I DIDN'T.
WAAHH! WHY'D YOU HIT ME?!
SOMEONE NEEDED TO! YOU LEARN THAT HABIT FROM GRANDMA?
EH, WHATEVER. I'M GONNA GET SOME REST.
ALL RIGHT, SLEEP TIGHT.
...
HMM,
ONIICHAN...

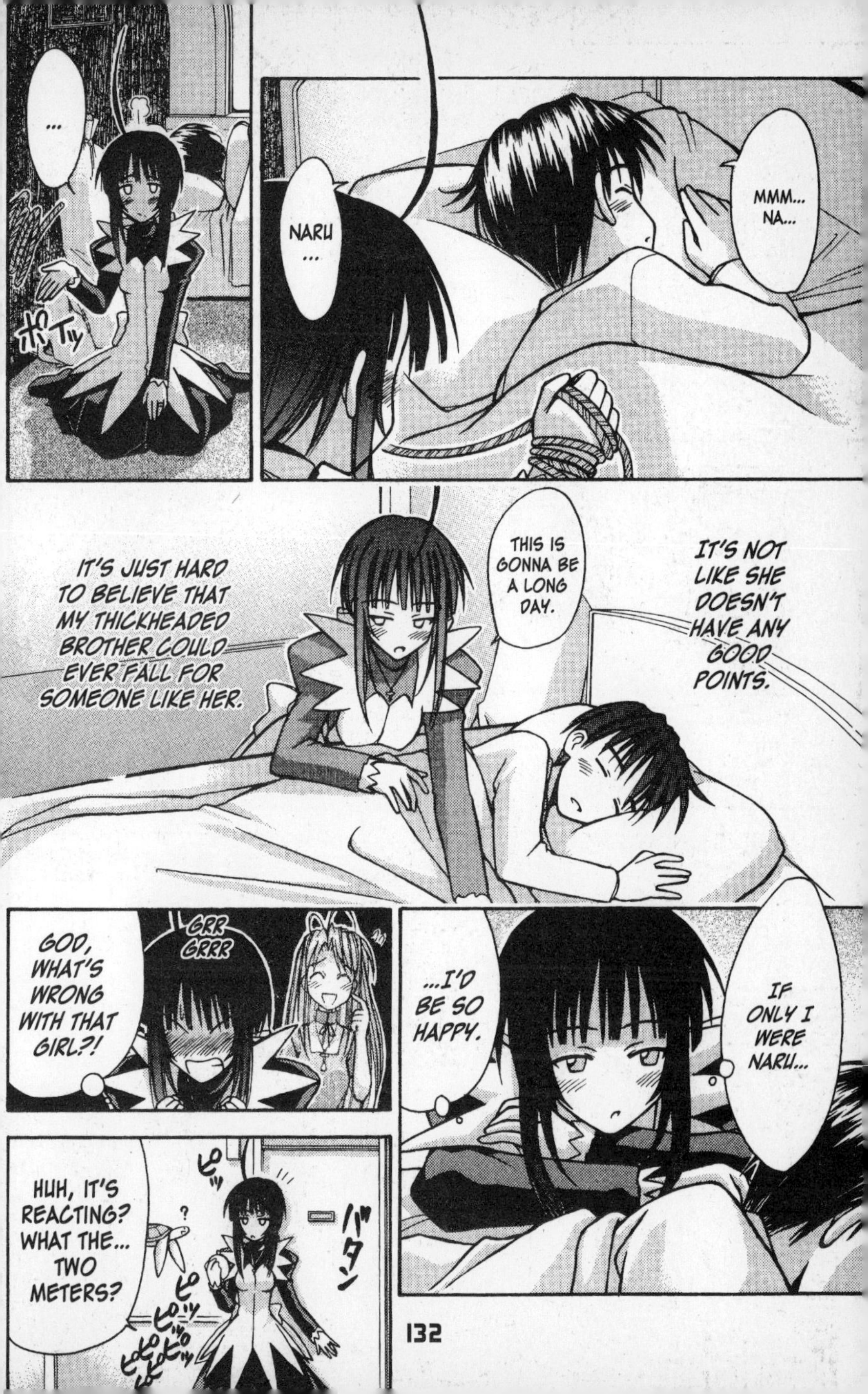
MMM... NA...
NARU ...
...
IT'S NOT LIKE SHE DOESN'T HAVE ANY GOOD POINTS.
THIS IS GONNA BE A LONG DAY.
IT'S JUST HARD TO BELIEVE THAT MY THICKHEADED BROTHER COULD EVER FALL FOR SOMEONE LIKE HER.
IF ONLY I WERE NARU...
...I'D BE SO HAPPY.
GRR GRRR
GOD, WHAT'S WRONG WITH THAT GIRL?!
ピッ
バタン
HUH, IT'S REACTING? WHAT THE... TWO METERS?

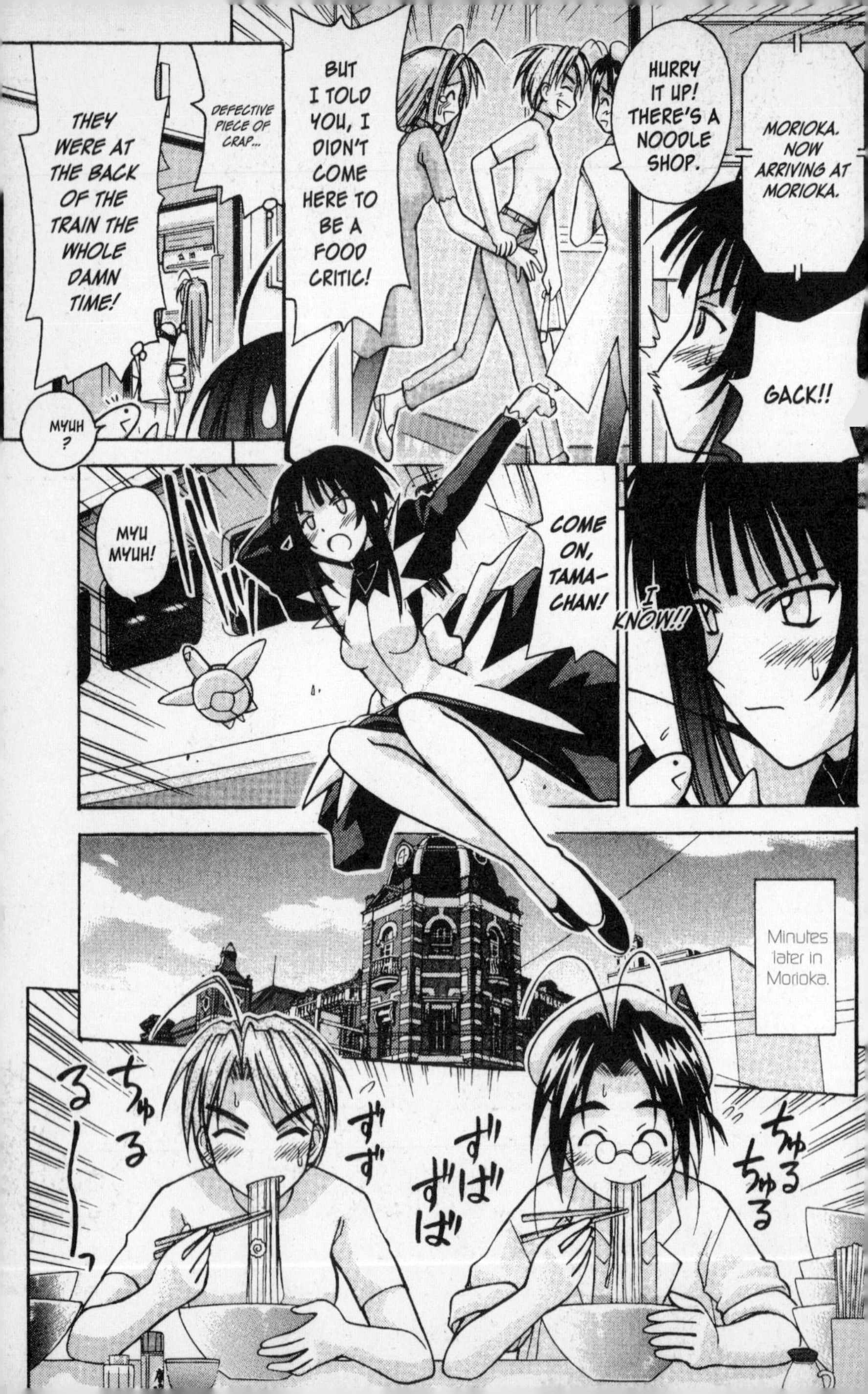
MORIOKA. NOW ARRIVING AT MORIOKA.
GACK!!
HURRY IT UP! THERE'S A NOODLE SHOP.
BUT I TOLD YOU, I DIDN'T COME HERE TO BE A FOOD CRITIC!
DEFECTIVE PIECE OF CRAP...
THEY WERE AT THE BACK OF THE TRAIN THE WHOLE DAMN TIME!
MYUH ?
I KNOW!!
COME ON, TAMA-CHAN!
MYU MYUH!
Minutes later in Morioka.
ちゅるちゅる
ずばずば
ずず
ちゅる
るーっ

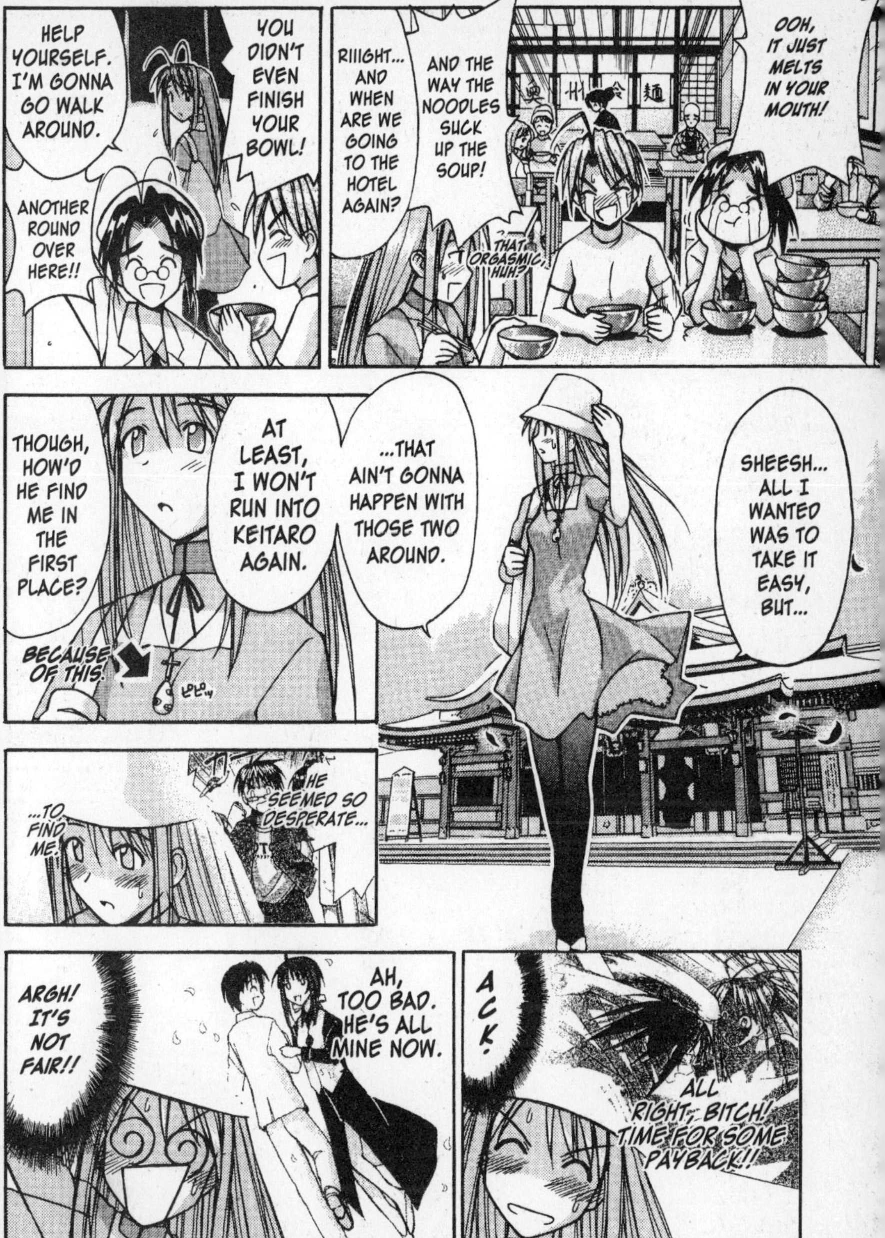
OOH, IT JUST MELTS IN YOUR MOUTH!
AND THE WAY THE NOODLES SUCK UP THE SOUP!
THAT ORGASMIC, HUH?
RIIIGHT... AND WHEN ARE WE GOING TO THE HOTEL AGAIN?
YOU DIDN'T EVEN FINISH YOUR BOWL!
HELP YOURSELF. I'M GONNA GO WALK AROUND.
ANOTHER ROUND OVER HERE!!
SHEESH... ALL I WANTED WAS TO TAKE IT EASY, BUT...
AT LEAST, I WON'T RUN INTO KEITARO AGAIN.
...THAT AIN'T GONNA HAPPEN WITH THOSE TWO AROUND.
THOUGH, HOW'D HE FIND ME IN THE FIRST PLACE?
BECAUSE OF THIS.
ピピッ
HE SEEMED SO DESPERATE...
...TO FIND ME.
ACK.
ALL RIGHT, BITCH! TIME FOR SOME PAYBACK!!
AH, TOO BAD. HE'S ALL MINE NOW.
ARGH! IT'S NOT FAIR!!

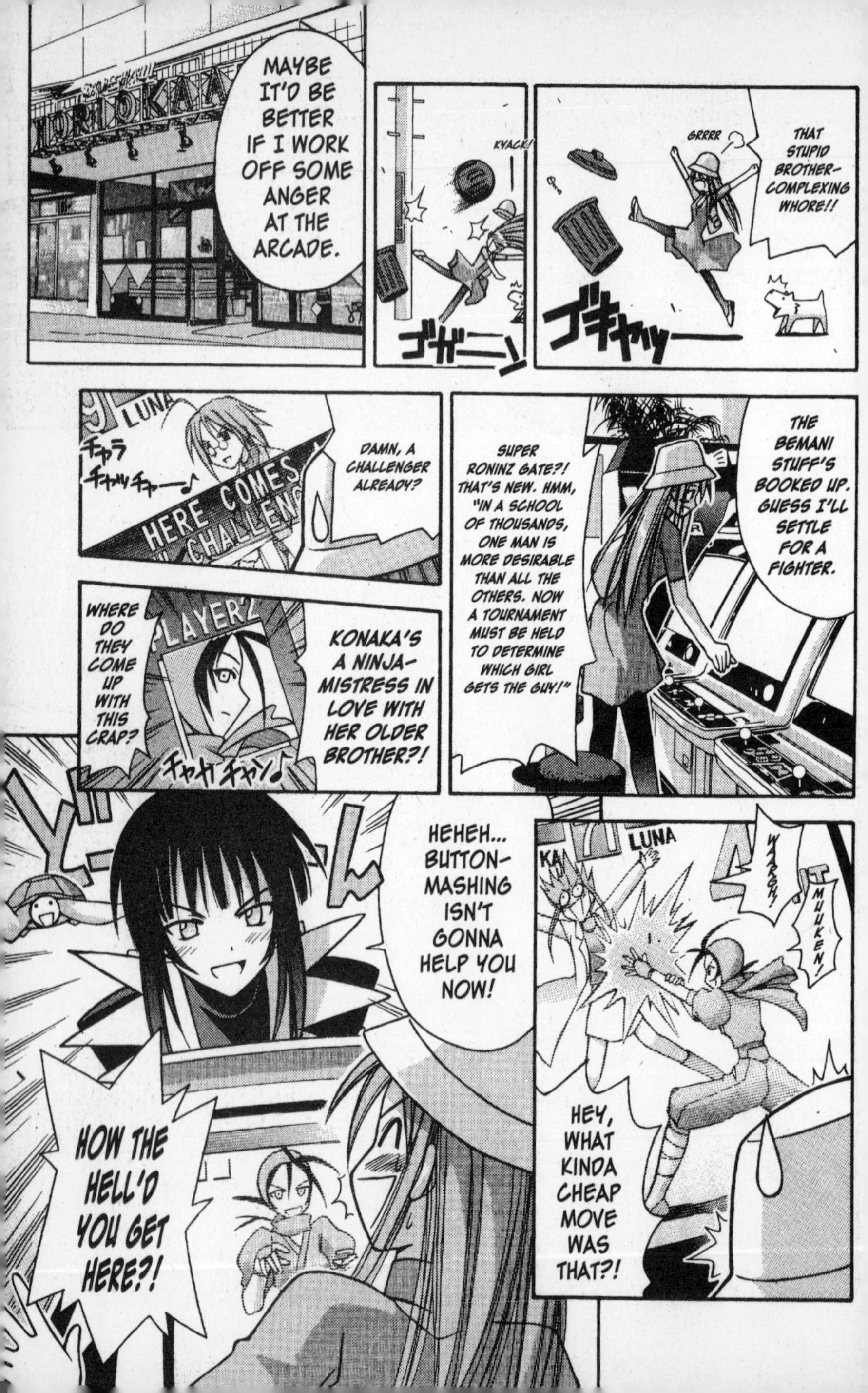
GRRRR
THAT STUPID BROTHER-COMPLEXING WHORE!!
ゴキャッー
KYACK!
ゴガーン
MAYBE IT'D BE BETTER IF I WORK OFF SOME ANGER AT THE ARCADE.
THE BEMANI STUFF'S BOOKED UP. GUESS I'LL SETTLE FOR A FIGHTER.
SUPER RONINZ GATE?! THAT'S NEW. HMM, "IN A SCHOOL OF THOUSANDS, ONE MAN IS MORE DESIRABLE THAN ALL THE OTHERS. NOW A TOURNAMENT MUST BE HELD TO DETERMINE WHICH GIRL GETS THE GUY!"
DAMN, A CHALLENGER ALREADY?
LUNA
チャラチャッチャー♪
HERE COMES
KONAKA'S A NINJA-MISTRESS IN LOVE WITH HER OLDER BROTHER?!
WHERE DO THEY COME UP WITH THIS CRAP?
PLAYER2
チャカチャン♪
LUNA
KA
WAAAGH!
MUUKEN!
HEY, WHAT KINDA CHEAP MOVE WAS THAT?!
HEHEH... BUTTON-MASHING ISN'T GONNA HELP YOU NOW!
HOW THE HELL'D YOU GET HERE?!

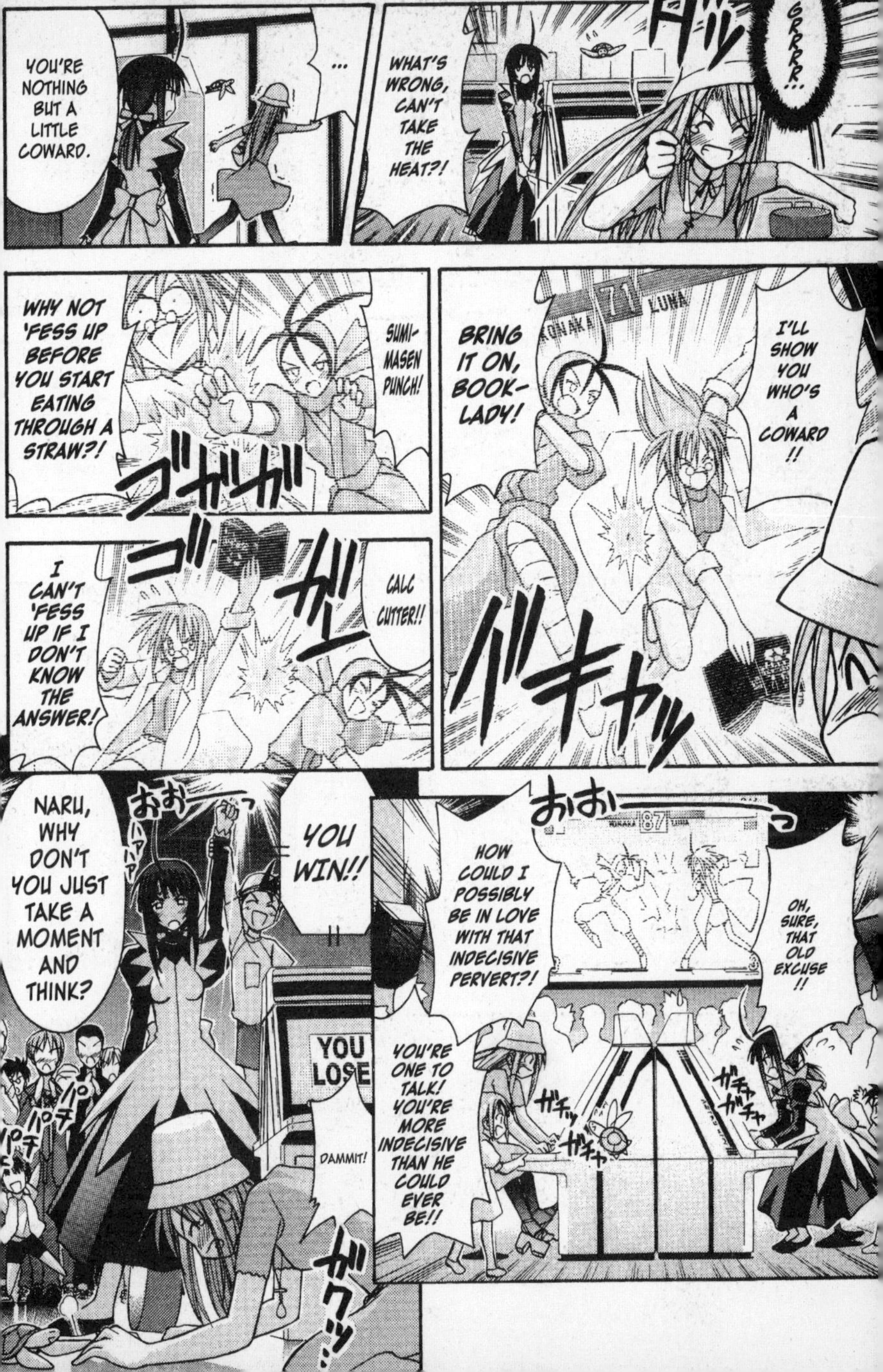
GRRRR!!
ダッ
WHAT'S WRONG, CAN'T TAKE THE HEAT?!
...
YOU'RE NOTHING BUT A LITTLE COWARD.
KONAKA 71 LUNA
I'LL SHOW YOU WHO'S A COWARD!!
BRING IT ON, BOOK-LADY!
ガチャッ
SUMI-MASEN PUNCH!
WHY NOT 'FESS UP BEFORE YOU START EATING THROUGH A STRAW?!
ゴガゴガ
CALC CUTTER!!
I CAN'T 'FESS UP IF I DON'T KNOW THE ANSWER!
おおーっ
OH, SURE, THAT OLD EXCUSE!!
HOW COULD I POSSIBLY BE IN LOVE WITH THAT INDECISIVE PERVERT?!
ガチャガチャ
ガチッ
ガチャ
YOU'RE ONE TO TALK! YOU'RE MORE INDECISIVE THAN HE COULD EVER BE!!
YOU WIN!!
おおーっ
ハァハァ
NARU, WHY DON'T YOU JUST TAKE A MOMENT AND THINK?
YOU LOSE
DAMMIT!
パチパチパチ
ガクッ

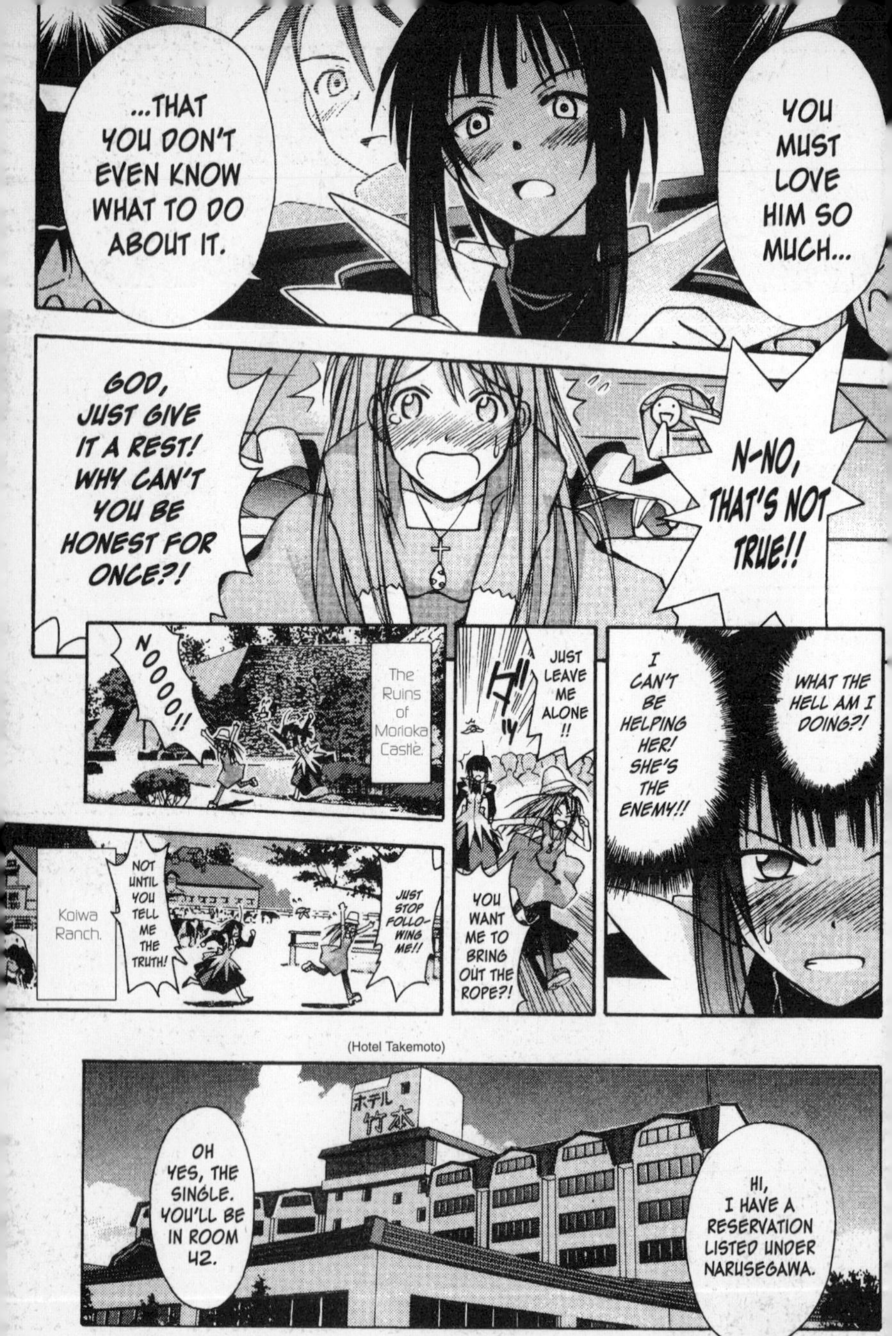
YOU MUST LOVE HIM SO MUCH...
...THAT YOU DON'T EVEN KNOW WHAT TO DO ABOUT IT.
N-NO, THAT'S NOT TRUE!!
GOD, JUST GIVE IT A REST! WHY CAN'T YOU BE HONEST FOR ONCE?!
WHAT THE HELL AM I DOING?!
I CAN'T BE HELPING HER! SHE'S THE ENEMY!!
JUST LEAVE ME ALONE!!
YOU WANT ME TO BRING OUT THE ROPE?!
The Ruins of Morioka Castle.
NOOOOO!!
JUST STOP FOLLOWING ME!!
NOT UNTIL YOU TELL ME THE TRUTH!
Koiwa Ranch.
(Hotel Takemoto)
ホテル竹本
HI, I HAVE A RESERVATION LISTED UNDER NARUSEGAWA.
OH YES, THE SINGLE. YOU'LL BE IN ROOM 42.

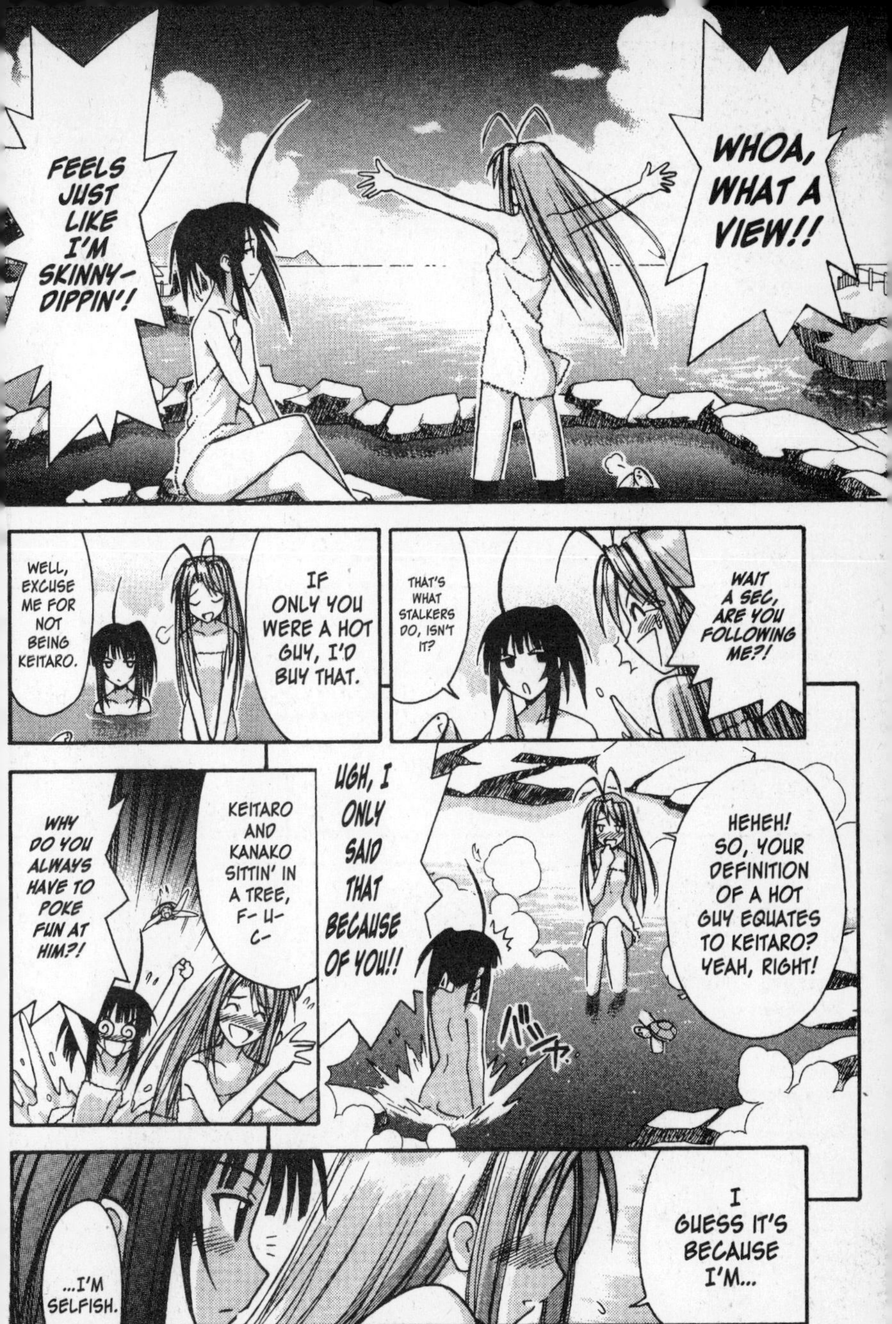
WHOA, WHAT A VIEW!!
FEELS JUST LIKE I'M SKINNY-DIPPIN'!
WAIT A SEC, ARE YOU FOLLOWING ME?!
THAT'S WHAT STALKERS DO, ISN'T IT?
IF ONLY YOU WERE A HOT GUY, I'D BUY THAT.
WELL, EXCUSE ME FOR NOT BEING KEITARO.
HEHEH! SO, YOUR DEFINITION OF A HOT GUY EQUATES TO KEITARO? YEAH, RIGHT!
UGH, I ONLY SAID THAT BECAUSE OF YOU!!
バシャ
KEITARO AND KANAKO SITTIN' IN A TREE, F- U- C-
WHY DO YOU ALWAYS HAVE TO POKE FUN AT HIM?!
I GUESS IT'S BECAUSE I'M...
...I'M SELFISH.

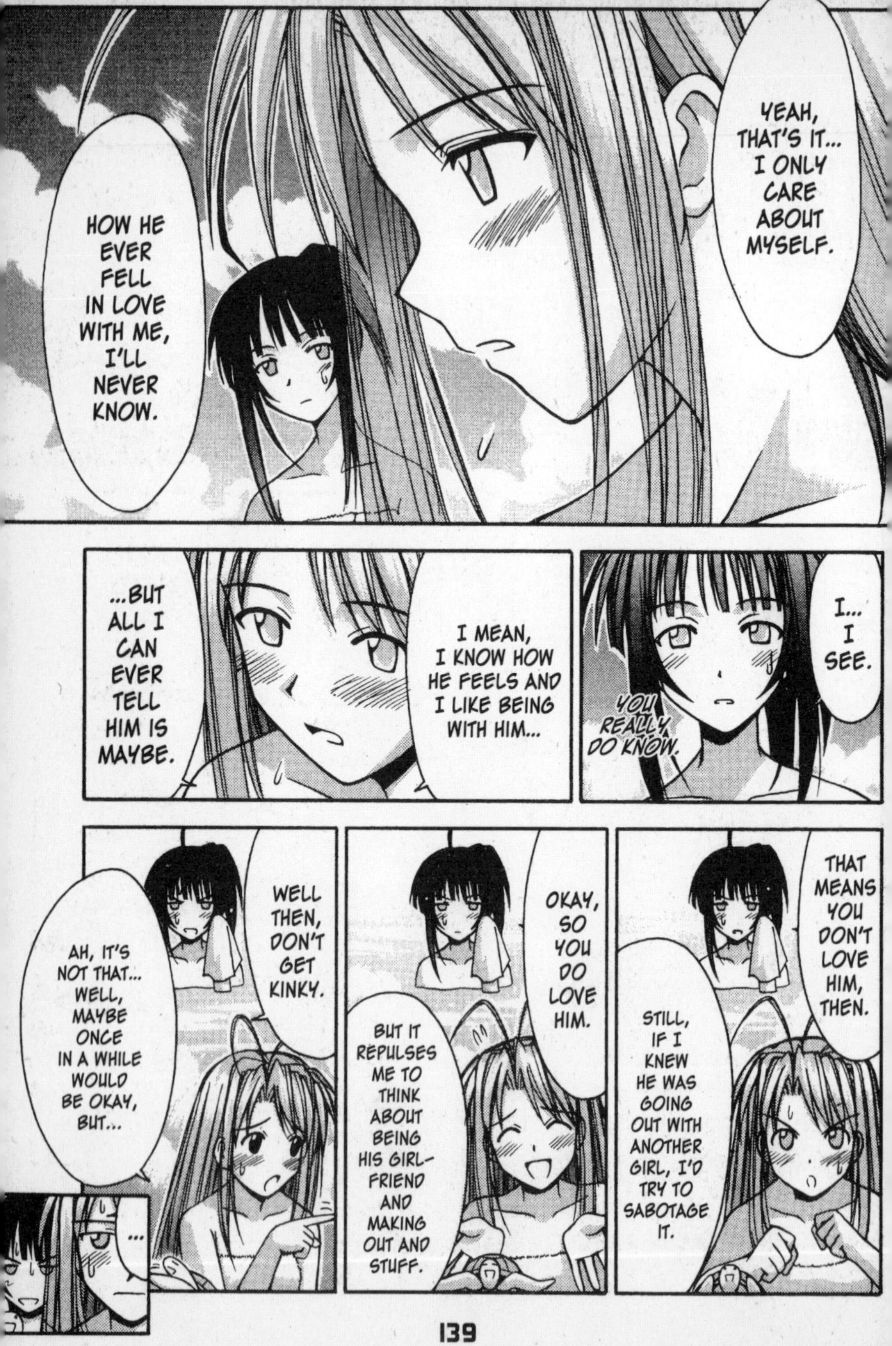
YEAH, THAT'S IT... I ONLY CARE ABOUT MYSELF.
HOW HE EVER FELL IN LOVE WITH ME, I'LL NEVER KNOW.
I... I SEE.
YOU REALLY DO KNOW.
I MEAN, I KNOW HOW HE FEELS AND I LIKE BEING WITH HIM...
...BUT ALL I CAN EVER TELL HIM IS MAYBE.
THAT MEANS YOU DON'T LOVE HIM, THEN.
STILL, IF I KNEW HE WAS GOING OUT WITH ANOTHER GIRL, I'D TRY TO SABOTAGE IT.
OKAY, SO YOU DO LOVE HIM.
BUT IT REPULSES ME TO THINK ABOUT BEING HIS GIRL-FRIEND AND MAKING OUT AND STUFF.
WELL THEN, DON'T GET KINKY.
AH, IT'S NOT THAT... WELL, MAYBE ONCE IN A WHILE WOULD BE OKAY, BUT...
...

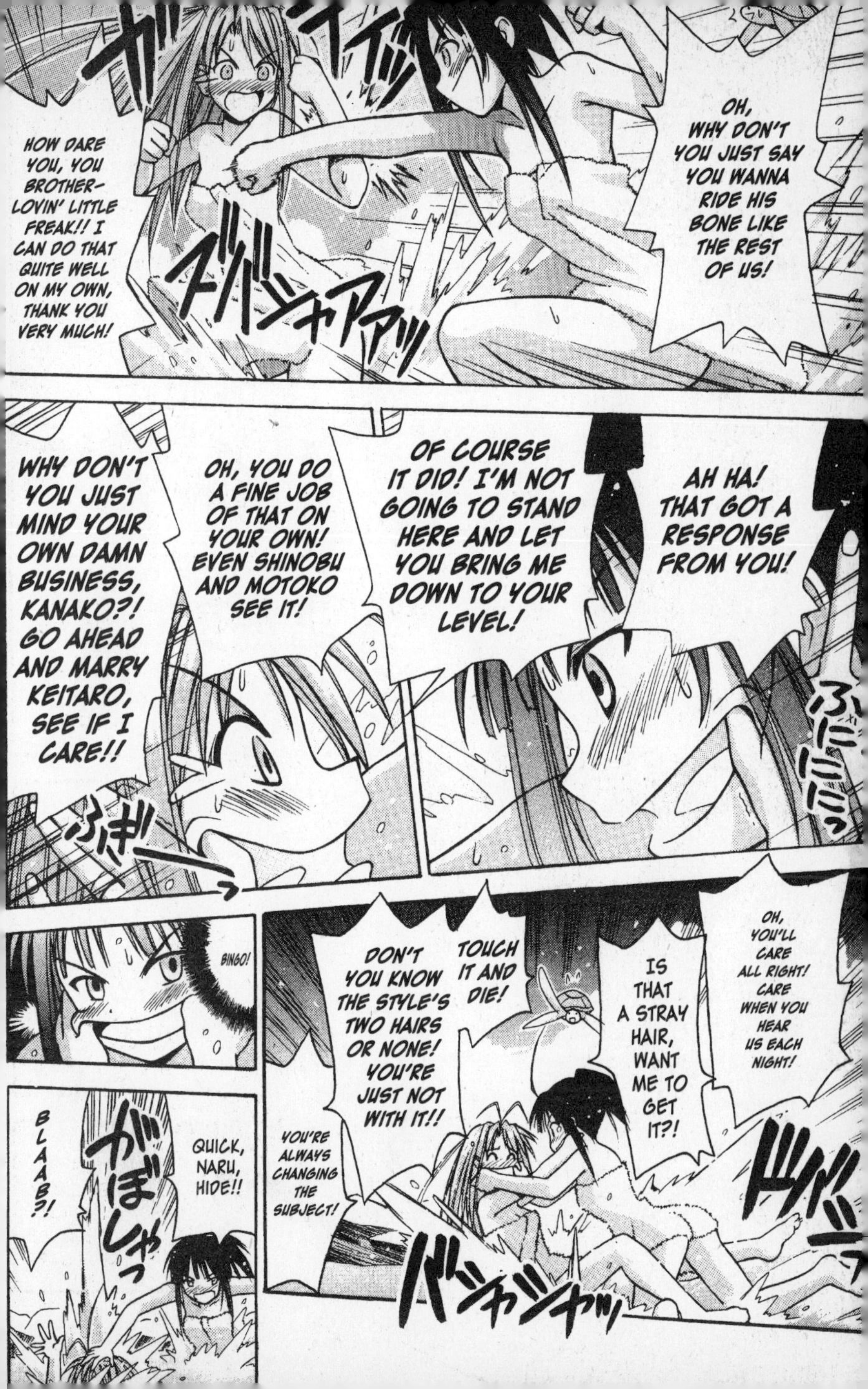
OH, WHY DON'T YOU JUST SAY YOU WANNA RIDE HIS BONE LIKE THE REST OF US!
HOW DARE YOU, YOU BROTHER-LOVIN' LITTLE FREAK!! I CAN DO THAT QUITE WELL ON MY OWN, THANK YOU VERY MUCH!
AH HA! THAT GOT A RESPONSE FROM YOU!
OF COURSE IT DID! I'M NOT GOING TO STAND HERE AND LET YOU BRING ME DOWN TO YOUR LEVEL!
OH, YOU DO A FINE JOB OF THAT ON YOUR OWN! EVEN SHINOBU AND MOTOKO SEE IT!
WHY DON'T YOU JUST MIND YOUR OWN DAMN BUSINESS, KANAKO?! GO AHEAD AND MARRY KEITARO, SEE IF I CARE!!
OH, YOU'LL CARE ALL RIGHT! CARE WHEN YOU HEAR US EACH NIGHT!
IS THAT A STRAY HAIR, WANT ME TO GET IT?!
TOUCH IT AND DIE!
DON'T YOU KNOW THE STYLE'S TWO HAIRS OR NONE! YOU'RE JUST NOT WITH IT!!
YOU'RE ALWAYS CHANGING THE SUBJECT!
BINGO!
QUICK, NARU, HIDE!!
BLAAB?!

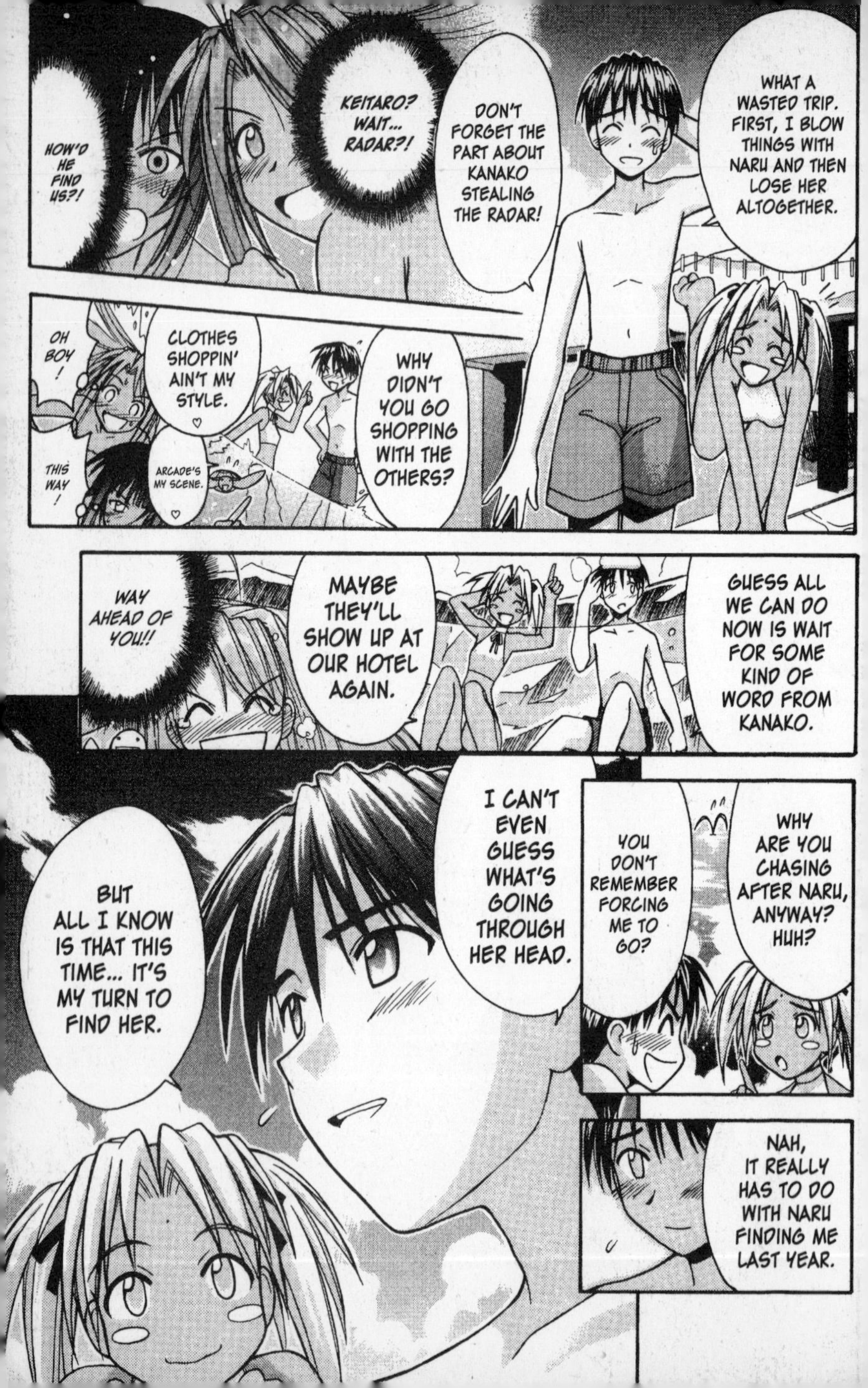
WHAT A WASTED TRIP. FIRST, I BLOW THINGS WITH NARU AND THEN LOSE HER ALTOGETHER.
DON'T FORGET THE PART ABOUT KANAKO STEALING THE RADAR!
KEITARO? WAIT... RADAR?!
HOW'D HE FIND US?!
WHY DIDN'T YOU GO SHOPPING WITH THE OTHERS?
CLOTHES SHOPPIN' AIN'T MY STYLE. ♡
ARCADE'S MY SCENE. ♡
OH BOY!
THIS WAY!
GUESS ALL WE CAN DO NOW IS WAIT FOR SOME KIND OF WORD FROM KANAKO.
MAYBE THEY'LL SHOW UP AT OUR HOTEL AGAIN.
WAY AHEAD OF YOU!!
WHY ARE YOU CHASING AFTER NARU, ANYWAY? HUH?
YOU DON'T REMEMBER FORCING ME TO GO?
NAH, IT REALLY HAS TO DO WITH NARU FINDING ME LAST YEAR.
I CAN'T EVEN GUESS WHAT'S GOING THROUGH HER HEAD.
BUT ALL I KNOW IS THAT THIS TIME... IT'S MY TURN TO FIND HER.

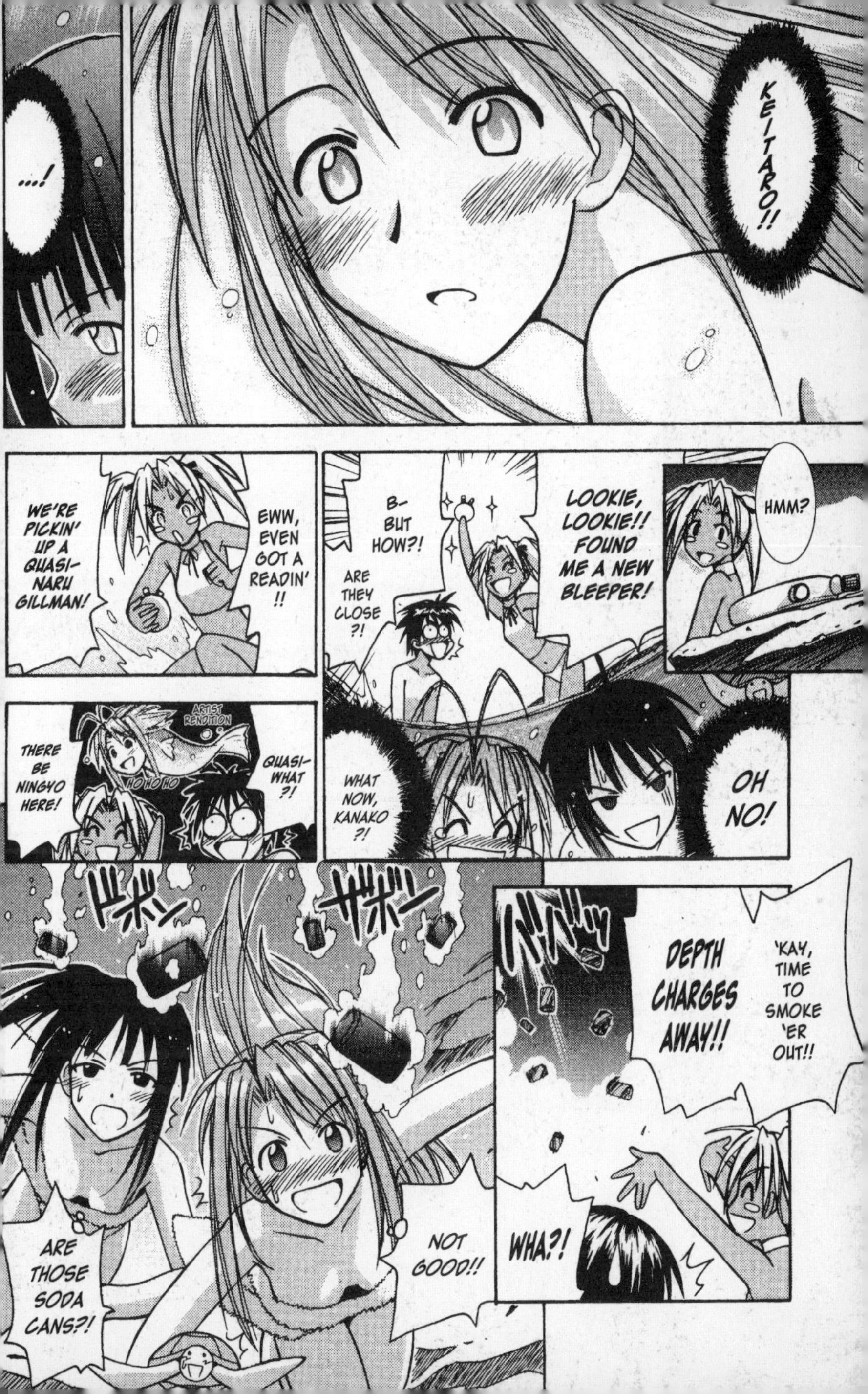
KEITARO!!
...!
HMM?
LOOKIE, LOOKIE!! FOUND ME A NEW BLEEPER!
B-BUT HOW?!
ARE THEY CLOSE?!
EWW, EVEN GOT A READIN'!!
WE'RE PICKIN' UP A QUASI-NARU GILLMAN!
OH NO!
WHAT NOW, KANAKO?!
QUASI-WHAT?!
ARTIST RENDITION
HO HO HO
THERE BE NINGYO HERE!
'KAY, TIME TO SMOKE 'ER OUT!!
DEPTH CHARGES AWAY!!
WHA?!
ザボーン
ドボン
NOT GOOD!!
ARE THOSE SODA CANS?!

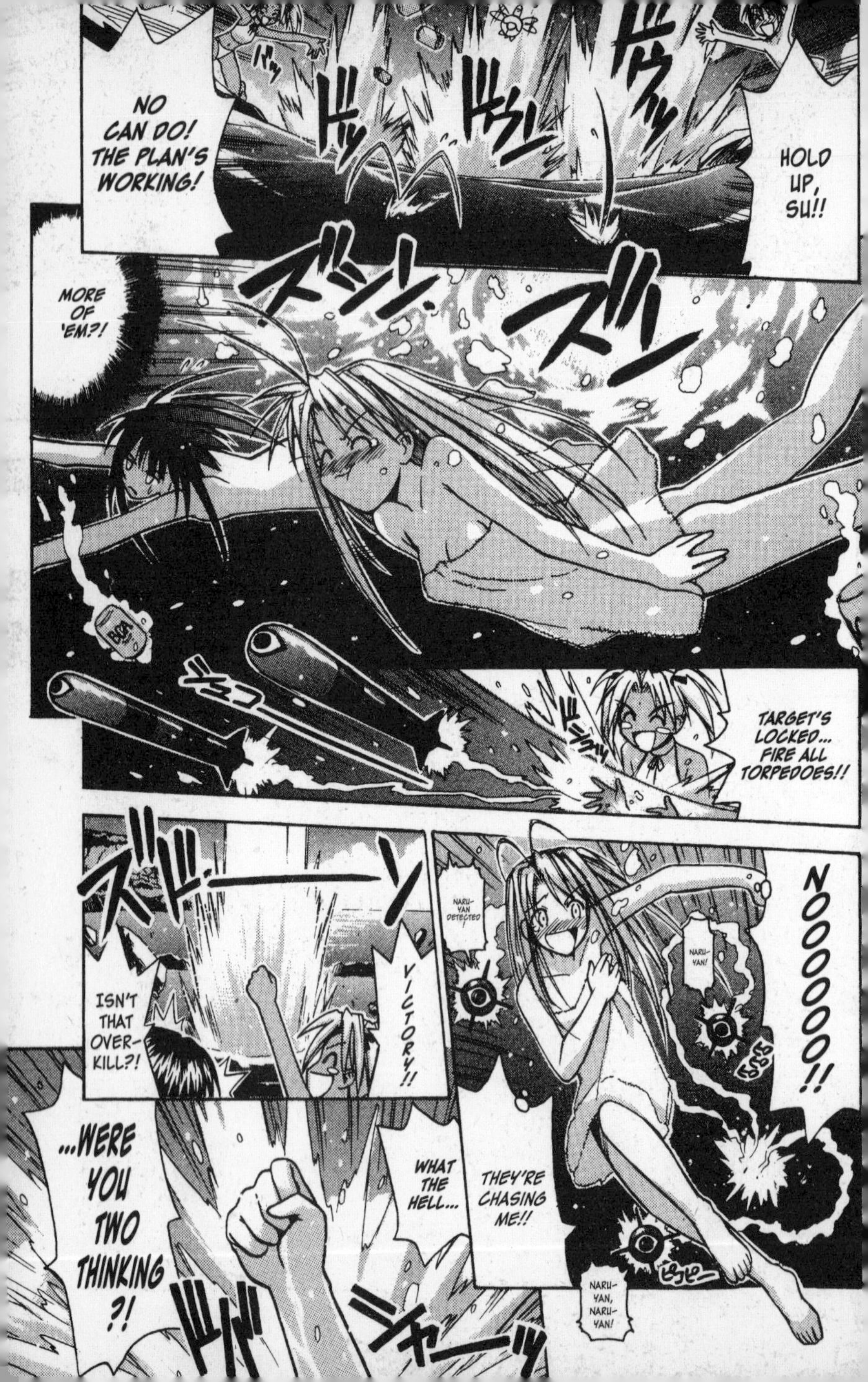
HOLD UP, SU!!
NO CAN DO! THE PLAN'S WORKING!
MORE OF 'EM?!
TARGET'S LOCKED... FIRE ALL TORPEDOES!!
NOOOOOOO!!
NARU-YAN!
NARU-YAN DETECTED!
THEY'RE CHASING ME!!
NARU-YAN, NARU-YAN!
VICTORY!!
ISN'T THAT OVER-KILL?!
WHAT THE HELL...
...WERE YOU TWO THINKING?!

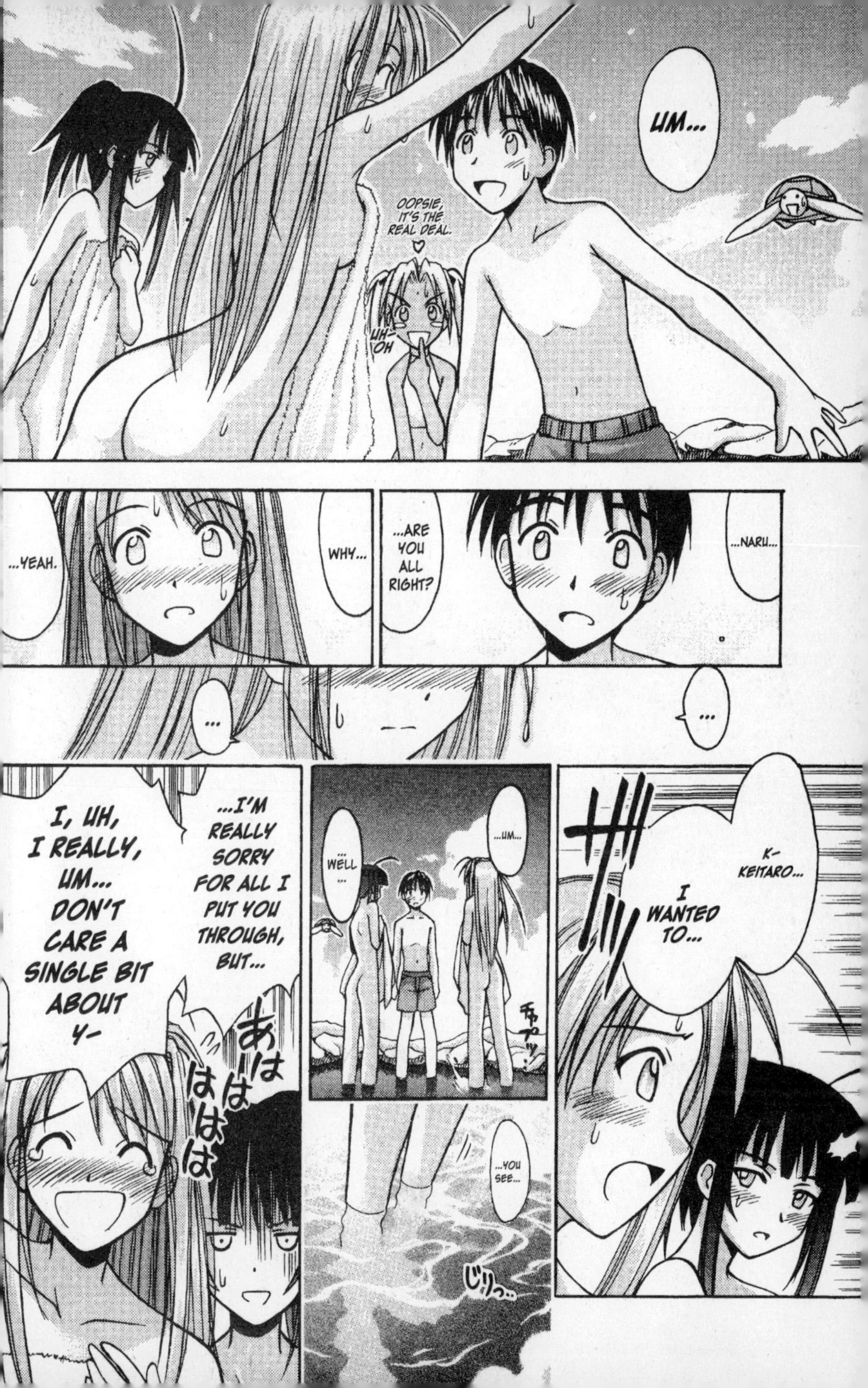
UM...
OOPSIE, IT'S THE REAL DEAL.
UH-OH
...NARU...
...ARE YOU ALL RIGHT?
WHY...
...YEAH.
...
...
K-KEITARO... I WANTED TO...
...UM...
... WELL ...
チャプッ
...YOU SEE...
じりっ
...I'M REALLY SORRY FOR ALL I PUT YOU THROUGH, BUT...
I, UH, I REALLY, UM... DON'T CARE A SINGLE BIT ABOUT Y-
あははははは

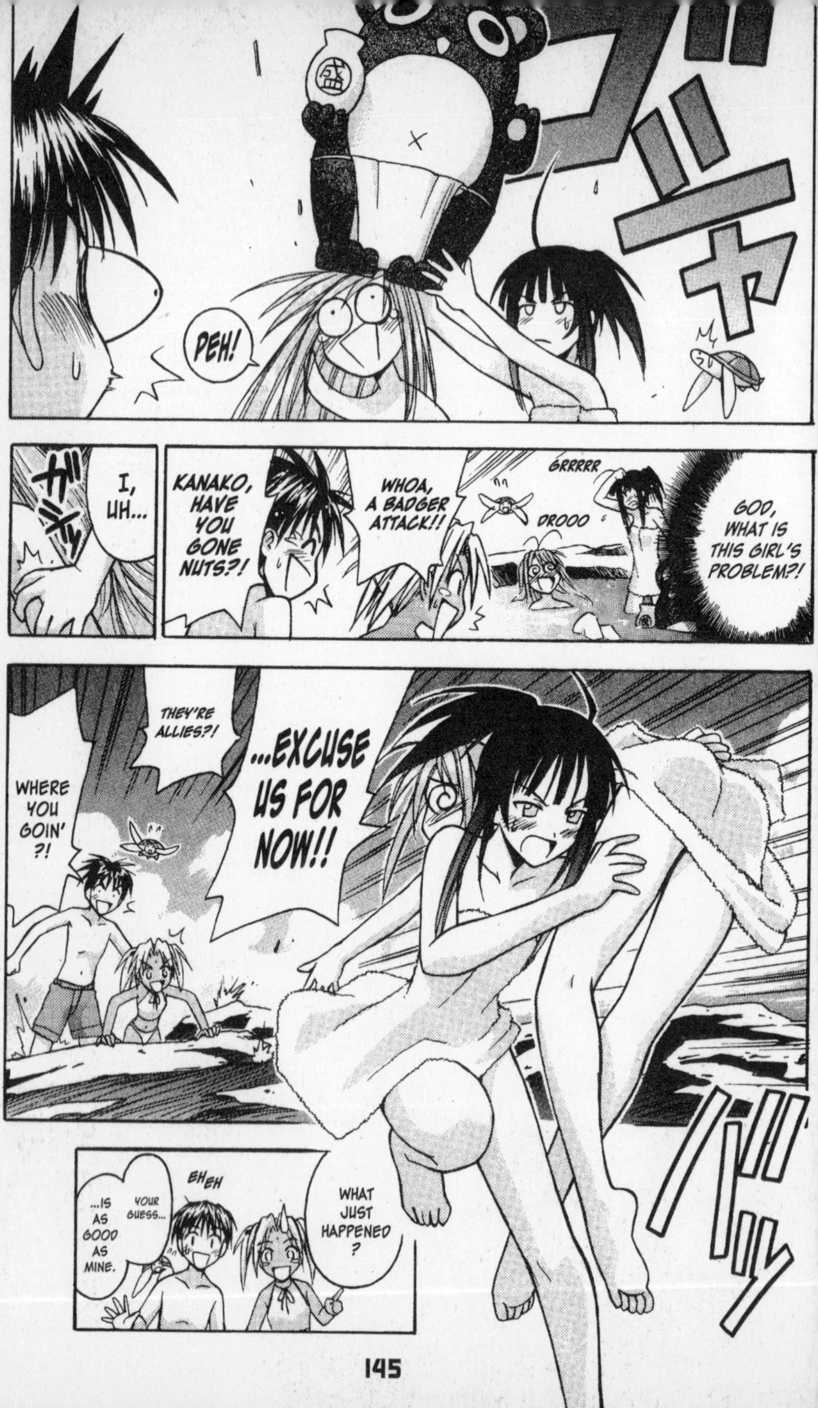
PEH!
GOD, WHAT IS THIS GIRL'S PROBLEM?!
GRRRRR
DROOO
WHOA, A BADGER ATTACK!!
KANAKO, HAVE YOU GONE NUTS?!
I, UH...
...EXCUSE US FOR NOW!!
THEY'RE ALLIES?!
WHERE YOU GOIN' ?!
WHAT JUST HAPPENED ?
EHEH
YOUR GUESS...
...IS AS GOOD AS MINE.

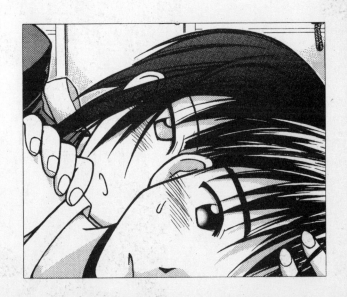

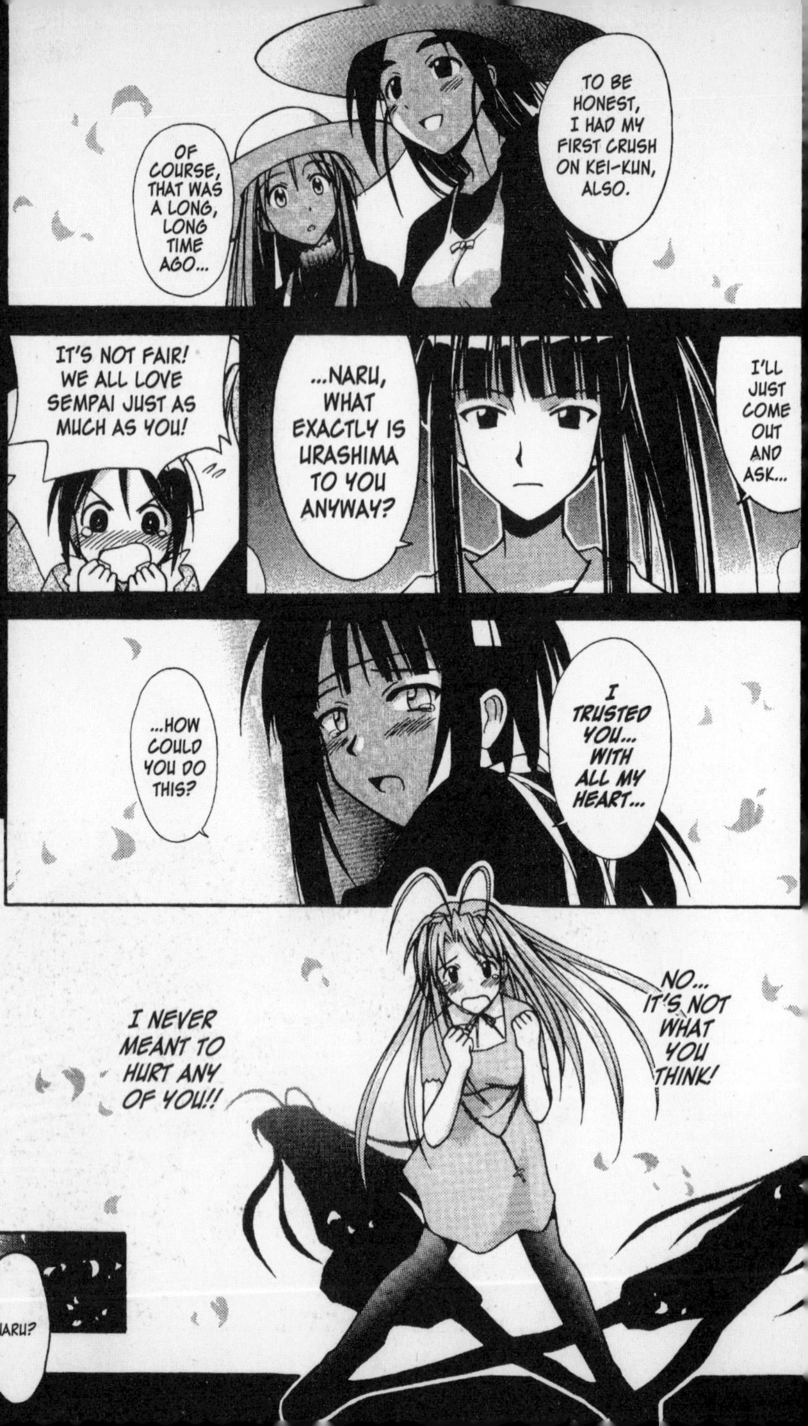
TO BE HONEST, I HAD MY FIRST CRUSH ON KEI-KUN, ALSO.
OF COURSE, THAT WAS A LONG, LONG TIME AGO...
I'LL JUST COME OUT AND ASK...
...NARU, WHAT EXACTLY IS URASHIMA TO YOU ANYWAY?
IT'S NOT FAIR! WE ALL LOVE SEMPAI JUST AS MUCH AS YOU!
I TRUSTED YOU... WITH ALL MY HEART...
...HOW COULD YOU DO THIS?
NO... IT'S NOT WHAT YOU THINK!
I NEVER MEANT TO HURT ANY OF YOU!!
NARU?

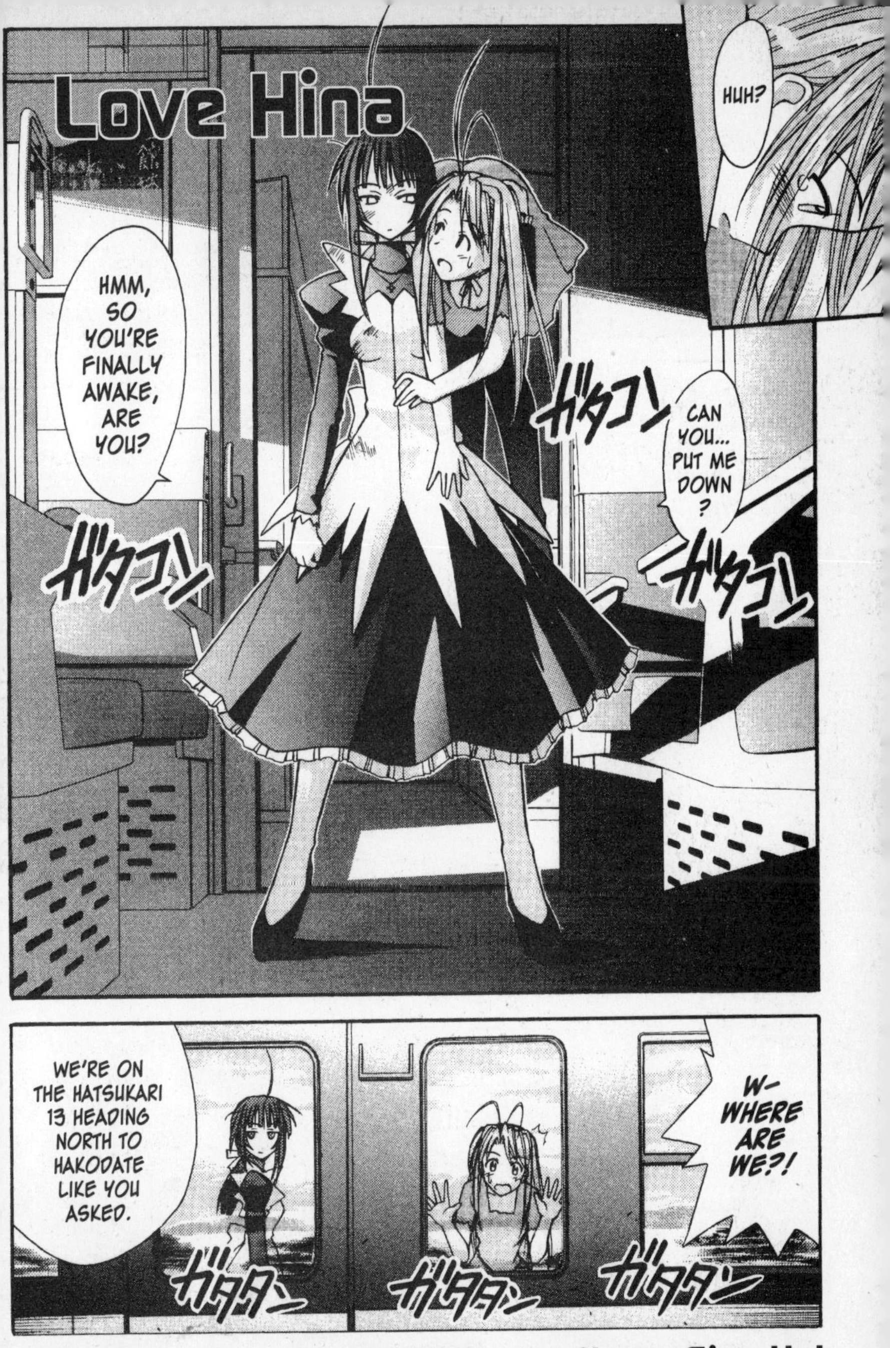
Love Hina
HUH?
HMM, SO YOU'RE FINALLY AWAKE, ARE YOU?
CAN YOU... PUT ME DOWN?
ガタコン
ガタコン
ガタコン
W- WHERE ARE WE?!
WE'RE ON THE HATSUKARI 13 HEADING NORTH TO HAKODATE LIKE YOU ASKED.
ガタタン
ガタタン
ガタタン

HINATA. 104 Never Give Up!

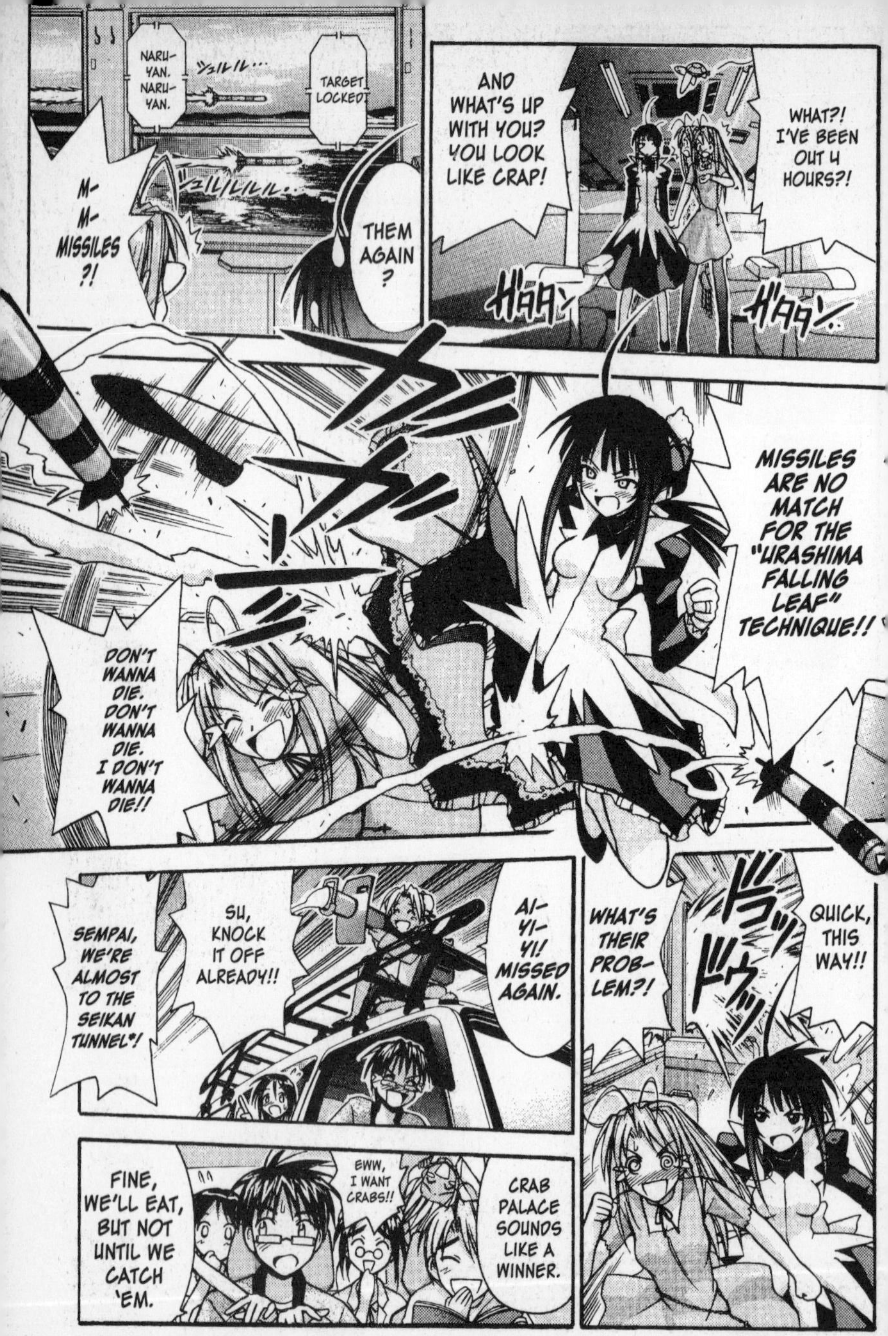
WHAT?! I'VE BEEN OUT 4 HOURS?!
AND WHAT'S UP WITH YOU? YOU LOOK LIKE CRAP!
TARGET LOCKED
THEM AGAIN ?
NARU-YAN. NARU-YAN.
M-M-MISSILES ?!
MISSILES ARE NO MATCH FOR THE "URASHIMA FALLING LEAF" TECHNIQUE!!
DON'T WANNA DIE. DON'T WANNA DIE. I DON'T WANNA DIE!!
QUICK, THIS WAY!!
WHAT'S THEIR PROB-LEM?!
AI-YI-YI! MISSED AGAIN.
SU, KNOCK IT OFF ALREADY!!
SEMPAI, WE'RE ALMOST TO THE SEIKAN TUNNEL*!
CRAB PALACE SOUNDS LIKE A WINNER.
EWW, I WANT CRABS!!
FINE, WE'LL EAT, BUT NOT UNTIL WE CATCH 'EM.

* THE TUNNEL CONNECTING AOMORI (HONSHU) TO HAKODATE (HOKKAIDO).

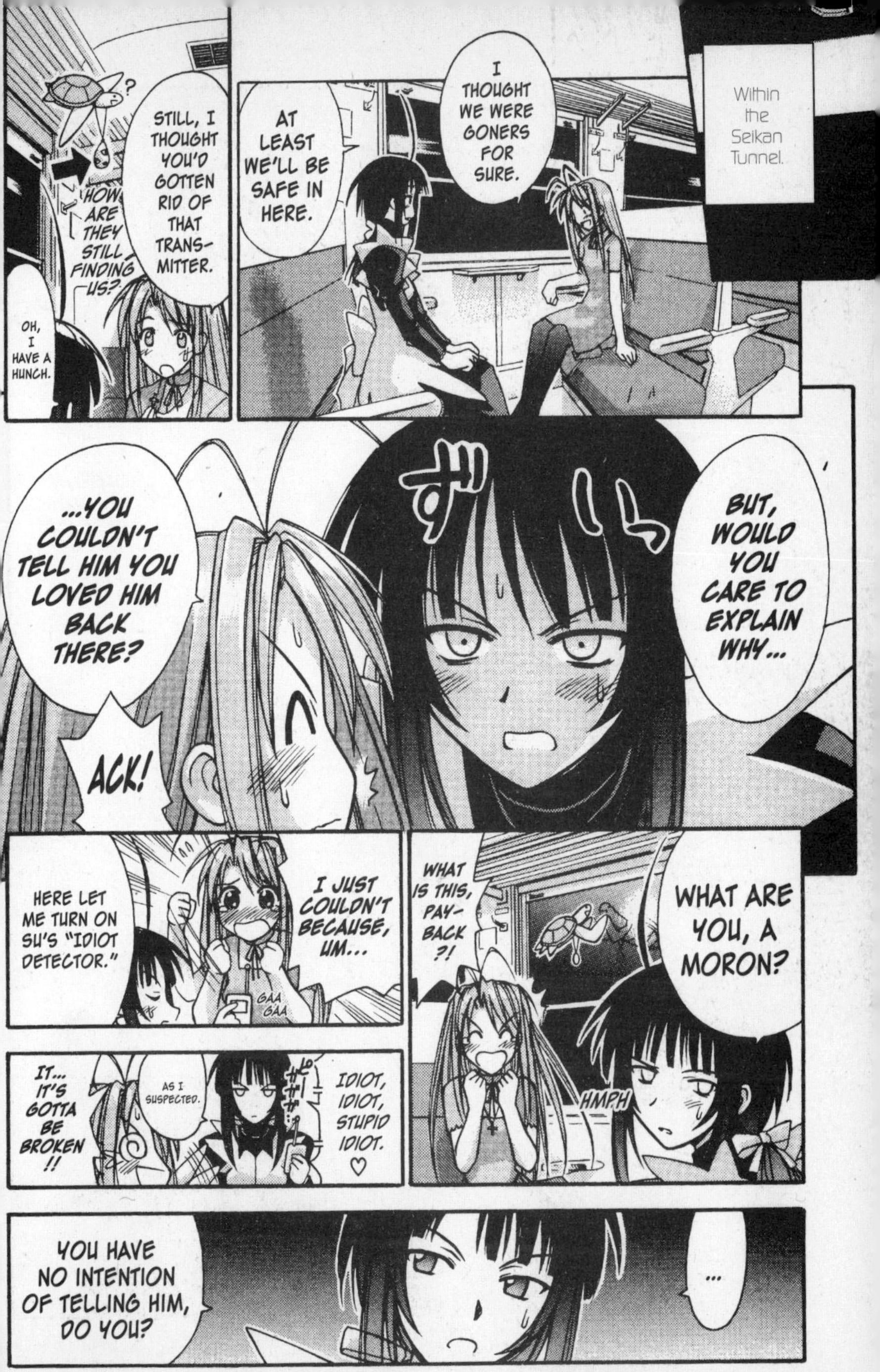

Within the Seikan Tunnel.
I THOUGHT WE WERE GONERS FOR SURE.
AT LEAST WE'LL BE SAFE IN HERE.
STILL, I THOUGHT YOU'D GOTTEN RID OF THAT TRANS-MITTER.
HOW ARE THEY STILL FINDING US?
OH, I HAVE A HUNCH.
ずい
BUT, WOULD YOU CARE TO EXPLAIN WHY...
...YOU COULDN'T TELL HIM YOU LOVED HIM BACK THERE?
ACK!
WHAT ARE YOU, A MORON?
WHAT IS THIS, PAY-BACK?!
HMPH
I JUST COULDN'T BECAUSE, UM...
HERE LET ME TURN ON SU'S "IDIOT DETECTOR."
GAA GAA
IDIOT, IDIOT, STUPID IDIOT. ♡
AS I SUSPECTED.
IT... IT'S GOTTA BE BROKEN!!
...
YOU HAVE NO INTENTION OF TELLING HIM, DO YOU?

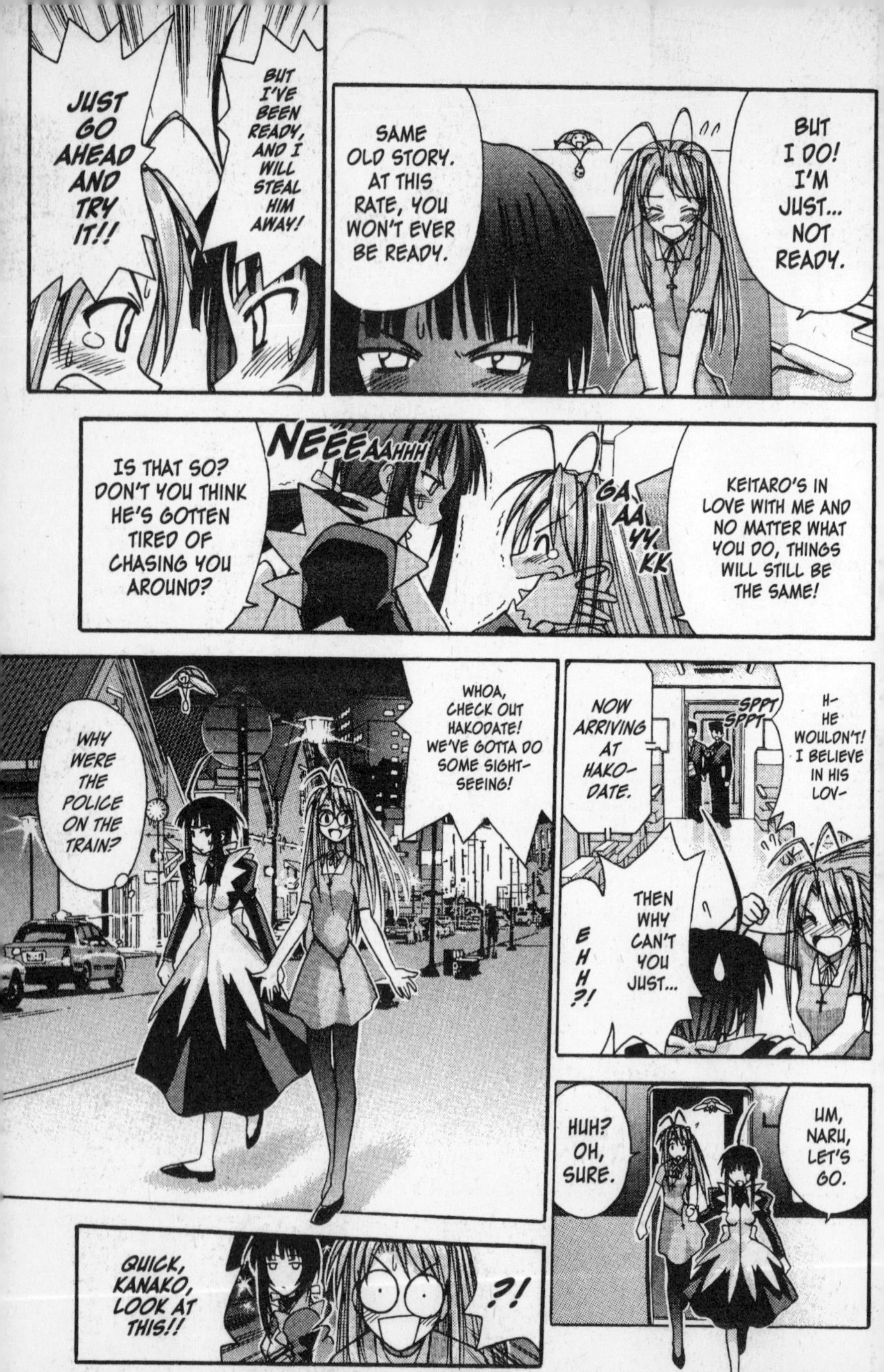
BUT I DO! I'M JUST... NOT READY.
SAME OLD STORY. AT THIS RATE, YOU WON'T EVER BE READY.
BUT I'VE BEEN READY, AND I WILL STEAL HIM AWAY!
JUST GO AHEAD AND TRY IT!!
KEITARO'S IN LOVE WITH ME AND NO MATTER WHAT YOU DO, THINGS WILL STILL BE THE SAME!
GAAAYYKK
NEEEAAHHH
IS THAT SO? DON'T YOU THINK HE'S GOTTEN TIRED OF CHASING YOU AROUND?
H-HE WOULDN'T! I BELIEVE IN HIS LOV-
SPPT SPPT
NOW ARRIVING AT HAKODATE.
THEN WHY CAN'T YOU JUST...
EHH?!
UM, NARU, LET'S GO.
HUH? OH, SURE.
WHOA, CHECK OUT HAKODATE! WE'VE GOTTA DO SOME SIGHT-SEEING!
WHY WERE THE POLICE ON THE TRAIN?
?!
QUICK, KANAKO, LOOK AT THIS!!

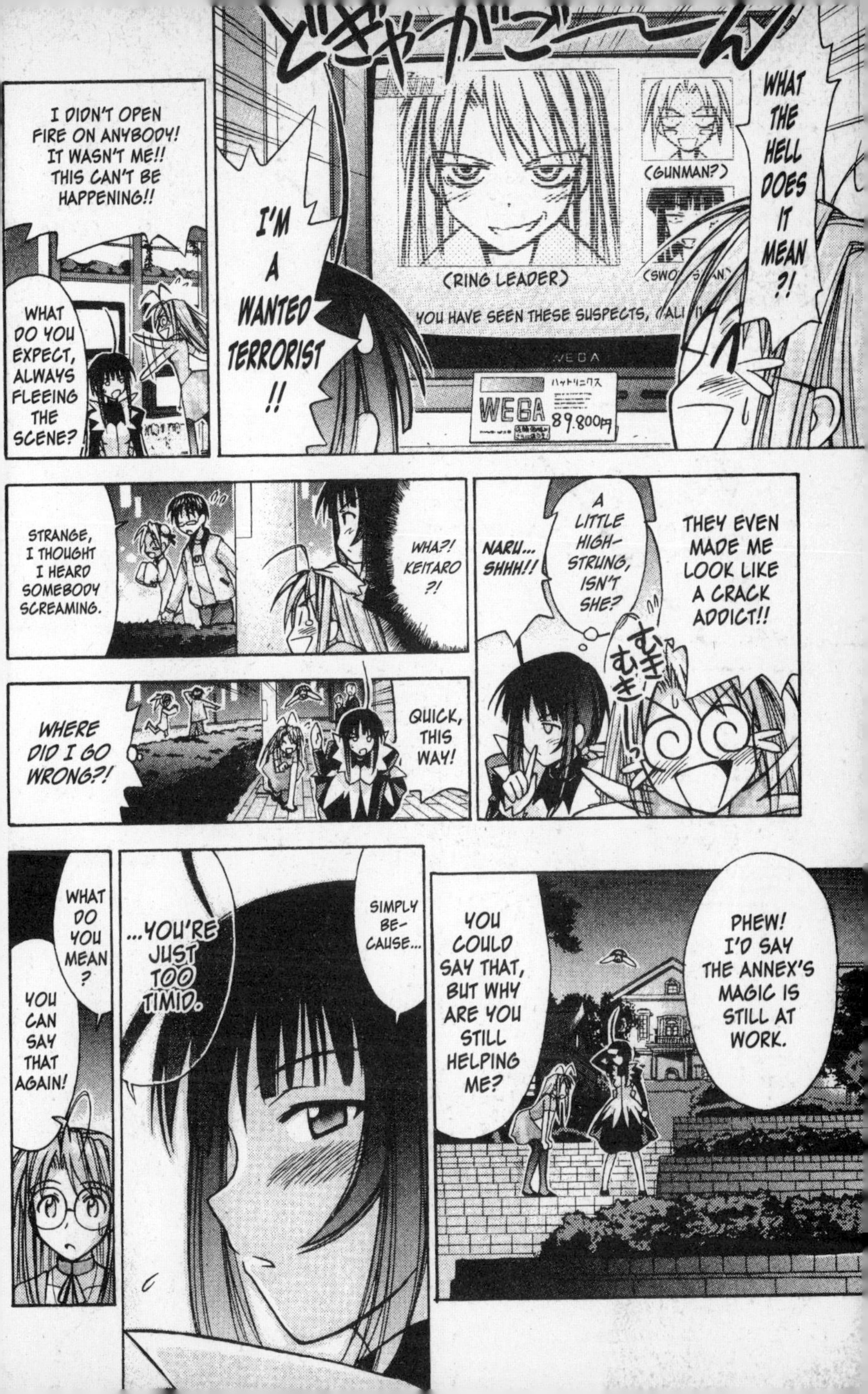
どぎゃがごーーん
WHAT THE HELL DOES IT MEAN?!
(GUNMAN?)
(RING LEADER)
YOU HAVE SEEN THESE SUSPECTS,
WEGA
ハットリニクス
89,800円
I'M A WANTED TERRORIST!!
I DIDN'T OPEN FIRE ON ANYBODY! IT WASN'T ME!! THIS CAN'T BE HAPPENING!!
WHAT DO YOU EXPECT, ALWAYS FLEEING THE SCENE?
THEY EVEN MADE ME LOOK LIKE A CRACK ADDICT!!
A LITTLE HIGH-STRUNG, ISN'T SHE?
NARU... SHHH!!
WHA?! KEITARO?!
STRANGE, I THOUGHT I HEARD SOMEBODY SCREAMING.
QUICK, THIS WAY!
WHERE DID I GO WRONG?!
PHEW! I'D SAY THE ANNEX'S MAGIC IS STILL AT WORK.
YOU COULD SAY THAT, BUT WHY ARE YOU STILL HELPING ME?
SIMPLY BE-CAUSE...
...YOU'RE JUST TOO TIMID.
WHAT DO YOU MEAN?
YOU CAN SAY THAT AGAIN!

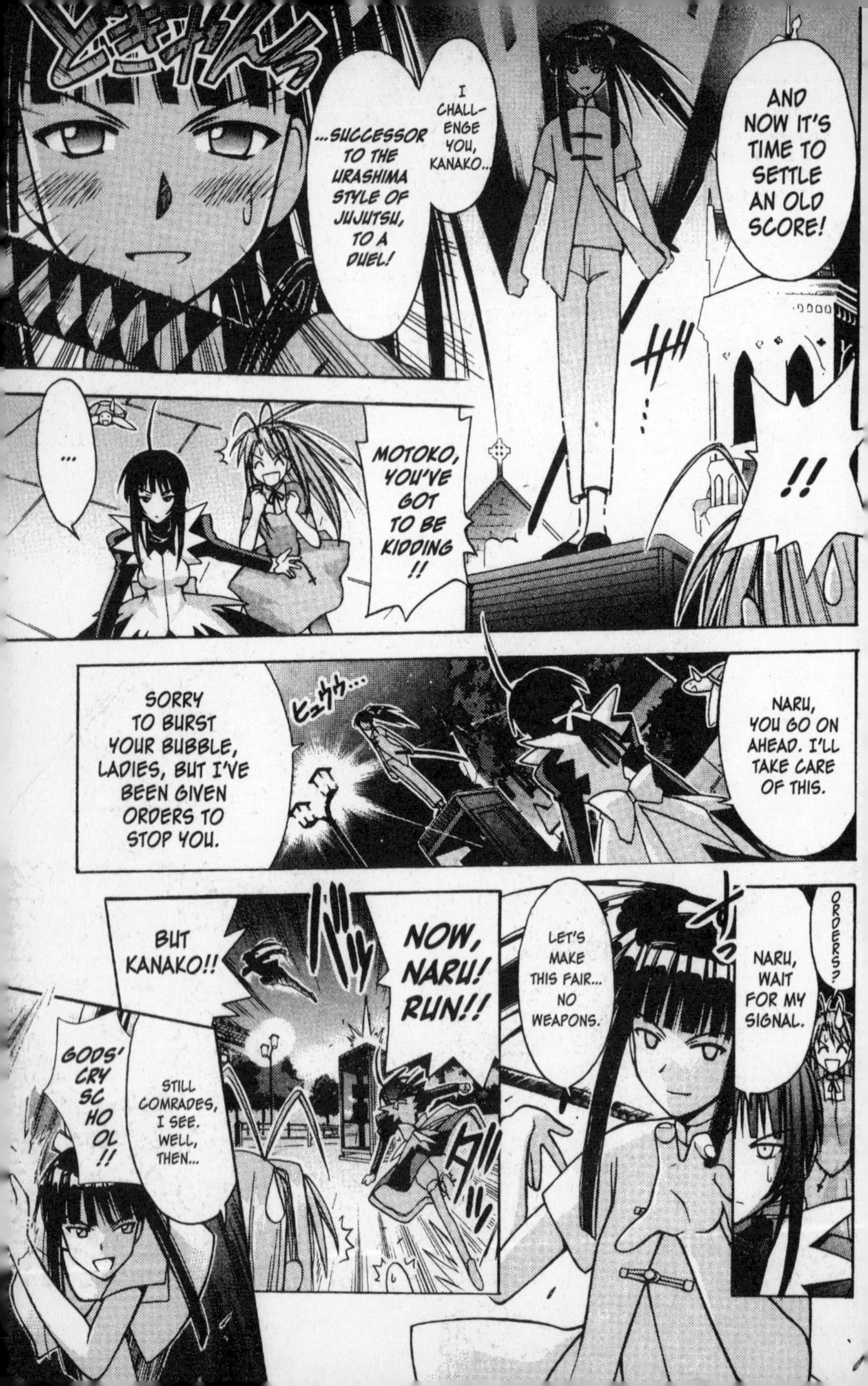
AND NOW IT'S TIME TO SETTLE AN OLD SCORE!
I CHALLENGE YOU, KANAKO...
...SUCCESSOR TO THE URASHIMA STYLE OF JUJUTSU, TO A DUEL!
!!
MOTOKO, YOU'VE GOT TO BE KIDDING!!
...
NARU, YOU GO ON AHEAD. I'LL TAKE CARE OF THIS.
SORRY TO BURST YOUR BUBBLE, LADIES, BUT I'VE BEEN GIVEN ORDERS TO STOP YOU.
ORDERS?
NARU, WAIT FOR MY SIGNAL.
LET'S MAKE THIS FAIR... NO WEAPONS.
NOW, NARU! RUN!!
BUT KANAKO!!
STILL COMRADES, I SEE. WELL, THEN...
GODS' CRY SCHOOL!!

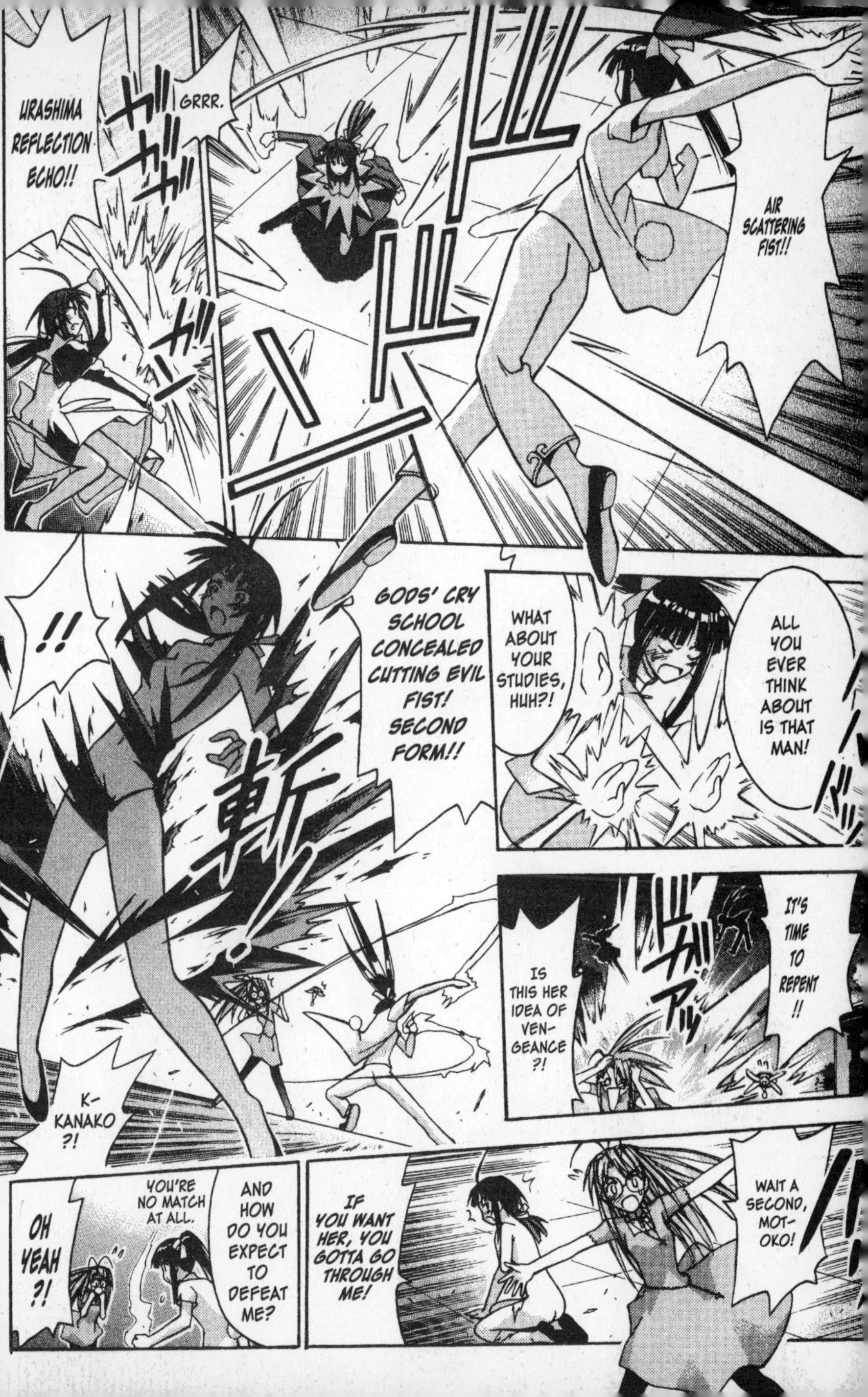
AIR SCATTERING FIST!!
GRRR.
URASHIMA REFLECTION ECHO!!
ALL YOU EVER THINK ABOUT IS THAT MAN!
WHAT ABOUT YOUR STUDIES, HUH?!
IT'S TIME TO REPENT!!
IS THIS HER IDEA OF VEN-GEANCE?!
GODS' CRY SCHOOL CONCEALED CUTTING EVIL FIST! SECOND FORM!!
!!
K-KANAKO?!
WAIT A SECOND, MOT-OKO!
IF YOU WANT HER, YOU GOTTA GO THROUGH ME!
YOU'RE NO MATCH AT ALL.
AND HOW DO YOU EXPECT TO DEFEAT ME?
OH YEAH?!

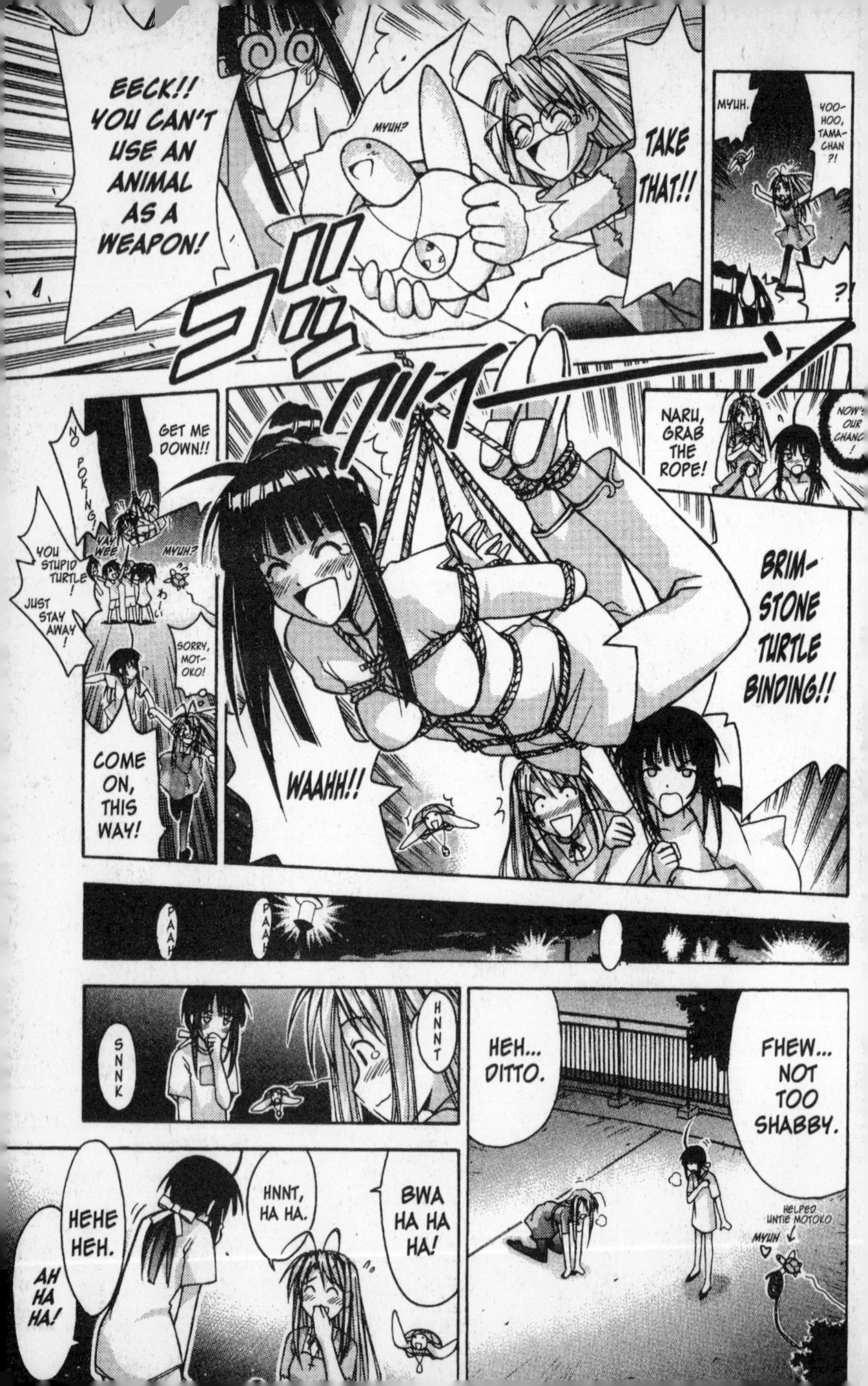
MYUH.
YOO-HOO, TAMA-CHAN?!
?!
TAKE THAT!!
MYUH?
EECK!! YOU CAN'T USE AN ANIMAL AS A WEAPON!
NOW'S OUR CHANC!
NARU, GRAB THE ROPE!
BRIM-STONE TURTLE BINDING!!
WAAHH!!
GET ME DOWN!!
NO POKING!
YAY WEE
MYUH?
YOU STUPID TURTLE!
JUST STAY AWAY!
SORRY, MOT-OKO!
COME ON, THIS WAY!
PAAH
PAAH
FHEW... NOT TOO SHABBY.
HEH... DITTO.
HELPED UNTIE MOTOKO
MYUH
HNNT
SNNK
BWA HA HA HA!
HNNT, HA HA.
HEHE HEH.
AH HA HA!

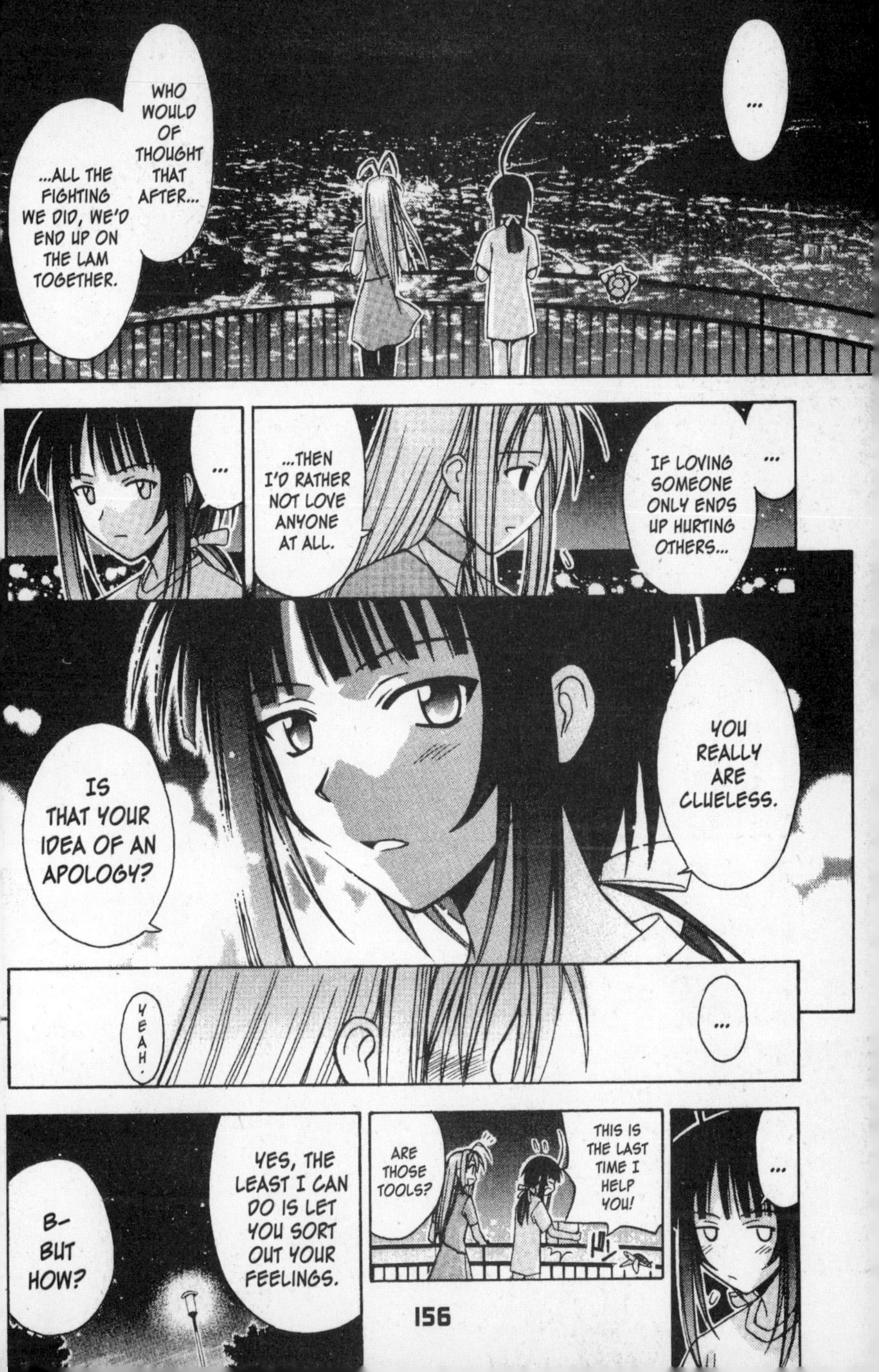
...
WHO WOULD OF THOUGHT THAT AFTER...
...ALL THE FIGHTING WE DID, WE'D END UP ON THE LAM TOGETHER.
...
IF LOVING SOMEONE ONLY ENDS UP HURTING OTHERS...
...THEN I'D RATHER NOT LOVE ANYONE AT ALL.
...
YOU REALLY ARE CLUELESS.
IS THAT YOUR IDEA OF AN APOLOGY?
...
YEAH.
...
THIS IS THE LAST TIME I HELP YOU!
ARE THOSE TOOLS?
YES, THE LEAST I CAN DO IS LET YOU SORT OUT YOUR FEELINGS.
B-BUT HOW?

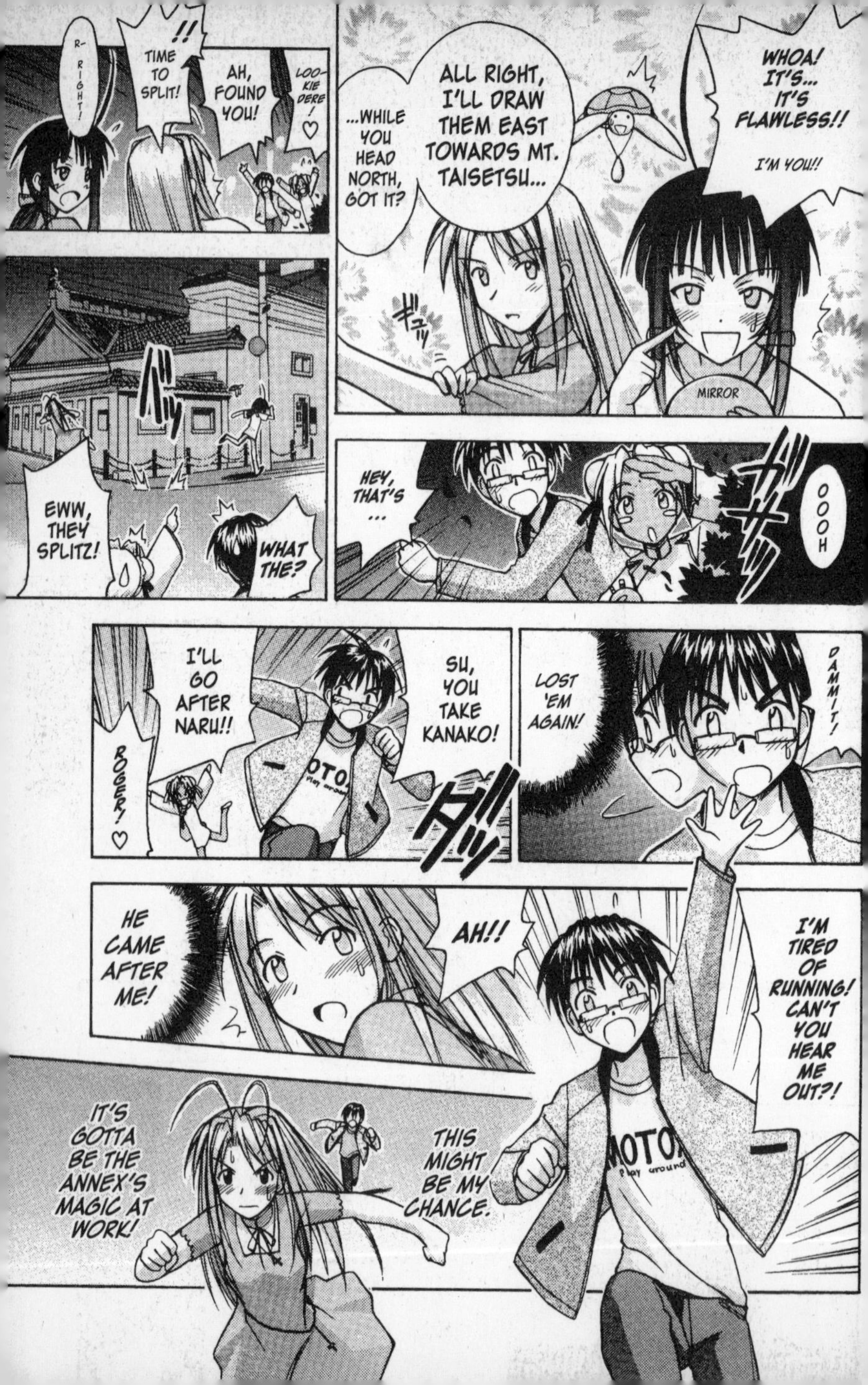
WHOA! IT'S... IT'S FLAWLESS!!
I'M YOU!!
ALL RIGHT, I'LL DRAW THEM EAST TOWARDS MT. TAISETSU...
...WHILE YOU HEAD NORTH, GOT IT?
MIRROR
OOOH
HEY, THAT'S ...
LOOKIE DERE! ♡
AH, FOUND YOU!
!! TIME TO SPLIT!
R-RIGHT!
WHAT THE?
EWW, THEY SPLITZ!
DAMMIT!
LOST 'EM AGAIN!
SU, YOU TAKE KANAKO!
I'LL GO AFTER NARU!!
ROGER! ♡
I'M TIRED OF RUNNING! CAN'T YOU HEAR ME OUT?!
AH!!
HE CAME AFTER ME!
THIS MIGHT BE MY CHANCE.
IT'S GOTTA BE THE ANNEX'S MAGIC AT WORK!

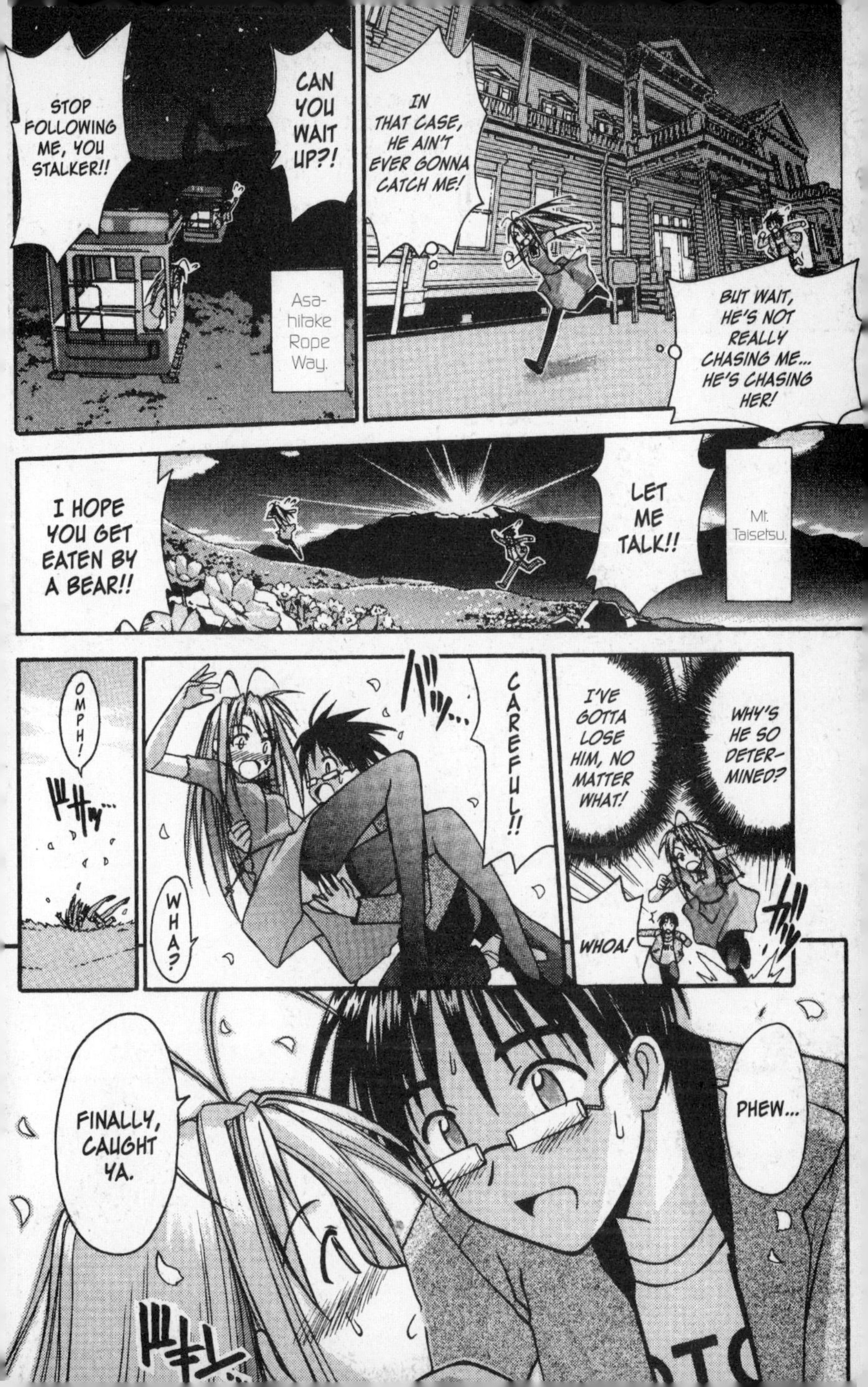

IN THAT CASE, HE AIN'T EVER GONNA CATCH ME!
BUT WAIT, HE'S NOT REALLY CHASING ME... HE'S CHASING HER!
CAN YOU WAIT UP?!
STOP FOLLOWING ME, YOU STALKER!!
Asa-hitake Rope Way.
Mt. Taisetsu.
LET ME TALK!!
I HOPE YOU GET EATEN BY A BEAR!!
WHY'S HE SO DETER-MINED?
I'VE GOTTA LOSE HIM, NO MATTER WHAT!
WHOA!
CAREFUL!!
WHA?
OMPH!
PHEW...
FINALLY, CAUGHT YA.

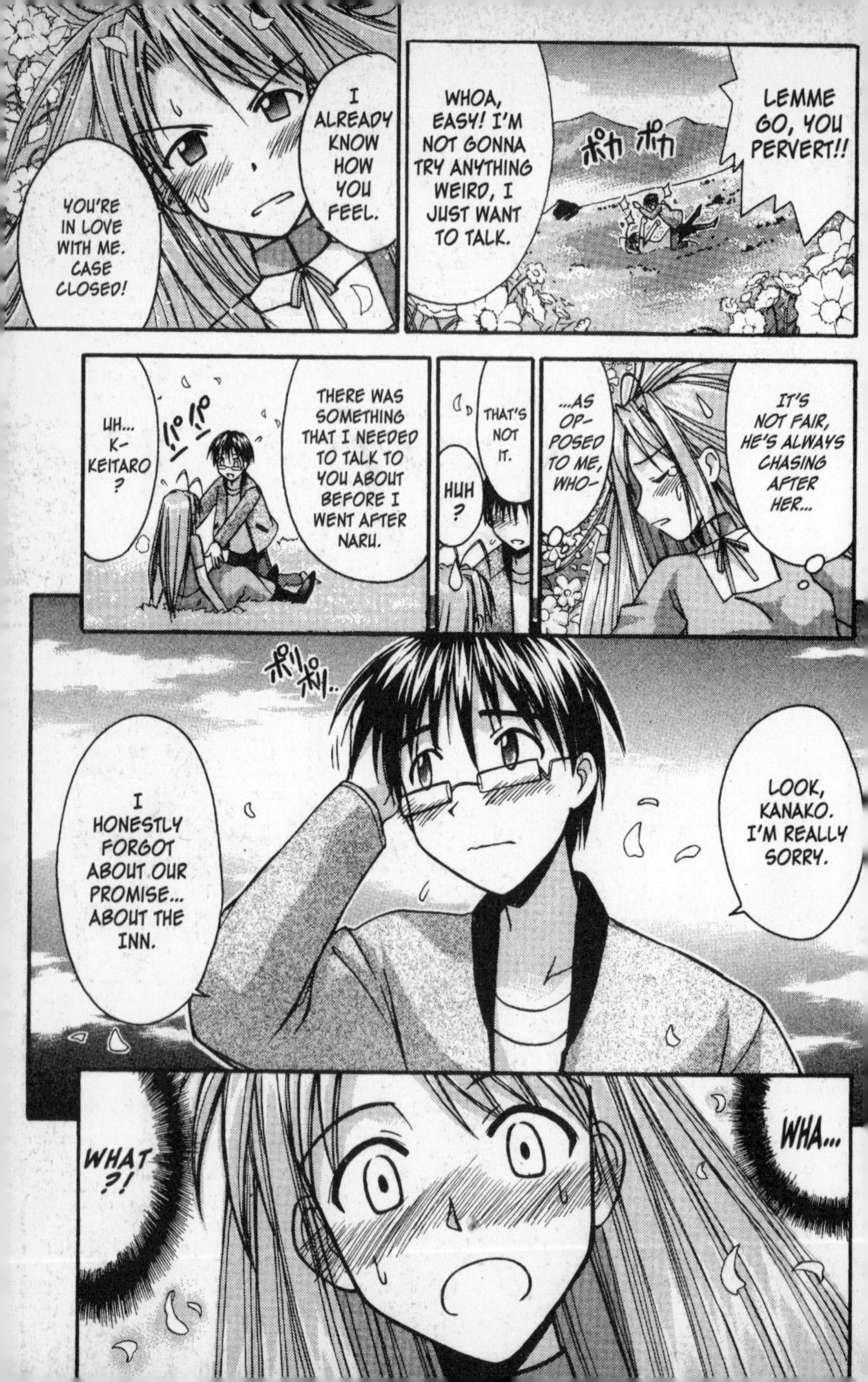
LEMME GO, YOU PERVERT!!
ポカ ポカ
WHOA, EASY! I'M NOT GONNA TRY ANYTHING WEIRD, I JUST WANT TO TALK.
I ALREADY KNOW HOW YOU FEEL.
YOU'RE IN LOVE WITH ME. CASE CLOSED!
IT'S NOT FAIR, HE'S ALWAYS CHASING AFTER HER...
...AS OP-POSED TO ME, WHO-
THAT'S NOT IT.
HUH?
THERE WAS SOMETHING THAT I NEEDED TO TALK TO YOU ABOUT BEFORE I WENT AFTER NARU.
UH... K-KEITARO?
ポリ ポリ..
LOOK, KANAKO. I'M REALLY SORRY.
I HONESTLY FORGOT ABOUT OUR PROMISE... ABOUT THE INN.
WHA...
WHAT?!

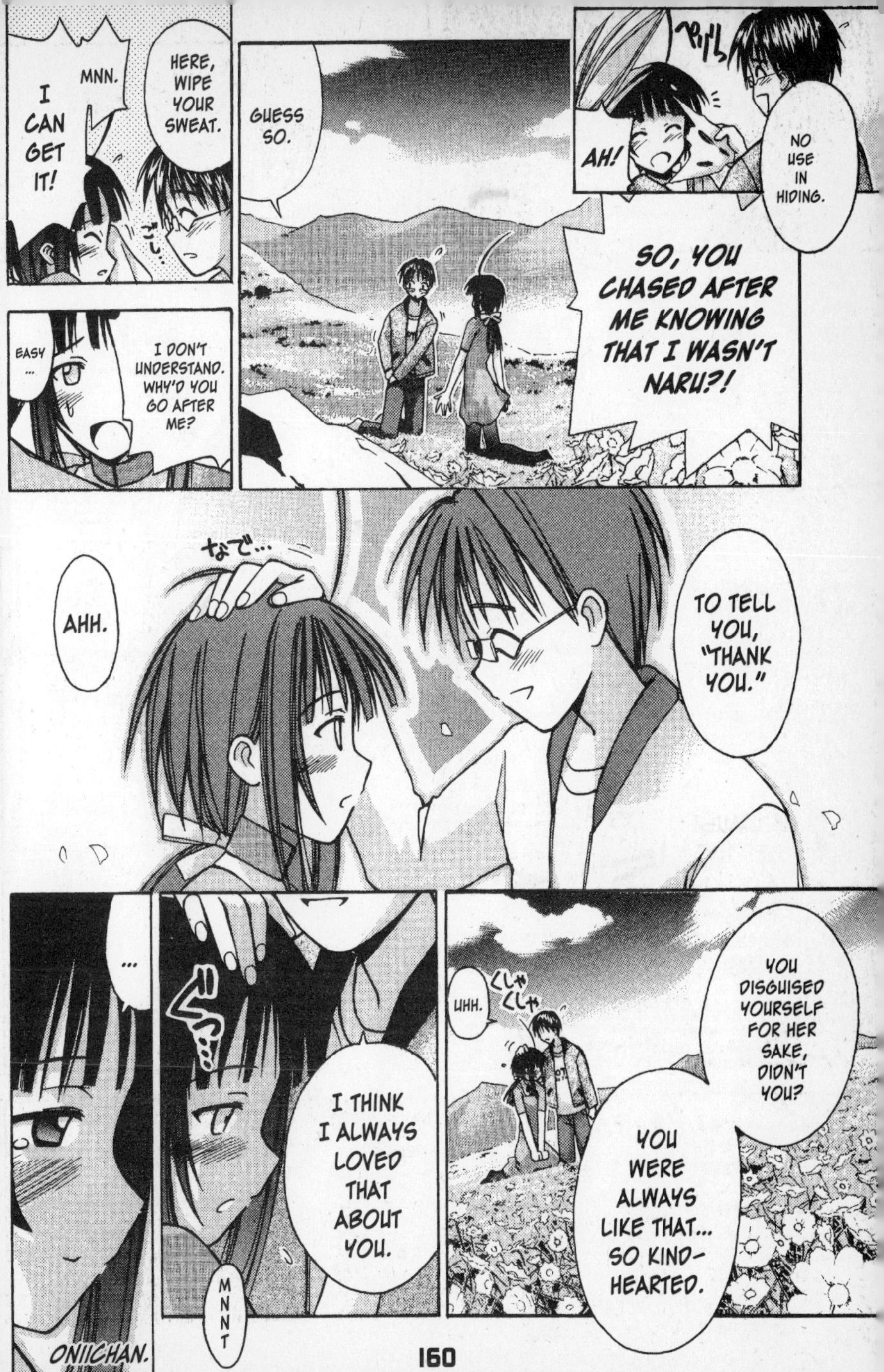
NO USE IN HIDING.
AH!
SO, YOU CHASED AFTER ME KNOWING THAT I WASN'T NARU?!
GUESS SO.
HERE, WIPE YOUR SWEAT.
MNN.
I CAN GET IT!
I DON'T UNDERSTAND. WHY'D YOU GO AFTER ME?
EASY ...
TO TELL YOU, "THANK YOU."
なで…
AHH.
YOU DISGUISED YOURSELF FOR HER SAKE, DIDN'T YOU?
YOU WERE ALWAYS LIKE THAT... SO KIND-HEARTED.
くしゃ くしゃ
UHH.
I THINK I ALWAYS LOVED THAT ABOUT YOU.
MNNT
...
ONIICHAN.

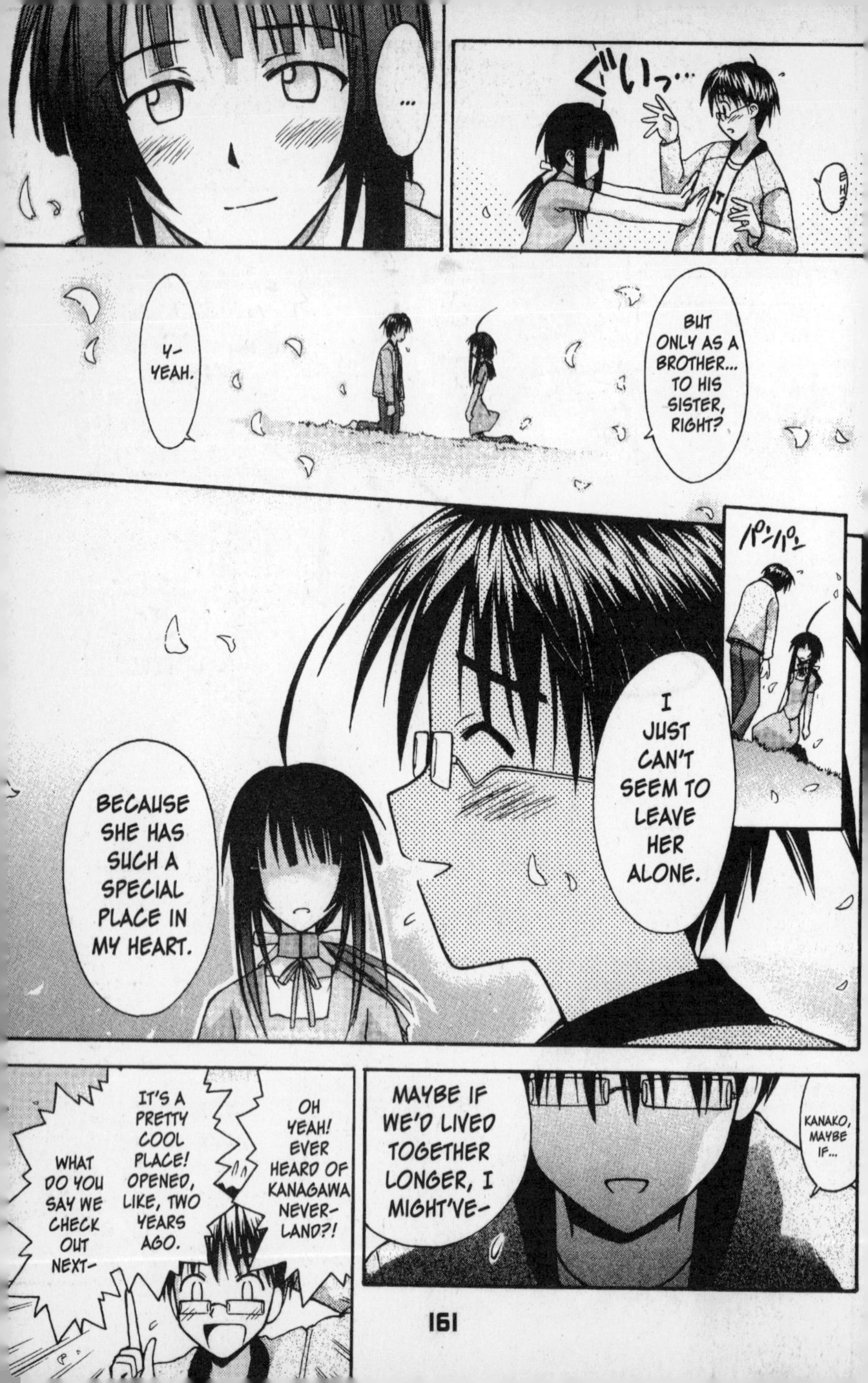
ぐいっ…
EH?
...
BUT ONLY AS A BROTHER... TO HIS SISTER, RIGHT?
Y-YEAH.
パンパン
I JUST CAN'T SEEM TO LEAVE HER ALONE.
BECAUSE SHE HAS SUCH A SPECIAL PLACE IN MY HEART.
KANAKO, MAYBE IF...
MAYBE IF WE'D LIVED TOGETHER LONGER, I MIGHT'VE-
OH YEAH! EVER HEARD OF KANAGAWA NEVER-LAND?!
IT'S A PRETTY COOL PLACE! OPENED, LIKE, TWO YEARS AGO.
WHAT DO YOU SAY WE CHECK OUT NEXT-

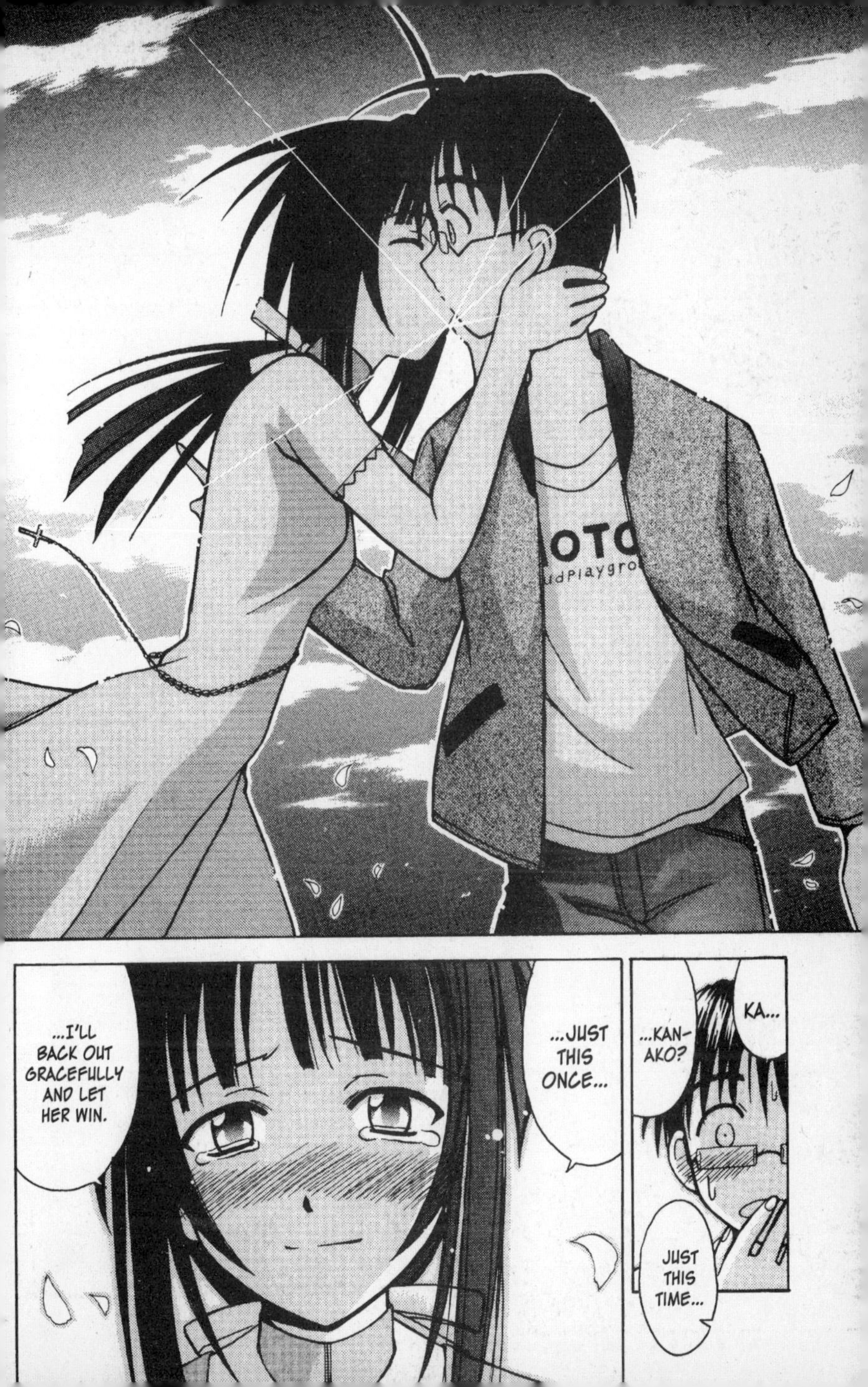
KA...
...KAN-AKO?
JUST THIS TIME...
...JUST THIS ONCE...
...I'LL BACK OUT GRACEFULLY AND LET HER WIN.

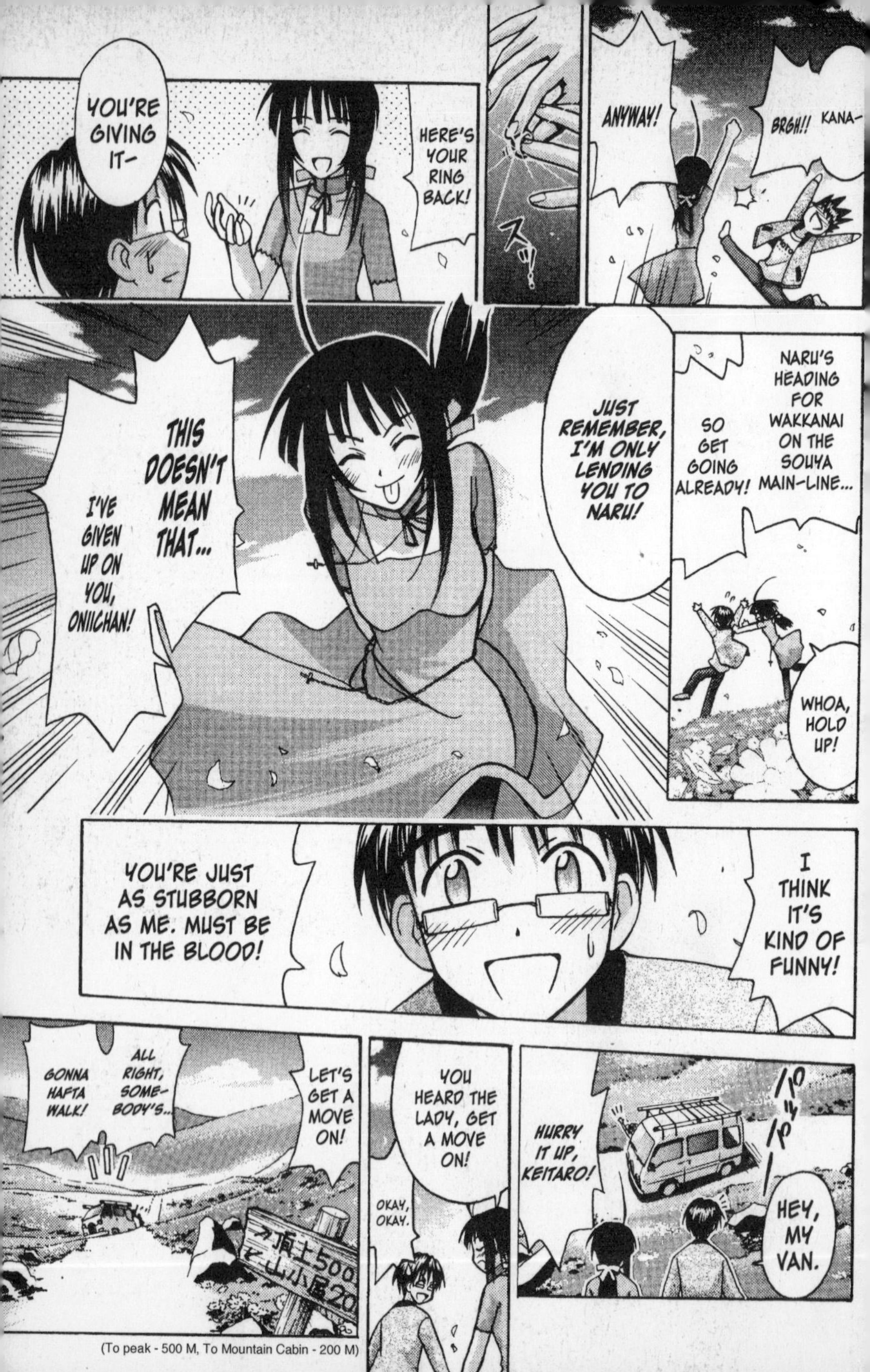
BRGH!! KANA-
ANYWAY!
HERE'S YOUR RING BACK!
YOU'RE GIVING IT-
NARU'S HEADING FOR WAKKANAI ON THE SOUYA MAIN-LINE...
SO GET GOING ALREADY!
WHOA, HOLD UP!
JUST REMEMBER, I'M ONLY LENDING YOU TO NARU!
THIS DOESN'T MEAN THAT...
I'VE GIVEN UP ON YOU, ONIICHAN!
I THINK IT'S KIND OF FUNNY!
YOU'RE JUST AS STUBBORN AS ME. MUST BE IN THE BLOOD!
HEY, MY VAN.
HURRY IT UP, KEITARO!
YOU HEARD THE LADY, GET A MOVE ON!
OKAY, OKAY.
LET'S GET A MOVE ON!
ALL RIGHT, SOME-BODY'S...
GONNA HAFTA WALK!

(To peak - 500 M, To Mountain Cabin - 200 M)

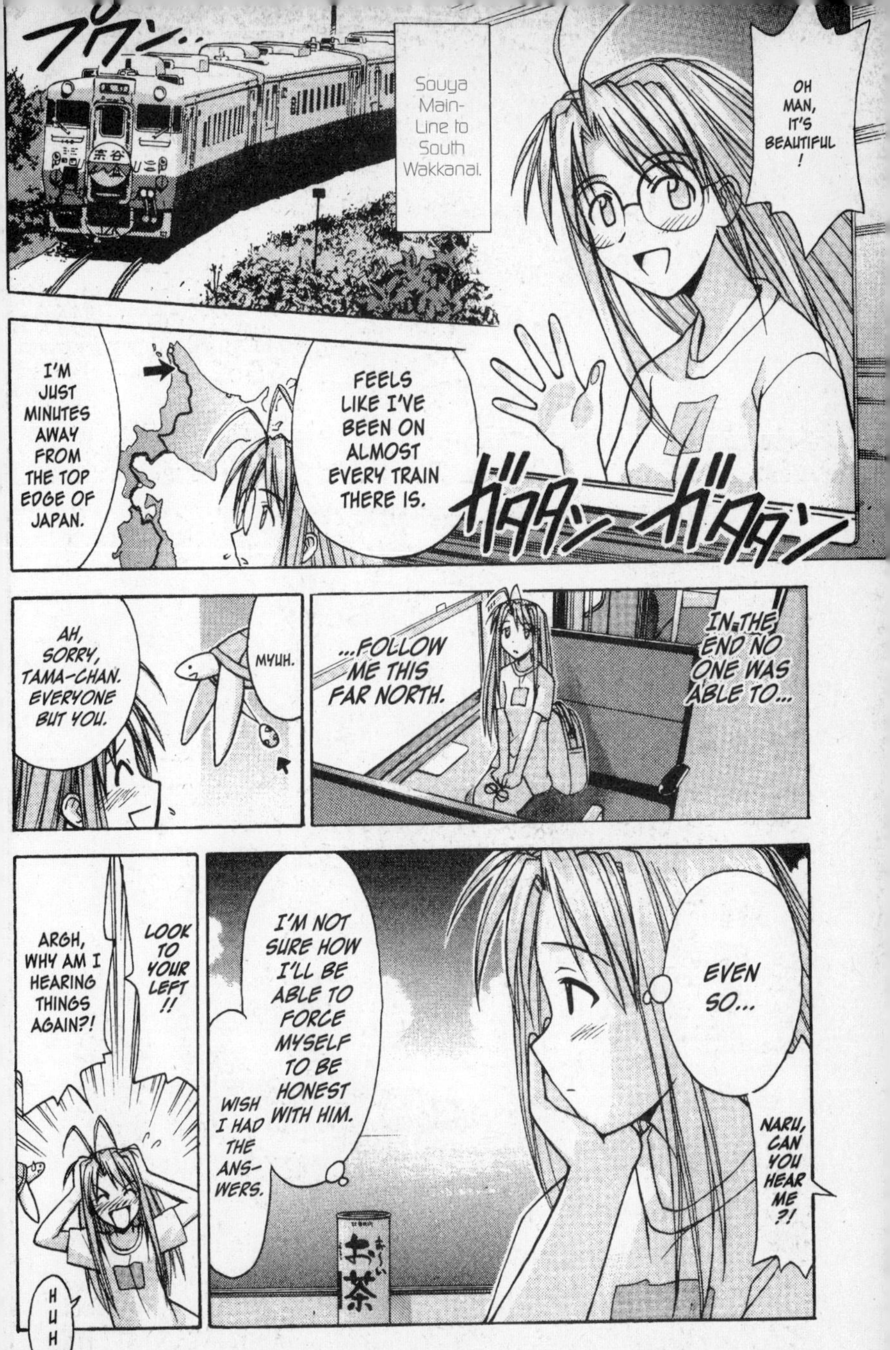

OH MAN, IT'S BEAUTIFUL!
ガタン ガタン
プワン…
Souya Main-Line to South Wakkanai.
FEELS LIKE I'VE BEEN ON ALMOST EVERY TRAIN THERE IS.
I'M JUST MINUTES AWAY FROM THE TOP EDGE OF JAPAN.
IN THE END NO ONE WAS ABLE TO...
...FOLLOW ME THIS FAR NORTH.
MYUH.
AH, SORRY, TAMA-CHAN. EVERYONE BUT YOU.
EVEN SO...
I'M NOT SURE HOW I'LL BE ABLE TO FORCE MYSELF TO BE HONEST WITH HIM.
WISH I HAD THE ANSWERS.
お茶
NARU, CAN YOU HEAR ME?!
LOOK TO YOUR LEFT!!
ARGH, WHY AM I HEARING THINGS AGAIN?!
HUH?

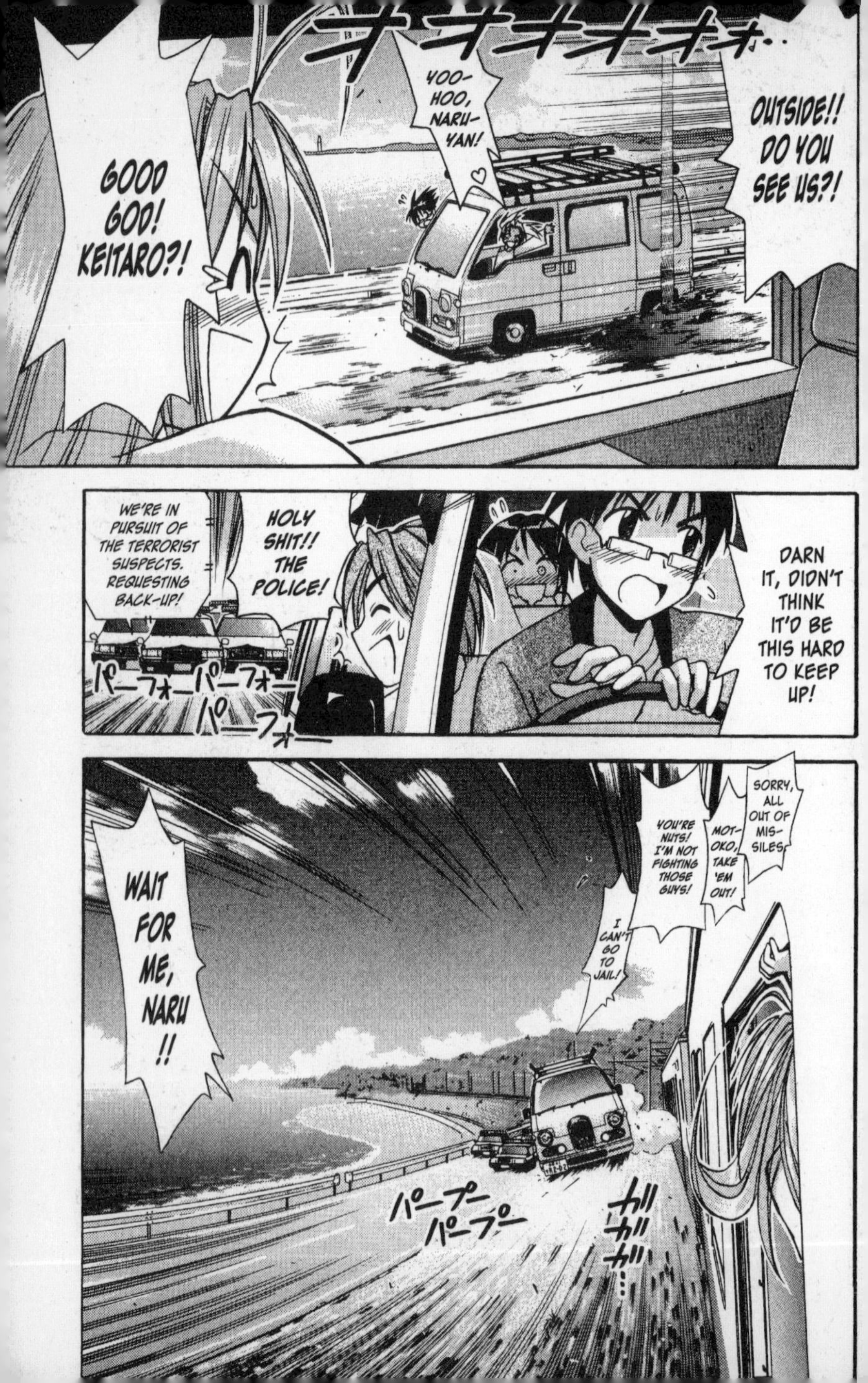
オオオオオォ…
OUTSIDE!! DO YOU SEE US?!
YOO-HOO, NARU-YAN!
GOOD GOD! KEITARO?!
DARN IT, DIDN'T THINK IT'D BE THIS HARD TO KEEP UP!
HOLY SHIT!! THE POLICE!
WE'RE IN PURSUIT OF THE TERRORIST SUSPECTS. REQUESTING BACK-UP!
パーフォーパーフォー
パーフォー
SORRY, ALL OUT OF MIS-SILES
MOT-OKO, TAKE 'EM OUT!
YOU'RE NUTS! I'M NOT FIGHTING THOSE GUYS!
I CAN'T GO TO JAIL!
WAIT FOR ME, NARU!!
ガガガガ…
パープー
パープー

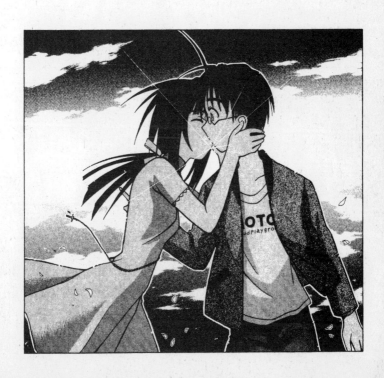

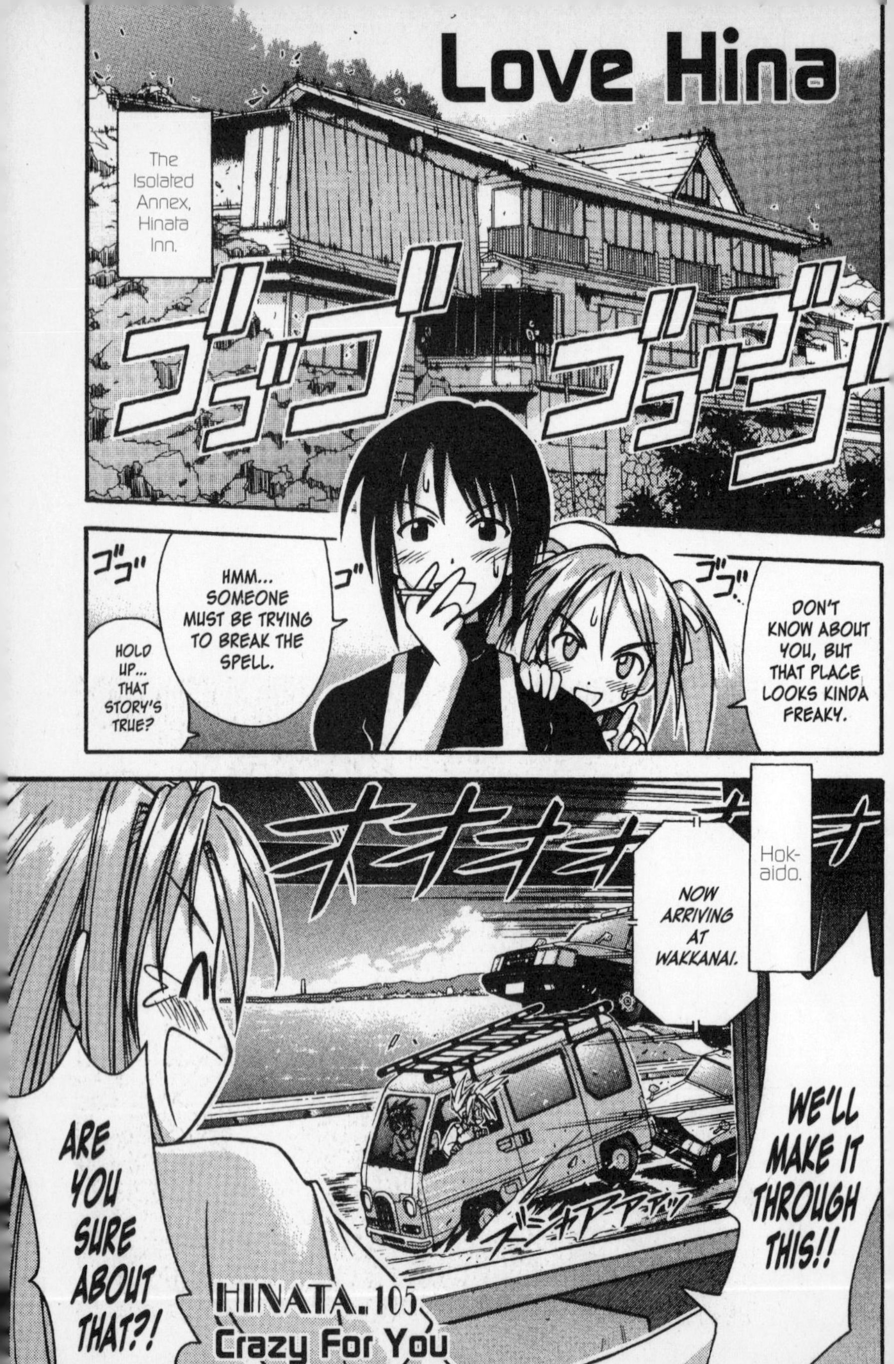
Love Hina
The Isolated Annex, Hinata Inn.
ゴゴゴ
ゴゴゴゴ
ゴゴ
DON'T KNOW ABOUT YOU, BUT THAT PLACE LOOKS KINDA FREAKY.
ゴ
HMM... SOMEONE MUST BE TRYING TO BREAK THE SPELL.
ゴゴ
HOLD UP... THAT STORY'S TRUE?
Hok-aido.
NOW ARRIVING AT WAKKANAI.
WE'LL MAKE IT THROUGH THIS!!
ARE YOU SURE ABOUT THAT?!
HINATA.105
Crazy For You to the Ends of the Earth

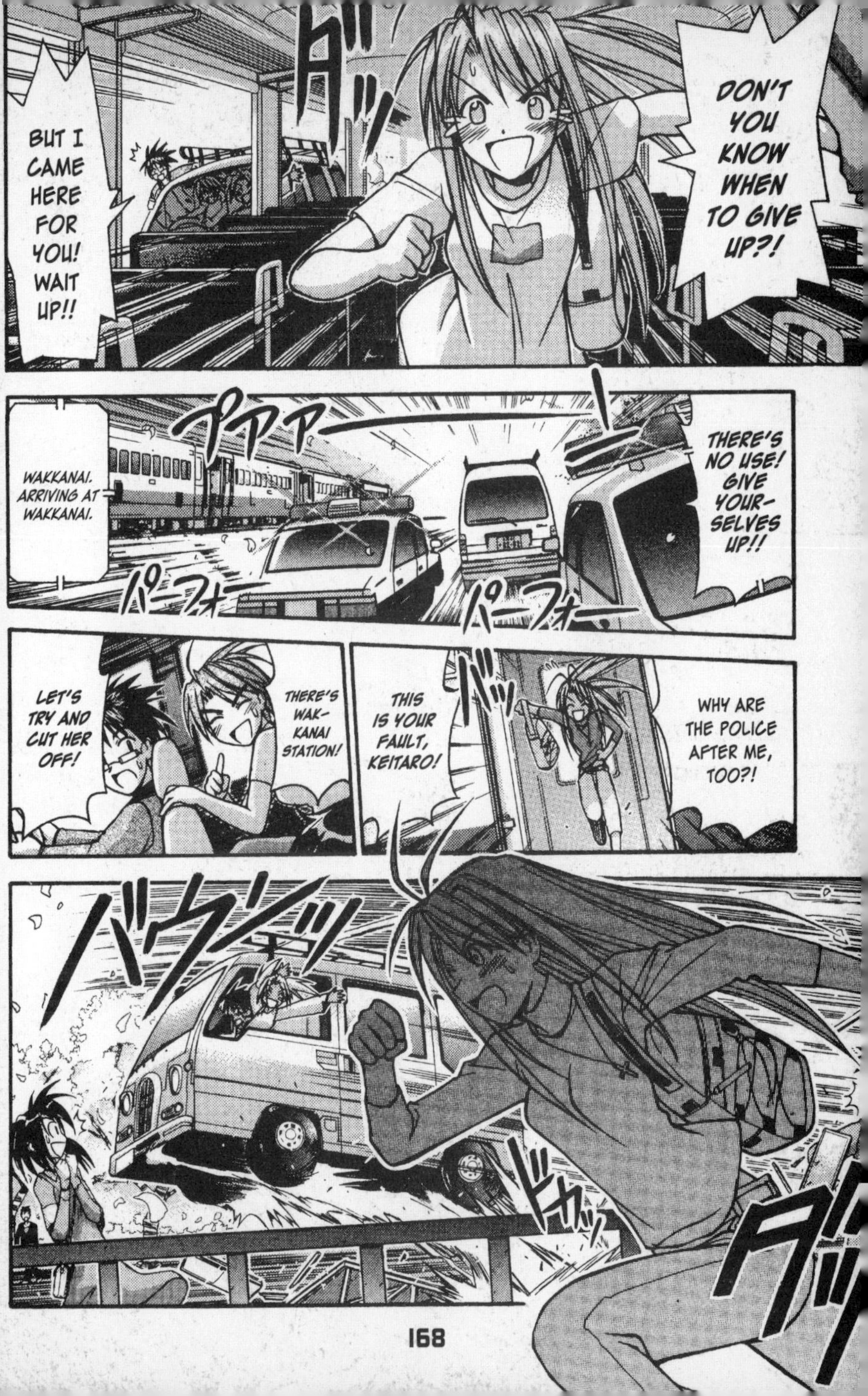
DON'T YOU KNOW WHEN TO GIVE UP?!
BUT I CAME HERE FOR YOU! WAIT UP!!
THERE'S NO USE! GIVE YOUR-SELVES UP!!
WAKKANAI. ARRIVING AT WAKKANAI.
WHY ARE THE POLICE AFTER ME, TOO?!
THIS IS YOUR FAULT, KEITARO!
THERE'S WAK-KANAI STATION!
LET'S TRY AND CUT HER OFF!

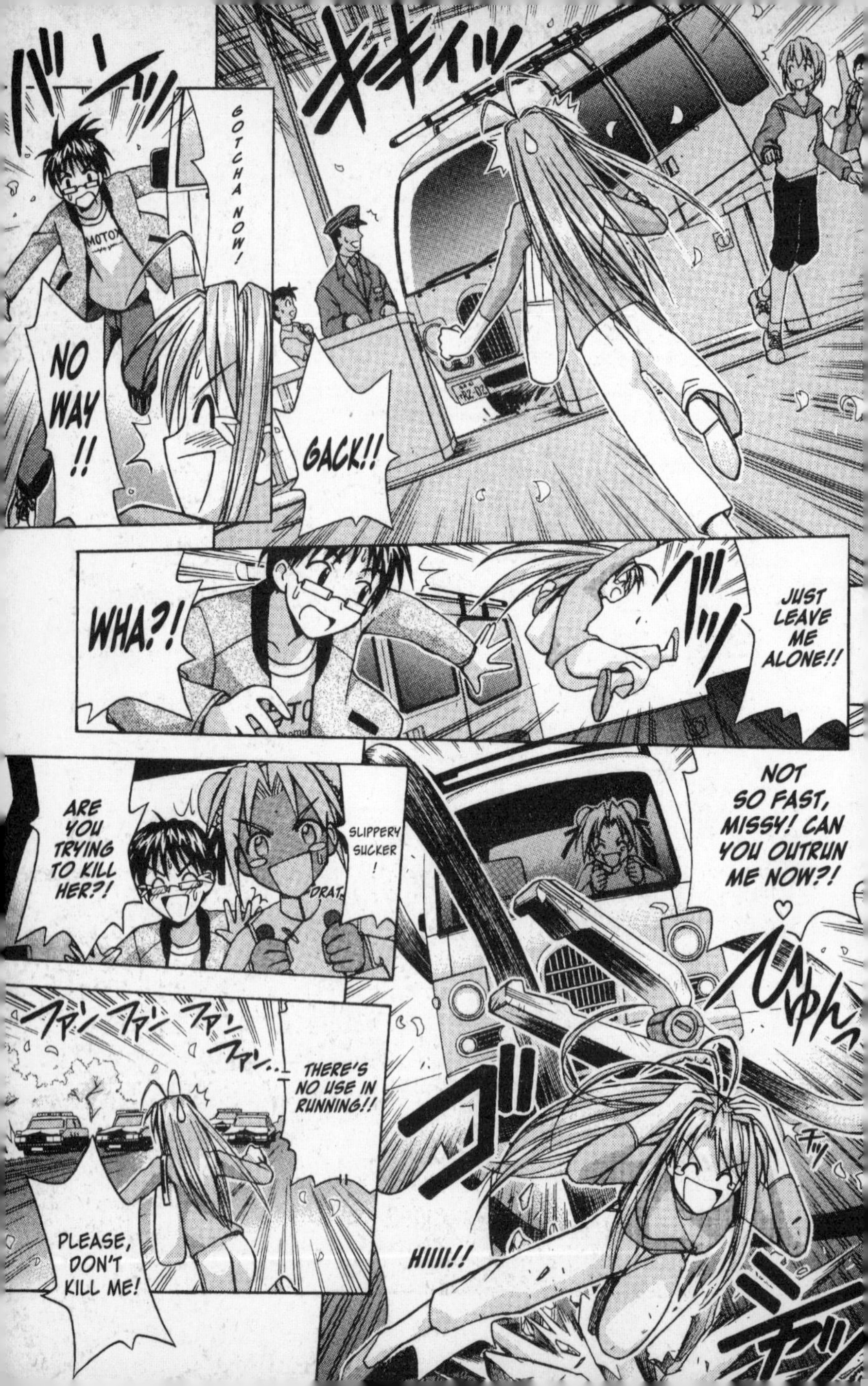

ギギイッ
GACK!!
バーンッ
GOTCHA NOW!
NO WAY!!
JUST LEAVE ME ALONE!!
WHA?!
NOT SO FAST, MISSY! CAN YOU OUTRUN ME NOW?!
SLIPPERY SUCKER!
DRAT.
ARE YOU TRYING TO KILL HER?!
HIIII!!
THERE'S NO USE IN RUNNING!!
PLEASE, DON'T KILL ME!

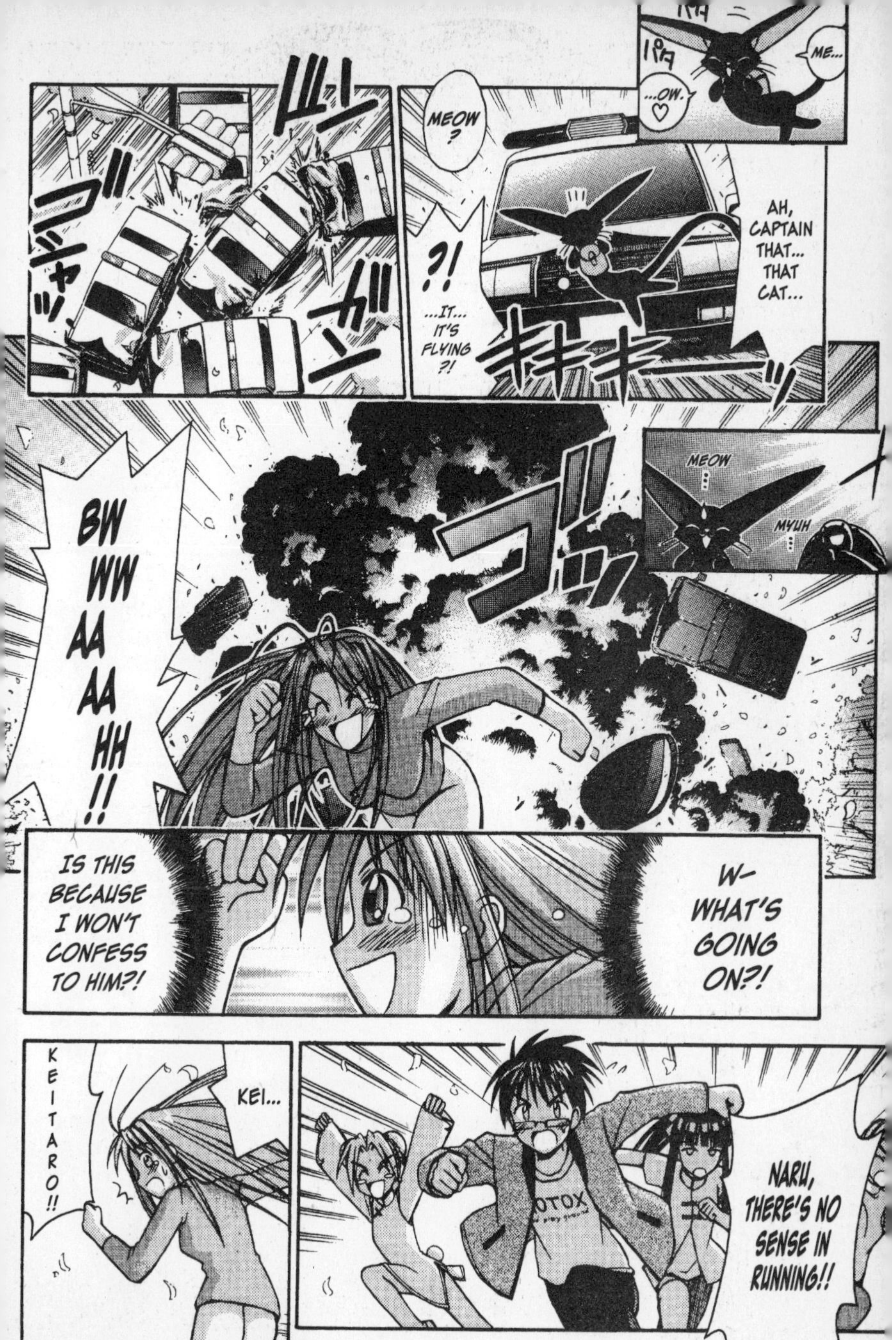
ME...
...OW. ♡
AH, CAPTAIN THAT... THAT CAT...
MEOW ?
?!
...IT... IT'S FLYING ?!
MEOW ...
MYUH ...
BWWWAAAAHH!!
W-WHAT'S GOING ON?!
IS THIS BECAUSE I WON'T CONFESS TO HIM?!
NARU, THERE'S NO SENSE IN RUNNING!!
KEI...
KEITARO!!

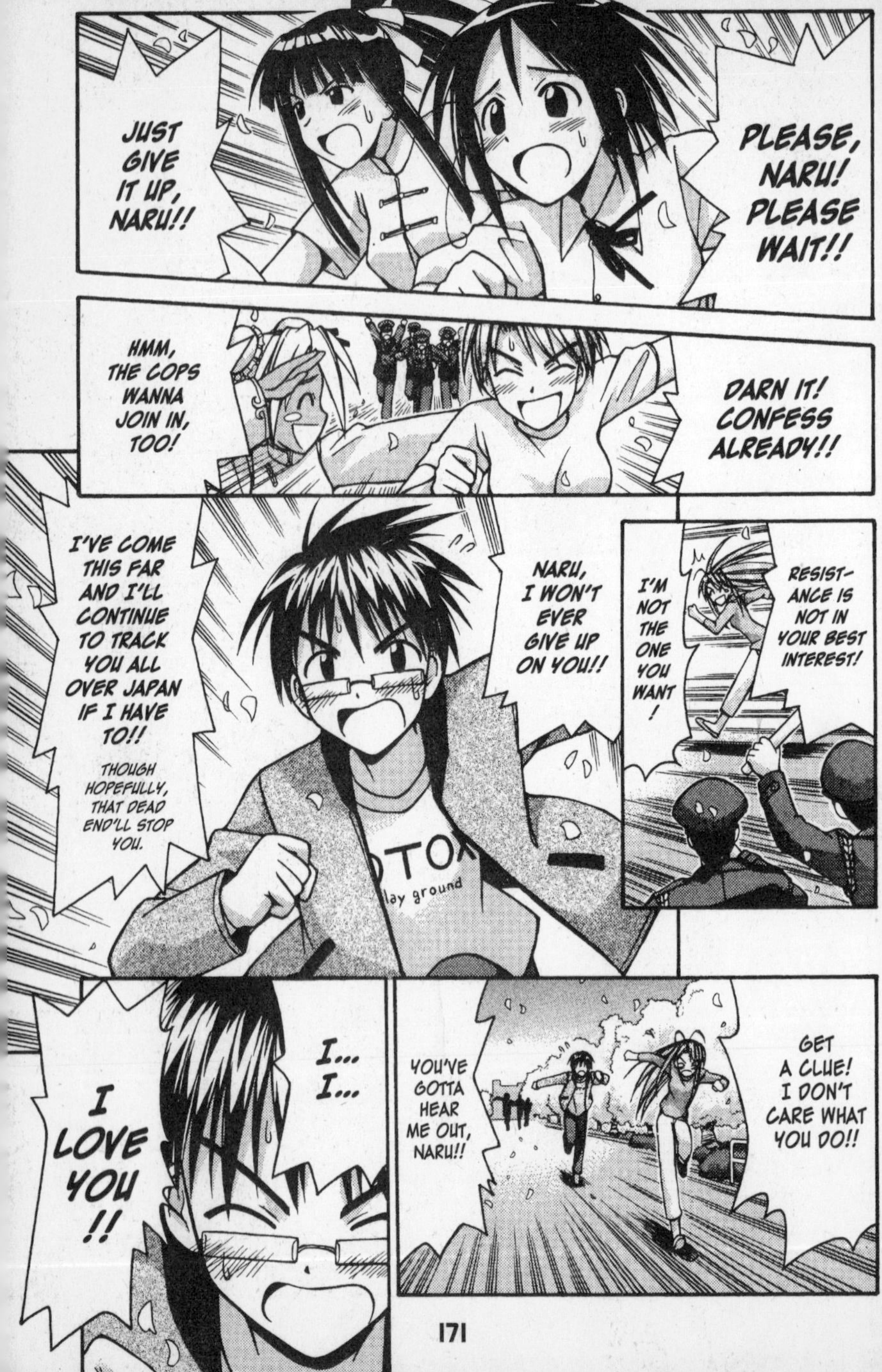
PLEASE, NARU! PLEASE WAIT!!
JUST GIVE IT UP, NARU!!
DARN IT! CONFESS ALREADY!!
HMM, THE COPS WANNA JOIN IN, TOO!
RESIST-ANCE IS NOT IN YOUR BEST INTEREST!
I'M NOT THE ONE YOU WANT!
NARU, I WON'T EVER GIVE UP ON YOU!!
I'VE COME THIS FAR AND I'LL CONTINUE TO TRACK YOU ALL OVER JAPAN IF I HAVE TO!!
THOUGH HOPEFULLY, THAT DEAD END'LL STOP YOU.
GET A CLUE! I DON'T CARE WHAT YOU DO!!
YOU'VE GOTTA HEAR ME OUT, NARU!!
I... I...
I LOVE YOU!!

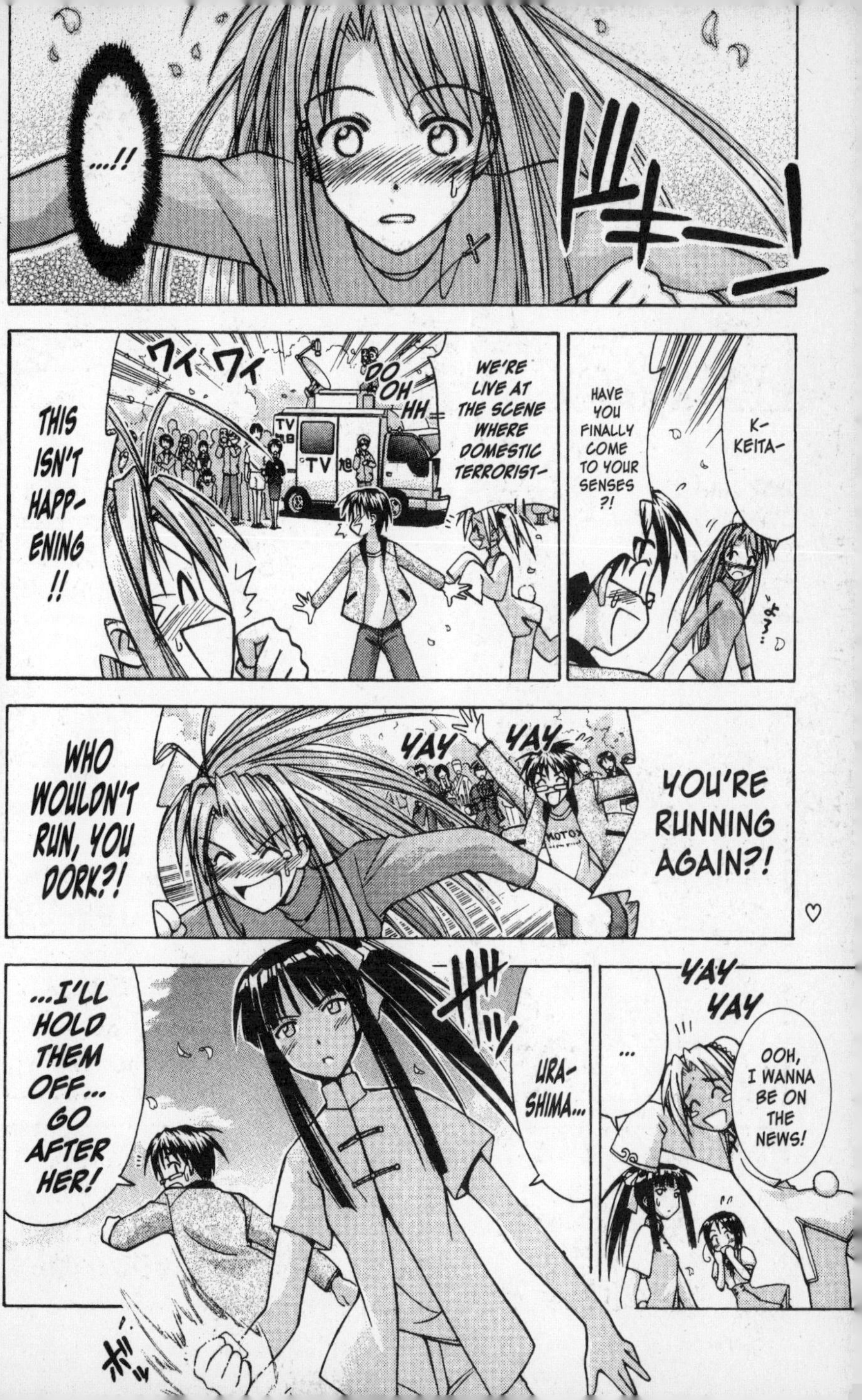

ドキーーッ
...!!
K-KEITA-
HAVE YOU FINALLY COME TO YOUR SENSES?!
よろ...
WE'RE LIVE AT THE SCENE WHERE DOMESTIC TERRORIST-
DOOOHH
ワイワイ
THIS ISN'T HAPPENING!!
YOU'RE RUNNING AGAIN?! ♡
YAY YAY
WHO WOULDN'T RUN, YOU DORK?!
YAY YAY
OOH, I WANNA BE ON THE NEWS!
...
URA-SHIMA...
ガッ
...I'LL HOLD THEM OFF... GO AFTER HER!
ボッ

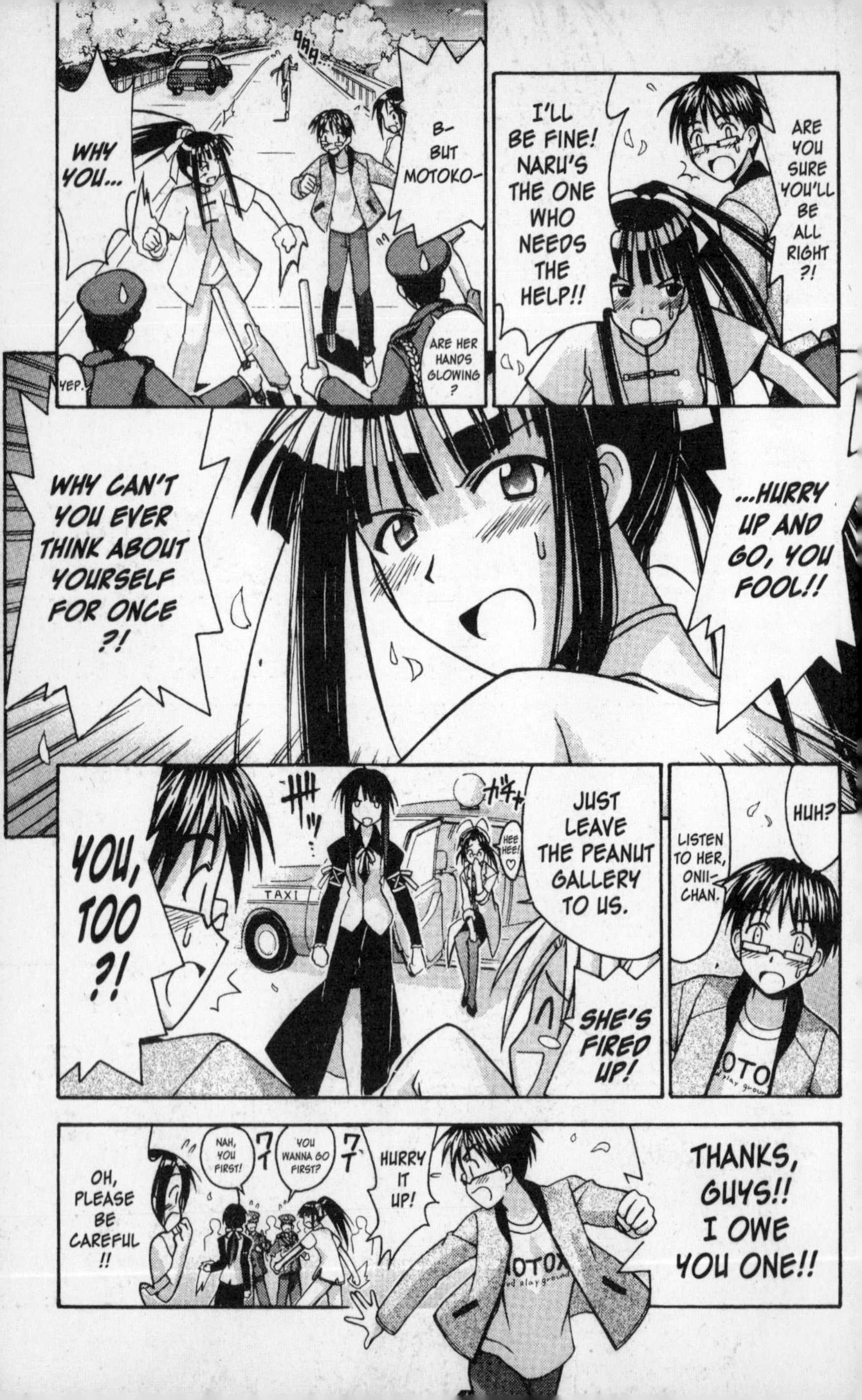
ARE YOU SURE YOU'LL BE ALL RIGHT?!
I'LL BE FINE! NARU'S THE ONE WHO NEEDS THE HELP!!
B-BUT MOTOKO-
WHY YOU...
ARE HER HANDS GLOWING?
YEP.
...HURRY UP AND GO, YOU FOOL!!
WHY CAN'T YOU EVER THINK ABOUT YOURSELF FOR ONCE?!
HUH?
LISTEN TO HER, ONII-CHAN.
JUST LEAVE THE PEANUT GALLERY TO US.
HEE HEE! ♥
TAXI
SHE'S FIRED UP!
YOU, TOO?!
THANKS, GUYS!! I OWE YOU ONE!!
HURRY IT UP!
YOU WANNA GO FIRST?
NAH, YOU FIRST!
OH, PLEASE BE CAREFUL!!

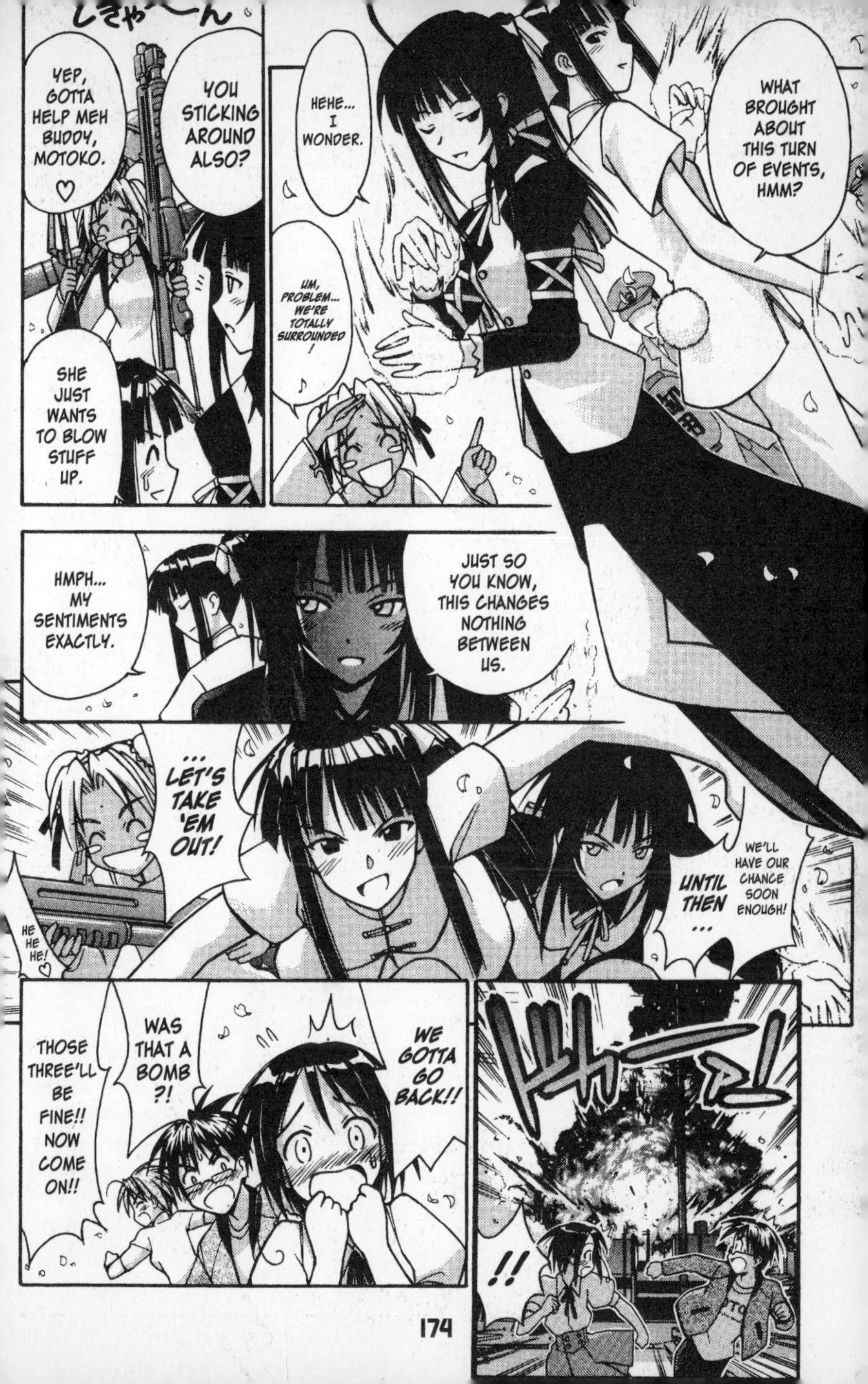
WHAT BROUGHT ABOUT THIS TURN OF EVENTS, HMM?
HEHE... I WONDER.
UM, PROBLEM... WE'RE TOTALLY SURROUNDED!
YOU STICKING AROUND ALSO?
YEP, GOTTA HELP MEH BUDDY, MOTOKO. ♡
SHE JUST WANTS TO BLOW STUFF UP.
JUST SO YOU KNOW, THIS CHANGES NOTHING BETWEEN US.
HMPH... MY SENTIMENTS EXACTLY.
WE'LL HAVE OUR CHANCE SOON ENOUGH!
UNTIL THEN ...
...LET'S TAKE 'EM OUT!
HE HE HE! ♡
!!
WE GOTTA GO BACK!!
WAS THAT A BOMB?!
THOSE THREE'LL BE FINE!! NOW COME ON!!

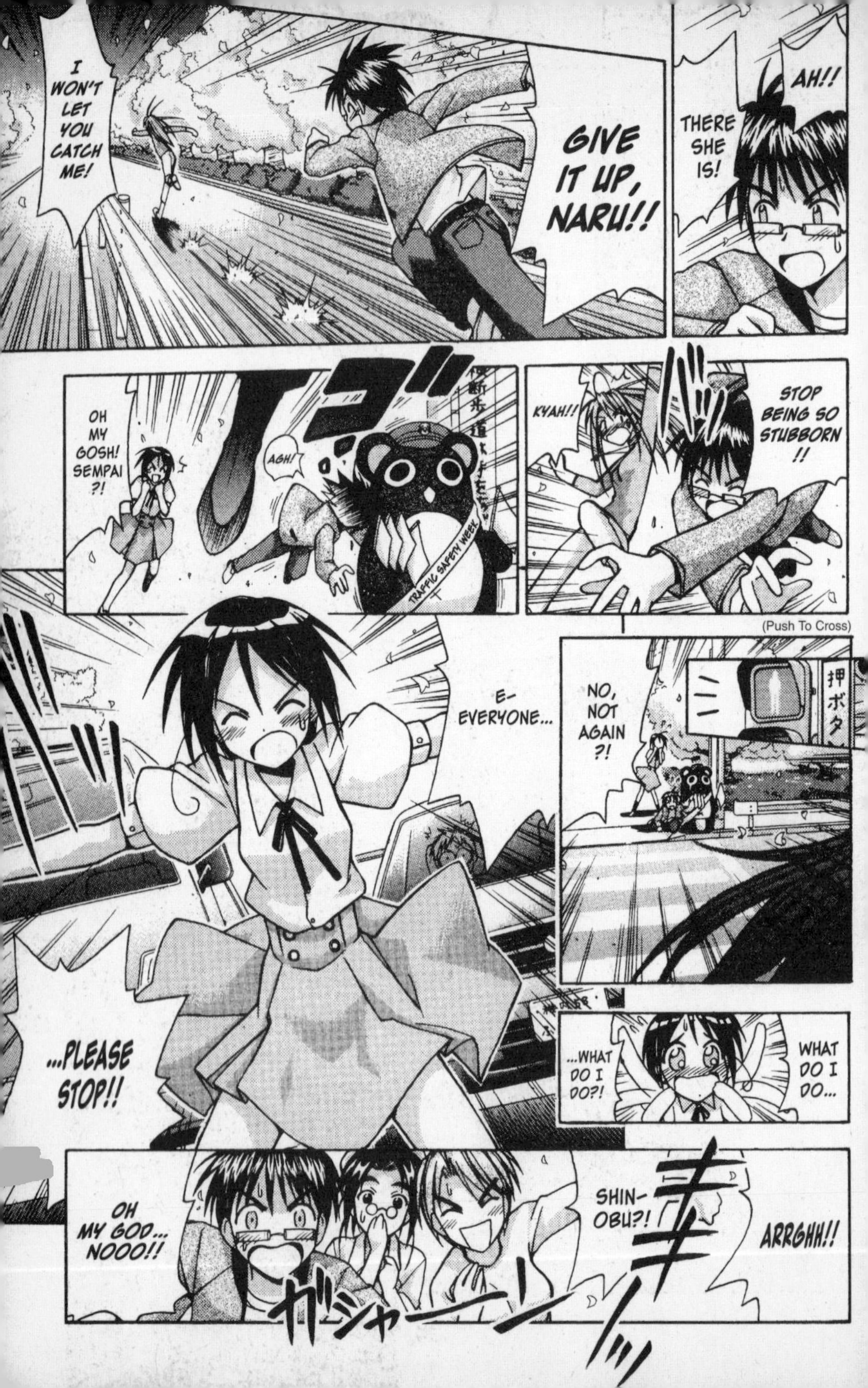
AH!!
THERE SHE IS!
GIVE IT UP, NARU!!
I WON'T LET YOU CATCH ME!
STOP BEING SO STUBBORN!!
KYAH!!
AGH!
TRAFFIC SAFETY WEEK
OH MY GOSH! SEMPAI?!
(Push To Cross)
押ボタ
NO, NOT AGAIN?!
WHAT DO I DO...
...WHAT DO I DO?!
E-EVERYONE...
...PLEASE STOP!!
ARRGHH!!
SHIN-OBU?!
OH MY GOD... NOOO!!

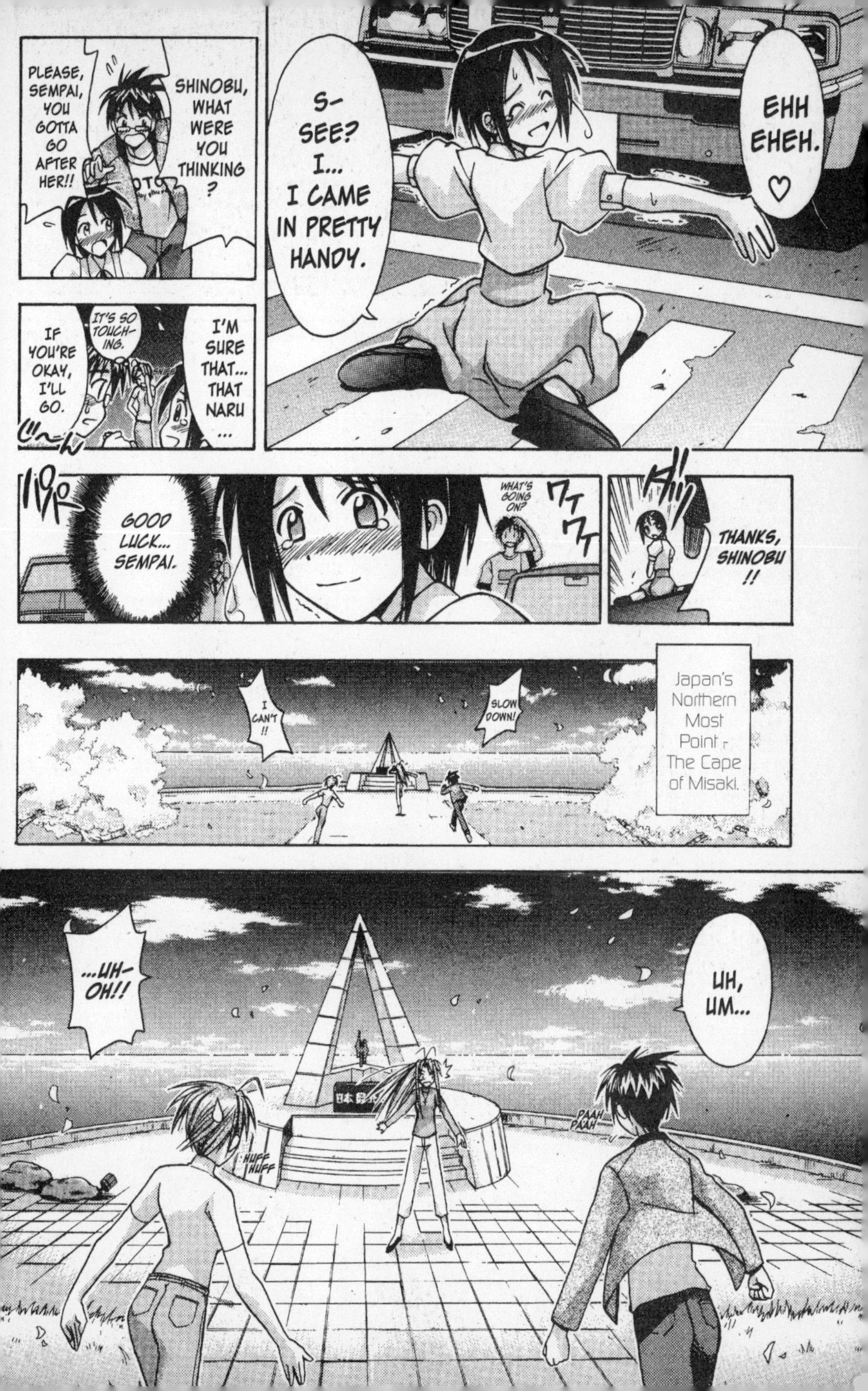
EHH EHEH. ♡
S-SEE? I... I CAME IN PRETTY HANDY.
SHINOBU, WHAT WERE YOU THINKING?
PLEASE, SEMPAI, YOU GOTTA GO AFTER HER!!
I'M SURE THAT... THAT NARU...
IT'S SO TOUCHING.
IF YOU'RE OKAY, I'LL GO.
THANKS, SHINOBU!!
WHAT'S GOING ON?
GOOD LUCK... SEMPAI.
Japan's Northern Most Point r The Cape of Misaki.
SLOW DOWN!
I CAN'T!!
UH, UM...
PAAH PAAH
HUFF HUFF
...UH-OH!!

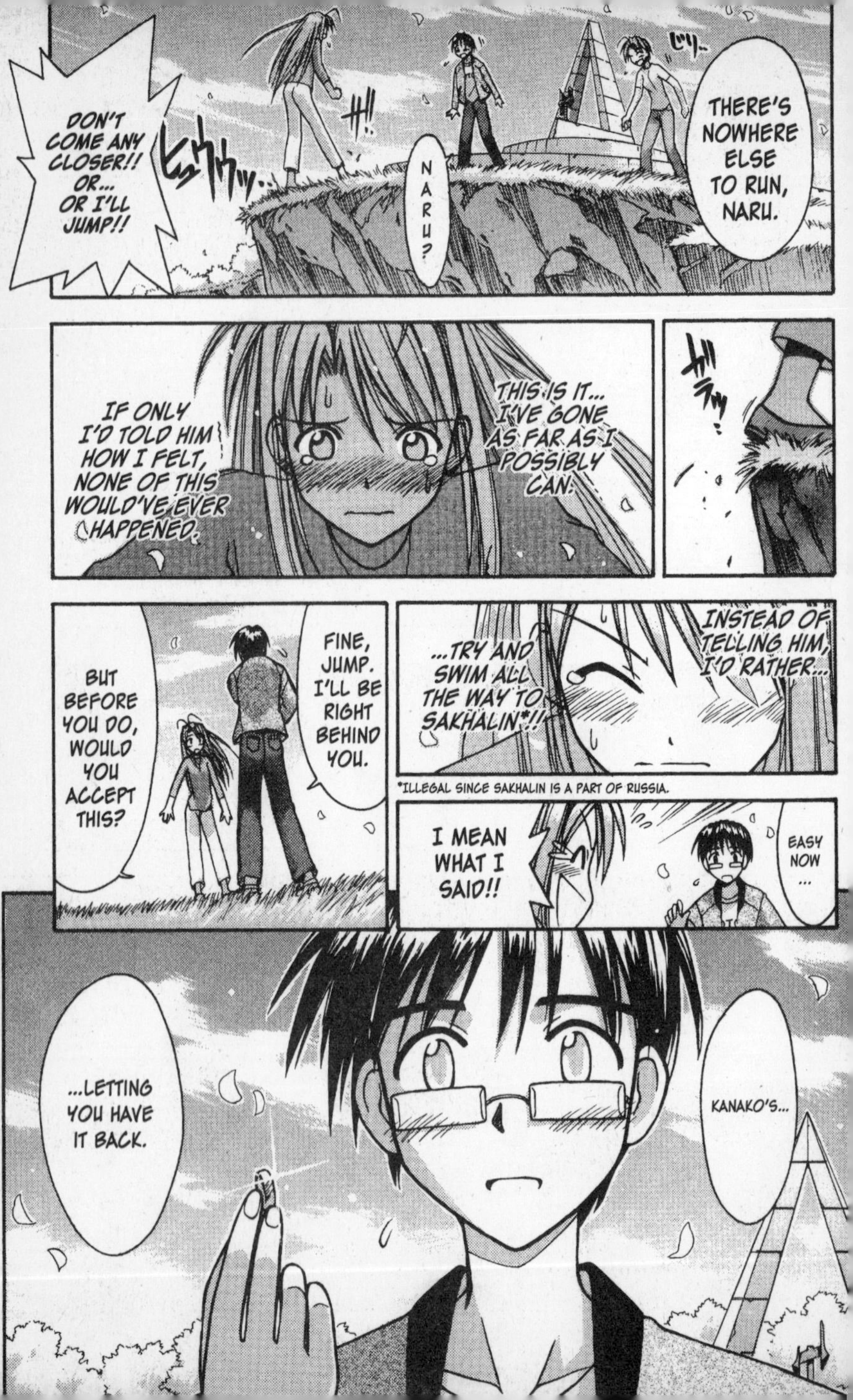
THERE'S NOWHERE ELSE TO RUN, NARU.
NARU?
DON'T COME ANY CLOSER!! OR... OR I'LL JUMP!!
THIS IS IT... I'VE GONE AS FAR AS I POSSIBLY CAN.
IF ONLY I'D TOLD HIM HOW I FELT, NONE OF THIS WOULD'VE EVER HAPPENED.
INSTEAD OF TELLING HIM, I'D RATHER...
...TRY AND SWIM ALL THE WAY TO SAKHALIN*!!
*ILLEGAL SINCE SAKHALIN IS A PART OF RUSSIA.
EASY NOW ...
I MEAN WHAT I SAID!!
FINE, JUMP. I'LL BE RIGHT BEHIND YOU.
BUT BEFORE YOU DO, WOULD YOU ACCEPT THIS?
KANAKO'S...
...LETTING YOU HAVE IT BACK.

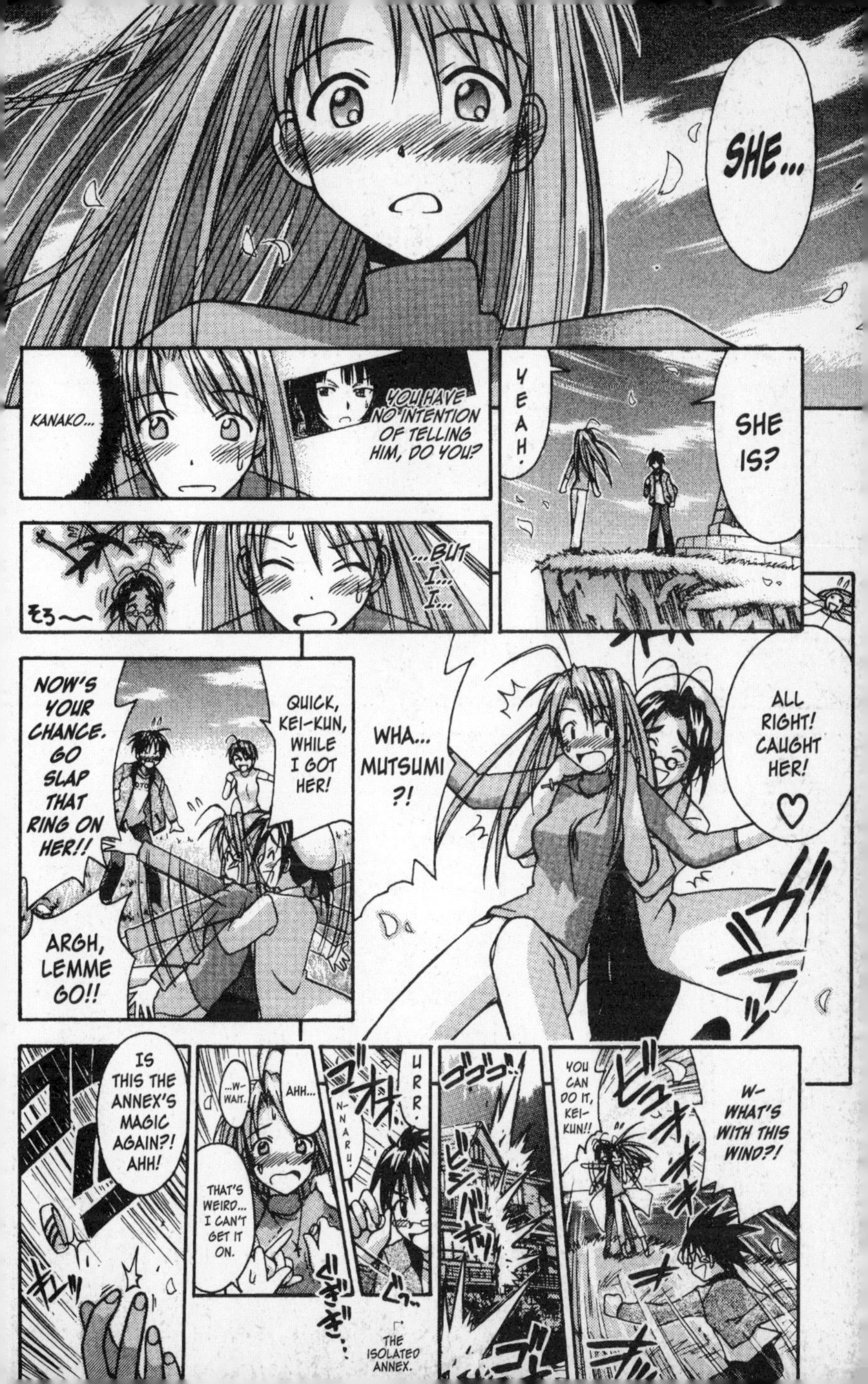
SHE...
SHE IS?
YEAH!
YOU HAVE NO INTENTION OF TELLING HIM, DO YOU?
KANAKO...
...BUT I... I...
そろ～～
ALL RIGHT! CAUGHT HER! ♡
WHA... MUTSUMI?!
QUICK, KEI-KUN, WHILE I GOT HER!
NOW'S YOUR CHANCE. GO SLAP THAT RING ON HER!!
ARGH, LEMME GO!!
W-WHAT'S WITH THIS WIND?!
YOU CAN DO IT, KEI-KUN!!
URR.
N-NARU!
AHH...
...W-WAIT.
THAT'S WEIRD... I CAN'T GET IT ON.
THE ISOLATED ANNEX.
IS THIS THE ANNEX'S MAGIC AGAIN?! AHH!

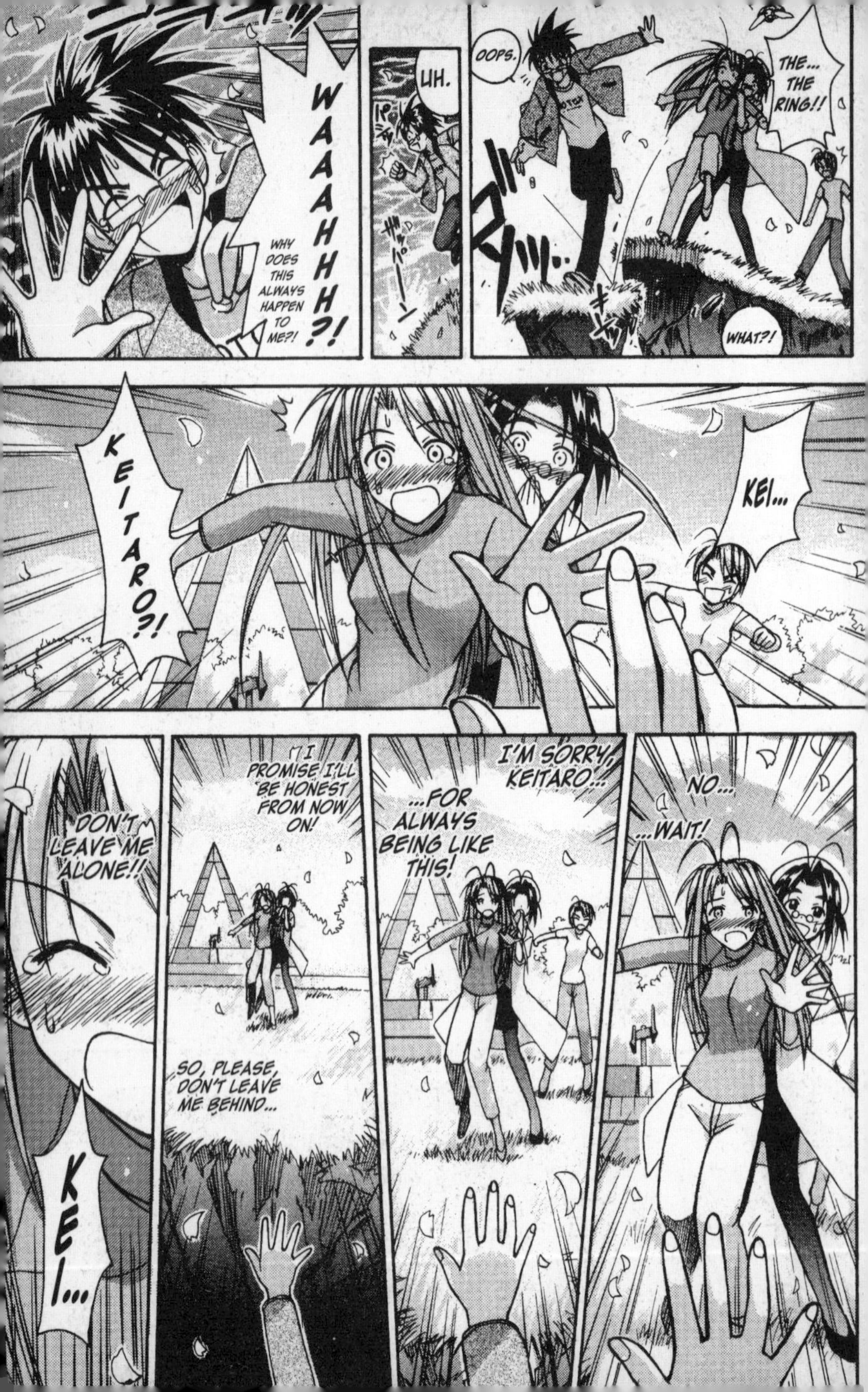
THE... THE RING!!
OOPS.
WHAT?!
UH.
WAAAAHHHH?!
WHY DOES THIS ALWAYS HAPPEN TO ME?!
KEI...
KEITARO?!
NO...
...WAIT!
I'M SORRY, KEITARO...
...FOR ALWAYS BEING LIKE THIS!
I PROMISE I'LL BE HONEST FROM NOW ON!
SO, PLEASE, DON'T LEAVE ME BEHIND...
DON'T LEAVE ME ALONE!!
KEI...

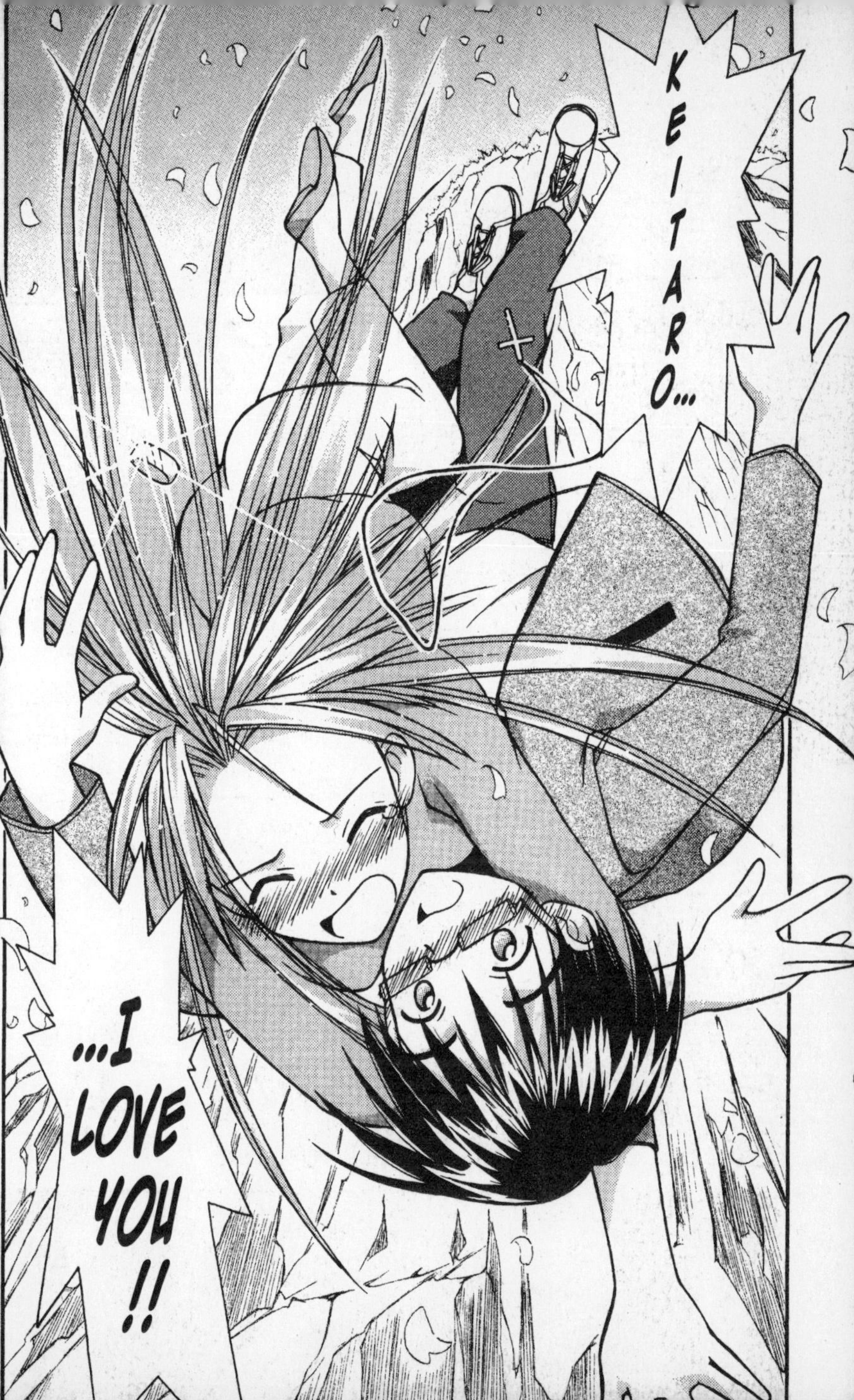
KEITARO...
...I LOVE YOU!!

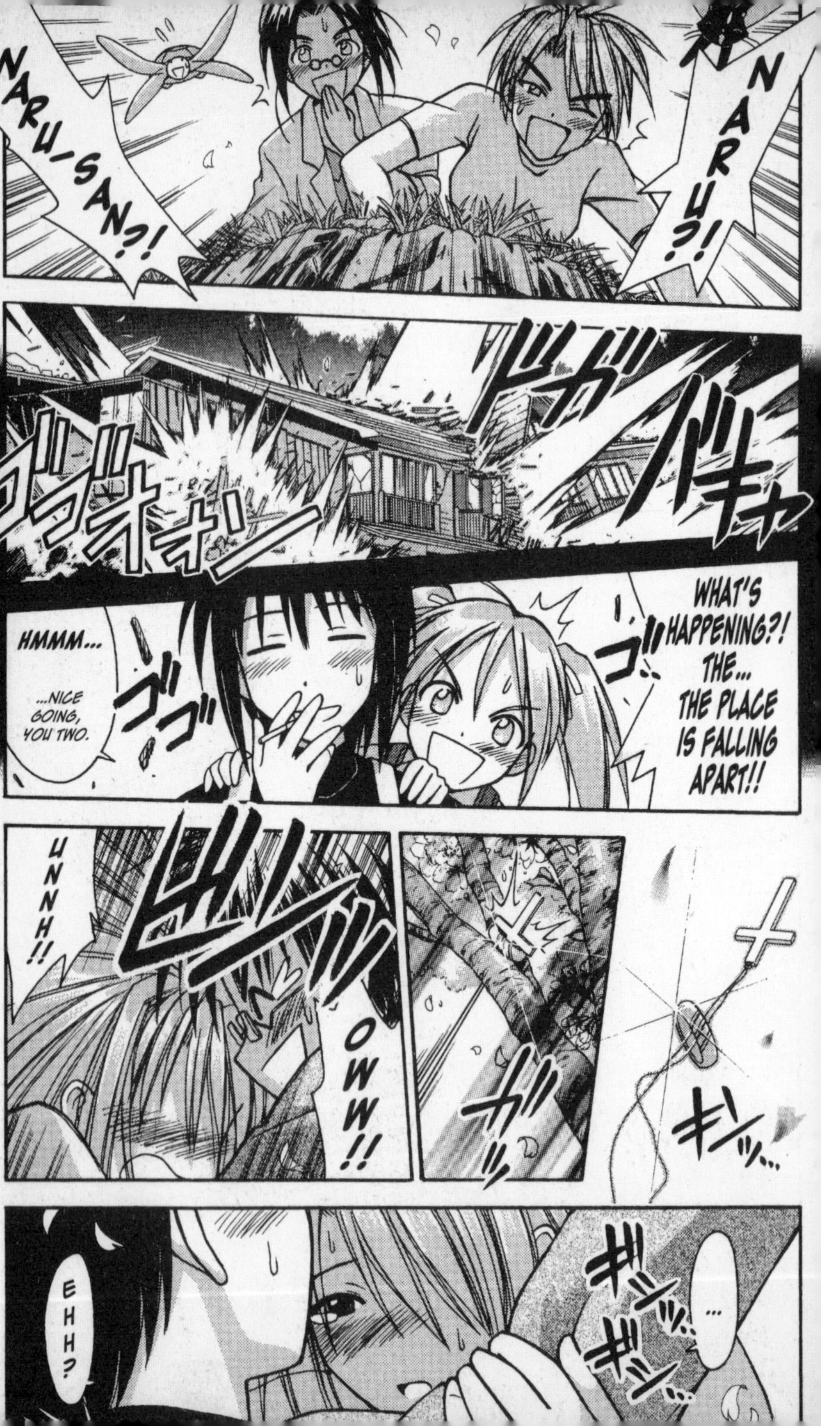
NARU?!
NARU-SAN?!
WHAT'S HAPPENING?! THE... THE PLACE IS FALLING APART!!
HMMM...
...NICE GOING, YOU TWO.
UNNNH!!
OWW!!
...
EHH?

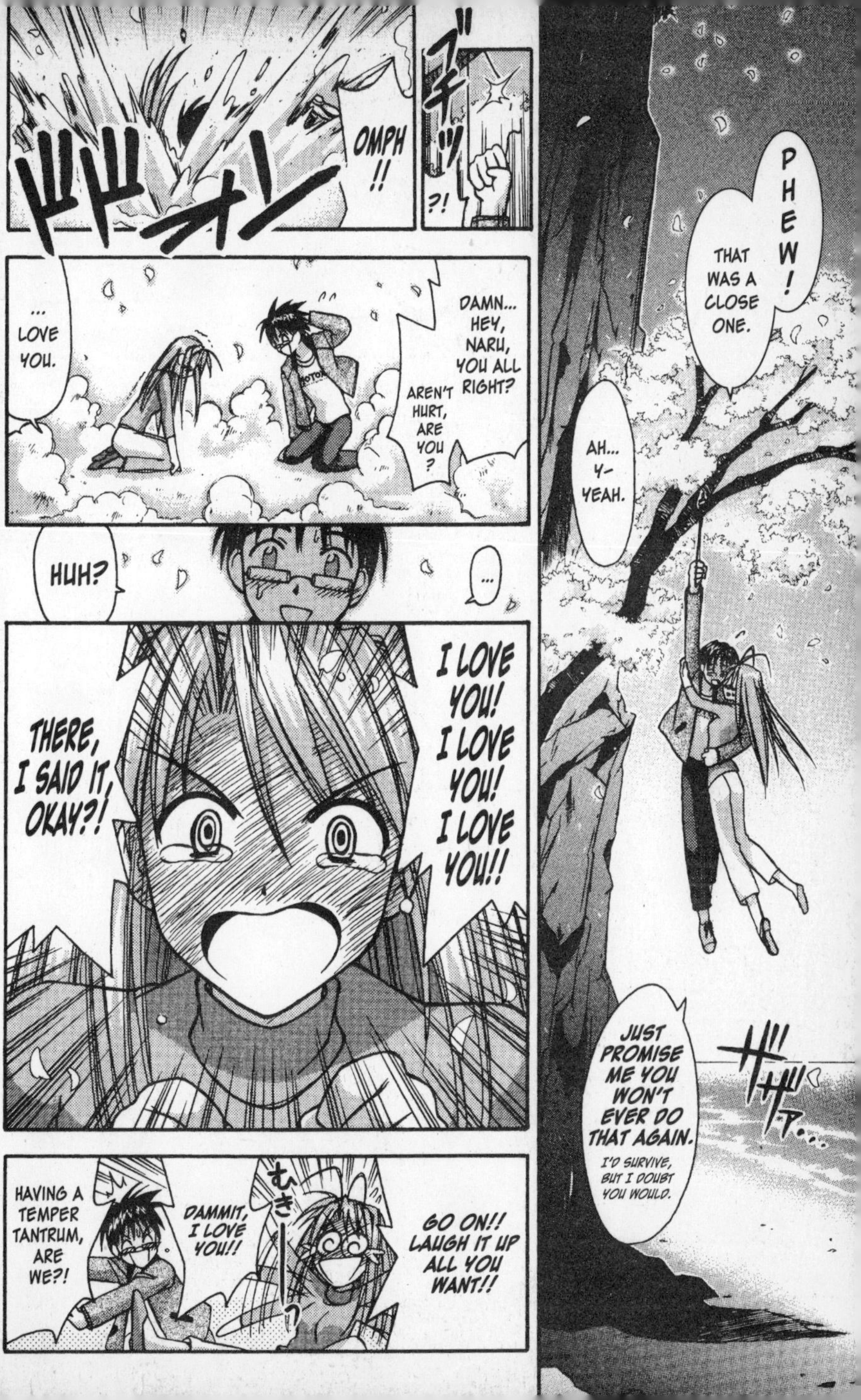
PHEW!
THAT WAS A CLOSE ONE.
AH... Y-YEAH.
ザザッ...
JUST PROMISE ME YOU WON'T EVER DO THAT AGAIN.
I'D SURVIVE, BUT I DOUBT YOU WOULD.
ゴチッ
?!
OMPH!!
ドドォン
DAMN... HEY, NARU, YOU ALL RIGHT?
AREN'T HURT, ARE YOU?
... LOVE YOU.
...
HUH?
I LOVE YOU! I LOVE YOU! I LOVE YOU!!
THERE, I SAID IT, OKAY?!
GO ON!! LAUGH IT UP ALL YOU WANT!!
むきーっ
DAMMIT, I LOVE YOU!!
HAVING A TEMPER TANTRUM, ARE WE?!

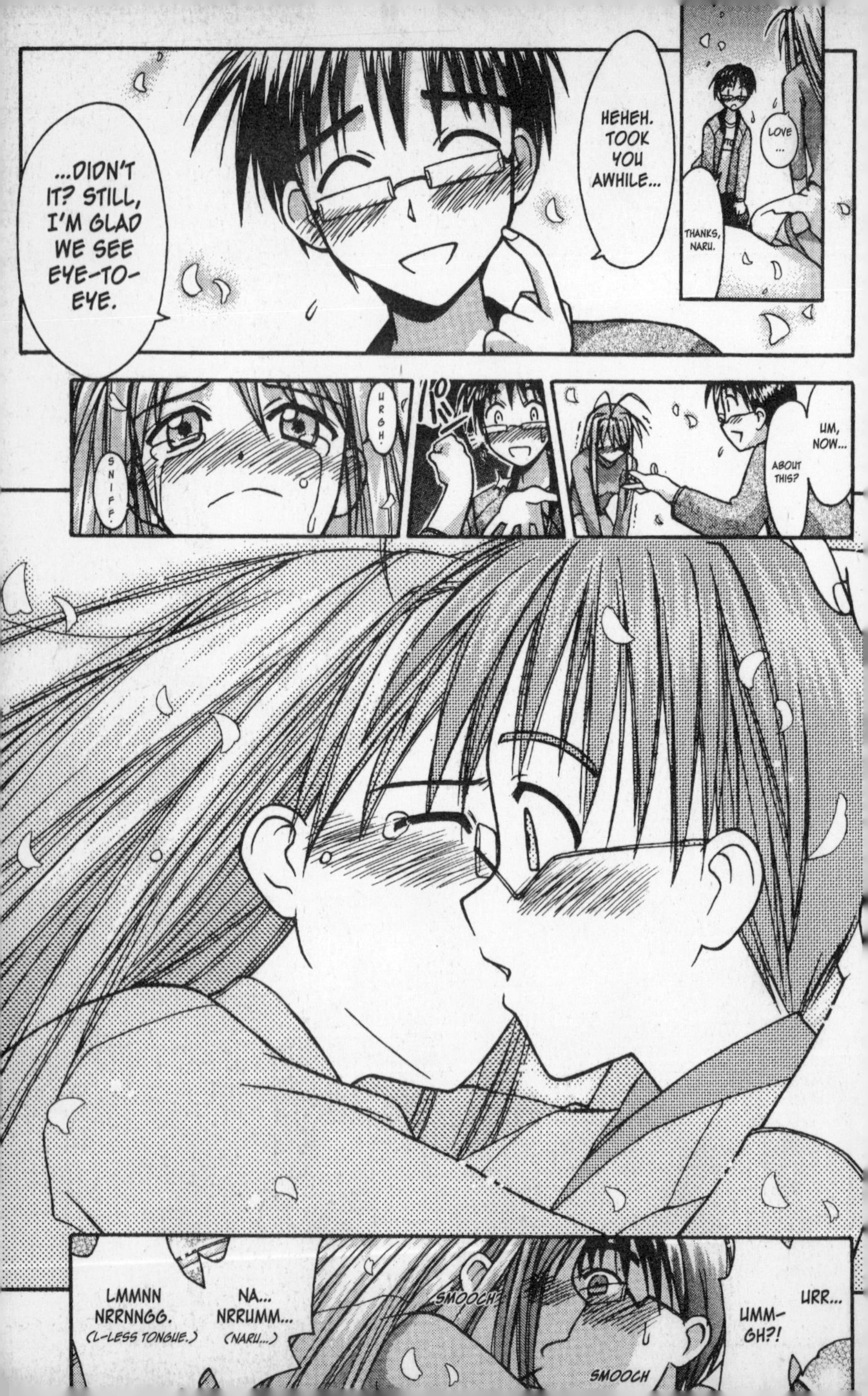
LOVE ...
THANKS, NARU.
HEHEH. TOOK YOU AWHILE...
...DIDN'T IT? STILL, I'M GLAD WE SEE EYE-TO-EYE.
UM, NOW...
ABOUT THIS?
URGH.
SNIFF.
URR... UMM-GH?!
SMOOCH
SMOOCH
NA... NRRUMM...
(NARU...)
LMMNN NRRNNGG.
(L-LESS TONGUE.)

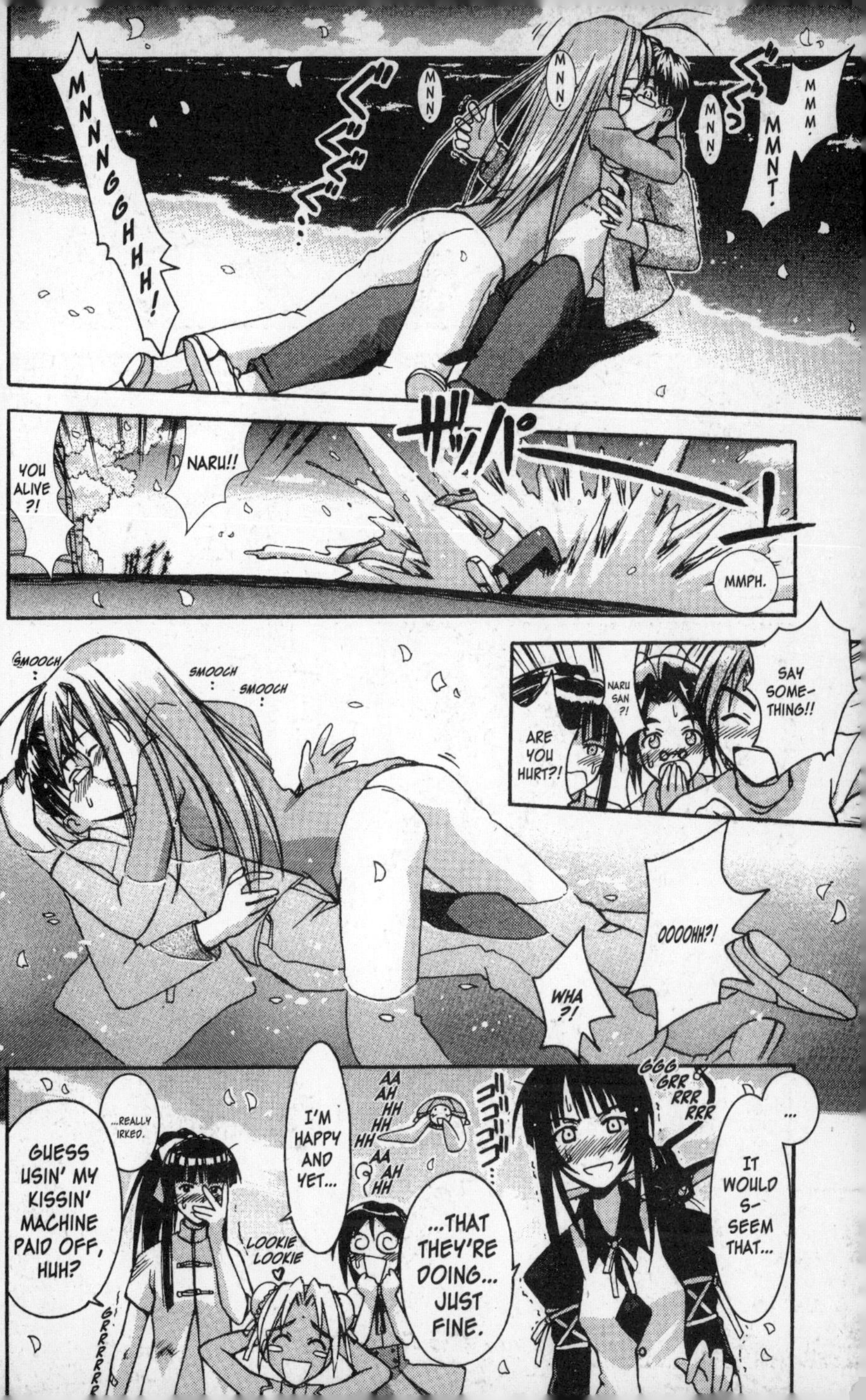
MMM.
MMNT.
MNN.
MNN.
MNNNGGHHHH!
!
MMPH.
NARU!!
YOU ALIVE ?!
SAY SOME-THING!!
NARU SAN ?!
ARE YOU HURT?!
SMOOCH
SMOOCH
SMOOCH
OOOOHH?!
WHA ?!
...
IT WOULD S-SEEM THAT...
GGG GRR RRR RRR
...THAT THEY'RE DOING... JUST FINE.
I'M HAPPY AND YET...
AA AH HH HH HH
AA AH HH
LOOKIE LOOKIE
...REALLY IRKED.
GUESS USIN' MY KISSIN' MACHINE PAID OFF, HUH?
GRRRRRRR

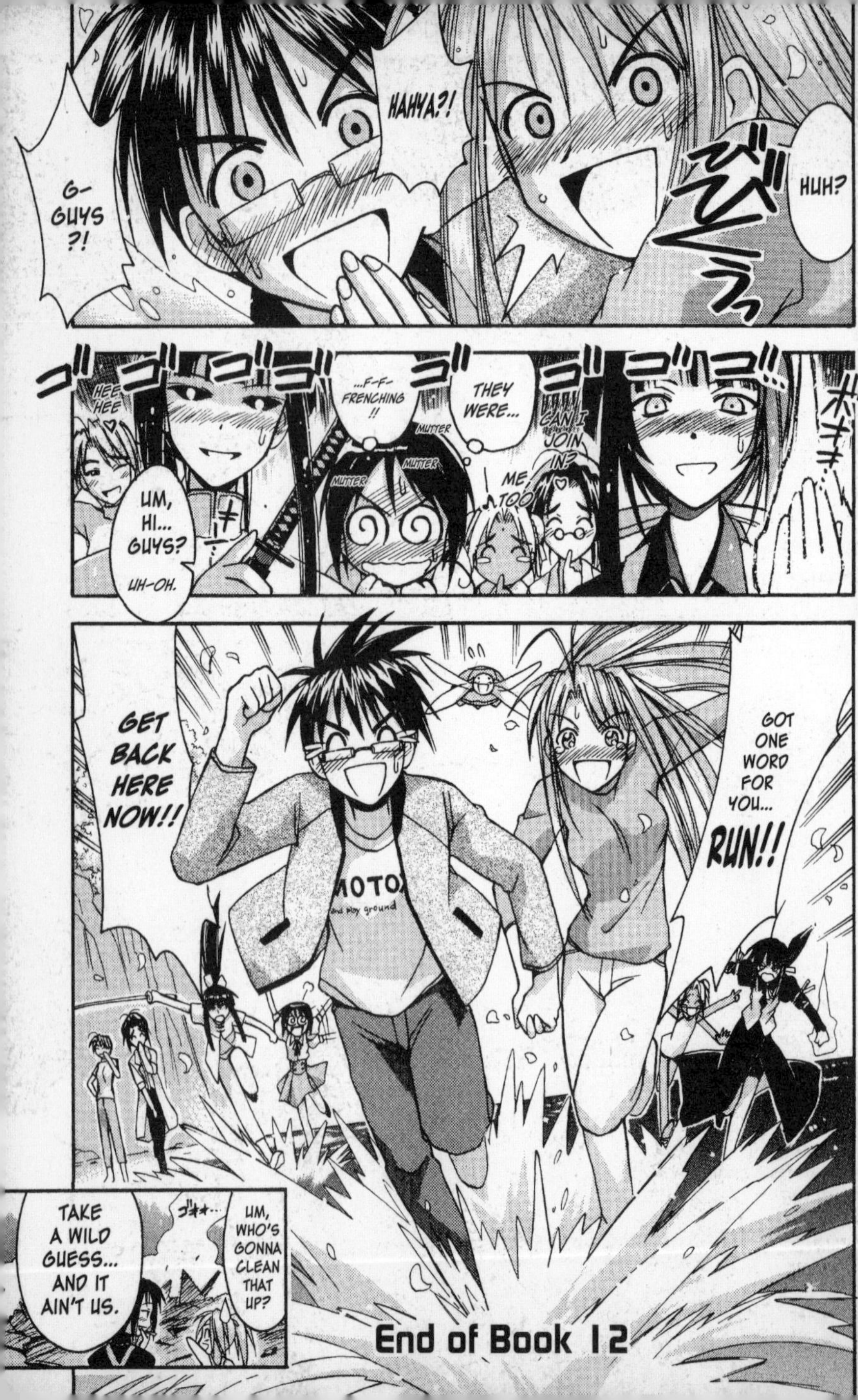
HUH?
HAHYA?!
G-GUYS?!
CAN I JOIN IN?
ME TOO
THEY WERE...
...F-F-FRENCHING!!
MUTTER
MUTTER
MUTTER
HEE HEE
UM, HI... GUYS?
UH-OH.
GOT ONE WORD FOR YOU... RUN!!
GET BACK HERE NOW!!
MOTOX
UM, WHO'S GONNA CLEAN THAT UP?
TAKE A WILD GUESS... AND IT AIN'T US.
End of Book 12

STAFF

Ken Akamatsu
Takashi Takemoto
Kenichi Nakamura
Takaaki Miyahara
Tomohiko Saito
Masaki Ohyama
Ran Ayanaga

EDITOR

Noboru Ohno
Masakazu Yoshimoto
Yasushi Yamanaka

KC Editor

Mitsuei Ishii

In the next volume of

Love Hina

Give Me Tokyo U or Give Me Death

For the moment, the chaos surrounding the Hinata crew has begun to settle down. And Keitaro and Naru have started to show the world that they are indeed a couple, though their relationship still has quite a bit of improving to do before it can move to the next level. But when Motoko realizes she harbors long-buried feelings for Keitaro, she attempts to break up the semi-happy couple.

As a result, Motoko finds herself in the same position Keitaro was once in--and her Tokyo U mock exams reflect it. It's at this pivotal time that her demented sister, Tsuruko, decides to make a surprise visit to Hinata House to congratulate Motoko on making it into Tokyo U! Forced to lie to her sister once again, the situation for Motoko snowballs out of control and the ramifications may leave her forever changed.

However, the problems that Motoko faces pale in comparison to the mammoth decision Keitaro must make when he's taken to the Kingdom of Molmol in this penultimate volume of Love Hina. The moment everyone has been waiting for arrives at last...Keitaro finally chooses the girl he wants to be with!

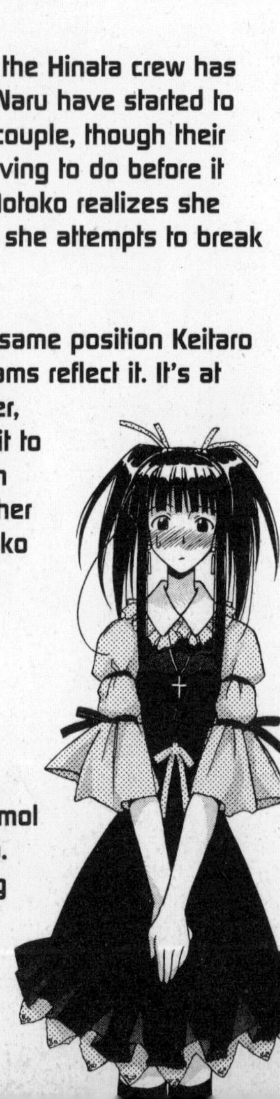

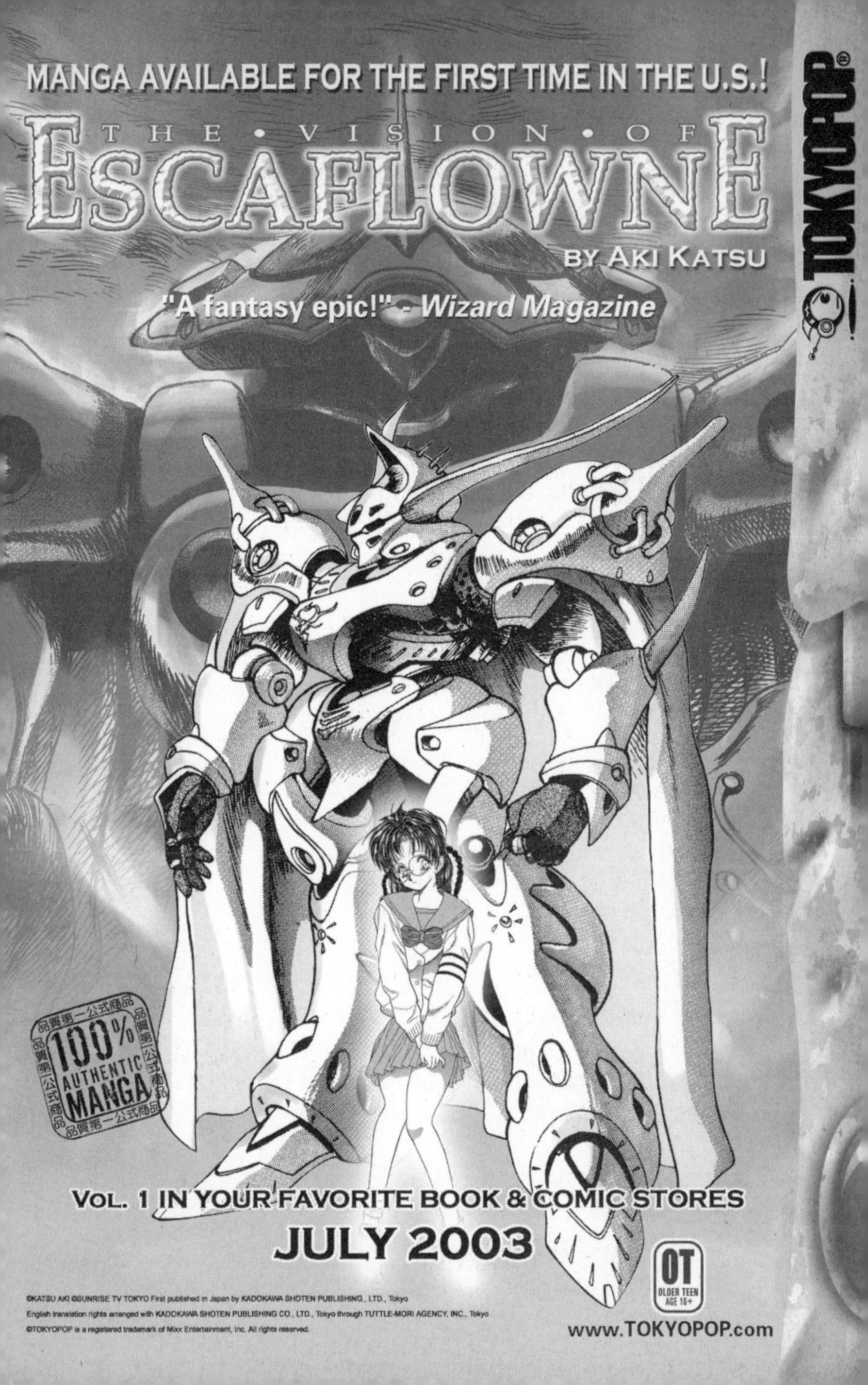

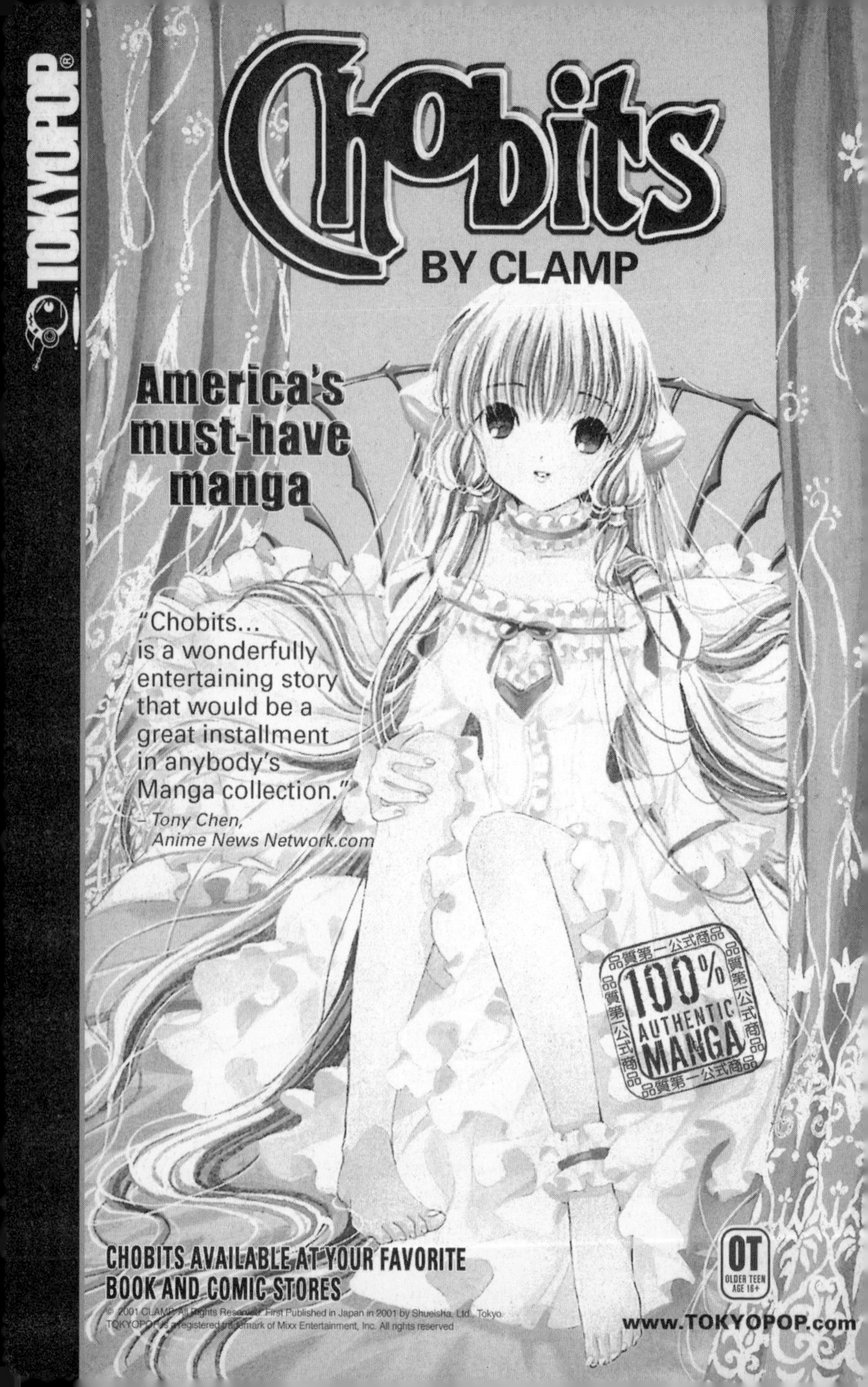
TOKYOPOP®
Chobits
BY CLAMP
America's must-have manga
"Chobits... is a wonderfully entertaining story that would be a great installment in anybody's Manga collection."
– Tony Chen, Anime News Network.com
100% AUTHENTIC MANGA
品質第一公式商品
OT
OLDER TEEN AGE 16+
CHOBITS AVAILABLE AT YOUR FAVORITE BOOK AND COMIC STORES
© 2001 CLAMP. All Rights Reserved. First Published in Japan in 2001 by Shueisha, Ltd., Tokyo.
TOKYOPOP is a registered trademark of Mixx Entertainment, Inc. All rights reserved
www.TOKYOPOP.com

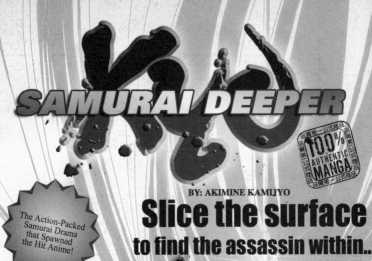

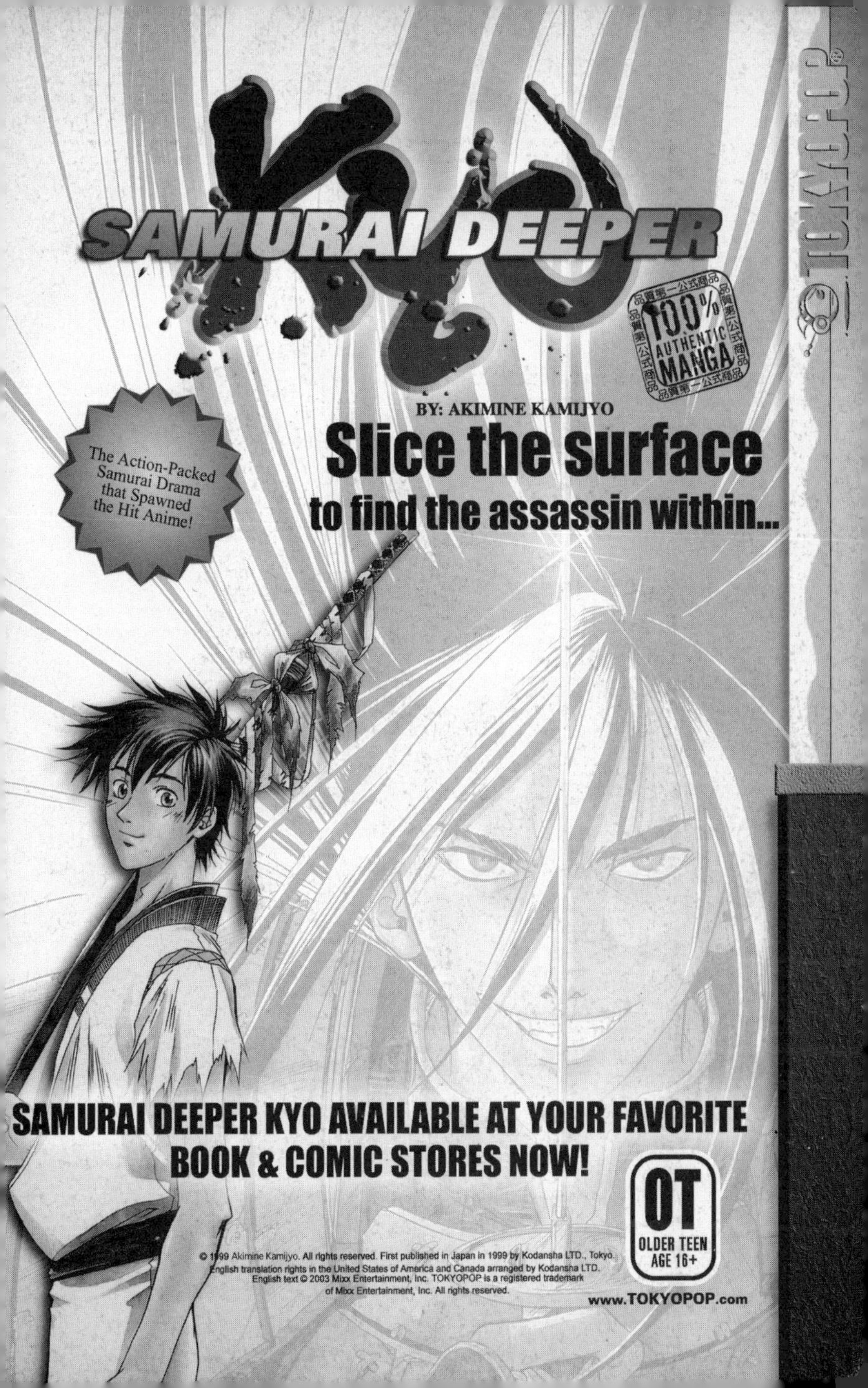

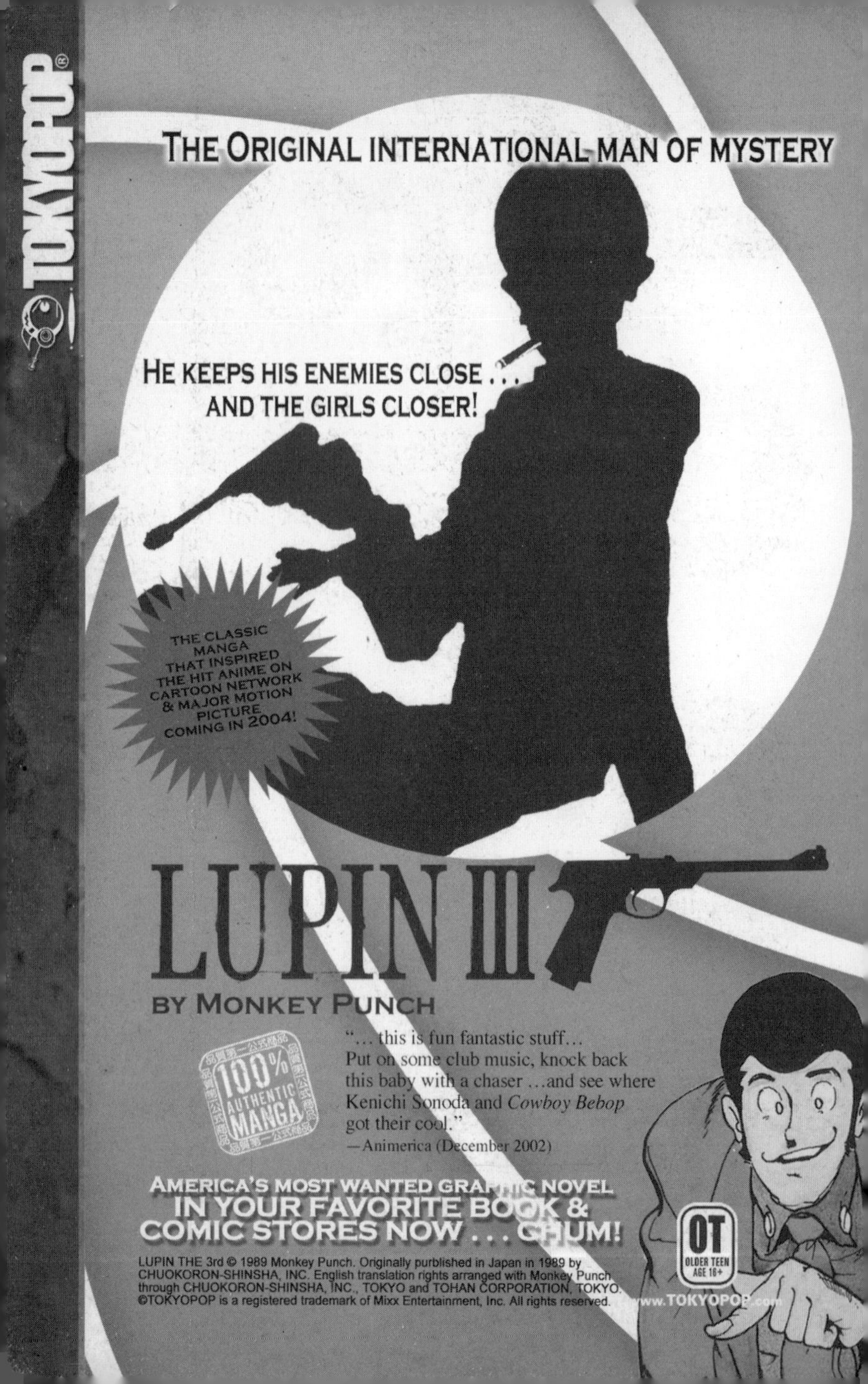
TOKYOPOP®
THE ORIGINAL INTERNATIONAL MAN OF MYSTERY
HE KEEPS HIS ENEMIES CLOSE . . .
AND THE GIRLS CLOSER!
THE CLASSIC MANGA THAT INSPIRED THE HIT ANIME ON CARTOON NETWORK & MAJOR MOTION PICTURE COMING IN 2004!
LUPIN III
BY MONKEY PUNCH
100% AUTHENTIC MANGA
"... this is fun fantastic stuff... Put on some club music, knock back this baby with a chaser ...and see where Kenichi Sonoda and Cowboy Bebop got their cool."
—Animerica (December 2002)
AMERICA'S MOST WANTED GRAPHIC NOVEL
IN YOUR FAVORITE BOOK &
COMIC STORES NOW . . . CHUM!
OT OLDER TEEN AGE 18+
LUPIN THE 3rd © 1989 Monkey Punch. Originally purblished in Japan in 1989 by CHUOKORON-SHINSHA, INC. English translation rights arranged with Monkey Punch through CHUOKORON-SHINSHA, INC., TOKYO and TOHAN CORPORATION, TOKYO. ©TOKYOPOP is a registered trademark of Mixx Entertainment, Inc. All rights reserved.
www.TOKYOPOP.com

KU-446-216

STOP!

This is the back of the book.
You wouldn't want to spoil a great ending!

This book is printed "manga-style," in the authentic Japanese right-to-left format. Since none of the artwork has been flipped or altered, readers get to experience the story just as the creator intended. You've been asking for it, so TOKYOPOP® delivered: authentic, hot-off-the-press, and far more fun!

DIRECTIONS

If this is your first time reading manga-style, here's a quick guide to help you understand how it works.

It's easy... just start in the top right panel and follow the numbers. Have fun, and look for more 100% authentic manga from TOKYOPOP®!

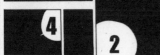

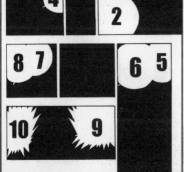

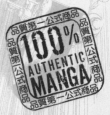